INTERNATIONAL FAMILY LAW

DATE DUE

GAYLORD		PRINTED IN U.S.A.

International Family Law

An Introduction

BARBARA STARK
Visiting Professor of Law, Hofstra Law School
Professor of Law, University of Tennessee

ASHGATE

© Barbara Stark 2005

Published by
Ashgate Publishing Limited
Gower House
Croft Road
Aldershot
Hants GU11 3HR
England

Ashgate Publishing Company
Suite 420
101 Cherry Street
Burlington, VT 05401-4405
USA

Ashgate website: http://www.ashgate.com

British Library Cataloguing in Publication Data
Stark, Barbara Kahn
    International family law : an introduction
    1. Domestic relations (International law)
    I. Title
    346'.015

Library of Congress Cataloging-in-Publication Data
Stark, Barbara, 1952-
    International family law : an introduction / by Barbara Stark.
        p. cm.
    Includes index.
    ISBN 0-7546-2341-6 (hardcover : alk. paper) -- ISBN 0-7546-2347-5 (pbk. : alk. paper)
        1. Domestic relations. 2. Conflict of laws--Domestic relations. 3. Legal polycentricity. I. Title.

    K670.S73 2005
    346.01'5--dc22

2005007441

ISBN (Hbk) 0 7546 2341 6
ISBN (Pbk) 0 7546 2347 5

Printed and bound in Great Britain by TJ International Ltd, Padstow, Cornwall.

Contents

Introduction

Why Study International Family Law?

Why Study 'International' Family Law?

This question contains three related but distinct questions, all of which pivot on the multiple meanings of 'international' in this context. First, why study *international* family law as opposed to *domestic* family law? Second, why study *international* family law as opposed to *comparative* family law? Third, why study *international* (i.e. private *and* public) family law rather than private family law? The answers to these questions explain the purpose, scope, and approach of this book.

'International' vs. 'Domestic' Family Law: The Importance of International Family Law

The answer here is pragmatic. International Family Law (IFL) is an essential part of any Family Law curriculum, or any family lawyer's library, because the practice of family law has in fact become globalized. Lawyers inevitably encounter clients whose family law problems extend beyond national boundaries, including problems in which the laws of more than one state must be taken into account. Lawyers everywhere are increasingly confronted with issues regarding international adoption, child abduction, divorce, custody and domestic violence, where the parties reside in, or are citizens of, different states.

This is not surprising. As the United Nations notes, families are the primary unit of social organization, and families are changing, trying to adapt to new demands and taking advantage of new mobility. Globalization is transforming family law. Women are seeking asylum as refugees, fleeing domestic violence. Workers are following jobs, leaving their families behind and sometimes starting new families in their new countries. Child abduction has become an increasing threat as parents of different nationalities divorce, and both want their children to be raised in their own national traditions.

Even as ties to such traditions become increasingly attenuated, their appeal may become stronger for some. Local religious leaders, similarly, may insist on even stricter adherence to local customs, especially those related to marriage, divorce, and the care and custody of children, as their authority is challenged by competing customs and international norms. In many States, such as Saudi Arabia, family law is basically left to religious authorities. This reflects both its relatively low importance to national governments (compared to matters of trade and finance, for example) and its paradoxically high importance to those who seek to shape the national identity. As Article 9 of the Basic Law of Saudi Arabia states, 'the family is the kernel of Saudi society, and its members shall be brought up on the basis of Islamic faith.' There are powerful trends and countertrends everywhere, and competing norms of family law are at the core of each.

These play out in a range of contexts, such as the recognition of marriage, child custody jurisdiction, enforcement of foreign support awards, and adoptions, which already claim a significant amount of class time in family law courses and account for a similarly significant number of hours in family law practice. The extraterritorial expansion of family law poses new challenges, but the basic analytic framework remains the same. First, we identify procedures that do not mesh, distinguishing those that are better characterized as procedural from those that reflect more substantive differences in underlying policy. Second, we find or create mechanisms for reconciliation, where possible, or for the orderly resolution of disputes where reconciliation is not possible.

While major issues in international family law, such as those addressed in the Hague Convention on Child Abduction, can be at least touched upon in a general course, growing numbers of students go on to specialize in family law. For these future lawyers, IFL is increasingly a necessity. In fact, the failure to anticipate international family law issues, such as the removal of children to another country during visitation, may well expose a lawyer to a malpractice claim.

'International' Family Law vs. 'Comparative' Family Law

Second, why study 'international family' as opposed to 'comparative' family law? 'International' here refers to shared or agreed upon rules and norms among a group of States, while 'comparative' refers to the respective rules and norms applicable in two or more particular States. Comparative family law is an essential component of IFL. The ways in which different domestic legal systems address custody disputes or invalidate marriages must be understood in the practice of IFL. The study of comparative law is also invaluable for gaining insight into other cultures and expanding horizons. Lawmakers increasingly look abroad for new approaches to intractable domestic problems.

They must keep in mind, however, that legal norms do not operate in the abstract, but in specific cultural contexts. A particular reform, such as retroactive laws opening adoption records, might be functional because it is compatible with the underlying social norms in one context but not in another. Comparative family law requires lawyers to focus on the ways in which culture supports or undermines law. The comparative perspective not only provides a window into another culture, but exposes the often unquestioned assumptions of one's own. Studying custodial presumptions in Islamic states, for example, exposes ways in which culture shapes such presumptions, which may not be as visible when dealing with the culture in which we are immersed.

Thus, the comparative element of international family law enables law students to gain a perspective on their own law. While comparative analysis is an integral part of IFL, the analytic and procedural processes which govern the interaction between national laws is the focus of this book. That is, the emphasis here is on the legal mechanisms devised by the international community to resolve or reconcile the different perspectives that a study of comparative family law reveals.

'International' Family Law vs. 'Private' International Family Law

'Private' international law historically referred to the rules regarding conflicts of law in disputes between private legal persons, including individuals or corporations. Public international law, in contrast, historically referred to the rules and norms governing disputes among nation States. As many commentators have observed, the distinction between public and private international law has steadily eroded. States increasingly engage in the same kinds of commercial activities as private entities. In addition, because of the growing influence of international human rights, the individual has increasingly become the subject of public international law.

Historically, IFL has been regarded primarily as the province of private international law, requiring familiarity with conflicts of law principles in general and the conventions promulgated by the Hague Conference on Private Law in particular. Public international law plays an increasingly important role, however. Even as the Hague Conference studies the problem of transnational child support, for example, States enter into growing numbers of bilateral treaties addressing the issue. (See Chapter 10, section 7.) Such treaties are governed by public international law.

International human rights law, moreover, has become an increasingly pervasive factor in international family law, from the refusal to recognize institutions such as polygamy (as a violation of human rights) to the recognition of reproductive rights. International human rights law also recognizes affirmative economic, social, and cultural rights, such as the right to maternal protection before and after the birth of a child, which are explicitly identified as rights owed to the family as such. Finally, rights of individuals within the family, such as the child's rights to freedom of religion, raise issues of State interference with family privacy. The State has an obligation to protect the child's rights without violating the rights of the family unit.

In sum, the erosion between public and private international law has been so thorough in the context of international family law that the subject can no longer be understood merely as a part of private international law. Rather, it requires a grasp of the applicable public international laws, especially human rights law, as well. Thus, this book addresses international family law, encompassing the principles of public as well as private international law.

The Approach

Each topic in IFL is addressed in a separate chapter. Each chapter takes the same basic approach, although different aspects of this basic approach are emphasized for different topics. In general, each chapter tracks the following outline:

1. The Problem
2. Overview
3. Cultural Variations
4. Private International Law
5. Public International Law
6. Regional Conventions
7. National Implementation
8. International Organizations (IOs) and Nongovernmental Organizations (NGOs)

The substantive content and objectives of each section are described below.

The Problem

Each chapter begins with one or two problems. There are concrete fact situations, often based on actual cases. The problem provides law students with a focus for the chapter and practitioners with analyses for some of the most common kinds of problems encountered in practice. The materials that follow explain the general principles to be applied and provide a few examples of local variations.

After reading the entire chapter the student should be able to answer the question posed or solve the problem presented in broad terms. It must be stressed, however, that local counsel should be consulted in actual practice. As a practical matter, foreign counsel is likely to be barred from actually representing a client under local or national rules governing the practice of law. As the problems indicate, however, legal representation is not always required in many cases where advice is sought. (At least no legal representation is required at that point.) The problem in Chapter 6, for example, presents a hypothetical in which the client wants to know which of three States is most likely to grant her asylum. Actually preparing an application for asylum would be the responsibility of the lawyer in the asylum State. Even where local counsel is necessary, moreover, a basic understanding of the substantive law and procedural posture will enable the lawyer to be more helpful to both the client and to local counsel.

Often, as in actual practice, there is not one correct answer but a range of possibilities. The question then becomes one of strategy, that is, how to present the case in a manner that is likely to lead to the client's desired outcome. Sometimes, of course, the client's desired outcome is not a realistic possibility. Then the question becomes: what is the best possible result for the client in this situation? How can other options be generated?

Overview

The purpose of this section is both to introduce the particular topic to those for whom family law is a new subject and to broaden the understanding of the topic for those who have studied or practiced in a single national context. It begins by describing the scope and function of the law, the circumstances in which it becomes important and the parties likely to be involved. Each section includes a range of perspectives to remind the reader that there is no 'neutral' overview; any orientation necessarily reflects some perspectives and omits others.

Cultural Variations

The third section discusses both specific national approaches and ethnic or religious approaches that cross national boundaries. In each chapter, this section focuses on one particular aspect of the law, such as the requirement of 'consent' in Chapter 1, to suggest the range of approaches to a single issue.

The point is to problematize what might otherwise be perceived as straightforward doctrine. The simple requirement of 'consent,' for example, may refer to the consent of the parties to the marriage, or it may refer to the consent of their fathers. Cultural variations are often expressed in the form of legal presumptions, that which a particular culture accepts as 'natural.' Under the Hanafi school of Islamic family law, for example, the assent of a virgin to a marriage may be presumed from her silence, her laughter, or her tears, which are interpreted as regret about leaving her parents (El Alami and Hinchcliff, 1996). The range of presumptions in a particular context illustrates the range of custom that has been naturalized. Indeed, in some cases, such as custody presumptions in favor of fathers or mothers, 'cultural variations' may include polar opposites.

Private International Law Conventions

Each chapter sets out the pertinent provisions of the private international law conventions, if any, that govern that particular issue in family law. Family law in many States is a matter of national or sub-national, i.e., state or provincial, law. A major exception is those States in which family law is basically delegated to religious authorities. IFL focuses on the ways in which these various systems are harmonized on the international level.

This has been accomplished through private international law conventions, such as the Hague Convention on Child Abduction, the Hague Convention on Intercountry Adoption, and the Convention on the Law Applicable to Maintenance Obligations Toward Children. A list of the Hague Conventions on Private International Law can be found at www.hcch.net/e/conventions/index.html. (Lists of States Parties are also available at this site.) These treaties are binding on States parties. In many States, such treaties become enforceable in national courts through implementing legislation. Under international law, a State is legally obligated under a convention it has ratified even if it has not yet enacted domestic law to implement that treaty.

An excellent introduction to the Hague Conference is available on its website. An excerpt is printed below.

Hague Conference InfoSheet[1]

> *Intro* The Hague Conference on private international law is an intergovernmental organization the purpose of which is 'to work for the progressive unification of the rules of private international law' (Statute, Article 1).

> *Background, Establishment and Status* The First Session of the Hague Conference on private international law was convened in 1893 by the Netherlands Government on the initiative of T.M.C. Asser. The Seventh Session in 1951 marked the beginning of a new era with the Plenary Sessions meet in principle every four years in ordinary diplomatic session. In case of need, as occurred in 1966 and 1985, an Extraordinary Session may be held. The Plenary Sessions discuss and adopt the draft Conventions (and sometimes Recommendations) prepared by the Special Commissions and take decisions on the subjects to be included in the agenda for the Conference's work. All of the texts adopted are brought together in a Final Act which is signed by the delegations. Under the rules of procedure of the Plenary Sessions each Member State has one vote. Decisions are taken by a majority of the votes cast by the delegations of Member States which are present at the vote. Non-Member States invited to participate on an equal footing with Member States also have the right to vote.
>
> * * *
>
> *Secretariat* The activities of the Conference are organized by a secretariat – the Permanent Bureau – which has its seat at The Hague and whose officials must be of different nationalities. The Secretary General is currently assisted by four lawyers: a Deputy Secretary General and three First Secretaries. The Permanent Bureau's main task is the preparation and organization of the Plenary Sessions and the Special Commissions. Its members carry out the basic research required for any subject that the Conference takes up.
>
> * * *
>
> *Methods of operation* The principal method used to achieve the purpose of the Conference consists in the negotiation and drafting of multilateral treaties or Conventions in the different fields of private international law (international judicial and administrative co-operation;
>
> * * *

maintenance obligations, status and protection of children, relations between spouses. After preparatory research has been done by the secretariat, preliminary drafts of the Conventions are drawn up by the Special Commissions made up of governmental experts. The drafts are then discussed and adopted at a Plenary Session of the Hague Conference, which is a diplomatic conference.

The secretariat of the Hague Conference maintains close contacts with the Governments of its <u>Member States</u> through National Organs designated by each Government. For the purpose of monitoring the operation of certain treaties involving judicial or administrative co-operation, the Permanent Bureau enters into direct contact from time to time with the <u>Central Authorities</u> designated by the States Parties to such treaties. In order to promote international co-operation and to ensure co-ordination of work undertaken by different bodies, the Hague Conference also maintains continuing contacts with a number of international organizations, including the United Nations – particularly its Commission of

International Trade Law (UNCITRAL), UNICEF, the Committee on the Rights of the Child (CRC) and the High Commissioner for Refugees (UNHCR) – the Council of Europe, the European Union, the Organization of American States, the Commonwealth Secretariat, the Asian-African Legal Consultative Committee, the International Institute for the Unification of Private Law (Unidroit) and others. Certain non-governmental organizations, such as the International Chamber of Commerce, the International Bar Association, International Social Service, the International Society of Family Law and the International Union of Latin Notaries also send observers to follow the meetings of the Hague Conference.

Achievements, monitoring of results and work in progress From 1951 to 2002 the Conference adopted 35 international Conventions. Until 1960 the Conventions were drafted only in French; since then they have been drawn up in French and English. Among those that have been the most widely ratified, the following Conventions should be mentioned: maintenance obligations, recognition of divorces, protection of minors, international child abduction and intercountry adoption. Some of the Hague Conventions deal with the determination of the applicable law, some with the conflict of jurisdictions, some with the recognition and enforcement of foreign judgments and some with administrative and judicial co-operation between authorities. Some of the Hague Conventions combine one or more of these aspects of private international law.

From time to time, Special Commissions are held at The Hague to monitor the practical operation of Hague Conventions. In the past, such Commissions have been convoked for the Child Abduction Convention, the Intercountry Adoption Convention and the Conventions on maintenance (support) obligations.

Public International Law

State family law is also subject to public international law, including international human rights law. As set out in the Statute of the International Court of Justice, there are three sources of international law. First, international law may be made by treaty; that is, a binding agreement entered into by two or more States. Examples include the U.N. Charter and the human rights conventions discussed below, all of which are multilateral treaties, and the bilateral treaties regarding child support (discussed in Chapter 10) and spousal maintenance (discussed in Chapter 5).

Second, international law may be found in customary international law, which has two elements: (1) State practice, and (2) *opinio juris*; that is, the belief that such State practice is legally mandated. Torture, for example, is a violation of customary international law. No State claims that it may legally engage in torture. On the contrary, all States have official policies against torture, reflecting their common understanding that it is prohibited in the international community. This does not mean, of course, that no State actually engages in torture. It simply means that it does so secretly, or contends that a particular practice is not in fact 'torture.' As discussed in Chapter 11, for example, domestic violence may amount to torture although this is not recognized by most States.

Customary international law may be shown through State practice over time, in the form of State adherence to international treaties, declarations, or General Assembly resolutions, through the enactment of domestic legislation, through executive action, and through a State's own judicial decisions. The accretion of such practice, accompanied by evidence that the State believed that such practice was legally mandated, constitutes customary international law. Where consensus among States is clear and no State objects, less practice may be needed.

Third, and finally, international law may be found in the 'general principles' of law recognized by States. These include principles such as *res judicata* or the commonly accepted understanding that statements made to one's lawyer are privileged. In the context of ILF, however, general principles may not be applicable. *Res judicata*, for example, may not apply to the custody determination of one State because another considers that determination subject to its modification, or contrary to the best interest of the child.

The major international human rights treaties affecting family law are the International Covenant on Civil and Political Rights ('ICCPR' or the 'Civil Covenant,') the International Covenant on Economic, Social, and Cultural Rights ('ICESCR' or the 'Economic Covenant'), the Convention on the Elimination of All Forms of Discrimination Against Women ('CEDAW' or the 'Women's Convention'), and the Convention on the Rights of the Child ('CRC' or the 'Child's Convention'). The pertinent sections of each of these instruments are set forth in the chapters in which they apply most directly. There is some cross-referencing in order to avoid repetition, but there is also some repetition for the reader's convenience. Complete texts of the instruments can be found in the treaty series cited in the chapters or at http://www1.umn.edu/humanrts/instree. (Lists of States Parties are also available at this site.)

Some States ratify human rights conventions subject to reservations regarding specific provisions. This means that the State accepts its obligations under the treaty with the exception of the particular article to which it has taken a reservation. Many Islamic States, for example, have taken reservations to Article 16 of the Women's Convention, addressing family rights. The usual reservation provides that the State accepts the cited article to the extent that it is consistent with Shari'ah, Islamic personal law.

Regional Conventions

This section sets forth the pertinent regional conventions, private and public, governing and harmonizing national family law. Most of the regional private law conventions involve European States.

The relevant provisions, if any, of the various regional public law conventions, establish another layer of human rights protection. The most important regional conventions for purposes of IFL include the European Convention on Human Rights, the Inter-American Convention on Human Rights, and the African Charter on the Rights and Welfare of Children. The European Convention has been useful in protecting the rights of sexual minorities, particularly gays, lesbians and transgendered persons. The Inter-American Convention has been used to establish State responsibility in connection with domestic violence. The African Charter restricts intercountry adoption in Africa, explicitly preferring institutionalization in the child's country of origin to intercountry adoption. Where there are no feasible alternatives, intercountry adoption may be considered, but even then, it is limited to those countries which are also parties to the Charter or to the CRC. This has recently been challenged under the South African Constitution, as discussed in Chapter 3.

National Implementation

This section considers the national implementation of international norms. Implementing legislation may be required in those States, like the United Kingdom and the United States, which do not incorporate international treaties as part of domestic law. Implementing legislation may be useful even in those States which do incorporate treaties, since it enables the State to tailor the treaty to national circumstances.

In addition, national laws often function on both a national (or federal) and a local level. While cooperation with a local lawyer will probably be necessary, an overview of the national family law system may facilitate such cooperation. The U.S. State Department maintains some useful sites, e.g., http://travel.state.gove/abduct.html (International Parental Child Abduction, with links to Application for Assistance; Booklet, Islamic Family Law, Judicial Education), and country-specific flyers.

Conflicts questions are apt to be decided under the national conflicts law of the State asserting jurisdiction. As in the domestic sphere, *forum non conveniens* arguments may sometimes prevail. In general, however, the foreign State is likely to retain jurisdiction where it believes that the issue raises important public policy concerns. Deference to foreign law, reasonably expected in a commercial context, is more elusive when matters involving highly-charged family issues are at stake.

IOs and NGOs

The last section describes some of the roles played by non-State actors in IFL. International organizations (IOs), that is, organizations comprised of States such as the United Nations or UNIFEM, often exert a strong influence in this area. As discussed in Chapter 6, for example, UNIFEM has established an internet working group to end violence against women. This represents a broad-based effort, which coordinates strategies involving education, training, mobilization, and changing male behavior. The World Health Organization ('WHO'), similarly, has supported efforts throughout the world to educate teenagers and young adults about reproduction and different forms of birth control. These are described in Chapter 7.

Non-governmental organizations (NGOs) are also increasingly important in lobbying for and raising consciousness about family law issues. The European Women's Lobby, for example, has taken strong positions on a number of issues from domestic violence to family leave. Non-State actors play important roles in establishing, maintaining, enforcing and challenging family law norms. In addition to NGOs, these may include religious and local communities which shape and support cultural norms. As noted above, for example, in some States family law is explicitly left to religious authorities. Cultural norms, such as the son's responsibility for aged parents in China and parts of India, may undermine or even negate more formal law.

An Approach to the Problem

Each chapter offers a possible approach to the Problem set out in the first section. Legal problem-solving is more of an art than a science and there are usually a range of possible approaches to any particular problem. Indeed, if there were only one, obvious solution, there would be no 'problem' to be solved, since there would be no basis for contesting that solution. The proposed approach, accordingly, is neither the only solution nor necessarily the optimal solution. It is, however, a solution that constructively deals with the material at hand, that is, the material set out in the preceding sections for that chapter.

For Further Research

Finally, each chapter concludes with suggestions for further research. These include the bibliographic material relied upon for that chapter. Sources relied upon for this chapter, for example, along with other helpful sources on international family law in general, are set out below. In addition, bibliographies have been compiled for several of the Hague Conventions. These can be accessed through the Hague Conference website.

For Further Research

1. For a comprehensive text on IFL, see Blair, D. Marianne and Weiner, Merle (2003), *Family Law in the World Community*, Carolina Academic Press, Durham. The International Society of Family Law publishes an annual survey, *The International Survey of Family Law*, providing information on current developments in family law throughout the world. Other noteworthy global surveys include Eeklaar, J. and Katz, S. (eds 1978), *Family Violence,* Butterworths, Canada; Eeklaar, J. and Katz, S. (eds. 1980), *Marriage and Cohabitation*, Butterworths, Canada; Eeklaar, J. and Katz, S. (eds 1984), *The Resolution of Family Conflict*, Butterworths, Canada; Meulders-Klein, M.T. and Eeklaar, J. (eds 1988), *Family, State, and Individual Economic Security*, Story Scientia and Kluwer, London; Lowe, N. and Douglas, G. (eds 1996), *Families Across Frontiers*, Martinus Nijhoff, London; Stark, B. (ed 1992), *Family Law and Gender Bias: Comparative Perspectives,* JAI, Greenwich.

2. For a current survey of family law in twenty-two Islamic States, in Africa and Asia as well as the Middle East, see Islamic Family Law http://www.law.emory.edu/ifl/legal/html. For an overview of Islamic laws, codified as well as uncodified, in the Arab world, see El Alimi, Dawoud and Hinchcliff, Doreen (1996), *Islamic Marriage and Divorce Laws of the Arab World*, Kluwer, London.

3. For an introduction to the harmonization and unification of family law in Europe, see *The European Family Law Series*, including Boele-woelki, K., Breat, B. and Summer, I. (eds 2003), *European Family Law in Action: Grounds for Divorce*, Interscientia, Antwerp.   For an analysis of the European Community's changing approach to family law, see McEleavy, P. (2002),'The Brussels II Regulation: How the European Community has moved into Family Law', *International & Comparative Law Quarterly*, Vol. 51, pp. 883-908.

Note

[1]   http://www.hcch.net/e/infosheet.html.

Chapter 1

Marriage

1. The Problem

Julia and Amitabh met when both were students at the London School of Economics. Julia is a citizen of the U.K. and an agnostic; Ami is a citizen of India and a Hindu. They fell in love and decided to marry. Julia wanted to marry in the Savoy Hotel in London. Ami wanted to marry in his village in India. They agreed to do both.

After a joyful wedding at the Savoy, they wrote to Ami's Uncle in India and asked him to arrange a wedding for them there. Ami's parents had died in an earthquake when he was 8 and he had been raised by his Uncle, who had quickly sent him off to boarding school in the U.K. Ami and Julia have just received the following letter from his Uncle:

> My Dear Nephew,
> I am very sorry to be the one to have to tell you this, but you should probably reconsider your desire to return to Rajasthan for your wedding. You were in fact married here 18 years ago, when you were just four years old. Your wife, Ratna, was sent to your father's house when she was 11, but you had already left for boarding school when you were 9. The dowry was paid in full and I never heard of any action for divorce or annulment. I do not know where she went when your parents died.
>
> I look forward to seeing you soon, but it would probably be unwise to attempt to marry here. Your Fond Uncle

Ami and Julia come to you. Assuming that his Uncle's statements are true, how does this affect their marriage in London? How does it affect their planned marriage in India? Does Ami have any obligation to Ratna? What are his options?

2. Overview

Anthropologists agree that the institution of marriage began as a way to connect the families of the bride and groom. It was usually arranged between the families and often accompanied by an exchange of property (usually from the wife's family to that of the husband, in the form of a 'bride price' or 'dowry') and the formation of alliances. In patriarchal societies, a young woman or girl would leave her family and join that of her husband.

The modern notion of companionate marriage is very different. It also involves a long-term commitment between a man and a woman, but it is a relationship which they enter into voluntarily. Unlike traditional marriage, modern marriage resembles a partnership, a relationship of equals. Many women in such marriages, for example, work outside the home. They are more likely to have some degree of economic independence, accordingly, although they usually earn less than their husbands.

Both kinds of marriages may be found throughout the world. Traditional marriages endure in traditional societies, such as Pakistan. They may also be found throughout Africa, parts of Asia, and the Middle East alongside modern marriages. In rural areas in Kenya, for example, traditional marriages persist while modern marriages are more common in the more cosmopolitan cities. Modern marriages are most common in the industrialized North, although more traditional groups within those societies may opt for some form of traditional marriage. Among fundamentalist religious groups, such as Christian Mormons in the United States or Orthodox Jews in Israel, for example, traditional marriage is often favored.

A crucial function of both traditional and modern marriage is to establish a stable framework in which children will be cared for and supported, emotionally as well as financially. Marriage rates are falling in some regions, however, especially in northern Europe. This reflects, in part, a growing number of couples who choose to live together without marrying. As discussed in Chapters 8-10, increasing numbers of children are born out of wedlock. In addition, a growing, but still small, number of couples opt for 'child free' marriages in the industrialized North. In the developing South, in contrast, barrenness is often a ground for annulment or divorce.

Many States recognize multiple forms of marriage, including religious and civil marriages. Traditional marriages usually involve a religious ceremony, while modern marriage is often entered into through a secular, civil ceremony. Czechoslovakia, for example, recognizes civil as well as religious forms of marriage, but both require a procedure before a civil registrar. India recognizes several different forms of marriage. Under Hindu law, marriage is viewed as a sacrament, in contrast to Muslim law, under which marriage is regarded as a contract. The Special Marriage Act authorizes some interreligious civil marriages. The 1937 Arya Marriage Validation Act recognizes the legality of intercaste marriages. The 1955 Hindu Marriages Act, which applies to any person in India who is not a Muslim, Christian, Parsi, or Jew, establishes the legal parameters of Hindu marriage, and prohibits bigamy as well as certain degrees of consanguinity.

Prerequisites

The prerequisites to marriage fall into three categories: eligibility, consent, and formalities. In general, States determine who is eligible to enter into marriage, and require freely given consent (although the 'consent' required may be that of the heads of the families rather than that of the parties). In addition, States often require some ceremony, registration or similar formality to distinguish marriage from other relationships and to impress this distinction upon the parties as well as their families and their communities.

'Eligibility' refers to a wide range of factors. Most States impose limits based on their laws on consanguinity; that is, laws which incorporate incest taboos and prohibit close relatives from marrying, although 'close' has different meanings in different cultures. In Asia, for example, marriages between cousins are common while in most parts of the United States such marriages are void. Virtually all States require that the spouses be different genders. While most States impose some age limit, this ranges from 'puberty' (which may be deemed to begin as early as nine years for girls) to 18 or 21 years. Some countries allow different ages for men and women. Others, such as the U.S. and Germany, require both parties to be at least 18, unless they have the consent of their parents.

Reforms in traditional societies often involve raising the marriage age. Under traditional Islamic law, for example, no minimum age is established. In codifying their marriage laws, however, several Islamic States have set a minimum age at which consent is valid. In Jordan, for example, the man must be 16 and the woman 15. Other traditional societies have similarly reformed their marriage laws. In Botswana, for example, the Marriage Bill 2000 establishes 18 as the minimum age for women as well as men to marry in order to conform to contemporary human rights instruments.

Former colonial powers, such as the U.K., also set minimum ages for marriage. In India and Pakistan, for example, the Child Marriage Restraint Act of 1929 set a minimum of 18 years for girls and 21 years for boys for contracting marriage. The Act also sought to deter arranged child marriages by punishing the parents or guardians who arranged them. The Act does not, however, invalidate the resulting marriage.

Most non-Muslim States require that a person be unmarried in order to be eligible for marriage. That is, most prohibit bigamy, and a prior existing marriage is a bar to a new one. Several Muslim States, however, permit polygamy, the practice of allowing a husband to marry more than one wife. Under some interpretations of Islamic law, a husband may marry up to four wives. Polyandry, in which a woman has more than one husband, is rare. It is said to persist in certain remote regions of Tibet, where an elder brother may share his wife with his younger brothers.

Additional eligibility requirements may be imposed by religious laws or other customs. Some religious laws, for example, require that the spouses be of the same religion. Customs that remain entrenched in certain societies, in some cases notwithstanding a legal bar, include: the requirement that a woman not marry below her own caste (certain Hindu castes in India), that the woman be a virgin (Iran and Saudi Arabia), and that a bride-price, or dowry be paid (Botswana). In general, as part of the marriage contract under Islamic law, the husband pays a dower, or *mahr*, to the wife. This is paid in cash or in kind and is the wife's sole property (El Alami and Hinchcliff, 1996).

Consent requirements refer to the consent of the spouses' families in traditional marriages or to consent of the spouses in a modern marriage. Under Muslim law, a woman who has not been married before needs a guardian (*wali*) before she can enter into marriage. The *wali's* authority varies under the interpretations of the different schools of Islam. Under the Hanafi view, for example, the *wali* advises the girl who has reached puberty and tries to guide her in the decisionmaking process. In Maliki, Shaf'i and Hanbali law, in contrast, a woman may never finalize her own marriage contract.

In the West, consent requirements are satisfied by the parties' sworn statements that they are entering into the marriage voluntarily, along with the absence of any obvious condition vitiating such consent. In the state of Georgia in the U.S., for example, drunkenness at the time of the marriage by either spouse may be used to show that the marriage was not in fact consensual.

One underlying purpose of formalities is to assure that the parties' marital status is known to the community and to the public at large. Ceremonies often reflect the traditional importance of marriage. Hindu ceremonies, for example, can last for days, but short versions with English translations are available on the Internet for contemporary British Hindus. The mix of customary and modern law which characterizes many States' systems is often expressed in the ceremony itself. In Israel, for example, although civil marriage is available, it is virtually unknown, the overwhelming majority of couples opting instead for 'white weddings' which include a religious ceremony.

Formalities may also include the requirement that the couple register with a government authority. In India, for example, the Compulsory Registration of Marriage Act passed in 2002 provides a means of monitoring child marriages or bigamist marriages. Several smaller Indian states, including Rajasthan, have declined to require compulsory registration because of the continuing popularity of child marriages. In 1993, a UNICEF survey in Rajasthan found that 50% of the population had married before the age of 15 and 17% of this group were under the age of 10.

In some countries, such as France, China, and Japan, registration is considered extremely important. In Japan and France, accurate record-keeping ensures the integrity of family lineage. In China, registration is necessary in order to qualify for State benefits, which may include housing and education. In other countries, failure to register may be regarded as a mere oversight with no legal consequences for the parties.

Consequences

Marriage affects the parties' personal status. Marital status has public consequences, such as nationality or citizenship status, eligibility for insurance coverage, entitlement to social security, intestacy, and inheritance rules. Marital status also has private, social consequences, such as the recognition by the community of the couple as a household unit.

Marriage may also involve contractual obligations between the husband and wife. The contractual aspects of the parties' relationship often includes support obligations, either mutual or unilateral, and other expectations, such as sexual fidelity and the establishment of a household, including children. In the U.S., for example, the husband was historically required to support the wife and provide her with 'necessaries', such as food and shelter. This obligation is now viewed as a mutual obligation; that is, either spouse may be required to support the other. Under traditional Islamic law, similarly, the husband was required to support the wife as long as she submitted to his control. Under recent codifications, the obligation has been made gender-neutral. Under the codified law of Libya, adopted in 1984, a wife 'who is wealthy shall be required to support her husband . . . during [his] hardship.' Under Islamic law, marriage is viewed as a civil contract, and either party, in theory, may stipulate the terms. In some countries, such as Nigeria, breach of the obligation of fidelity by the woman is considered a crime, even if it is involuntary. Adultery by the woman, which may include rape, may be punishable by death. In other States sexual infidelity is considered a breach of the agreement between the parties, rather than a criminal offense against the State. Thus, adultery may be grounds for divorce (see Chapter 4) or it may have a bearing on a property award in connection with divorce (see Chapter 5).

Void Marriages

The failure to comply with the prerequisites of marriage may render the marriage void or voidable. A void marriage is one which is regarded as a nullity; a voidable marriage is one which may be considered a nullity but only if a court or similar authority so determines. In some parts of the United States, for example, a marriage in which one of the spouses is underage is considered voidable. The spouse or her parents may petition a court to declare the marriage a nullity. A voidable marriage may be ratified, however, by the parties' continuing cohabitation until the condition which rendered the marriage voidable is removed; that is, until the underage party attains the legal age for marriage.

Recognition of Foreign Marriages

In general, a marriage which is valid under the law of the State where it is entered into will be recognized as valid by another State. The exception to this is that if a marriage is void as a matter of public policy in the second State, it may not be recognized even if it were valid under the laws of the State in which it was entered into. In countries where bigamy is unlawful, for example, polygamous marriages may be regarded as null and void. In France, for example, the second and third wives of Muslim immigrants from Northern Africa or the Middle East are not considered the wives of their husbands even though they were recognized as legal wives in the State in which they were married. Because polygamy is barred as a matter of public policy in France, they are not entitled to the legal protections accorded legal wives under French law.

3. Cultural Variations

The consent of at least two parties is necessary for a valid marriage, but it need not be the consent of the prospective husband and wife. Syria, for example, follows the Muslim law of the Hanafi school, which has been modified to allow a judicial override. That is, under Syrian law, a *wali* (guardian) cannot unfairly block or delay the marriage of a woman who has attained majority. If he does so, the woman can complain to a judge, who can override the *wali's* decision and perform the marriage himself.

In Cameroon, couples can choose to be married under statutory law or customary law. The latter permits polygamous marriages and requires the payment of a bride-price. Since the bride-price is paid to the family, represented by the family head, parental consent is implicitly required. Customary law marriages join the two families as well as the two spouses.

An unusual local custom regarding consent may be found on the Indonesian island of Lombok, where parents traditionally arranged their daughters' marriages. If a lover broke into the daughter's bedroom, however, and kidnaped her, the parents would condone their marriage. Although globalization has eroded traditional customs, and arranged marriages are no longer the norm, many couples still carry out the charade of kidnaping because it is considered thrilling and romantic.

A recent report by UNICEF on Early Marriage Child Spouse, including a detailed discussion of consent, is reproduced in Section 8 of this Chapter.

4. Private International Law Conventions

Convention on Celebration and Recognition of the Validity of Marriages[1]

> *Article 2* The formal requirements for marriages shall be governed by the law of the State of celebration.
>
> * * *
>
> *Article 5* The application of a foreign law declared applicable by this Chapter may be refused only if such application is manifestly incompatible with the public policy ('ordre public') of the State of celebration.
>
> * * *
>
> *Article 8* This Chapter shall not apply to –
> (1) marriages celebrated by military authorities;
> (2) marriages celebrated aboard ships or aircraft;
> (3) proxy marriages;
> (4) posthumous marriages;
> (5) informal marriages.
>
> * * *
>
> *Article 9* A marriage validly entered into under the law of the State of celebration or which subsequently becomes valid under that law shall be considered as such in all Contracting States, subject to the provisions of this Chapter.
>
> * * *
>
> *Article 11* A Contracting State may refuse to recognize the validity of a marriage only where, at the time of the marriage, under the law of that State –
> (1) one of the spouses was already married; or
> (2) the spouses were related to one another, by blood or by adoption, in the direct line or as brother and sister; or
> (3) one of the spouses had not attained the minimum age required for marriage, nor had obtained the necessary dispensation; or
> (4) one of the spouses did not have the mental capacity to consent; or
> (5) one of the spouses did not freely consent to the marriage.

However, recognition may not be refused where, in the case mentioned in sub-paragraph 1 of the preceding paragraph, the marriage has subsequently become valid by reason of the dissolution or annulment of the prior marriage.

* * *

Article 14 Contracting State may refuse to recognize the validity of a marriage where such recognition is manifestly incompatible with its public policy ('ordre public').

5. Public International Law

Universal Declaration of Human Rights[2]

Article 16 1. Men and women of full age, without any limitation due to race, nationality or religion, have the right to marry and to found a family. They are entitled to equal rights as to marriage, during marriage and at its dissolution.
2. Marriage shall be entered into only with the free and full consent of the intending spouses.
3. The family is the natural and fundamental group unit of society and is entitled to protection by society and the State.

International Convenant on Economic, Social and Cultural Rights[3]

* * *

Article 10.1. The States Parties to the present Covenant recognize that the widest possible protection and assistance should be accorded to the family, which is the natural and fundamental group unit of society, particularly for its establishment and while it is responsible for the care and education of dependent children. Marriage must be entered into with the free consent of the intending spouses.

International Covenant on Civil and Political Rights[4]

Article 23 1. The family is the natural and fundamental group unit of society and is entitled to protection by society and the State.
2. The right of men and women of marriageable age to marry and to found a family shall be recognized.
3. No marriage shall be entered into without the free and the full consent of the intending spouses.
4. States Parties to the present Covenant shall take appropriate steps to ensure equality of rights and responsibilities of spouses as to marriage, during marriage and at its dissolution. In the case of dissolution, provision shall be made for the necessary protection of any children.

Convention on the Elimination of All Forms of Discrimination Against Women[5]

Article 16 1. States Parties shall take all appropriate measures to eliminate discrimination against women in all matters relating to marriage and family relations and in particular shall ensure, on a basis of equality of men and women:

(a) The same right to enter into marriage;

(b) The same right freely to choose a spouse and to enter into marriage only with their free and full consent;

(c) The same rights and responsibilities during marriage and at its dissolution;

(d) The same rights to decide freely and responsibly on the number and spacing of their children and to have access to the information, education and means to enable them to exercise these rights;

(e) The same personal rights as husband and wife, including the right to choose a family name, a profession and an occupation;

(f) The same rights for both spouses in respect of the ownership, acquisition, management, administration, enjoyment and disposition of property, whether free of charge or for a valuable consideration.

2. The betrothal and the marriage of a child shall have no legal effect and all necessary action, including legislation, shall be taken to specify a minimum age for marriage and to make the registration of marriages in an official registry compulsory.

Convention on Consent to Marriage, Minimum Age for Marriage and Registration of Marriages[6]

Article 1 (1) No marriage shall be legally entered into without the full and free consent of both parties, such consent to be expressed by them in person after due publicity and in the presence of the authority competent to solemnize the marriage and of witnesses, as prescribed by law.

(2) Notwithstanding anything in paragraph 1 above, it shall not be necessary for one of the parties to be present when the competent authority is satisfied that the circumstances are exceptional and that the party has, before a competent authority and in such manner as may be prescribed by law, expressed and not withdrawn consent.

Article 2 States parties to the present Convention shall take legislative action to specify a minimum age for marriage. No marriage shall be legally entered into by any person under this age, except where a competent authority has granted a dispensation as to age, for serious reasons, in the interest of the intending spouses.

Article 3 All marriages shall be registered in an appropriate official register by the competent authority.

6. Regional Conventions

European Convention for the Protection of Human Rights and Fundamental Freedoms[7]

Article 8 – 1. Everyone has the right to respect for his private and family life, his home and his correspondence.

2. There shall be no interference by a public authority with the exercise of this right except such as is in accordance with the law and is necessary in a democratic society in the interests of national security, public safety or the economic well-being of the country, for the prevention of disorder or crime, for the protection of health or morals, or for the protection of the rights and freedoms of others.

American Declaration of the Rights and Duties of Man[8]

> *Article V* – Every person has the right to the protection of the law against abusive attacks upon his honor, his reputation, and his private and family life.
>
> *Article VI* – Every person has the right to establish a family, the basic element of society, and to receive protection therefor.

American Convention on Human Rights[9]

> *Article 17* – Rights of the Family
> 1. The family is the natural and fundamental group unit of society and is entitled to protection by society and the state.
> 2. The right of men and women of marriageable age to marry and to raise a family shall be recognized, if they meet the conditions required by domestic laws, insofar as such conditions do not affect the principle of nondiscrimination established in this Convention.
> 3. No marriage shall be entered into without the free and full consent of the intending spouses.
> 4. The States Parties shall take appropriate steps to ensure the equality of rights and the adequate balancing of responsibilities of the spouses as to marriage, during marriage, and in the event of its dissolution. In case of dissolution, provision shall be made for the necessary protection of any children solely on the basis of their own best interests.

Additional Protocol to the American Convention on Human Rights in the Area of Economic, Social and Cultural Rights ('Protocol of San Salvador')[10]

> *Article 15.* – Right to the formation and the protection of families. 1. The family is the natural and fundamental element of society and ought to be protected by the State, which should see to the improvement of its spiritual and material conditions.
> 2. Everyone has the right to form a family, which shall be exercised in accordance with the provisions of the pertinent domestic legislation.

African Charter on Human and Peoples' Rights (Banjul Charter)[11]

> *Article 18* – 1. The family shall be the natural unit and basis of society. It shall be protected by the State which shall take care of its physical health and morals.
> 2. The State shall have the duty to assist the family which is the custodian of morals and traditional values recognized by the community.

African Charter on the Rights and Welfare of the Child[12]

> *Article 21*: Protection against Harmful Social and Cultural Practices
> * * *
> 2. Child marriage and the bethrothal of girls and boys shall be prohibited and effective action, including legislation, shall be taken to specify the minimum age of marriage to be 18 years and make registration of all marriages in an official registry compulsory.

7. National Implementation

Following a regime change in 1991 in Ethiopia, the new government adopted a Charter which explicitly affirmed the rights set out in the Universal Declaration. Ethiopia subsequently ratified the ICCPR, the ICESCR, the CRC, and the Women's Convention. In the new Constitution of 1995, Ethiopia reaffirmed its commitment to women's equality and the rights of children. The Revised Family Code (RFC) of 2000 was enacted in order to conform family law to the Constitution.

Under the RFC, the age of marriage is set at 18, rather than 15, in accordance with the CRC. The new law recognizes three forms of marriage: customary, civil, and religious. There are ongoing tensions between customary and religious norms, on one hand, and the norm of gender equality, on the other. Laws from the 1961 Civil Code establishing the husband as head of the family, a duty of wifely obedience, wifely performance of household duties, and the husband's right to choose the family residence, guide the wife in her conduct, and manage common property (not including the wife's earnings), have all been repealed.

The RFC, in contrast, requires the husband and wife to jointly manage the family, which includes jointly choosing the family's place of residence. In addition, the parties have mutual support obligations and they are to cooperate with respect to child rearing and management of family property. The latter, however, may be modified by contract.

8. IOs and NGOs

IOs

IOs and NGOs have increasingly focused on marriage, exposing the ways in which it has operated to effectively deny the human rights of women and children. In the excerpt below, for example, UNICEF describes the effects of early marriage, that is, marriage below the age of 18.

From UNICEF, Early Marriage Child Spouses (March 2001)
Birth, marriage and death are the standard trio of key events in most people's lives. But only one – marriage – is a matter of choice. The right to exercise that choice was recognized as a principle of law even in Roman times and has long been established in international human rights instruments. Yet many girls, and a smaller number of boys, enter marriage without any chance of exercising their right to choose.

Some are forced into marriage at a very early age. Others are simply too young to make an informed decision about their marriage partner or about the implications of marriage itself. They may have given what passes for 'consent' in the eyes of custom or the law, but in reality, consent to their binding union has been made by others on their behalf.

The assumption is that once a girl is married, she has become a woman – even if she is only 12. Equally, where a boy is made to marry, he is now a man and must put away childish things. While the age of marriage is generally on the rise, early marriage – marriage of children and adolescents below the age of 18 – is still widely practised.

While early marriage takes many different forms and has various causes, one issue is paramount. Whether it happens to a girl or a boy, early marriage is a violation of human rights. The right to free and full consent to a marriage is recognized in the 1948 Universal Declaration of Human Rights (UDHR) and in many subsequent human rights instruments – consent that cannot be 'free and full' when at least one partner is very immature. For both girls and boys, early marriage has profound physical, intellectual, psychological and emotional impacts, cutting off educational opportunity and chances of personal growth. For girls, in addition, it will almost certainly mean premature pregnancy and childbearing, and is likely to lead to a lifetime of domestic and sexual subservience over which they have no control.

Yet many societies, primarily in Africa and South Asia, continue to support the idea that girls should marry at or soon after puberty. Their spouses are likely to be a few years older than they are, but may be more than twice their age. Parents and heads of families make marital choices for daughters and sons with little regard for the personal implications. Rather, they look upon marriage as a family-building strategy, an economic arrangement or a way to protect girls from unwelcome sexual advances.

Neglect of the Rights Perspective

Social reformers in the first part of the 20th century were concerned about early marriage, especially in India, and influenced the UDHR and other human rights conventions of the 1950s and 1960s. In the latter part of the 20th century, interest centred on the behavioural determinants fuelling rapid population growth, for obvious reasons. Early marriage extends a woman's reproductive span, thereby contributing to large family size, especially in the absence of contraception.

More recently, advocates of safe motherhood have turned their attention to this issue. Pregnancies that occur 'too early' – when a woman's body is not fully mature – constitute a major risk to the survival and future health of both mother and child. Concern with the special health needs of adolescents has also recently been growing in a world where young people are particularly vulnerable to HIV/AIDS.

However, from a demographic health perspective, early marriage is seen primarily as a contributory factor to early child-bearing. And sometimes, even in this context, its role is overlooked: the phrase 'teenage pregnancy' is typically understood to mean pregnancy outside marriage. Yet far more adolescent or teenage pregnancies occur within marriage than outside it.

During the past decade, the movement for 'Education for All' has stressed the need to enroll more girls in school and to keep them from dropping out before completion. In this context, the custom of early marriage is acknowledged as one of the reasons for girls' exclusion from school, especially in cultural settings where girls are raised for a lifetime confined to household occupations and are expected to marry very young.

Very recently, the situation of children in need of special protection, notably girls vulnerable to sexual abuse and HIV/AIDS, suggests that early marriage is being used as a strategy to protect girls from sexual exposure, or to pass the economic burden for their care to others. Thus, early marriage lingers on as a culturally and socially sanctioned practice according to some traditional sets of values and, among some highly stressed populations, it may even be on the rise.

Despite the efforts of reformers in the early part of the 20th century, early marriage has received scant attention from the modern women's rights and children's rights movements. There has been virtually no attempt to examine the practice as a human rights violation in itself. Children and teenagers married at ages well below the legal minimum become statistically invisible as 'children'. Thus, in the eyes of the law, an adult male who has sex with a girl of 12 or 13 outside marriage may be regarded as a criminal, while the same act within marriage is condoned.

To date, most studies on the effects of early marriage have focused on premature sex and pregnancy and school drop-out. Much work remains to be done, therefore, to analyse the full impact of this practice.

* * *

Sanctions Against Early Marriage – The Legal Context

In many countries, early marriage falls into what amounts to a sanctions limbo. It may be prohibited in the existing civil or common law, but be widely condoned by customary and religious laws and practice. This is common where marriages typically take place according to customary rites and remain unregistered.

The situation is further complicated in countries where legislation was introduced by the colonizing power on the understanding that many customary practices would continue even if they were inconsistent with new laws. Some were even codified to make them legal. In Benin, for example, Article 68 of the 1931 'Coutumier du Dahomey' regulating customary marriage states that: 'A marriage is not settled by the interested parties, but by their father, or in his absence by his older brother, or failing him, by the head of the family'. In Suriname, the legal minimum age of marriage is 15 according to the Civil Code; but under the Asian Marriage Act, which codifies practice for a particular group, the minimum age for girls is 13.

Although most countries have laws that regulate marriage, both in terms of minimum age and consent, these laws may not be applied and few prosecutions are ever brought against lawbreakers – parents, officiators or spouses. Some laws do not prescribe sanctions; the only outcome of a case would be to declare the marriage invalid, leaving the wife without legal protection. Moreover, such laws usually do not apply to customary marriages.

In some countries, the legal minimum age of marriage set for boys and girls is clearly aspirational. Thus, the minimum age in two countries with a high prevalence of HIV/AIDS – Uganda, where 50 per cent of girls aged 15-19 are married, and Zambia, where the figure is 27 percent – has been set at 21 for both males and females.

In most cases where a minimum age is set, it is 18 or above for both males and females. In 15 countries, it is 16. A number of countries nonetheless allow marriages to take place at much younger ages with parental consent.

In cases where there is a discrepancy between the minimum age of marriage for boys and girls, it is consistently lower for girls. However, at least 20 countries either do not have legislation to regulate marriage, or do not set any minimum age for either girls or boys.

The situation is exacerbated by the fact that birth registration is so irregular that age at marriage may not be known. In addition, many marriages go unregistered; if there are problems in the marriage, the wife has no means of legal redress.

Thus, the use of law as a means of regulating early marriage is in no way sufficient. This does not mean that legal reform should not be sought. The Indian *Child Marriage Restraint Act*, 1929 stemmed from a campaign that helped reposition women, family life, and childbearing within modern India. While the Act did not declare child marriages invalid, it helped pave the way for change. In 1978 it was strengthened to inhibit marriage of girls until the age of 18 and boys until age 21. However, the number of prosecutions under the Act did not exceed 89 in any year between 1994 and 1998. Some governments have taken steps to unify their customary law and civil or common law, or have passed legislation designed to protect those in customary marriages: South Africa's *Recognition of Customary Marriages Act* of 1998 sets 18 as the minimum age for such unions and requires their registration.

In keeping with the spirit of the CRC, an increasing number of laws fix the minimum age at 18 years – the standard also set by the *1990 African Charter on the Rights and Welfare of the Child* and suggested by the CEDAW Committee in its general recommendation 21 and by the UN Special Rapporteur on Violence against Women. This standard responds to the growing consensus that the period of adolescence needs special support and protection.

The Inter-African Committee (IAC) on Traditional Practices Affecting the Health of Women and Children states that early marriage is: 'Any marriage carried out below the age of 18 years, before the girl is physically, physiologically, and psychologically ready to shoulder the responsibilities of marriage and childbearing.' The Forum on Marriage echoes this position.

In their observations on States Parties' reports, the CEDAW and CRC Committees have both consistently recommended that states adopt higher minimum ages of marriage and ensure that these are the same for boys and girls. The CRC Committee also takes the view that, in cases where girls are considered adults before the law upon marriage, they would be deprived of the comprehensive protection of the CRC.

Consent: Law and Practice

The second issue at the heart of a rights approach to early marriage is that of consent. The picture is similar to that concerning minimum age: in the vast majority of countries the law grants women the right to consent. Only in Cameroon, Jordan, Morocco, Uganda and Yemen are women specifically not granted by law the right to 'full, free and informed consent' to their marriage. But in a large number of countries, these legal provisions are merely symbolic.

The more important practical issue is, therefore, whether or not the idea of consent is socially rated. Difficult questions arise around the age a child should be before he or she can 'consent' as a mature, cognisant and independent being to sexual relations or marriage, but where no clear consent has been given by one or other partner, the marriage is clearly forced.

In the case of marriages under the age of 10, consent – other than to dress up and play a game – is not a consideration. Toddlers married at *Akha Teej* ceremonies in Rajasthan cannot 'consent'. Nor is consent given in the cases of young girls from very poor homes in the Indian city of Hyderabad, Andhra Pradesh, sold as wives to rich men in the Middle East. In Gojam, Ethiopia, marriages may be imposed from birth, with the girl sent to her future husband's home at around the age of seven to begin her integration into her marriage family. Here again, consent by the girl does not enter the picture. Similarly, in marriages at or around puberty – from roughly ages 10 to 14 – 'consent' cannot be said to have been given since, at such an early age, a child cannot be expected to understand the implications of accepting a lifetime partner.

The question of marital consent becomes more difficult at age 15 or 16, by which stage a girl may have reached the legal age of sexual consent. In the CEDAW Committee's recommendation that the minimum age for marriage of both men and women should be 18, it commented that, 'When men and women marry, they assume important responsibilities. Consequently, marriage should not be permitted before they have attained full maturity and capacity to act.' The Committee also observed that, 'Some countries provide for different ages for marriage for men and women. As such provisions assume incorrectly that women have a different rate of intellectual development from men, or that their stage of physical and intellectual development at marriage is immaterial, these provisions should be abolished.'

It could be argued that even older children cannot be said to give informed consent to such a potentially damaging practice as early marriage. Beyond the issues of maturity and non discrimination, any argument for a child's ability to consent to marriage is further undermined by the risk that marriage represents to his or her well-being. Many international bodies consider early marriage to be one of the 'traditional practices prejudicial to the health of children' cited in article 24(3) of the Convention on the Rights of the Child. Indeed, one of the key messages contained in this Digest is that both the physical and psychological impacts of early marriage may have serious implications for the well-being of those married.

Furthermore, while in many countries a girl or boy may have reached the legal age of sexual consent at the age of 15 or 16, this should not be taken to mean that they are ready to enter marriage. A lack of legislative clarity over the different implications of consent to sexual activity and consent to marriage can result in strange anomalies. In Maryland, USA, the state law defines statutory rape as sex with a child younger than 14 by someone four or more years older. However, another law allows children under 16 (with no minimum) to marry with proof of pregnancy and parental permission, and this provision is sometimes used – in one notorious case to allow a 29-year-old man to marry a 13-year-old girl.

In 1997, the Committee on the Rights of the Child protested a similar situation in Algeria. Here, as in other countries such as Chad, Costa Rica, Lebanon, Libya, Romania and Uruguay, the law allows a perpetrator of rape, including statutory rape of a minor, to be excused of his crime if he marries his victim; a judge simply legitimizes the union. This has also happened in California in cases of under-age pregnancies where the man is willing to 'stand by' the girl. In effect, the state welfare agency supports what is seen as a viable partnership as an alternative to costly state care for mother and child.

In a number of countries, it takes only the parents' consent to override the legal age of marriage – a judge is not required. In Colombia, the legal age is 18, but with parents' permission girls of 12 and boys of 14 can be married. In the Dominican Republic there is no minimum age in exceptional circumstances and with parental consent.

The UK Home Office Report into forced marriages of British girls of South Asian parentage distinguishes between 'forced' and 'arranged' marriages. In arranged marriages, the initiative is taken by the parents of the couple, but consent is required from both partners and either has the right to withdraw. However, the pressures from parents may be very high, and the younger the bride or groom the less real chance there is to exercise this right. Both types of marriage indicate the degree to which many societies view marriage as a family affair in which the views of people other than the couple are given priority. Parents' views will override children's, and men's will override women's – even taking precedence over the law.

Cases of runaway brides highlight the issue of consent – or lack of it. In Pakistan, the Commission on the Status of Women reported in 1989: 'Men are constantly fighting to retrieve their women because they have run away.' There are reports of young wives being locked up by their husbands in India, and in Zimbabwe it is often forbidden for a young bride to visit her own family until she goes there to give birth to her first child. In one tragic case in Nigeria, a 12-year-old girl unhappy with her new husband ran away so often that he cut off her legs to prevent her absconding. She subsequently died.

The CRC Committee has focused on laws and customs in its observations to a number of countries. Its most common complaints are low minimum age for girls and disparate – therefore discriminatory – marriage ages for girls and boys.

NGOs

Human Rights Watch World Report 2002: Women's Human Rights[13] Women's Status in the Family/Law and practices governing women's personal status – their legal capacity and role in the family – continued to deny women rights. While the type of discrimination varied from region to region, women throughout the world found that their relationship to a male relative or husband determined their rights.

* * *

Personal status laws in Syria and Morocco, among other countries, continued to curtail women's rights entering into marriage, during marriage, and the dissolution of marriage. In Syria, the minimum age for marriage was eighteen for boys and seventeen for girls. If a woman over the age of seventeen married without the consent of a male guardian, the guardian could demand the annulment of the marriage if the husband was not of the same social standing as the wife, and as long as the wife were not pregnant. Further, a Muslim Syrian woman could not marry a non-Muslim, while a Muslim man had absolute freedom to choose a spouse. Syrian law also assigned different rights and responsibilities for women and men during marriage. A wife's 'disobedience' could lead to forfeiture of her husband's responsibility to provide support. A man could legally have up to four wives simultaneously, while a woman could have only one husband.

9. A Possible Approach to the Problem

As suggested in the Overview, the major question here is whether Ami's marriage to Ratna was valid. If it was, it was a bar to his marriage to Julia and Ami is in fact a bigamist (p. 15). Although India recognizes multiple forms of marriage (p. 14), it seems unlikely that the early marriage to Ratna would be recognized for a range of practical as well as doctrinal reasons.

First, the Child Marriage Restraint Act of 1929 explicitly sets minimum ages for marriages (p. 15). Although the Act does not invalidate the resulting marriage, it is evidence of the public policy against it. The Compulsory Registration of Marriage Act of 2002 (p. 16) would obviously not cover Ami and Ratna's marriage sixteen years earlier, but it suggests the ongoing tension between culture and legal norms in Rajasthan, where the marriage took place, and where UNICEF found that half of the population had married before the age of 15.

Information about Ratna's current situation would be helpful. If she is married, for example, she may agree to an annulment. Underage marriages are voidable, and there has been no ratification (by continuing cohabitation) here (p. 17). On the other hand, if Ratna hopes for British citizenship (or support from Ami), she may argue that the marriage was valid. Further research would be necessary to determine whether the U.K. would refuse to recognize the marriage as void as a matter of public policy.

If the U.K. is a party to the Convention on Celebration, set out in Section 4, it is required to recognize foreign marriages unless 'manifestly incompatible' with the law of the State of celebration (India). While the Convention explicitly exempts underage marriage, the exemption itself may be avoided by the 'necessary dispensation.' In the U.S., this would refer to the consent of the parents of an underage spouse. While further research would be necessary to ascertain the substance of 'necessary dispensation' under other States' law, an interpretation of this phrase that validated a marriage entered into without the actual consent of the parties (Ami and Ratna) would arguably vitiate the Convention.

The excerpts from the human rights conventions set out in Section 5 show that the 'free consent' of the parties to a marriage (as opposed to their families) is a widely recognized human rights norm. As set out in Section 8, the rights of the girl child are a particular concern. The regional conventions confirm the geographical scope of the norm, with some significant variations. Under the European Convention, for example, the privacy protections of Article 8 would probably not bar a claim against Ami by Ratna. The protection of 'honor' and family privacy under Article V of the American Convention, in contrast, might deter such threats by an outsider against the family.

Section 7 highlights the political significance of the laws against child marriage in the developing world. The new government in Ethiopia made a dramatic break with the past, affirming its commitment to human rights. In India, on the other hand, as noted at page 15 and described in greater detail in Section 8, efforts to restrict child marriage have long been linked to colonialism. While the national government has ratified many human rights instruments, local governments may resist 'western' restriction as a matter of cultural pride.

For Further Research

1. R.J. Scholes with the assistance of Phataralaoha, A., 'The Mail-Order Bride Industry and its impact on U.S. Immigration. http://www.ins.usdoj.gov/graphics/aboustins/repsstudies/Mobappa.htm.

2. For a comprehensive overview of Islamic marriage laws, see El Alami, Dawoud and Hinchcliffe, Doreen (1996), *Islamic Marriage and Divorce Laws of the Arab World*, Kluwer, London; Al-Hibri, A.Y. (1992), 'Marriage Laws in Muslim Countries: A Comparative Study of Certain Egyptian, Syrian, Moroccan, and Tunisian Marriage Laws,' in B. Stark (ed), *Family Law and Gender Bias: Comparative Perspectives*, JAI, Greenwich pp. 231-233.

3. For useful overviews of contemporary marriage law in particular countries, see Ngwafor, E.N. (2000), 'Cameroon: Customary Law Versus Statutory Law: An Unresolved Second Millennium Moral Quagmire,' in A. Bainham (ed), *The International Survey of Family Law: 2000 Edition*, Jordan, Bristol, pp. 55-64; Molokomme, A. (2000), 'Overview of Family Law in Botswana,' in A. Bainham (ed), *The International Survey of Family Law: 2000 Edition*, Jordan, Bristol pp. 43-54;

Haderka, J.F. (2000), 'Czech Republic: A Half-Hearted Family Law Reform of 1998,' in A. Bainham (ed), *The International Survey of Family Law: 2000 Edition*, Jordan, Bristol pp. 119-130;   Palmer, M. (2000), 'China: Caring for Young and Old: Developments in the Family Law of the People's Republic of China, 1996-1998,' in A. Bainham (ed), *The International Survey of Family Law: 2000 Edition*, Jordan, Bristol, pp. 95-108.

Notes

[1]   Concluded March 14, 1978.
[2]   G.A. Res. 217, adopted by the UN General Assembly on December 10, 1948.
[3]   993 U.N.T.S. 3, 6 I.L.M. 360 (1967), entered into force on January 3, 1976.
[4]   999 U.N.T.S. 171, 6 I.L.M. 368 (1967), entered into force on March 23, 1976.
[5]   G.A. Res. 100 (1979), 19 I.L.M. 38 (1980), entered into force September 3, 1981.
[6]   Adopted by the General Assembly on 7 November 1962 U.N.T.S. 231, No. 7525.
[7]   213 U.N.T.S. 221.
[8]   O.A.S. Res. XXX, adopted by the Ninth International Conference of American States. (March 30–May 2, 1948), Bogota, O.A.S. Off. Rec. OEA/Ser. L/V/I.4 Rev. (1965).
[9]   O.A.S. Official Records OEA/Ser. K/XVI/1.1, Doc. 65, Rev. 1, Corr. 1, January 7, 1970, 9 I.L.M. 101 (1970), 65 A.J.I.L. 679 (1971), 9 I.L.M. 673 (1970).
[10]   Reprinted at 29 I.L.M. 1447 (1990). Done on June 8, 1990; entered into force August 28, 1991. Costa Rica and Panama are the only parties to ratify the Protocol.
[11]   OAU Doc. CAB/LEG/67/3/Rev. 5; reprinted at, 21 I.L.M. 58 (1982).
[12]   OAU Doc. CAB/LEG/24.9/49 (1990) *entered into force* Nov. 29, 1999.
[13]   http://www.hrw.org/wr2k2/women.html.

Chapter 2

Partnerships Other Than Marriage

1. The Problem

David and Keith have lived together in the Hague, the Netherlands, for the past nine years. When the Dutch Parliament enacted legislation opening civil marriage to same gender couples in April, 2001, they decided to get married. Their wedding was a glorious occasion, although it did not change their relationship.

Keith is a freelance writer, who has been specializing in tour guides for the past few years. He can work anywhere, but his job has no benefits. David is a math professor. His job provides the couple with health insurance and retirement benefits. David has recently been offered positions in the United States and Canada. Both pay more than his present job and he is seriously considering a change. He and Keith are concerned, however, about the recognition of their marriage in either of these countries. Would they be treated as a married couple in either of these countries? What benefits or rights, if any, would they lose?

2. Overview

Domestic partnerships are generally intended for same-sex partners in marriage-like relationships. They provide such partners with many of the legal protections of marriage, although the symbolic impact, in terms of social status and acceptance, varies as a function of culture. Legal rights include those available through the State, such as nationality, social security benefits, and tax advantages. In addition, recognition of domestic partnerships by the State has consequences in the private sector, including benefits and insurance. Even where the State does not provide for the recognition of domestic partnerships, political entities within the State, such as provinces or municipalities, may do so. Even where political entities do not recognize domestic partnerships, similarly, private corporations may.

Some countries and some states in the United States explicitly prohibit same-sex marriage. The usual rule that a marriage which is valid in a State in which it is entered into will be recognized in other States, accordingly, does not follow in this context because same-sex marriages are considered void as a matter of public policy. A void marriage, as noted in Chapter 1, is not entitled to recognition anywhere. Recognition of same-sex marriages in States that neither recognize nor preclude such marriages is an open issue. Domestic partnerships, in contrast to 'marriage', are generally beyond the scope of such laws. Nor do they trigger the presumption of validity.

Some countries recognize domestic partnerships which are generally marriage-like, but do not contemplate parenthood. Denmark, the Netherlands, Norway, Sweden, Hungary, Iceland, and Spain, for example, have instituted registered domestic partnerships. British Columbia, in Canada, added gays and lesbians to the definition of spouse and parent, giving them rights and obligations with respect to custody, access, guardianship, spousal and child support, support enforcement, domestic contract enforcement, and possessory rights to property.[1]

3. Cultural Variations

As noted above, homosexual relationships are widely recognized as entitled to some legal status throughout Europe. This widespread acceptance results in detailed regimes of legal rights and obligations, like that of Germany, set out below. Where there is less acceptance, as in South America, the result is very different, as Brazil's experience demonstrates.

Germany

In 2001, the German Parliament passed a registered partnership act. Registered partnership is available only to two people of the same gender, unlike the Pacte Civil de Solidarité in France, which is open to all unmarried persons. Like those entering into marriage, those entering into a registered partnership must freely consent, cannot be within a prohibited degree of blood relationship (consanguinity), and neither can be a party to an existent marriage or registered partnership. Like parties seeking to enter into marriage, parties seeking to enter into a registered partnership must have attained majority. Unlike those entering into marriage, however, attainment of majority cannot be waived in the case of domestic partnerships.

The domestic partnership establishes mutual obligations of care and support. This explicitly includes a mutual duty of financial support (the 'obligation of solidarity'). Both parties are responsible for the necessaries of the other, including food, clothing, and household items. This is predicated on a traditional gendered division of labor, in which one partner is a breadwinner and the other a homemaker, although it is not at all clear that this pattern will prevail in the case of same sex couples. The parties may keep their own names or they may choose a new partnership name. A registered partnership may be terminated through dissolution, but there is no procedure for annulment.

Brazil

Comprehensive legislation legalizing civil unions between same sex partners was introduced in Brazil in 1995, although it has not been enacted.

The Civil Unions Bill provides specific benefits for gay and lesbian couples who register, including social security, health insurance, and the right to residence and nationality if one of the partners is not Brazilian. It further provides for the judicial termination of such unions, upon the demand of one or both of the partners, and the division of partnership assets upon such termination.

Unlike Brazilian Law governing unmarried heterosexual couples, the proposed Bill does not create any rights or duties regarding financial support. In the absence of binding federal law, the courts and administrative agencies have addressed some of the issues raised by gay and lesbian couples in a piecemeal fashion.

4. Private International Law Conventions

Although there are no private international law conventions governing recognition of domestic partnerships, there are literally thousands of private law policies, regulations, and agreements doing so. A few samples of such policies are excerpted below.[2]

American Association of University Professors, Statement of Domestic Partnership

I. *Declaration* We (employee) and, (domestic partner) certify that we are domestic partners in accordance with the following criteria and eligible for an annual contribution from the American Association of University Professors to defray the costs of the domestic partner's own purchase of health insurance:

II. *Status*

1. Neither of us is married or related to the other by blood or marriage.

2. We are each other's sole domestic partner.

3. We live together in the same residence and intend to do so indefinitely.

4. We are responsible for each other's welfare and share financial obligations, as evidenced by three of the following types of documentation, which we will provide if requested:

    a. Joint mortgage or lease

    b. Designation of domestic partner as beneficiary for life insurance conform

    c. Designation of domestic partner as primary beneficiary in employee's will

    d. Domestic partnership agreement

    e. Powers of attorney for property and health care

    f. Joint ownership of motor vehicle, joint checking account, or joint credit account

5. We certify that the subsidy will be used solely to purchase health insurance for the domestic partner. We agree to furnish the Association evidence of insurance payments.

AFSCME (American Federation of State, County, and Municipal Employees) Local 57 Side Letter on Domestic Partners

Effective May 1, 1998, UCSF Stanford Health Care implemented a policy which provided employees the opportunity to enroll same-sex domestic partners, and the children of domestic partners, in UCSF Stanford Health Care employee benefits plans available to spouses and dependent children of UCSF Stanford employees, excluding life insurance benefits. Domestic partners are also eligible for pension benefits when designated as a beneficiary by the employee.

In order to enroll a same-sex domestic partner in a benefit plan, the employee must certify that he/she shares a long-term committed relationship with the domestic partner. A domestic partnership must meet the following criteria: partners must have been living together for at least six months prior to enrollment; have an exclusive mutual commitment similar to that of marriage; and be financially responsible for each other's well-being and debts to third parties. Neither partner may be married to anyone else or have another domestic partner. Dependent children of a same-sex domestic partner may also be eligible for benefits under this plea. In general, unmarried natural or adopted children, or children for whom an employee or his/her partner has legal guardianship, who live with and are dependent on an employee or his/her partner for support, are eligible to receive benefits. Although employees are not eligible for Family and Medical Leave Act (FMLA) leave to care for a domestic partner or dependent child of a domestic partner under federal law, UCSF Stanford Health Care will provide an equivalent type leave to employees who must care for a same-sex domestic partner or dependent child of that partner, who otherwise would be eligible for FMLA leave.

Merrill Lynch, Questions & Answers on Qualified Adult Health Coverage (For U.S. Employees Only)

The attached letter announces an enhancement to the Merrill Lynch Health Care Program, which expands dependent eligibility under most available plans, including the Merrill Lynch Medical Plan, the Merrill Lynch Dental Plan, and most HMOs. Beginning January 1, 1999, eligible employees can cover *either* their spouse or one other qualified adult member of their household. Qualified adult means a domestic partner of the same or opposite sex, or an extended family member who lives with you and who meets the definition of a dependent under the Internal Revenue Code. This change means you can cover up to one adult (your spouse or a qualified adult) in addition to yourself.

The following questions and answers were developed to help you better understand this new coverage. If eligible, you can enroll a qualified adult under most of the Medical Program options and the Dental Plan during the annual enrollment period in October 1998. You will receive more information at that time.

Q: What does Merrill Lynch mean by a qualified adult?

A: For the purposes of coverage under the Merrill Lynch Health Care Program, a qualified adult may either be a domestic partner (same or opposite sex) or an extended family member.

Q: What is Merrill Lynch's definition of a domestic partner?

A: To meet eligibility requirements as a same- or opposite-sex domestic partner under the Merrill Lynch Health Care Program, you and your domestic partner must:

- Be age 18 or older;
- Have lived together for at least one year, and have an exclusive, committed relationship;
- Be mutually responsible for each other's welfare on a continuing basis;
- Not be related to each other; and
- Not be legally married to anyone else.

Q: Why is there a distinction between a domestic partner and an extended family member?

A: This distinction exists because of the way current tax law requires Merrill Lynch to treat the value of benefits provided by the company to a domestic partner. For example, if you cover your spouse, an extended family member, or a domestic partner who satisfied the definition of a tax dependent, there is no additional taxable income. However, if your domestic partner does not satisfy the definition of a tax dependent under the Internal Revenue Code, the company is required to report the value of your domestic partner's health care coverage which is paid by Merrill Lynch as taxable income to you.

5. Public International Law

Sexual orientation is not *per se* protected under international human rights law. However, in Toonen v. Australia the Human Rights Committee recognized a right to be free of criminal prosecution under Articles 2 and 26 of the Civil Covenant.

International Covenant on Civil and Political Rights[3]

Article 2 1. Each State Party to the present Covenant undertakes to respect and to ensure to all individuals within its territory and subjected to its jurisdiction the rights recognized in the present Covenant, without distinction of any kind, such as race, colour, sex, language, religion, political or other opinion, national or social origin, property, birth or other status. 2. Where not already provided for by existing legislative or other measures, each State Party to the present Covenant undertakes to take the necessary steps, in accordance with its constitutional processes and with the provisions of the present Covenant, to adopt such legislative or other measures as may be necessary to give effect to the rights recognized in the present Covenant.
3. Each State Party to the present Covenant undertakes:
(a) To ensure that any person whose rights or freedoms as herein recognized are violated shall have an effective remedy, notwithstanding that the violations has been committed by persons acting in an official capacity;
(b) To ensure that any person claiming such a remedy shall have his right thereto determined by competent judicial, administrative or legislative authorities, or by any other competent authority provided for by the legal system of the State, and to develop the possibilities of judicial remedy:
(c) To ensure that the competent authorities shall enforce such remedies when granted.

* * *

Article 26 All persons are equal before the law and are entitled without any discrimination to the equal protection of the law. In this respect, the law shall prohibit any discrimination and guarantee to all persons equal and effective protection against discrimination on any ground such as race, colour, sex, language, religion, political or other opinion, national or social origin, property, birth or other status.

While the recognition of same-sex couples as 'families' under Article 23 has not yet been generally recognized in international law, torture, cruel, inhuman, or degrading treatment of homosexuals is prohibited under the Civil Covenant.

The following report by the NGO Amnesty International illustrates some of the issues.

Egypt: Torture and imprisonment for actual or perceived sexual orientation[4] Gays in Egypt suffer discrimination, persecution and violence simply for being who they are. Those who are detained because their actual or perceived sexual orientation is deemed to threaten socially accepted norms are at particular risk of torture and ill-treatment and other human rights violations.

Around the world, countless people are targeted simply because of their perceived or self-expressed sexual orientation. Their vulnerability to human rights violations is underpinned by a web of laws and social practices which deny them an equal right to life, liberty and physical security as well as other fundamental rights such as freedom of association, freedom of expression and rights to privacy, employment, education and health care. The degree to which discrimination is institutionalized varies from country to country, but almost nowhere are they treated as equal before the law.

Discrimination is an assault on the very notion of human rights. It systematically denies certain people or groups their full human rights just because of who they are or what they believe. It is an attack on the fundamental principle underlying the Universal Declaration of Human Rights: that human rights are everyone's birthright and apply to all without distinction.

Amnesty International calls on all governments to make the principle of non-discrimination a reality in practice as well as law. No one shall be discriminated on any grounds such as race, colour, sex, language, religion, political or other opinion, national or social origin, property, birth or other status.

In Egypt in 2001 alone, dozens of men, including at least one juvenile, have been held for months in detention solely on the grounds of their actual or perceived sexual orientation. The effective criminalization of consensual sexual relations between adults of the same sex is discriminatory and violates international human rights standards. The right to freedom from discrimination on the basis of sex, which includes sexual orientation, is recognized in international treaties, including the International Covenant on Civil and Political Rights (ICCPR), to which Egypt is a State Party.

On 14 November 2001 23 men were sentenced to prison terms of between one and five years by the (Emergency) State Security Court for Misdemeanours in Cairo; 29 others in the same trial were acquitted. Twenty-one men were convicted of 'habitual debauchery', one of 'contempt of religion' and another of both charges. Amnesty International has adopted 22 of the 23 men as prisoners of conscience. The case of the twenty-third is still under consideration by the organization. In a related case, on 19 September 2001, Cairo Juvenile Court handed down a three-year prison term for 'habitual debauchery' to a juvenile. This was subsequently reduced by the Cairo Juvenile Appeal Court for Misdemeanours to a six-month prison sentence on 19 December 2001.

Amnesty International considers all those who are detained solely on the grounds of their identity, including their actual or perceived sexual orientation, to be prisoners of conscience and calls for their immediate and unconditional release.

Trinidad & Tobago/A summary of Concerns[5] *Criminalization of homosexual acts*
Amnesty International is concerned that sexual acts in private between consenting male adults and between consenting female adults remain criminalized and punishable by imprisonment, pursuant to Sections 60 and 61 of the Offences against the Person Act No. 10 (1925). Under the Sexual Offences Act No. 27 of 1986, such individuals can be charged under Sections 13 and 16. Article 16 punishes with up to five years imprisonment anyone convicted of committing any act of 'serious indecency'. 'Serious indecency' is defined in law as, 'an act, other than sexual intercourse (whether natural or unnatural), by a person involving the use of the genital organ for the purpose of arousing or gratifying sexual desire.' The Act specifically excludes private acts of 'serious indecency' between a man and a woman over 16 years of age.

Amnesty International considers that the existence of such laws violate the prohibition against discrimination, the right to privacy and the right to equal protection under the law enshrined, respectively, in Articles 2(1), 17 and 26 of the ICCPR.

Both the Attorney General and the Minister for Trade have recently issued strong verbal criticisms of Amnesty International because of the organization's support for the repeal of laws criminalizing consensual gay relations. In an interview on BBC World Service (Caribbean) on 28 September 2000, the Attorney General suggested that the existence of such a law was not a human rights issue and was a matter for the people of Trinidad and Tobago to decide.(23)

Amnesty International does not have information about recent successful prosecutions of men for consensual homosexual activity in private in Trinidad and Tobago. However, if a person were to be imprisoned under these provisions as a result of consensual sexual activity between adults conducted in private, the organization would regard him or her as a prisoner of conscience, imprisoned in violation of Articles 2, 17 and 26 of the ICCPR, and would call for the immediate and unconditional release of individuals concerned.

6. Regional Conventions

The descriptions of the difficulties confronting gays and lesbians before two major regional human rights bodies is revealing.

From The International Lesbian and Gay Association, Finding a Place in International Law[6]

Regional treaty-based human rights bodies In 1992 the refusal of the Government of Argentina to grant legal status to the non-governmental organisation Comunidad Homosexual Argentina was taken to the Inter-American Commission of Human Rights. The refusal had been confirmed in a decision of the Supreme Court of Argentina. Later that year the government granted legal recognition to the organisation, an act which the Commission considered an 'amicable settlement' of the matter. The same problem was repeated in 1995 with the refusal of government agencies to register the Costa Rican group Abraxas and the Association of Honduran Homosexuals Against Aids. After protest, the Costa Rican organisation has been registered.

In 1995 a petition was submitted to the African Commission on Human Rights asking it to open an inquiry into Zimbabwe's laws and policies on homosexual conduct. The communication was withdrawn at the request of the country's largest lesbian and gay organisation out of concern for possible reprisals by the government. Later in 1995, a large book fair, annually held in Harare, banned a gay rights exhibit under pressure from the government. Four organisations boycotted the fair in protest. President Robert Mugabe in a speech opening the fair denounced homosexuals, saying 'We do not believe they have any rights at all.' Later he called for an international campaign 'to oppose those who support homosexuality.' He said that homosexuality was not part of African culture. The barring of the lesbian and gay group from the book fair was repeated in 1996.

European Convention on Human Rights and Fundamental Freedoms[7]

Article 8 of the European Convention on Human Rights has been held by the European Court on Human Rights in Strasbourg to prohibit the criminalization of homosexual practices between consenting adults.

Dudgeon v. United Kingdom The Government right affected by the impugned legislation protects an essentially private manifestation of the human personality (see paragraph 52, third sub-paragraph, above). As compared with the era when that legislation was enacted, there is now a better understanding, and in consequence an increased tolerance, of homosexual behaviour to the extent that in the great majority of the member States of the Council of Europe it is no longer considered to be necessary or appropriate to treat homosexual practices of the kind now in question as in themselves a matter to which the sanctions of the criminal law should be applied; the Court cannot overlook the marked changes which have occurred in this regard in the domestic law of the member States (see, mutatis mutandis, the above-mentioned Marckx judgment, p. 19, par. 41, and the Tyrer judgment of 25 April 1978, Series A no. 26, pp. 15-16, par. 31). In Northern Ireland itself, the authorities have refrained in recent years from enforcing the law in respect of private homosexual acts between consenting males over the age of 21 years capable of valid consent (see paragraph 30 above). No evidence has been adduced to show that this has been injurious to moral standards in Northern Ireland or that there has been any public demand for stricter enforcement of the law. It cannot be maintained in these circumstances that there is a 'pressing social need' to make such acts criminal offences, there being no sufficient justification provided by the risk of harm to vulnerable sections of society requiring protection or by the effects on the public. On the issue of proportionality, the Court considers that such justifications as there are for retaining the law in force unamended are outweighed by the detrimental effects which the very existence of the legislative provisions in question can have on the life of a person of homosexual orientation like the applicant. Although members of the public who regard homosexuality as immoral may be shocked, offended or disturbed by the commission by others of private homosexual acts, this cannot on its own warrant the application of penal sanctions when it is consenting adults alone who are involved.

61. Accordingly, the reasons given by the Government, although relevant, are not sufficient to justify the maintenance in force of the impugned legislation in so far as it has the general effect of criminalizing private homosexual relations between adult males capable of valid consent. In particular, the moral attitudes towards male homosexuality in Northern Ireland and the concern that any relaxation in the law would tend to erode existing moral standards cannot, without more, warrant interfering with the applicant's private life to such an extent. 'Decriminalization' does not imply approval, and a fear that some sectors of the population might draw misguided conclusions in this respect from reform of the legislation does not afford a good ground for maintaining it in force with all its unjustifiable features. To sum up, the restriction imposed on Mr. Dudgeon under Northern Ireland law, by reason of its breadth and absolute character, is, quite apart from the severity of the possible penalties provided for, disproportionate to the aims sought to be achieved.

62. In the opinion of the Commission, the interference complained of by the applicant can, in so far as he is prevented from having sexual relations with young males under 21 years of age, be justified as necessary for the protection of the rights of others (see especially paragraphs 105 and 116 of the report). This conclusion was accepted and adopted by the Government, but disputed by the applicant who submitted that the age of consent for male homosexual relations should be the same as that for heterosexual and female homosexual relations, that is, 17 years under current Northern Ireland law (see paragraph 15 above). The Court has already acknowledged the legitimate necessity in a democratic society for some degree of control over homosexual conduct notably in order to provide safeguards against the exploitation and corruption of those who are specially vulnerable by reason, for example, of their youth (see paragraph 49 above). However, it falls in the first instance to the national authorities to decide on the appropriate safeguards of this kind required for the defence of morals in their society and, in particular, to fix the age under which young people should have the protection of the criminal law (see paragraph 52 above).

D. Conclusion

63. Mr. Dudgeon has suffered and continues to suffer an unjustified interference with his right to respect for his private life. There is accordingly a breach of Article 8 .

* * *

For those Reasons, the Court
1. Holds by fifteen votes to four that there is a breach of Article 8 (art. 8) of the Convention;
The Court has recently upheld France's decision to bar adoption by a homosexual, holding that France must be allowed 'a certain leeway' and noting that 'child psychiatrists and psychologists are divided about the consequences of a child being raised by one or more homosexual parents'.

Parliamentary Assembly of the Council of Europe, Thirty-Third Ordinary Session Recommendation 924 (1981)[8] on discrimination against homosexuals

The Assembly
1. Recalling its firm commitment to the protection of human rights and to the abolition of all forms of discrimination;
2. Observing that, despite some efforts and new legislation in recent years directed towards eliminating discrimination against homosexuals, they continue to suffer from discrimination and even, at time, from oppression;
3. Believing that, in the pluralistic societies of today, in which of course traditional family life has its own place and value, practices such as the exclusion of persons on the grounds of their sexual preferences from certain jobs, the existence of acts of aggression against them or the keeping of records on those persons, are survivals of several centuries or prejudice;
4. Considering that in a few member states homosexual acts are still a criminal offence and often carry severe penalties:
5. Believing that all individuals, male or female, having attained the legal age of consent provided by the law of the country they live in, and who are capable of valid personal consent, should enjoy the right to sexual self-determination;
6. Emphasizing, however, that the state has a responsibility in areas of public concern such as the protection of children,
7. Recommends that the Committee of Ministers:
   i. Urge those member states where homosexual acts between consenting adults are liable to criminal prosecution, to abolish those laws and practices;
   ii. urge member states to apply the same minimum age of consent for homosexual and heterosexual acts;
   iii. call on the governments of the member states:
   a. to order the destruction of existing special records on homosexuals and to abolish the practice of keeping records on homosexuals by the police or any other authority;
   b. to assure equality of treatment, no more no less, for homosexuals with regard to employment, pay and job security, particularly in the public sector;
   c. to ask for the cessation of all compulsory medical action or research designed to alter the sexual orientation of adults;
   d. to ensure that custody, visiting rights and accommodation of children by their parents should not be restricted on the sole grounds of the homosexual tendencies of one of them;
   e. to ask prison and other public authorities to be vigilant against the risk of rape, violence and sexual offences in prisons.

7. National Implementation

In North America, recent decisions by the high courts of both Canada and the United States have reflected and reinforced growing acceptance of homosexuality. Resistance to same-sex marriage remains, however, especially in the United States. As set forth in the *Lawrence* decision below, the Supreme Court of the United States has only recently held that states cannot criminalize consensual homosexual acts.

Canada

Vriend v. Alberta[9] The violation of s.15(1) of the *Charter* created by the omission of sexual orientation from the Act could not be saved by s.1 in that the two requirements for the application of the latter section were not met. First, there was no evidence of a pressing and substantive objective in excluding sexual orientation from the Act. Even if that objective could be determined by examining the Act as a whole, the exclusion of sexual orientation was antithetical to the Act's overall goal of protecting the dignity and rights of all persons living in Alberta. Further, even if the omission was for a pressing and substantive objective, the omission did not meet the second requirement of attempting to achieve that objective through means that were reasonable and demonstrably justifiable in a free and democratic society. First, there was no rational connection between the omission and the objective of the Act of protecting all Albertans from discrimination. The argument that the objective of the Act could be met by incrementally expanding the scope of the Act was rejected, as there was no evidence of the Alberta legislature adopting such an approach with the Act. Further, government incrementatalism is an inappropriate justification for *Charter* violations, especially with respect to human rights legislation. Second, the omission did not meet the minimal impairment requirement. The argument that the legislature's exclusion of sexual orientation was for the purpose of mediating between the conflicting interests of religious freedom and homosexuality was rejected in that there were provisions in the Act to deal with this conflict. As well, since the exclusion in this case was total, this was an inappropriate case for judicial deference. Finally, there was no evidence of any proportionality between the objective of the Act and the infringement of the appellant's equality rights.

Reading in sexual orientation as a prohibited grounds of discrimination into the impugned sections of the Act was the best remedy for the Charter violation. Case law has established that before choosing this remedy, a court must give regard to guiding principles of respect for the role of legislatures and respect for the purposes of the Charter. With respect to the first principle, reading in sexual orientation into the Act minimized interference with the Alberta legislature's goal as set out in the Act of recognizing and protecting the inherent dignity and inalienable rights of Albertans through the elimination of discriminatory practices. In contrast, striking down the impugned sections would have, in effect, gutted the Act and thereby deprived all Albertans of human rights protection. This would have constituted an excessive intrusion into the legislative scheme enacted by the legislature. With respect to the second principle, adding to the list of prohibited grounds of discrimination found in the Act was consistent with the purposes of the Charter, while the other option of striking down the impugned sections would have been inconsistent with the Charter in that it would have denied all Albertans protection from marketplace discrimination. With respect to the need for remedial precision before adopting the reading in remedy, the expression 'sexual orientation' is a term with an easily discernible common sense meaning. In terms of budgetary repercussions, they were not sufficiently significant in this case to avoid the reading in remedy. As for the effect of reading in on the thrust of the legislation, there was no deleterious impact. It was reasonable to assume that the legislature would prefer to include sexual orientation in the Act than to having no human rights legislation. As well, reading in did not interfere with the legislative objective, as the evidence indicated that the legislature decided to defer to the courts on this controversial issue. Finally, reading in did not constitute judicial interference with democratic principles. Democracy involves more than majority rule and involves legislators taking into account the interests of majorities and minorities alike. Judicial interference is warranted where the interest of minorities have not been considered. As well, there were procedures in place, such as the s. 33 of the Charter override provision which allowed the legislature to override the reading in.

Law Commission of Canada, Beyond Conjugality[10] *Introduction* Canadians enjoy a wide variety of close personal relationships – many marry or live with conjugal partners while others may share a home with parents, grandparents or a caregiver. The diversity of these relationships is a significant feature of our society, to be valued and respected. For many Canadians, the close personal relationships that they hold dear constitute an important source of comfort and help them to be productive members of society.

The law has not always respected these choices, however, or accorded them full legal recognition. While the law has recently been expanding its recognition beyond marriage to include other marriage-like relationships, it continues to focus its attention on conjugality. The Law Commission believes that governments need to pursue a more comprehensive and principled approach to the legal recognition and support of the full range of close personal relationships among adults. This requires a fundamental rethinking of the way in which governments regulate relationships.

The Diversity of Personal Adult Relationships The diversity of personal relationships formed by Canadian adults is not a new phenomenon. Alongside the nuclear family centred on the conjugal couple, there have always been a variety of other living arrangements, including adult siblings sharing a home, widows and widowers forming blended families and multi-generational households. While domestic relationships appear to have become more diverse over the past thirty years, it may simply be that public awareness has increased as a result of the increased availability of statistical data. For example, the 2001 census was the first time that Statistics Canada collected data on same-sex unions. Many non-conjugal relationships are still largely invisible in mainstream social science research. As well, we have only limited information about relationships where adults are economically, emotionally and even physically interdependent, but do not share a residence.

Conjugal Relationships A majority of Canadians form a conjugal union at some point in their lives. While the marriage rate has declined steadily since 1971, marriages still constitute a predominant choice for opposite-sex conjugal unions. Nevertheless, opposite-sex cohabitation – whether as an alternative to marriage, as a prelude to marriage or as a sequel to marriage – is a growing phenomenon that now has widespread social acceptance.

There is as yet no census data or reliable studies on the number of lesbian and gay couples living together in Canada. The available data from small-scale studies suggests that gays and lesbians form enduring conjugal relationships in numbers comparable to the population as a whole. It appears that a significant minority of Canadian households consists of same-sex couples.

Non-Conjugal Households and Non-Conjugal Relationships A substantial minority of Canadian households involves adults living alone, lone-parent families or adults living together in non-conjugal relationships. Households centred around a conjugal relationship may also include other adults with no conjugal ties to the couple, such as relatives or close friends. In addition, adult children are often returning home to live with their parents, principally for financial reasons caused by unemployment or the need to complete their education.

The concept of the economic family encompasses all relatives living in the same household, regardless of how they are related. Adult siblings living together form the largest component of this group.

We know little about non-conjugal relationships between non-relatives, since the 1996 census did not differentiate between same-sex conjugal relationships and non-conjugal relationships between non-relatives. We do know that 'families of friends' can be of great importance, particularly within the gay and lesbian communities and among older adults, especially older women.

Designing a Registration Scheme
1. *Formal Attributes* There is no reason for governments to restrict a registration scheme to conjugal couples or only to same-sex couples. We also see no compelling reason to impose a residential requirement on registrations, just as there is no requirement that married couples live together. Registrations should be terminable by mutual agreement. Registered partners should also be able to register a unilateral dissolution of their registration. The state should ensure that the legal obligations and reasonable expectations of the registrants are respected when the relationship breaks down.
2. *Legal Implications of Registrations* Registration should provide options to registrants: for example, models of predetermined rights and responsibilities reflecting a conjugal relationship or a variety of caregiving relationships.
The legal consequences of registration might be limited to the private rights and responsibilities within the relationship – both during and after the relationship. Registration would be about clarifying the mutual responsibilities each party is voluntarily assuming, both for the parties themselves and for potentially interested third parties.
3. *Intergovernmental and International Implications* Although the federal government has constitutional jurisdiction over marriage and divorce, including support and custody issues, it is unlikely that this jurisdiction would allow it to enact a registration regime that regulates the private legal obligations between adults in close personal relationships or to pass legislation regulating entry into, or exit from, this new civil arrangement. The best scenario would be a coordinated initiative among the federal, provincial and territorial governments.
On the international level, Canada should participate in the efforts toward international recognition of registration systems. It should also attempt to design its international arrangements on the basis of the existence of a variety of relationships and move toward an international recognition of registrations.

Marriage In assessing whether our marriage laws continue to meet the needs of our evolving society, a first fundamental question is whether we need marriage laws at all. Could registration replace marriage, for all legal purposes? Would this better serve the objectives of the state?

Registration Instead of Marriage A registration scheme could be used to replace marriage as a legal institution. Religious marriage ceremonies would continue to exist, but they would no longer have legal consequences. Only a system of civil registration would bind two people to a range of legal rights and responsibilities, and any two people who wanted to obtain public recognition and support of their relationship could register. We conclude that, while further debate about the appropriate role of the state in marriage is worthwhile, removing marriage as a legal mechanism for expressing commitment in a personal relationship is unlikely to be an attractive option for the majority of Canadians currently.

Adequacy of Current Marriage Laws An historical overview of marriage in the Western world shows that church and state have had varying degrees of control over this institution. In some countries, like France, the state has had exclusive jurisdiction over marriage for centuries, although of course people continue to participate in religious ceremonies. In Canada, civil marriage and religious marriage co-exist. Although it may be appropriate to revisit the role of religious authorities as state-delegates for the purpose of marriage celebrations, and consider adopting a regime that requires a civil ceremony for the marriage to have legal effect, it does lead to duplication for those who want a religious ceremony.

The state's interest in marriage is not connected to the promotion of a particular conception of appropriate gender roles, nor is it to reserve procreation and the raising of children to marriage. The state's objectives underlying contemporary regulation of marriage relate essentially to the facilitation of private ordering: providing an orderly framework in which people can express their commitment to each other, receive public recognition and support, and voluntarily assume a range of legal rights and obligations. As the Supreme Court of Canada recognized in 1999 (M. v. H.), the capacity to form conjugal relationships characterized by emotional and economic interdependence has nothing to do with sexual orientation. If governments are to continue to maintain an institution called marriage, they cannot do so in a discriminatory fashion. Accordingly, the Report recommends that Parliament and provincial/territorial legislatures move toward repealing legislative restrictions on marriages between persons of the same sex.

Conclusion In this Report, we argue that governments have tended to rely too heavily on conjugal relationships in accomplishing important state objectives. Rather than advocating simply that the law cover a broader range of relationships, the Law Commission is of the view that it is time for governments to re-evaluate the way in which they regulate personal adult relationships.

We are suggesting a new methodology for addressing the legal regulation of these relationships, consisting of four questions. Are the objectives of the legislation legitimate? If so, are relationships relevant to achieving them? If they are relevant, can individuals themselves choose which relationships should be subject to the law? Finally, if relationships are relevant and self-designation is not feasible, is there a better way for governments to include relationships?

Implementation of this methodology would greatly diminish government reliance on relationship status. However, the state would still have an important role to play with respect to personal relationships, providing the legal framework for the voluntary assumption of rights and obligations between the two parties. It should broaden the range of relationships that receive this kind of state recognition and support through the creation of a registration scheme and the legalization of same-sex marriage.

United States

Supreme Court of the United States, Syllabus, Lawrence et al. v. Texas[11] Responding to a reported weapons disturbance in a private residence, Houston police entered petitioner Lawrence's apartment and saw him and another adult man, petitioner Garner, engaging in a private, consensual sexual act. Petitioners were arrested and convicted of deviate sexual intercourse in violation of a Texas statute forbidding two persons of the same sex to engage in certain intimate sexual conduct. In affirming, the State Court of Appeals held, *inter alia*, that the statute was not unconstitutional under the Due Process Clause of the Fourteenth Amendment. The court considered *Bowers* v. *Hardwick,* 478 U. S. 186, controlling on that point.

Held: The Texas statute making it a crime for two persons of the same sex to engage in certain intimate sexual conduct violates the Due Process Clause. Pp. 3-18.

* * *

In *Carey v. Population Services Int'l,* 431 U. S. 678 (1977), the Court confronted a New York law forbidding sale or distribution of contraceptive devices to persons under 16 years of age. Although there was no single opinion for the Court, the law was invalidated. Both *Eisenstadt* and *Carey,* as well as the holding and rationale in *Roe,* confirmed that the reasoning of *Griswold* could not be confined to the protection of rights of married adults. This was the state of the law with respect to some of the most relevant cases when the Court considered *Bowers v. Hardwick.*

The facts in *Bowers* had some similarities to the instant case. A police officer, whose right to enter seems not to have been in question, observed Hardwick, in his own bedroom, engaging in intimate sexual conduct with another adult male. The conduct was in violation of a Georgia statute making it a criminal offense to engage in sodomy. One difference between the two cases is that the Georgia statute prohibited the conduct whether or not the participants were of the same sex, while the Texas statute, as we have seen, applies only to participants of the same sex. Hardwick was not prosecuted, but he brought an action in federal court to declare the state statute invalid. He alleged he was a practicing homosexual and that the criminal prohibition violated rights guaranteed to him by the Constitution. The Court, in an opinion by Justice White, sustained the Georgia law. Chief Justice Burger and Justice Powell joined the opinion of the Court and filed separate, concurring opinions. Four Justices dissented. 478 U. S., at 199 (opinion of Blackmun, J., joined by Brennan, Marshall, and STEVENS, JJ.); *id.,* at 214 (opinion of STEVENS, J., joined by Brennan and Marshall, JJ.).

The Court began its substantive discussion in *Bowers* as follows: 'The issue presented is whether the Federal Constitution confers a fundamental right upon homosexuals to engage in sodomy and hence invalidates the laws of the many States that still make such conduct illegal and have done so for a very long time.' *Id.,* at 190. That statement, we now conclude, discloses the Court's own failure to appreciate the extent of the liberty at stake. To say that the issue in *Bowers* was simply the right to engage in certain sexual conduct demeans the claim the individual put forward, just as it would demean a married couple were it to be said marriage is simply about the right to have sexual intercourse. The laws involved in *Bowers* and here are, to be sure, statutes that purport to do no more than prohibit a particular sexual act. Their penalties and purposes, though, have more far-reaching consequences, touching upon the most private human conduct, sexual behavior, and in the most private of places, the home. The statutes do seek to control a personal relationship that, whether or not entitled to formal recognition in the law, is within the liberty of persons to choose without being punished as criminals.

This, as a general rule, should counsel against attempts by the State, or a court, to define the meaning of the relationship or to set its boundaries absent injury to a person or abuse of an institution the law protects. It suffices for us to acknowledge that adults may choose to enter upon this relationship in the confines of their homes and their own private lives and still retain their dignity as free persons. When sexuality finds overt expression in intimate conduct with another person, the conduct can be but one element in a personal bond that is more enduring. The liberty protected by the Constitution allows homosexual persons the right to make this choice.

Having misapprehended the claim of liberty there presented to it, and thus stating the claim to be whether there is a fundamental right to engage in consensual sodomy, the *Bowers* Court said: 'Proscriptions against that conduct have ancient roots.' *Id.*, at 192. In academic writings, and in many of the scholarly *amicus* briefs filed to assist the Court in this case, there are fundamental criticisms of the historical premises relied upon by the majority and concurring opinions in *Bowers*. Brief for Cato Institute as *Amicus Curiae* 16-17; Brief for American Civil Liberties Union et al. as *Amici Curiae* 15-21; Brief for Professors of History et al. as *Amici Curiae* 3-10. We need not enter this debate in the attempt to reach a definitive historical judgment, but the following considerations counsel against adopting the definitive conclusions upon which *Bowers* placed such reliance.

* * *

To the extent *Bowers* relied on values we share with a wider civilization, it should be noted that the reasoning and holding in *Bowers* have been rejected elsewhere. The European Court of Human Rights has followed not *Bowers* but its own decision in *Dudgeon v. United Kingdom*. See *P. G. & J. H. v. United Kingdom*, App. No. 00044787/98, ¶56 (Eur. Ct. H. R., Sept. 25, 2001); *Modinos v. Cyprus*, 259 Eur. Ct. H. R. (1993); *Norris v. Ireland*, 142 Eur. Ct. H. R. (1988). Other nations, too, have taken action consistent with an affirmation of the protected right of homosexual adults to engage in intimate, consensual conduct. See Brief for Mary Robinson et al. as *Amici Curiae* 11-12. The right the petitioners seek in this case has been accepted as an integral part of human freedom in many other countries. There has been no showing that in this country the governmental interest in circumscribing personal choice is somehow more legitimate or urgent.

* * *

In his dissenting opinion in *Bowers* JUSTICE STEVENS came to these conclusions:

'Our prior cases make two propositions abundantly clear. First, the fact that the governing majority in a State has traditionally viewed a particular practice as immoral is not a sufficient reason for upholding a law prohibiting the practice; neither history nor tradition could save a law prohibiting miscegenation from constitutional attack. Second, individual decisions by married persons, concerning the intimacies of their physical relationship, even when not intended to produce offspring, are a form of "liberty" protected by the Due Process Clause of the Fourteenth Amendment. Moreover, this protection extends to intimate choices by unmarried as well as married persons.' 478 U. S., at 216 (footnotes and citations omitted).

JUSTICE STEVENS' analysis, in our view, should have been controlling in *Bowers* and should control here.

Bowers was not correct when it was decided, and it is not correct today. It ought not to remain binding precedent. *Bowers v. Hardwick* should be and now is overruled.

The present case does not involve minors. It does not involve persons who might be injured or coerced or who are situated in relationships where consent might not easily be refused. It does not involve public conduct or prostitution. It does not involve whether the government must give formal recognition to any relationship that homosexual persons seek to enter. The case does involve two adults who, with full and mutual consent from each other, engaged in sexual practices common to a homosexual lifestyle. The petitioners are entitled to respect for their private lives. The State cannot demean their existence or control their destiny by making their private sexual conduct a crime. Their right to liberty under the Due Process Clause gives them the full right to engage in their conduct without intervention of the government. 'It is a promise of the Constitution that there is a realm of personal liberty which the government may not enter.' *Casey, supra*, at 847. The Texas statute furthers no legitimate state interest which can justify its intrusion into the personal and private life of the individual.

After the Lawrence case, the Massachusetts Supreme Court became the first to find a right to marriage for same sex partners under the state constitution.

Goodridge & others vs. Department of Public Health & another[12]
Unofficial Synopsis Prepared by the Reporter of Decisions
The Supreme Judicial Court held today that 'barring an individual from the protections, benefits, and obligations of civil marriage solely because that person would marry a person of the same sex violates the Massachusetts Constitution.' The court stayed the entry of judgment for 180 days 'to permit the Legislature to take such action as it may deem appropriate in light of this opinion.'

'Marriage is a vital social institution,' wrote Chief Justice Margaret H. Marshall for the majority of the Justices. 'The exclusive commitment of two individuals to each other nurtures love and mutual support; it brings stability to our society. For those who choose to marry, and for their children, marriage provides an abundance of legal, financial, and social benefits. In turn it imposes weighty legal, financial, and social obligations.' The question before the court was 'whether, consistent with the Massachusetts Constitution,' the Commonwealth could deny those protections, benefits, and obligations to two individuals of the same sex who wish to marry.

In ruling that the Commonwealth could not do so, the court observed that the Massachusetts Constitution 'affirms the dignity and equality of all individuals,' and 'forbids the creation of second-class citizens.' It reaches its conclusion, the court said, giving 'full deference to the arguments made by the Commonwealth.' The Commonwealth, the court ruled, 'has failed to identify any constitutionality adequate reason for denying civil marriage to same-sex couples.' The court affirmed that it owes 'great deference to the Legislature to decide social and policy issues.' Where, as here, the constitutionality of a law is challenged, it is the 'traditional and settled role' of courts to decide the constitutional question. The 'marriage ban' the court held, 'works a deep and scarring hardship' on same-sex families 'for no rational reason.' It prevents children of same-sex couples 'from enjoying the immeasurable advantages that flow from the assurance of "a stable family structure in which children will be reared, educated, and socialized".' 'It cannot be rational under our laws,' the court held, 'to penalize children by depriving them of State benefits' because of their parents' sexual orientation.

The court rejected the Commonwealth's claim that the primary purpose of marriage was procreation. Rather, the history of the marriage laws in the Commonwealth demonstrates that 'it is the exclusive and permanent commitment of the marriage partners to one another, not the begetting of children, that is the sine qua non of marriage.'

The court remarked that its decision 'does not disturb the fundamental value of marriage in our society.' 'That same-sex couples are willing to embrace marriage's solemn obligations of exclusivity, mutual support, and commitment to one another is a testament to the enduring place of marriage in our laws and in the human spirit,' the court stated.

The opinion reformulates the common-law definition of civil marriage to mean 'the voluntary union of two persons as spouses, to the exclusion of all others. Noting that 'civil marriage has long been termed a "civil right",' the court concluded that 'the right to marry means little if it does not include the right to marry the person of one's choice, subject to appropriate government restrictions in the interests of public health, safety, and welfare.'

8. IOs and NGOs

IOs

The Human Rights Committee has heard testimony regarding the persecution of homosexuals, as set forth in the following briefing.

Trinidad & Tobago/A Summary of Concerns[13] Amnesty International welcomes the opportunity to submit a summary of its concerns on human rights issues in Trinidad and Tobago to the Human Rights Committee for the consideration of Trinidad and Tobago's combined third and fourth periodic reports submitted under article 40 of the International Covenant on Civil and Political Rights (ICCPR), acceded to by the Government of Trinidad and Tobago on 21 December 1978. Amnesty International notes that the third and fourth reports were due in 1990 and 1995 respectively.

The organisation recently met with members of the Human Rights Unit, operating under the office of the Attorney General of Trinidad and Tobago. Amnesty International notes that the Unit's responsibilities include coordination of reports to the Human Rights Committee. Amnesty International welcomes this step as a means of ensuring that the state party's commitments under Article 40 are met. Amnesty also welcomes the commitment given by members of the unit to ensuring that Trinidad and Tobago is up to date with all its international reporting obligations by the end of the year.

Amnesty International reiterates its hope that the filing of the combined periodic report currently under examination by the Human Rights Committee is a signal that the Government of Trinidad and Tobago is prepared to take measures to ensure fuller implementation of the provisions of the ICCPR in line with the observations of the Human Rights Committee, to provide information to the Human Rights Committee and to implement recommendations of the Human Rights Committee in the context of individual cases.

Amnesty International conducted research missions to Trinidad and Tobago in February and September 2000. Amnesty International's requests for meetings with government officials were declined by the government, although a meeting did take place between the Human Rights Unit and AI researchers in September 2000.

This document summarizes Amnesty International's concerns regarding human rights violations in Trinidad and Tobago.

Article 17 (1) and 26 (right to privacy; prohibition of discrimination; right to equality before the law)

NGOs

NGOs stress the human rights implications of ongoing discrimination on the basis of sexual orientation.

The International Lesbian and Gay Association[14] ILGA's aim is to work for the equality of lesbians, gay men, bisexuals and transgendered people and their liberation from all forms of discrimination. We seek to achieve this aim through the worldwide cooperation and mutual support of our members.

We focus public and government attention on cases of discrimination against lesbians, gay men, bisexuals and transgendered people by supporting programs and protest actions, asserting diplomatic pressure, providing information and working with international organisations and the international media.

* * *

Many of ILGA's international campaigns have helped to win major victories. Our pressure contributed to the legalisation of homosexuality in New Zealand, Russia, Ireland and other countries, repeal of the discriminatory US immigration policy and compliance by various nations with the decisions of the European Court of Human Rights. ILGA highlights the vicious oppression of sexual minorities in countries where it is too dangerous for any organised movement to exist, such as Iran.

Support for emerging lesbian and gay movements. In many countries ILGA has supported the emergence of the first autonomous lesbian and gay groups. ILGA has given impetus and support to groups in Latin America and Asia, and contributed to the growth of a democratic multiracial lesbian and gay movement in South Africa. ILGA also played a crucial role in the development of the first gay and lesbian organisations in the former East-Bloc countries through its 'Eastern Europe Information Pool', which operated from 1982 to 1990, despite the surveillance of the secret police in these countries. ILGA also helped organise ten sub-regional conferences for Eastern Europe in the years 1987 to 1996 to allow the participation of people who could not travel to conferences in the West and to address the problems and needs specific to this part of Europe.

Lobbying of International Organisations. ILGA lobbies international organisations such as the United Nations, the Organisation for Security and Cooperation in Europe (OSCE), the Council of Europe, and the European Union.

ILGA has participated in many of the United Nations' human rights activities, including the 2nd UN World Conference on Human Rights in Vienna (1993) and the 4th UN World Conference on Women in Beijing (1995), as well as in regional preparatory conferences which preceded these world conferences. ILGA's representatives have regularly presented evidence on human rights violations to the annual hearings in Geneva of the UN's Sub-Commission on Prevention of Discrimination and Protection of Minorities.

ILGA has taken part in the so-called Helsinki Process since 1980. At the Organisation for Security and Cooperation in Europe's 1993 Implementation Meeting in Warsaw, ILGA persuaded the OSCE that its commitments in the area of non-discrimination should also cover sexual orientation.

ILGA has promoted lesbian and gay rights within the framework of the Council of Europe in many ways, including lobbying the Parliamentary Assembly, putting forward proposals for the extension of the European Convention on Human Rights to cover sexual orientation, and supporting member organisations in taking test cases under the Convention. ILGA persuaded the Council of Europe to make the repeal of laws banning homosexuality a pre-condition for membership of the Council. This put significant pressure on membership applicants such as Lithuania, Romania, Albania, Moldova, and Macedonia to repeal their discriminatory laws. In 1998 ILGA was granted Consultative Status with the Council of Europe.

* * *

ILGA was also instrumental in the deletion of homosexuality from the World Health Organisation's International Classification of Diseases, again, after many years of campaigning.

HIV/AIDS. The issue of AIDS has been another focus of ILGA and has always been an integral part of ILGA conferences. ILGA has co-operated closely with the Global Programme on AIDS of the World Health Organization and later with its successor, the joint UN agency to fight AIDS, UNAIDS.

The ILGA Conference. Our World Conference attracts delegates from all over the globe. It provides international activists with the opportunity to learn from other countries, to present achievements, collaborate with other groups on national and international projects, and to help to set the international gay and lesbian agenda. The conferences are also a celebration of the diversity of the international gay, lesbian, bisexual and transgendered movement as we welcome representatives from a wide range of countries and constituencies.

ILGA is registered as a non-governmental non-profit international association under Belgian law.

9. A Possible Approach to the Problem

As indicated in the Overview, Keith and David are more likely to obtain benefits than recognition of their marital status. Domestic partnerships are more widely recognized than same-sex marriage. David and Keith may be willing to enter into such a partnership in a new location in order to be recognized as a couple and to obtain specified benefits, or they may view such partnerships as a second class status, but they should be aware of their options.

As noted in Section 3, Cultural Variations, domestic partnerships are widely recognized throughout Europe, indicating widespread recognition of legally sanctioned, same-sex relationships. Such recognition is less widespread in Canada, and even more rare in the U.S., as set out in Section 7, National Implementation. Even if benefits for Keith are not provided under local laws, they may be available through a private law policy adopted by David's employer. The specific benefits available under such policies are suggested in Section 4, Private International Law Conventions. As indicated in Section 5, Public International Law, Keith and David have no right under international human rights law to have their relationship recognized, although criminalization of homosexual relationships has been condemned as violative of human rights. As set out at Section 7, criminal prosecution is no longer an issue in Canada or the U.S. Section 6, Regional Conventions, again highlights the very progressive approach of the European region compared to the Inter-American and African regional human rights authorities.

The point is that by leaving Europe, David and Keith should be prepared to be faced with less enlightened legal regimes. More specifically, as set out in Section 7, the U.S. has only recently barred state laws criminalizing homosexuality. Unless they relocate to Massachusetts, where the state Supreme Court held that homosexuals could not be prohibited from marrying under the state constitution, recognition of their marriage is at best an open question in most states. In Canada, in contrast, discrimination on the basis of sexual orientation has been held to violate the Charter. Opening marriage to gays and lesbians is one way a province can address this violation, but as the Report of the Law Commission of Canada, 'Beyond Conjugality' points out, it is not necessarily the only way. After *Vriend*, Canada seems generally more hospitable to homosexuals, but David and Keith should note that local law (and culture) may be more important. Massachusetts, for example, may well be a better choice for them than Alberta.

For Further Research

1. For comprehensive overview of same sex partnerships, see Wintemute, R. and Andenaes, M. (2001), *Legal Recognition of Same Sex Partnership: A Study of National, European and International Law*, Hart, Portland. On the exclusion from marriage of homosexual couples, see Strasser, M. (1997), *Legally Wed–Same-Sex Marriage and the Constitution*; Arriola, E. (1997), Law and the Family of Choice and Need; *Brandeis Journal of Family Law*, Vol. 35, p. 691; West, R. (1998), Universalism, Liberal Theory, and the Problem of Gay Marriage, *Florida State University Law Review*, Vol. 45, p. 705; Coombs, M. (1998), Sexual Dis-Orientation: Transgendered People and Same-Sex Marriage, *UCLA Women's Law Journal*, Vol. 8, p. 219.

2. For studies regarding homosexuals as parents, see American Psychological Association, *Lesbian and Gay Parenting: a Resource for Psychologists* (1995) (reviewing 43 empirical studies as well as other articles and concluding that '[N]ot a single study has found children of gay and lesbian parents to be disadvantaged in any significant respect relative to children of heterosexual parents.') (cited in Chambers, D. and Polikoff, M. (1999) 'Family Law and Gay and Lesbian Family Issues in the 20th Century', *Family Law Quarterly*, Vol. 33, 539 and n.50); Maxwell, N. et al. (2000), 'Legal Protection for All the Children: Dutch-United States Comparison of Lesbian and Gay Parent Adoptions,' *Arizona Journal of International and Comparative Law*, Vol. 17, p. 309 (comparing Dutch and American law on adoption by homosexuals).

3. Sadtler, E. (1999), 'A Right to Same-Sex Marriage Under International Law: Can It Be Vindicated in the United States?' *Virginia Journal of International Law*, Vol. 40, p. 405.

Notes

[1] Family Relations Act, RSC 1996, c. 128, as am. by Family Relations Amendment Act, 1997 (proclaimed by February 4, 1998); Family Maintenance Enforcement Act, R.S.B.C. 1996, c. 127 as am. by Family Maintenance Enforcement Amendment ct, 1997 (proclaimed February 4, 1998).

[2] All of the following excerpts are from *Sample Workplace Policies*, http://www.hrc.org/worknet/samples/index.asp.

[3] G.A. res. 2200A (XXI), 21 U.N. GAOR Supp. (No.16) at 52, U.N. Doc. A/6316 (1966), 999 U.N.T.S. 171, *entered into force Mar.* 23, 1976.

4   http://web.amnesty.org/LIBRARY/INDEXPRINT/ENGMDE120332001   (last   visited   3/30/03).

5   Briefing for the Human Rights Committee UNCR, 70th Session, October 2000, Geneva.

6   http://www.ilga.org/Information/international/finding_a_place_in_international.htm#   Non-Governmental%20Organisations.

7   213 U.N.T.S. 221, E.T.S. 5, entered into force on September 3, 1953.

8   Assembly debate on October 1981 (10th Sitting) (see Doc. 4755, report of the Committee on Social and Health Question). Text adopted by the Assembly on 1 October 19981 (10th Sitting).

9   156 D.L.R. (4th) 385.

10 http://www.lcc.gc.ca/en/themes/pr/cpra/report.asp.

11 Certiorari to the Court of Appeals of Texas, Fourteenth District No. 02-102. Argued March 26, 2003 – Decided June 26, 2003.

12 SJC-08860 November 18, 2003.

13 Briefing for the Human Rights Committee UNCR, 70th Session, October 2000, Geneva.

14 http://www.ilga.org/About%20ILGA/A_overview.htm.

Chapter 3

Adoption

1. The Problems

Sergei

You are a lawyer in Boston, Massachusetts (U.S.) and you receive a telephone call from Allie, another lawyer in your office. She is in Romania at the office of the State Agency, holding ten month old Sergei and sobbing into the phone. She has just been advised that the government has imposed a complete bar on all foreign adoptions, including those in progress. The State Agency has no idea when the bar might be lifted.

What can she do? Does it matter whether there is a U.S. agency involved? Whether Romania is a party to the Hague Convention on Protection of Children and Cooperation in Respect of Intercountry Adoption ('Hague Convention on Adoption')? The International Covenant on Economic, Social and Cultural Rights (ICESCR)? The International Covenant on Civil and Political Rights (ICCPR)? The International Convention on the Rights of the Child (CRC)?

Carlos

Jean-Paul and Sophie live in Aix-en-Provence, France. They have recently adopted Carlos, a four year old boy from Colombia. They received a detailed social and medical history of Carlos's biological mother, a terse description of his biological father as a 'healthy twenty-six year old,' and no specific identifying information. They have been reading about the importance of roots and cultural identity for many adopted children, and have decided that they want more information. Can they get it? To whom can they address their request, and what law (if any) supports it?

2. Overview

Adoption is the process through which a legal relationship is established between a child and a person or couple who are not her biological parents. The primary purpose of adoption is to assure an otherwise parentless child a stable, secure and loving home. In addition, adoption enables those who want a child, or more children, to create or enlarge their families.

In intercountry adoption, this may be achieved through a simple adoption, in which the relationship with the child's biological parents is not completely severed, or a full adoption, in which it is. Termination of the parent/child relationship may be involuntary, initiated by the State in cases of neglect or abuse. In the alternative, the biological parents may terminate the relationship voluntarily, through abandonment of the child, or by surrendering the child to an agency or to the adoptive parents. In many States, a surrender is not valid unless it occurs after the birth. That is, a biological mother cannot be held to a pre-birth agreement to give the child up for adoption. This reflects the belief that a mother cannot agree to give up the baby in the abstract; only after the birth can she fully understand what she is giving up. Often there is an additional period in which she can revoke her decision.

This kind of protection may be extended to both parents. In the Czech Republic, for example, under the Family Law Reform of 1998, the parents may submit a written declaration to a court or appropriate agency in which they agree to their infant's adoption. This consent is not valid, however, unless it is given after the infant is six weeks old. In general, if the biological father is married to the child's mother, he also has rights to the child. If he is not married to the child's mother, he usually has fewer rights and may have none. If he has parental rights but does not want to exercise them, it is usually a simple matter for him to relinquish them. In many States, for example, he need only sign a statement to that effect.

Once the child's relationship with the biological parents is legally terminated, the child is eligible for adoption. Standards for those who are eligible to adopt are established by the national law of the country in which the adoption will take place. This may be the child's country of origin, the adoptive parents' country of residence, or both. These standards for adoptive parents vary widely, but may include: minimum (or maximum) age, proof of the ability to financially care for the child, and the absence of other children in the family.

Screening is often delegated to public or private agencies, which may impose additional requirements. In China, for example, adoptive parents are likely to be asked why they are adopting a Chinese child, whether they have any children now (either adopted or birth), details regarding their family background, an explanation as to their childlessness, and for assurances that the adopted child will be well-treated. A home study, in which a social worker visits the parents in the home where they plan to raise the child, is frequently part of the screening process. In countries where there are more parents seeking babies than babies needing parents, screening can become quite restrictive.

Once the parents have been screened, the child may be placed with them and the adoption provisionally granted. There may be a mandatory waiting period, typically between six months and a year, before the order of adoption is finalized. This final order typically gives the parents and child all of the legal rights and obligations of a biological family.

Intercountry adoption raises many important legal issues, some of which may be very sensitive. National laws regarding the disclosure of the identity of the biological parents vary widely, for example, as discussed in Section 3. The requirement of voluntary relinquishment, similarly, may be presumed from the circumstances or may be satisfied only by a formal oath before a court. In addition to the distinction between 'full' and 'simple' adoptions, noted above, some States create other categories for adoptions. The Czech Republic, for example, allows two types of adoption, one revocable on 'important grounds,' the other irrevocable. The legal issues which must be addressed in intercountry adoption are complicated, finally, by the emigration and citizenship laws of the involved States. These may require that a child be adopted before leaving her State of origin, and be adopted again under the laws of the parents' State.

Agency or Independent Adoption

Some States allow adoptions to be arranged independently, that is, without the supervision of a State-authorized agency. In an independent adoption, the prospective parents may deal directly with the biological parent, or they may hire an intermediary. Independent adoptions must comply with all applicable local or national laws governing adoption in general, such as prohibitions against baby-selling and requirements for voluntary consent. But they are free of the additional requirements that may be imposed by agencies, whether as part of an effort to reduce the pool of applicants or to further what the agency views as the best interests of the child. Instead of agency criteria, independent adoptions may be based on the specific preferences of the parties, such as a biological mother's preference for parents of a particular religious denomination.

A major risk in an independent adoption is that if the adoption is not finalized – for whatever reason – the prospective parents, as well as the biological parent, must begin the process all over again. The prospective parents may lose any money advanced – for counseling, legal fees or medical care – depending on the terms of the contract between the parties. Even if they are entitled to reimbursement, as a practical matter it may be impossible to recover funds already spent by an impoverished mother. The psychological costs of a failed adoption may be devastating, especially where the prospective parents have bonded with the child.

While these psychological costs are not entirely avoided in an agency adoption, they may be reduced. Once the prospective parents are approved to receive a baby, the agency will generally find them another baby if an initial placement is not finalized through no fault of the parents. This should be explicitly set out in the agreement with the agency, however. Agency obligations vary from State to State, so prospective parents, as well as surrendering parents, must be wary. Risk-averse prospective parents may decide to work through two agencies, one in the sending and one in the receiving State. A domestic agency with a history of successfully finalized adoptions from the sending country – and with ties to agencies there – is a relatively safe choice, but it is not always an option.

Alternatives to Adoption

It should be noted that some States, particularly Muslim States in the Middle East, do not recognize 'adoption' as described here. In such States responsibility for a parentless child is established through a system of kafalah, or guardianship, in which relatives of the child assume responsibility for the care of the child, who remains identified with the biological family. Kafalah is not subject to the Hague Convention on Intercounty Adoption and it will not be addressed in this chapter.

3. Cultural Variations

There is a broad range of cultural views as to the importance of blood ties, the stigma attached to non-marital births, and the privacy rights of all parties in the adoption triad. This is reflected in the broad range of approaches to the question of access to information regarding the child's biological family. Legal approaches to such identifying information range from complete secrecy to complete openness. In China, for example, the birth of an 'unauthorized' child may result in onerous fines and other penalties for the parents. In India, the birth of an out-of-wedlock child carries enormous social stigma. Children born under these circumstances in these countries are likely to be abandoned. They are often left in some public place, such as a public marketplace, where it is hoped that they will be found. Identifying information for such children is simply unavailable.

In New South Wales and Tennessee (U.S.), in contrast, relinquishing parents are expected to provide detailed information, including their names, addresses and telephone numbers. The purpose of such laws is to make it possible for the child to contact the biological parents upon majority if the child chooses to do so. The biological parent may veto such contact, however, and the adoptee may be subject to sanctions for violating a contact veto.

State approaches to the disclosure of identifying information are also shaped by politics and history. In Argentina, for example, the 1996 Adoption Act assures adoptees access to their original birth records. This law was passed following extensive lobbying by the Mothers of the Disappeared, whose adult children had been illegally detained and subsequently murdered by the military police ('disappeared'), during Argentina's 'dirty war' in the 1970s and early 1980s. Many of the children of the Disappeared, including infants born while their mothers were in police custody, had been adopted by the same military police who killed their parents. A few of these children were returned to their families of origin under the 'best interests of the child' standard during the 1980s, but the overwhelming majority was never found. The 1996 Act enabled the adult children of the Disappeared to discover the identities of their biological parents.

While few scandals on this scale have been exposed, Argentina is not the only State in which a traumatic history has shaped attitudes about a child's right to identity. In Poland, for example, many Jewish children were informally adopted by non-Jews during World War II when their parents fled or were taken away by the Nazis. A few of these parents returned to claim their children after the war. While Polish law did not allow adult adoptees access to identifying information until 1995, in 1986 Poland joined with Argentina to propose that the Convention on the Rights of the Child (CRC) requires States to assist any child 'illegally deprived of . . . his identity.'

Except in such cases of egregious State action, the rights of biological parents are rarely guaranteed. Rather, the emphasis is on the adoptee's right of access to information. Access to birth records is assured for adult adoptees in France, Germany, Denmark, Iceland, Norway, Sweden and the Netherlands. In England, there is a passive registry through which birth parents may be located, but there is no comparable registry through which birth parents can locate the biological children they surrendered. In Croatia, adoption records may be made available to the adoptive and the biological parents, as well as to the minor adoptee, if it is determined that disclosure is in the best interest of the child.

4. Private International Law

The Hague Convention on Protection of Children and Cooperation in Respect of Intercountry Adoption ('The Hague Convention on Adoption')

The full text of the Hague Convention on Adoption can be found at http://www.hcch.net/e/ conventions/text33e.html. Rather than setting forth detailed substantive law, the Convention takes into account the different approaches of State parties to issues such as independent adoptions, the use of private intermediaries and the disclosure of identifying information. These differences are resolved by allocating responsibility for different stages of the adoption process to the sending or receiving State. In addition, the Convention allows either State to veto the action of the other at various points during the process, or under the comprehensive veto power of Art. 17(c), which requires the Central Authorities of both States to affirmatively agree that the adoption should proceed.

Chapter I sets forth the scope of the Convention, which applies to adoptions involving residents of different Contracting States. Art. 2. Chapter I also clarifies the Convention's objectives, specifically, 'to ensure that intercountry adoptions take place in the best interests of the child and with respect for his or her fundamental rights as recognized in international law.' Art. 1(a).

Chapter II establishes the requirements for intercountry adoptions, including, importantly, a determination 'that an intercountry adoption is in the child's best interest . . . [*after*] possibilities for placement of the child within the State of origin have been given due consideration' (emphasis added). This provision reflects the assumption that it is in the child's best interest to remain in her country of origin, if she can be properly cared for there. Unlike the Convention on the Rights of the Child (CRC, Art. 21), however, the Hague Convention assumes that it is better for a child to be adopted abroad than raised in an institution in her country of origin.

Chapter II further requires the freely given consent, after counseling if needed, of all persons 'whose consent is necessary,' including that of a mature child. It expressly prohibits 'payment or compensation of any kind' to induce such consents. These provisions prevent the kind of problems that followed the U.S. 'Operation Baby Lift' at the end of its war in Vietnam. Babies were 'rescued' from orphanages in the final days of the war and placed with families in the U.S. It was later discovered that many of these babies had been placed in orphanages by their families with the understanding that such placement would be temporary, and that the child would be returned to its family when it was safe. The premature 'rescue' of these children resulted in several lawsuits, and courts ordered some of these babies returned to their biological parents (see Note 6, in For Further Research at the end of this chapter). Finally, Chapter II addresses the placement of the child in the receiving State (Art. 5), requiring that the competent authorities of that State 'have determined that the prospective adoptive parents are eligible and suited to adopt' and that the children will be 'authorized to enter and reside permanently in that State.' Art. 5.1(c).

Chapter III requires the Contracting State to designate a Central Authority which will carry out the State's duties under the Convention. This allows other States, as well as agencies and prospective adoptive parents, to know who they should be dealing with in what is often a complex bureaucracy. The Central Authority is also responsible for providing information regarding national adoption laws and otherwise cooperating with their counterparts in other Contracting States. This includes the duty to 'reply, in so far as is permitted by the law of their State, to justified requests from other Central Authorities or public authorities for information about a particular adoption situation.' Art. 9(e).

The Central Authority is ultimately responsible for ensuring that adoptions proceed in accordance with Chapter IV of the Convention. These duties may be delegated to other public authorities or 'duly accredited' bodies, such as private adoption agencies. Under Art. 22(2), a State may declare that these functions may also be performed by other 'qualified' bodies or persons, such as lawyers or social workers. A sending State may specify, however, that adoption of its children may only take place where such functions are performed by public or accredited bodies.

The Procedural Requirements set out in Chapter IV include the preparation of a report about the applicants 'including information about their identity, eligibility and suitability to adopt, background, family and medical history, social environment, reasons for adoption, ability to undertake an intercountry adoption, as well as the characteristics of the children for whom they would be qualified to care.' Art. 15. This report is to be prepared by the Central Authority of the receiving State. After determining that a child is adoptable, the Central Authority of the child's State of origin is required to 'transmit to the Central Authority of the receiving State its report on the child, . . . taking care not to reveal the identity of the mother and the father if, in the State of origin, these identities may not be disclosed.' Art. 16(d).

Chapter V requires Contracting States to recognize and give full legal effect to adoptions made in accordance with the Convention. Art. 23. Such recognition may be refused 'only if the adoption is manifestly contrary to its public policy, taking into account the best interests of the child.' Art. 24. This contemplates simple as well as full adoptions. Under Art. 26, recognition explicitly includes recognition of the 'legal parent-child relationship between the child and his or her adoptive parents' and 'the termination of a pre-existing relationship between the child and his or her mother and father, if the adoption has this effect in the Contracting State where it was made.' Under Art. 26, the law of the State of adoption governs. Under Art. 27, however, if the sending State grants a simple adoption, the receiving State may convert such adoption to a full adoption *unless* the consents were specifically limited.

Limited deference to the domestic laws of the Contracting States is also shown in Art. 29, which prohibits contact between the perspective adoptive parents and the biological parents until the required consents have been given, *unless* such contact is 'pursuant to conditions' established by the State of origin. Thus, independent adoptions are allowed under the Convention if such adoptions are allowed in the child's State of origin. Art. 30.1, similarly, requires the State to 'preserve' identifying information and medical histories of the child's biological parents, but leaves the question of actual access to such information to State law:

(1) The competent authorities of a Contracting State shall ensure that information held by them concerning the child's origin, in particular information concerning the identity of his or her parents, as well as the medical history, is preserved.

(2) They shall ensure that the child or his or her representative has access to such information, under appropriate guidance, in so far as is permitted by the law of that State.

Other provisions reflect greater consensus among Contracting States, and their shared intention to establish some common standards. Article 32, for example, provides that: '(1) No one shall derive improper financial or other gain from an activity related to an intercountry adoption. (2) Only costs and expenses, including reasonable professional fees may be charged or paid.' Art. 40, similarly, prohibits States from taking reservations to the Convention. Some of the Convention's requirements are vague and the Convention expressly contemplates variations in domestic law. The Convention nevertheless establishes clear bottom lines – with regard to the parents' and child's rights, reporting requirements, monitoring and administration – to which all Contracting Parties are bound.

U.S. State Department, Summary of the Convention's Provisions[1]

- The Convention will apply to all adoptions between countries becoming parties to it.
- An adoption will take place only if: 1) **the country of origin** has established that the child is adoptable, that an intercountry adoption is in the child's best interests, and that after counseling, the necessary consents to the adoption have been given freely, AND, **the receiving country** has determined that the prospective adoptive parents are eligible and suited to adopt, and that the child they wish to adopt will be authorized to enter and reside permanently in that country.
- Every country must establish a national government-level Central Authority to carry out certain non-delegable functions which include cooperating with other Central Authorities, overseeing the implementation of the Convention in its country, and providing information on the laws of its country.
- Other functions under the Convention are delegable to public authorities and, in many cases, to adoption agencies and other international adoption service providers.
- Services provided by persons/entities other than adoption agencies are permitted if both

the country of origin and the receiving country permit them.

- Persons wishing to adopt a child resident in another party country must apply to a designated authority in their own country.
- The Convention provides that, with limited exceptions, there can be no contact between the prospective adoptive parents and any person who cares for the child until certain requirements are met.
- All adoption service providers must be accredited/approved to provide services under the Convention.

5. Public International Law

A broad range of human rights may be implicated in international adoption. First, rights denied a mother, such as procreational rights, may affect, if not determine, whether there is a baby at all. Second, other rights denied a mother, such as prenatal care, may result in infants with special needs. Third, gender discrimination, in the form of sex-selective abortion and female infanticide, may affect the number and gender of babies available for adoption. Finally, the rights climate may affect the mother's decision to relinquish the infant. Indeed, the rights climate may be so oppressive that the 'voluntary' relinquishment required under the Hague Convention may in fact be impossible.

International Covenant on Economic, Social and Cultural Rights[2]

Article 3. The States Parties to the present Covenant undertake to ensure the equal right of men and women to the enjoyment of all economic, social and cultural rights set forth in the present Covenant.

Article 4. The States Parties to the present Covenant recognize that, in the enjoyment of those rights provided by the State in conformity with the present Covenant, the State may subject such rights only to such limitations as are determined by law only in so far as this may be compatible with the nature of these rights and solely for the purpose of promoting the general welfare in a democratic society.

* * *

Article 10. The States Parties to the present Covenant recognize that: 1. The widest possible protection and assistance should be accorded to the family, which is the natural and fundamental group unit of society, particularly for its establishment and while it is responsible for the care and education of dependent children. Marriage must be entered into with the free consent of the intending spouses.

2. Special protection should be accorded to mothers during a reasonable period before and after childbirth. During such period working mothers should be accorded paid leave or leave with adequate social security benefits.

3. Special measures of protection and assistance should be taken on behalf of all children and young persons without any discrimination for reasons of parentage or other conditions. Children and young persons should be protected from economic and social exploitation. Their employment in work harmful to their morals or health or dangerous to life or likely to hamper their normal development should be punishable by law.

* * *

Article 11. 1. The States Parties to the present Covenant recognize the right of everyone to an adequate standard of living for himself and his family, including adequate food, clothing and housing, and to the continuous improvement of living conditions. The States Parties will take appropriate steps to ensure the realization of this right, recognizing to this effect the essential importance of international cooperation based on free consent.

* * *

Article 12. 1. The States Parties to the present Covenant recognize the right of everyone to the enjoyment of the highest attainable standard of physical and mental health.

2. The steps to be taken by the States Parties to the present Covenant to achieve the full realization of this right shall include those necessary for:

(a) The provision for the reduction of the stillbirth-rate and of infant mortality and for the healthy development of the child;

International Covenant on Civil and Political Rights[3]

Article 17. 1. No one shall be subjected to arbitrary or unlawful interference with his privacy, family, home or correspondence, nor to unlawful attacks on his honour and reputation.

2. Everyone has the right to the protection of the law against such interference or attacks.

* * *

Article 23. 1. The family is the natural and fundamental group unit of society and is entitled to protection by society and the State.

Article 24. 1. Every child shall have, without any discrimination as to race, colour, sex, language, religion, national or social origin, property or birth, the right to such measures of protection as are required by his status as a minor, on the part of his family, society and the State.

2. Every child shall be registered immediately after birth and shall have a name.

3. Every child has the right to acquire a nationality.

Convention on the Elimination of All Forms of Discrimination Against Women[4]

Article 1. For the purposes of the present Convention, the term 'discrimination against women' shall mean any distinction, exclusion or restriction made on the basis of sex which has the effect or purpose of impairing or nullifying the recognition, enjoyment or exercise by women, irrespective of their marital status, on a basis of equality of men and women, of human rights and fundamental freedoms in the political, economic, social, cultural, civil or any other field.

Article 2. States Parties condemn discrimination against women in all its forms, agree to pursue by all appropriate means and without delay a policy of eliminating discrimination against women and, to this end, undertake:

(a) To embody the principle of the equality of men and women in their national constitutions or other appropriate legislation if not yet incorporated therein and to ensure, through law and other appropriate means, the practical realization of this principle;

(b) To adopt appropriate legislative and other measures, including sanctions where appropriate, prohibiting all discrimination against women;

(c) To establish legal protection of the rights of women on an equal basis with men and to ensure through competent national tribunals and other public institutions the effective protection of women against any act of discrimination;

(d) To refrain from engaging in any act or practice of discrimination against women and to ensure that public authorities and institutions shall act in conformity with this obligation;

(e) To take all appropriate measures to eliminate discrimination against women by any person, organization or enterprise;

(f) To take all appropriate measures, including legislation, to modify or abolish existing laws, regulations, customs and practices which constitute discrimination against women;

(g) To repeal all national penal provisions which constitute discrimination against women.

Article 3. States Parties shall take in all fields, in particular in the political, social, economic and cultural fields, all appropriate measures, including legislation, to ensure the full development and advancement of women, for the purpose of guaranteeing them the exercise and enjoyment of human rights and fundamental freedoms on a basis of equality with men.

Article 4. 1. Adoption by States Parties of temporary special measures aimed at accelerating de facto equality between men and women shall not be considered discrimination as defined in the present Convention, but shall in no way entail as a consequence the maintenance of unequal or separate standards; these measures shall be discontinued when the objectives of equality of opportunity and treatment have been achieved.

2. Adoption by States Parties of special measures, including those measures contained in the present Convention, aimed at protecting maternity shall not be considered discriminatory.

Article 5. States Parties shall take all appropriate measures: (a) To modify the social and cultural patterns of conduct of men and women, with a view to achieving the elimination of prejudices and customary and all other practices which are based on the idea of the inferiority or the superiority of either of the sexes or on stereotyped roles for men and women;

(b) To ensure that family education includes a proper understanding of maternity as a social function and the recognition of the common responsibility of men and women in the upbringing and development of their children, it being understood that the interest of the children is the primordial consideration in all cases.

* * *

Article 11. 2. In order to prevent discrimination against women on the grounds of marriage or maternity and to ensure their effective right to work, States Parties shall take appropriate measures:

(a) To prohibit, subject to the imposition of sanctions, dismissal on the grounds of pregnancy or of maternity leave and discrimination in dismissals on the basis of marital status;

(b) To introduce maternity leave with pay or with comparable social benefits without loss of former employment, seniority or social allowances;

(c) To encourage the provision of the necessary supporting social services to enable parents to combine family obligations with work responsibilities and participation in public life, in particular through promoting the establishment and development of a network of child-care facilities;

(d) To provide special protection to women during pregnancy in types of work proved to be harmful to them.

3. Protective legislation relating to matters covered in this article shall be reviewed

periodically in the light of scientific and technological knowledge and shall be revised, repealed or extended as necessary.

* * *

Convention on the Rights of the Child[5]

* * *

Article 1. For the purposes of the present Convention, a child means every human being below the age of eighteen years unless under the law applicable to the child, majority is attained earlier.

Article 2. 1. States Parties shall respect and ensure the rights set forth in the present Convention to each child within their jurisdiction without discrimination of any kind, irrespective of the child's or his or her parent's or legal guardian's race, colour, sex, language, religion, political or other opinion, national, ethnic or social origin, property, disability, birth or other status.
2. States Parties shall take all appropriate measures to ensure that the child is protected against all forms of discrimination or punishment on the basis of the status, activities, expressed opinions, or beliefs of the child's parents, legal guardians, or family members.

Article 3. 1. In all actions concerning children, whether undertaken by public or private social welfare institutions, courts of law, administrative authorities or legislative bodies, the best interests of the child shall be a primary consideration.
2. States Parties undertake to ensure the child such protection and care as is necessary for his or her well-being, taking into account the rights and duties of his or her parents, legal guardians, or other individuals legally responsible for him or her, and, to this end, shall take all appropriate legislative and administrative measures.
3. States Parties shall ensure that the institutions, services and facilities responsible for the care or protection of children shall conform with the standards established by competent authorities, particularly in the areas of safety, health, in the number and suitability of their staff, as well as competent supervision.

* * *

Article 5. States Parties shall respect the responsibilities, rights and duties of parents or, where applicable, the members of the extended family or community as provided for by local custom, legal guardians or other persons legally responsible for the child, to provide, in a manner consistent with the evolving capacities of the child, appropriate direction and guidance in the exercise by the child of the rights recognized in the present Convention.

Article 6. 1. States Parties recognize that every child has the inherent right to life.
2. States Parties shall ensure to the maximum extent possible the survival and development of the child.

Article 7. 1. The child shall be registered immediately after birth and shall have the right from birth to a name, the right to acquire a nationality and. as far as possible, the right to know and be cared for by his or her parents.
2. States Parties shall ensure the implementation of these rights in accordance with their national law and their obligations under the relevant international instruments in this field, in particular where the child would otherwise be stateless.

Article 8. 1. States Parties undertake to respect the right of the child to preserve his or her identity, including nationality, name and family relations as recognized by law without unlawful interference.

2. Where a child is illegally deprived of some or all of the elements of his or her identity, States Parties shall provide appropriate assistance and protection, with a view to reestablishing speedily his or her identity.

Article 9. 1. States Parties shall ensure that a child shall not be separated from his or her parents against their will, except when competent authorities subject to judicial review determine, in accordance with applicable law and procedures, that such separation is necessary for the best interests of the child. Such determination may be necessary in a particular case such as one involving abuse or neglect of the child by the parents, or one where the parents are living separately and a decision must be made as to the child's place of residence.

2. In any proceedings pursuant to paragraph 1 of the present article, all interested parties shall be given an opportunity to participate in the proceedings and make their views known.

3. States Parties shall respect the right of the child who is separated from one or both parents to maintain personal relations and direct contact with both parents on a regular basis, except if it is contrary to the child's best interests.

4. Where such separation results from any action initiated by a State Party, such as the detention, imprisonment, exile, deportation or death (including death arising from any cause while the person is in the custody of the State) of one or both parents or of the child, that State Party shall, upon request, provide the parents, the child or, if appropriate, another member of the family with the essential information concerning the whereabouts of the absent member(s) of the family unless the provision of the information would be detrimental to the well-being of the child. States Parties shall further ensure that the submission of such a request shall of itself entail no adverse consequences for the person(s) concerned.

Article 10. 1. In accordance with the obligation of States Parties under article 9, paragraph 1, applications by a child or his or her parents to enter or leave a State Party for the purpose of family reunification shall be dealt with by States Parties in a positive, humane and expeditious manner. States Parties shall further ensure that the submission of such a request shall entail no adverse consequences for the applicants and for the members of their family.

2. A child whose parents reside in different States shall have the right to maintain on a regular basis, save in exceptional circumstances personal relations and direct contacts with both parents. Towards that end and in accordance with the obligation of States Parties under article 9, paragraph 1, States Parties shall respect the right of the child and his or her parents to leave any country, including their own, and to enter their own country. The right to leave any country shall be subject only to such restrictions as are prescribed by law and which are necessary to protect the national security, public order (ordre public), public health or morals or the rights and freedoms of others and are consistent with the other rights recognized in the present Convention.

Article 11. 1. States Parties shall take measures to combat the illicit transfer and non-return of children abroad.

2. To this end, States Parties shall promote the conclusion of bilateral or multilateral agreements or accession to existing agreements.

Article 12. 1. States Parties shall assure to the child who is capable of forming his or her own views the right to express those views freely in all matters affecting the child, the views of the child being given due weight in accordance with the age and maturity of the child.

2. For this purpose, the child shall in particular be provided the opportunity to be heard in any judicial and administrative proceedings affecting the child, either directly, or through a representative or an appropriate body, in a manner consistent with the procedural rules of national law.

* * *

Article 16. 1. No child shall be subjected to arbitrary or unlawful interference with his or her privacy, family, home or correspondence, nor to unlawful attacks on his or her honour and reputation.

2. The child has the right to the protection of the law against such interference or attacks.

* * *

Article 20. 1. A child temporarily or permanently deprived of his or her family environment, or in whose own best interests cannot be allowed to remain in that environment, shall be entitled to special protection and assistance provided by the State.

2. States Parties shall in accordance with their national laws ensure alternative care for such a child.

3. Such care could include, inter alia, foster placement, kafalah of Islamic law, adoption or if necessary placement in suitable institutions for the care of children. When considering solutions, due regard shall be paid to the desirability of continuity in a child's upbringing and to the child's ethnic, religious, cultural and linguistic background.

* * *

Article 21. States Parties that recognize and/or permit the system of adoption shall ensure that the best interests of the child shall be the paramount consideration and they shall:

(a) Ensure that the adoption of a child is authorized only by competent authorities who determine, in accordance with applicable law and procedures and on the basis of all pertinent and reliable information, that the adoption is permissible in view of the child's status concerning parents, relatives and legal guardians and that, if required, the persons concerned have given their informed consent to the adoption on the basis of such counseling as may be necessary;

(b) Recognize that inter-country adoption may be considered as an alternative means of child's care, if the child cannot be placed in a foster or an adoptive family or cannot in any suitable manner be cared for in the child's country of origin;

(c) Ensure that the child concerned by inter-country adoption enjoys safeguards and standards equivalent to those existing in the case of national adoption;

(d) Take all appropriate measures to ensure that, in inter-country adoption, the placement does not result in improper financial gain for those involved in it;

(e) Promote, where appropriate, the objectives of the present article by concluding bilateral or multilateral arrangements or agreements, and endeavour, within this framework, to ensure that the placement of the child in another country is carried out by competent authorities or organs.

* * *

Article 27. 1. States Parties recognize the right of every child to a standard of living adequate for the child's physical, mental, spiritual, moral and social development.

2. The parent(s) or others responsible for the child have the primary responsibility to secure, within their abilities and financial capacities, the conditions of living necessary for the child's development.

3. States Parties, in accordance with national conditions and within their means, shall take appropriate measures to assist parents and others responsible for the child to implement this right and shall in case of need provide material assistance and support programmes, particularly with regard to nutrition, clothing and housing.
4. States Parties shall take all appropriate measures to secure the recovery of maintenance for the child from the parents or other persons having financial responsibility for the child, both within the State Party and from abroad. In particular, where the person having financial responsibility for the child lives in a State different from that of the child, States Parties shall promote the accession to international agreements or the conclusion of such agreements, as well as the making of other appropriate arrangements.

6. Regional Conventions

Two major regional agreements address the adoption of minors, the European Convention on the Adoption of Children, E.S.T. no. 58, 1967, and the Inter-American Convention on Conflict of Laws Concerning the Adoption of Minors (1984) (http://www.oas.org/juridico/english/treaties/b-48.htm) (last visited 6/9/02). In addition, the African Charter on the Rights and Welfare of the Child, OAU Doc. C.A.B./L.E.G./24.9/49 (1990), *entered into force* Nov. 29, 1999, addresses adoption in Article 24. While the regional conventions are neither as important in establishing procedures and substantive norms as national law, nor as comprehensive and widely-ratified as the Hague Convention on Adoption, they indicate the range of problems that are addressed in intercountry adoptions, as well as those that are limited to a particular region. Even where common problems are recognized, moreover, they suggest a range of approaches.

The European and the Inter-American Conventions have similar approaches to the following issues: revocability, succession, the adoptees's ties with the family of origin, and disclosure of identifying information. Under Article 12 of the Inter-American Convention, only full adoptions, in which ties to the biological family are completely severed, are irrevocable. Under Article 13 of the European Convention, adoptions are revocable 'only on serious grounds,' by judicial or administrative authorities, where explicitly permitted by national law.

Under both the Inter-American and European Conventions, adopted children are treated the same as legitimate family members for purposes of succession. The only exception is the adopted child born into lawful wedlock. Under the European Convention, the adopter's rights to inherit from the child may be restricted under these limited circumstances. This presumably refers to the adopter's right to inherit any property of the child received from the child's family of origin.

Under both the European Convention (Article 10) and the Inter-American Convention (Article 9), the adopted child's ties with the family of origin are terminated. The Inter-American Convention notes that 'impediments to marriage shall continue.' The European Convention specifies that the spouse of the adopter retains rights regarding his or her own legitimate, illegitimate or adopted child; that is, step-parent adoption does not affect the pre-existing relationship between the other parent and the child.

Both the Inter-American and the European Conventions permit, but do not require, secrecy with respect to disclosure of identifying information. The European Convention seems to leave the choice to the adopting family: 'Provision shall be made to enable an adoption to be completed without disclosing to the child's family the identity of the adopter.' Art. 20.1. Under the Inter-American Convention, in contrast, Article 7 guarantees secrecy 'where called for' under national law, but requires medical information regarding the minor and the birth parents – without identifying information – to be communicated to the adopting family.

Under Article 24(a) of the African Charter, States are to establish 'competent authorities.' Under Article 4 of the European Convention, similarly, an adoption is valid *only* if granted by a 'competent authority.' The African Charter, like the European Convention, prohibits trafficking or 'improper financial gain.' While Article 15 of the European Convention applies generally, however, Article 24(d) of the African Charter prohibits 'improper financial gain for *those who try to adopt a child*' (emphasis added).

Under the African Charter, unlike the European and Inter-American Conventions, intercountry adoption is a 'last resort,' to be utilized only if a child cannot be placed in a foster or adopted family or 'in any suitable manner,' including institutionalization, be cared for in the country of origin. Art. 24(b). (Recall the Hague Convention's preference for adoption over institutionalization, including adoption outside the country of origin over institutionalization within it.) The African Convention further restricts intercountry adoption to those countries which have ratified either the International Convention on the Rights of the Child (CRC) or the African Charter.

The regional conventions differ in their approaches to the law which should govern the adoption. The European Convention (Art. 8) merely requires that the adoption be in the 'best interest of the child,' leaving more specific criteria to the States involved. Appropriate screening mechanisms, or enquiries to be made at the time of adoption, are suggested in Article 9.2, with the understanding that these will be tailored to individual circumstances.

Under the Inter-American Convention, in contrast, responsibilities are allocated between the sending and receiving States. The authorities of the habitual residence of the adoptee are competent to grant the adoption under Article 15, or to convert a simple adoption into a full adoption. The law of the minor's habitual residence, similarly, governs capacity, consent and procedure. The law of the adopter's domicile governs capacity to adopt, including the age and marital status requirements to be met by adopters, but if the adopter's law is 'manifestly less strict,' the law of the adoptee's habitual residence governs these issues as well.

With respect to the required consents, the European Convention requires the consent of the mother, not less than six weeks after birth, and the father, but only if the child is legitimate. As noted above, under the Inter-American Convention, consents are governed by the national law of the adoptee's habitual residence. Under Article 18, however, 'The authorities of a State Party may refuse to apply the law declared applicable under this Convention when the law is manifestly contrary to its public policy.'

Both the European and the Inter-American Convention require that any reservations be addressed to specific provisions. Under the European Convention, moreover, a State may not take more than two reservations with respect to Part II, *Essential Provisions*. Reservations are in effect only for five years under the European Convention.

As set forth in the *Explanatory Report on the European Convention*, the objective was to establish 'a minimum of essential principles of adoption practice.' Para. 5(a). The Inter-American Convention takes a different approach. Rather than seeking to establish agreed-upon minimum standards, it sets out rules for governing conflicts between national laws.

7. National Implementation

The Hague Convention on Adoption does not provide a model which States can adapt to serve as their national adoption law. Rather, it provides a framework within which a broad range of national, and sub-national, laws can coexist. Since it sets forth no substantive norm with respect to the release of identifying information, for example, requiring merely that such information be 'preserved,' neither States which require identifying information nor those which prohibit it are required to change their domestic law upon ratifying the Convention.

Canada and the U.S.

Ratification of the Convention may nevertheless encourage domestic reform. In Canada and the United States, for example, ratification of the Convention was followed by the amendment of domestic law to extend the rights of citizenship to children adopted abroad. After ratifying the Hague Convention on December 19, 1996, Canada amended its federal Immigration Act on April 1, 1997. Under the amended Act, however, adopted children were still treated as immigrants. In 1998, accordingly, the Citizenship Act was amended to treat children adopted abroad by Canadian citizens the same as children of Canadian citizens born abroad.

The United States, similarly, enacted the Child Citizenship Act of 2000, which became effective on February 27, 2001, after ratifying the Convention. Under this Act, a child who is born abroad and adopted by a U.S. citizen automatically becomes a U.S. citizen, whether the adoption is finalized abroad or in the United States. The child must be in the physical custody of the U.S. parent in the United States, having been lawfully admitted. The Act amends § 320 of the Immigration and Nationality Act.

Romania

Some States find that they are either unable to meet international standards or to adequately protect their own nationals. Romania, for example, following a period of embarrassing scandal and unwanted international attention, recently announced a moratorium.

Update on Romanian Moratorium on International Adoption (6/1/02)[6]

The Romanian Adoption Committee (RAC) announced a one-year moratorium on inter-country adoption beginning June 21, 2001. That decision formalized a de facto suspension of international adoptions that had been in effect since Prime Minister Nastase's government took office in December 2000. The government subsequently extended that moratorium until as late as October 8, 2002, pending passage and implementation of new legislation intended to eliminate corruption from Romania's adoption system.

We know that this issue is a difficult one for the many Americans who are interested in adopting Romanian children. . . . In our dialogue with Romania on this issue, we have focused on two tracks:

First, we have pressed the Romanian government to allow those children whose matches with prospective parents have been approved by the government, and whose adoptions thus are in the final stages, to be exempt from the current moratorium. In response, the Romanian government announced on October 29, 2001 its intention to review these so-called 'pipeline' cases with a view to their early resolution, even while the moratorium remains in effect.

Second, there is widespread agreement that the prior Romanian legal framework did not always protect the best interests of children, creating opportunities for corruption at many levels. Reforms underway now will, we hope, lead to the creation of a more transparent inter-country adoption system that safeguards children while preventing fraud. The United States government . . . has made recommendations to the Romanian government on how to improve its adoption process and has offered to assist in drafting a new adoption law. We intend to continue our close and frank dialogue with Romanian officials on these issues. However, fundamental decisions on these issues are the purview of the Romanian government.

We know that there are disappointed prospective parents whose plans to adopt Romanian children have been adversely affected by this moratorium. The U.S. Government places great importance on resolving this issue so that these children can be placed in loving homes. We will continue to press for prompt completion of the new adoption law that is needed before international adoptions can resume. This will remain a high priority until the moratorium is lifted. This site will be updated as new information becomes available.

8. IOs and NGOs

IOs

The UN High Commissioner for Refugees has established a policy against the adoption of refugee children in emergency contexts for the reasons set forth below:

Office of the United Nations High Commissioner for Refugees Geneva, UNHCR Policy on Adoption of Refugee Children (August 1995) UNHCR's Policy on Adoption:
1. UNHCR's policy on adoption is set out on pages 130-133 of the Guidelines on protection and Care of Refugee Children. It is the Office's policy that refugee children in an emergency context are not available for adoption. Since most unaccompanied children are

not orphans, what they need is suitable interim care with a view to possible reunification with their families, not adoption. Staying with relatives in extended family units is a better solution than uprooting the child completely. Serious efforts to trace family members are essential before a child is considered eligible for adoption, and these are impossible in an emergency. Any adoption of an unaccompanied child of concern to the High Commissioner must be determined as being in the child's best interests and carried out in accordance with applicable national and international law.

2. It is UNHCR's policy that adoption should not be carried out if: a. there is reasonable hope for successful tracing and family reunification in the child's best interests;

    b. a reasonable period (normally at least two years) has not yet elapsed during which time all feasible steps to trace the parents or other surviving family members have been carried out;

    c. it is against the expressed wishes of the child or the parent; or voluntary repatriation in conditions of safety and dignity appears feasible in the near future and options in the child's country of origin would better provide for the psychosocial and cultural needs of the child than adoption in the country of asylum or a third country.

NGOs

Even in States which are parties to the Hague Convention, and have established Central Authorities to facilitate and coordinate intercountry adoptions, NGOs play a crucial role. Families with Children from China (FWCC), for example, is a U.S. NGO for families adopting from China, the major source of adoptees in the United States (surpassing Russia with 5,053 children to Russia's 4,269 in 2000). Through FWCC, its members network, lobby, and engage in a wide range of social and educational activities. FWCC also provides its members with access to a wide variety of goods and services. FWCC shows how useful, and influential, NGOs can be in the adoption context.

First, FWCC serves as an information clearinghouse for prospective adoptive parents. Its web site (www.fwcc.org) provides links to agencies which facilitate adoptions in China, information about the process, message boards and listserves for those who are going through the process, links to Internet sources about adoption, and Internet sources about China.

Second, FWCC offers adoptive families social, professional and commercial contacts. There are links to more than 40 local chapters. While many are relatively small, similar to an extended family, others are large and active, and function more like a community. The Greater New York chapter, for example, recently invited members to participate in six events over a one-month period. These ranged from play groups to parenting panels, culminating in an all-day celebration of Chinese Culture Day on Liberty Island, home of the Statute of Liberty. Throughout the year, families have a wide choice of events, from informal get-togethers to highly organized conferences, to discuss and exchange information about their experiences. The Greater New York group is a distinct community, with its own social networks, in which biracial families are the norm rather than the exception.

FWCC also provides its members with commercial contacts. 'The Mall' link on the FWCC website leads to a list of over one hundred links to companies that sell items related to Chinese adoption, from a bagel shop near the White Swan Hotel ('100 yards from the U.S. Consulate where every family adopting from China must go for INS paperwork') in Guangzhou to nutrition counseling for developmentally delayed babies.

FWCC also lobbies the U.S. government, including in its web site a link to pending U.S. legislation affecting adoptions from China. Members were urged to express their support for the Child Citizenship Act discussed above, for example. There is no lobbying aimed at the Chinese government, however. This is consistent with U.S. State Department warnings that adoptions are extremely sensitive in China and may be curtailed, to the detriment of all, if adoptive parents offend the government.

Rather, FWCC focuses on charitable initiatives benefitting Chinese orphanages. There are also links to ongoing academic research projects on Chinese adoptions, such as a study conducted by the University of Georgia on the bonding process in families with children from China.

Finally, a major purpose of the NGO is to assure that babies adopted from China, most of whom are ethnically different from their adoptive parents and the larger communities in which they live, have a strong and positive sense of the culture of their State of origin. Thus, while the U.S. has not ratified the ICESCR, the New York Chapter of FCC has in effect undertaken to assure the Article 16 'cultural rights' of these children, as set forth in its Mission Statement:

> Our mission is to provide a loving community that nurtures the adoption and parenting of children from China. We celebrate our cultural and racial differences to help one another fully integrate into our families the diverse roots, cultures and contexts from which we and our children come.

9. Possible Approaches to the Problems

Sergei

As set out in the Overview, if there is a U.S. agency involved, it may place another baby with Allie is she is unable to adopt Sergei. As described in Section 4, if Romania is a party to the Hague Convention Allie should be able to deal with the designated Central Authority (which may well have delegated authority to the State Agency as described in Section 4). Under Chapter V, moreover, Romania would be required to 'recognize and give full legal effect to adoptions made in accordance with the Convention.' Unfortunately, Sergei's adoption has not been finalized. Allie has no 'right' to Sergei under any of the cited human rights instruments because there is no legal parent/child relationship.

Indeed, it can be argued that the number of children available for adoption would be drastically reduced if the rights set out in the excerpted provisions were in fact enjoyed by biological parents, including the 'special protection' to be accorded mothers under Article 10 of the Economic Covenant, the child's right, under Article 7 of the Children's Convention, 'to know and be cared for by his or her parents,' and the

State's obligations to parents under Article 27 of the Children's Convention.

Section 7 provides more detail about the situation in Romania. Since the moratorium was initiated to eliminate corruption, the situation may be too sensitive for diplomatic intervention, but Allie should contact her senator or congressperson and explain her situation. The critical question is whether Sergei would be considered a 'pipeline' case. This requires more information about the precise status of the adoption. Hopefully, it has already been approved. In any case, the web site set out in footnote 8 should be checked for updated information.

Carlos

As indicated in Section 3, there is a broad range of cultural approaches to the question of access to information regarding the child's biological family. While it may be necessary to consult a Columbian lawyer, accordingly, the first step is to find out if Columbia is a party to the Hague Convention. If so, as set out in Section 4, Article 30.1 requires Columbia to preserve identifying information, but leaves the question of actual access to such information to State law (Columbian law or French law).

The adoptive parents' request for information is further supported by Article 7 of the Children's Convention, which affirms the 'right to know ... his or her parents [as far as possible']. As set out in Section 6, moreover, the Inter-American Convention guarantees secrecy if required under Columbian law, but requires non-identifying medical information to be communicated. (Jean-Paul and Sophie have only received such information about Carlos' biological mother.) The lawyer should check, of course, whether Columbia is a party to the Inter-American Convention.

For Further Research

1. On intercountry adoption generally, see Altstein, H. and Simon, R.J. (eds) (1991), *Intercountry Adoption: A Multinational Perspective*; Bartholet, E. (1999), *Family Bonds: Adoption, Infertility, and the New World of Child Production*, Beacon Press, Boston; Carlson, R.R. (1994), 'The Emerging Law of Intercountry Adoptions: An Analysis of the Hague Conference on Intercountry Adoption,' *Tulsa Law Journal*, Vol. 30, pp. 243-93; D'Amato, A. (1998), 'Cross-Country Adoption: A Call to Action,' *Notre Dame Law Review*, Vol. 73, pp. 1239-49; Jaffe, E.D. (ed) (1995), *Intercountry Adoptions: Laws and Perspectives of 'Sending' Countries*, Martinus Nijhoff, Dordrecht; Posner, R.A. (1987), 'The Regulation of the Market in Adoption,' *Boston University Law Review*, Vol. 67, pp. 59-72.

2. For descriptions of adoption in China, see Bouman, R.A. (2000), 'China's Attempt to Promote Domestic Adoptions: How Does China's One-Child Policy Affect Recent Revisions in China's Adoption Law and Measure Up to the Hague Convention?,' *Transnational Law*, Vol. 13, pp. 91-134; Gates, C.J. (1999), 'China's Newly Enacted Intercountry Adoption Law: Friend or Foe?,' *Indiana Journal of Global Legal Studies*, Vol. 7, pp. 369-92; Gordon, R.S. (1997), 'The New Chinese Export:

Orphaned Children, An Overview of Adopting Children from China,' *Transnational Law*, Vol. 10, pp. 121-150; Singer, J.L. (1998), 'Intercountry Adoption Laws: How Can China's One-Child Policy Coincide with the 1993 Hague Convention on Adoption?,' *Suffolk Transnational Law Review*, Vol. 22, pp. 283-310; Van Leeuwen, M. (1999), 'The Politics of Adoption Across Borders: Whose Interests Are Served?,' *Pacific Rim Law & Policy Journal*, Vol. 8, pp. 189-218.

3. For descriptions of intercountry adoption in other countries, see Masson, J. (2000), 'The 1999 Reform of Intercountry Adoption in the United Kingdom: New Solutions and Old Problems,' *Family Law Quarterly*, Vol. 34, pp. 221, 227 (explaining that UK agencies avoid intercountry adoption because the UK was a sending country until 1968, when it became known that it had sent thousands of children overseas into neglectful or abusive situations); Simov, J.P. (1999), Comment, 'The Effects of Intercountry Adoptions on Biological Parents' Rights,' *Loyola of Los Angeles International & Comparative Law Review*, Vol. 22, pp. 251-287 (analysing Hungarian law regarding intercountry adoptions); Thompson, S. (1999), Note, 'The 1998 Russian Federation Family Code Provisions on Intercountry Adoption Break the Hague Convention Ratification Gridlock: What Next? An Analysis of Post-Ratification Ramifications on Securing a Uniform Process of International Adoption,' *Transnational Law & Contemporary Problems*, Vol. 9, pp. 703-726 (setting out modifications to Russian Federation Family Code with respect to international adoptions).

4. For discussions of human rights issues in connection with adoption, see Brower Blair, D.M. (2001), 'The Impact of Family Paradigms, Domestic Constitutions, and International Conventions on Disclosure of an Adopted Person's Identities and Heritage: A Comparative Examination,' *Michigan Journal of International Law*, Vol. 22, pp. 587-671; Hillis, L. (1999), 'Intercountry Adoption Under the Hague Convention: Still an Attractive Option for Homosexuals Seeking to Adopt?' *Global Legal Studies Journal*, Vol. 6, p. 236; Oren, L. (2001), 'Righting Child Custody Wrongs: The Children of the "Disappeared" in Argentina,' *Harvard Human Rights Journal*, Vol.14, pp. 123-195; Perry, T.L. (1998), 'Transracial and International Adoption: Mothers, Hierarchy, Race, and Feminist Legal Theory,' *Yale Journal of Law and Feminism*, Vol. 10, pp. 101-164.

5. For insightful explications of the Hague Convention, see Silberman, L. (2000), 'The Hague Children's Conventions: The Internationalization of Child Law,' in Katz, S.N. et al. (eds) *Cross Currents*, pp. 589-617, Oxford, New York; Pfund, P.H. (1993), 'Introduction: Hague Conference on Private International Law, Final Act of the 17th Session, Including the Convention on Protection of Children and Cooperation in Respect of Intercountry Adoption,' *International Legal Materials*, Vol. 32, p. 1134.

6. The lawsuits filed in response to 'Operation Baby Lift,' described in Section 4 include: *Nguyen Da Yen v. Kissinger*, 528 F.2d 1194, 1197 (9th Cir. 1975; *Huynh Thi*

Anh v. Levi, 427 F. Supp. 1281 (E.D. Mich. 1977); *Hao Thi Popp v. Lucas*, 438 A.2d 755 (Conn. 1980).

7. For personal narratives by all of the females in the adoption triad, see Wadia-Ells, S. (ed 1995), *The Adoption Reader: Birth Mothers, Adoptive Mothers, and Adopted Daughters Tell Their Stories*.

Notes

[1] http://travel.state.gov/adoption_info_sheet.html (3/30/02).
[2] 933 U.N.T.S. 3, 6 I.L.M. 360 (1967). Adopted by the General Assembly of the United Nations on December 16, 1966; entered into force on January 3, 1976.
[3] 1999 U.N.T.S. 171, 6 I.L.M. 368 (1967). Adopted by the General Assembly of the United Nations on December 16, 1966; entered into force on March 23, 1976.
[4] 19 I.L.M. 33 (1980). Adopted by the General Assembly of the United Nations on December 18, 1979, entered into force on September 3, 1981.
[5] G.A. Res. 44/25, November 20, 1989; entered into force September 2, 1990.
[6] http://travel.state.gov/adoption_romania.html.

Chapter 4

Divorce/Marital Status

1. The Problem

Azizah married Abu in 1997 in Egypt. He was 56 years old and a successful lawyer; she was 20 years old and eager to marry a rich, handsome man like Abu. He had a magnificent house on the outskirts of Cairo and her quarters were luxurious. She knew that she was Abu's second wife and that his first wife, Zahra, was still living. Zahra was the same age as her husband, however, and had gone through menopause. She seemed like an old woman next to her fit, vibrant husband. Abu mentioned that she had been involved in a serious car accident several years earlier and had never regained her health. Although she seemed vague and distracted, she and Azizah got along well. Azizah became pregnant within three months of the wedding and gave birth to a son, Nasr.

Two years later, Abu informed his wives that the family was moving to France. Abu had been appointed to a prominent post with UNESCO in Paris. Azizah was unhappy about leaving her parents and her brothers, but excited about the move to a city she had heard much about. Zahra cried when she said good-bye to her three grown children, but she did not complain.

After eight months in Paris, Abu began staying late at the office every night. Once he mentioned a 'business meeting', but usually he gave no explanation. Azizah was shocked when he brought a woman about her age to their home one weekend and perfunctorily introduced Azizah and Zahra to her as 'mes soeurs.' Then they left in his new BMW.

You are not admitted to the French Bar but you are doing some consulting work with a French firm in Paris. Azizah was given your name by a mutual friend at UNESCO. She and Zahra want divorces. Zahra would like to return to Egypt; Azizah wants to stay in Paris with her son. What do you advise?

2. Overview

Divorce is the legal mechanism through which parties change their legal status from married to single. They are 'free of the bonds of matrimony' and free of marriage's rights and obligations, except as specifically provided in the decree of divorce. Although property rights and ongoing support obligations are separate matters, treated in Chapters 5 and 6, in many States a court will only decide these issues in the context of divorce.

Thus, if the State does not recognize a marriage or a particular form of marriage, divorce – and the determination of these issues – may not be available. This has serious consequences for women in customary or polygamous marriages, which many States refuse to recognize. Even in those States that may address issues of property distribution and support absent an extant marriage, in the interest of fairness or as a matter of equity, the rules and principles applied are different from those applied at divorce.

In general, the availability of divorce means better protections for the economically vulnerable party, although these protections may be minimal. In some States, those concerned with the welfare of economically vulnerable spouses, usually women, have sought to make divorce difficult to obtain, on the theory that women were likely to be better off economically if they remained married.

Divorce is also important because it enables the parties to re-marry. In Kabul, Afghanistan, for example, most of the 15 women in the Kabul jail in 2003 were accused, or convicted, of marrying a second time. Some had refused to live in marriages arranged by their parents and married for love instead. Others claimed that they had in fact obtained divorces, but that their first husbands were attempting to extort money from their second husbands. Absent formal proof of divorce, a second marriage was a crime for women under Afghan and Islamic law. Under Islamic law, a woman may have only one husband, although a man may have four wives.

Because divorce is viewed as a question of status, in some States any court having jurisdiction over the party seeking divorce can grant it. Under some interpretations of Muslim law, a husband may unilaterally divorce the wife (*talaq*) by unambiguously telling his wife, in writing or verbally, that they are divorced. A woman can divorce her husband under Islamic law by obtaining a decree from a Muslim judge (*Khul*).

Recognition of a foreign divorce depends on the law of the State in which such recognition is sought. This may be governed by any treaties, such as those excerpted in Sections 4 and 6, below, to which the State is a party. In determining whether to recognize a foreign divorce, a civil law country will generally look to the national law of the spouses. In common law countries, in contrast, the question is whether the court which granted the divorce had jurisdiction to do so.

Historically, the availability of divorce has been related to the role of marriage in a particular society. When marriage was a means of forming alliances among families, for example, divorce was unknown in the Western world. When marriage served a larger societal purpose, the couples' interests were secondary. Once companionate marriage became the norm; that is, when people began to marry for love, divorce became easier because there were no overarching societal interests at stake.

Divorce may be adversarial or by consent. When divorce is adversarial, or contested, one party asserts that the other is responsible for the breakdown of the marriage. Common grounds include adultery, desertion, cruelty, drunkenness, or failure to support. Under Islamic law, the wife's disobedience is also a ground.

Fault grounds have been criticized, however, as an unrealistic understanding of the marital relationship. All of the grounds for divorce occur in some enduring marriages; those that do break up do so because the parties are unable or uninterested in continuing the marriage. In addition, assigning fault has been viewed as arbitrary and artificial by some because spouses can grow apart without either being at fault.

Under no-fault divorce laws, guilt need not be established in court. Acts of misconduct need not be proven unless required to show 'irreconcilable differences' between the parties or that the marriage is 'irretrievably broken', or if such acts are relevant to the issue of child custody. Some States have pure no-fault laws while others have added no-fault or 'incompatibility' grounds to their preexisting law. A few States still prohibit divorce, and marriage can be ended only by death or annulment.

3. Cultural Variations

While fault is generally recognized as a ground for divorce, what constitutes fault varies by culture. Even adultery, possibly the most widely accepted ground for divorce, is interpreted differently in different cultures. In Nigeria, for example, a woman who has been raped may nevertheless be guilty of adultery. The practice of polygamy, similarly, which allows men in some Islamic states to take up to four wives, means that men may have multiple partners without committing adultery while women may not.

In Egypt, following reforms in 1979, a woman had an automatic right to a divorce from a husband who took another wife. The 1985 law, in contrast, removed the presumption of injury and required the wife to prove that she had suffered harm by reason of her husband's subsequent marriage. This represented a return to the classical position.

In 2000, Egypt adopted a version of no-fault divorce under which a woman, for the first time, can obtain a divorce without proving abuse, adultery or some other ground. Proceedings for establishing such grounds often took years because of the rights granted husbands to appeal. Under the new law, upon a wife's petition the matter is submitted to court-supervised mediation. If the divorce is granted, the wife must return any property given her under the marriage contract.

In India, in addition to divorce by mutual consent, divorce is available for fault for adultery, cruelty, desertion, or if the spouse has 'ceased to be a Hindu by conversion to another religion'; or 'has been suffering continuously or intermittently from mental disorder of such a kind and to such an extent that the petitioner cannot reasonably be expected to live with the respondent.'

In Uganda, fault is still required for divorce. While adultery is grounds for a divorce for either a wife or a husband, the wife must also prove that the husband was cruel or had deserted her. The Ugandan Law Reform Commission has recommended that the law should allow divorce on no-fault grounds, which could be claimed by either spouse.

In Ethiopia, in contrast, divorce law was reformed following the change of government in 1991. The new government ratified the International Bill of Rights, the Convention on the Rights of the Child and the Convention on the Elimination of All Forms of Discrimination Against Women, and enacted the 1995 Constitution, under which women are equal to men. The Revised Family Code (RFC) of 2000, in accordance with these reforms, now provides for no-fault divorce. While divorce was available under the old Civil Code, it was complicated and difficult to obtain.

In France, in addition to divorce on joint petition and divorce for separation for over six years, divorce is available for fault making it 'intolerable to continue conjugal life' and amounting to a grave or persistent violation of the duties of marriage (Rubellin-Devichi, 2000).

Under Islamic law, the husband has the unilateral right to terminate a marriage without a showing of fault on the part of the wife. This is known as 'talaq'. Upon exercise of the husband of his right of talaq, he must pay the wife her dowry. In 1961, in the Muslim Family Laws Ordinance, Pakistan restricted the right to triple talaq, under which the husband could immediately obtain a divorce upon the repetition of an unequivocal pronouncement of his intention to divorce his wife. In addition, a husband who wanted to marry more than one wife had to seek permission of the existing wives and the Arbitration Council. Upon contracting a polygamous marriage, moreover, he was liable for payment of dower to his existing wives.

4. Private International Law Conventions

As divorce becomes more common, and more accepted, it becomes increasingly important that legal mechanisms be available for assuring transnational recognition of divorce. As populations become increasingly mobile as a result of globalization, such mechanisms become even more necessary. There are problems, however, because differences remain about the underlying meaning of 'marriage.' Does it include polygamous marriages, for example? The following Convention is an early effort to address these issues.

Convention on the Recognition of Divorces and Legal Separations (concluded June 1st, 1970)[1]

The States signatory to the present Convention,
Desiring to facilitate the recognition of divorces and legal separations obtained in their respective territories,
Have resolved to conclude a Convention to this effect, and have agreed on the following provisions:

* * *

Article 1 The present Convention shall apply to the recognition in one Contracting State of divorces and legal separations obtained in another Contracting State which follow judicial or other proceedings officially recognized in that State and which are legally effective there.

The Convention does not apply to findings of fault or to ancillary orders pronounced on the making of a decree of divorce or legal separation; in particular, it does not apply to orders relating to pecuniary obligations or to the custody of children.

Article 2 Such divorces and legal separations shall be recognized in all other Contracting States, subject to the remaining terms of this Convention, if, at the date of the institution of the proceedings in the State of the divorce or legal separation (hereinafter called 'the State of origin') –

(1) the respondent had his habitual residence there; or
(2) the petitioner had his habitual residence there and one of the following further conditions was fulfilled –
    a) such habitual residence had continued for not less than one year immediately prior to the institution of proceedings;
    b) the spouses last habitually resided there together; or
(3) both spouses were nationals of that State; or
(4) the petitioner was a national of that State and one of the following further conditions was fulfilled –
    a) the petitioner had his habitual residence there; or
    b) he had habitually resided there for a continuous period of one year falling, at least in part, within the two years preceding the institution of the proceedings; or
(5) the petitioner for divorce was a national of that State and both the following further conditions were fulfilled –
    a) the petitioner was present in that State at the date of institution of the proceedings and
    b) the spouses last habitually resided together in a State whose law, at the date of institution of the proceedings, did not provide for divorce.

* * *

Article 6 Where the respondent has appeared in the proceedings, the authorities of the State in which recognition of a divorce or legal separation is sought shall be bound by the findings of fact on which jurisdiction was assumed.

The recognition of a divorce or legal separation shall not be refused –
    a) because the internal law of the State in which such recognition is sought would not allow divorce or, as the case may be, legal separation upon the same facts, or,
    b) because a law was applied other than that applicable under the rules of private international law of that State.

Without prejudice to such review as may be necessary for the application of other provisions of this Convention, the authorities of the State in which recognition of a divorce or legal separation is sought shall not examine the merits of the decision.

Article 7 Contracting States may refuse to recognize a divorce when, at the time it was obtained, both the parties were nationals of States which did not provide for divorce and of no other State.

Article 8 If, in the light of all the circumstances, adequate steps were not taken to give notice of the proceedings for a divorce or legal separation to the respondent, or if he was not afforded a sufficient opportunity to present his case, the divorce or legal separation may be refused recognition.

Article 9 Contracting States may refuse to recognize a divorce or legal separation if it is incompatible with a previous decision determining the matrimonial status of the spouses and that decision either was rendered in the State in which recognition is sought, or is recognized, or fulfils the conditions required for recognition, in that State.

5. Public International Law

The right to equal rights of the spouses at divorce, as well as during the marriage, has been recognized in international human rights law since its inception. The meaning of 'equality' in this context, however, remains contested.

International Covenant on Civil and Political Rights[2]

> *Article 23* 4. States parties to the present Covenant shall take appropriate steps to ensure equality of rights and responsibilities of spouses as to marriage, during marriage and at its dissolution. In the case of dissolution, provision shall be made for the necessary protection of any children.

CEDAW, General Recommendation No. 21 (13th session, 1994)[3]

> *Equality in marriage and family relations* 1. The Convention on the Elimination of All Forms of Discrimination against Women (General Assembly resolution 34/180, annex) affirms the equality of human rights for women and men in society and in the family. The Convention has an important place among international treaties concerned with human rights.
>
> 2. Other conventions and declarations also confer great significance on the family and woman's status within it. These include the Universal Declaration of Human Rights (General Assembly resolution 217/A (III)), the International Covenant on Civil and Political Rights (resolution 2200 A (XXI), annex), the Convention on the Nationality of Married Women (resolution 1040 (XI), annex), the Convention on Consent to Marriage, Minimum Age for Marriage and Registration of Marriages (resolution 1763 A (XVII), annex) and the subsequent Recommendation thereon (resolution 2018 (XX)) and the Nairobi Forward-looking Strategies for the Advancement of Women.
>
> 3. The Convention on the Elimination of All Forms of Discrimination against Women recalls the inalienable rights of women which are already embodied in the above-mentioned conventions and declarations, but it goes further by recognizing the importance of culture and tradition in shaping the thinking and behaviour of men and women and the significant part they play in restricting the exercise of basic rights by women.
>
> (c) *Background* 4. The year 1994 has been designated by the General Assembly in its resolution 44/82 as the International Year of the Family. The Committee wishes to take the opportunity to stress the significance of compliance with women's basic rights within the family as one of the measures which will support and encourage the national celebrations that will take place.
>
> 5. Having chosen in this way to mark the International Year of the Family, the Committee wishes to analyze three articles in the Convention that have special significance for the status of women in the family:

* * *

Article 16 1. States parties shall take all appropriate measures to eliminate discrimination against women in all matters relating to marriage and family relations and in particular shall ensure, on a basis of equality of men and women:

* * *

(c) The same rights and responsibilities during marriage and at its dissolution;

* * *

Various forms of family 13. The form and concept of the family can vary from State to State, and even between regions within a State. Whatever form it takes, and whatever the legal system, religion, custom or tradition within the country, the treatment of women in the family both at law and in private must accord with the principles of equality and justice for all people, as article 2 of the Convention requires.

Polygamous marriages 14. States parties' reports also disclose that polygamy is practised in a number of countries. Polygamous marriage contravenes a woman's right to equality with men, and can have such serious emotional and financial consequences for her and her dependants that such marriages ought to be discouraged and prohibited. The Committee notes with concern that some States parties, whose constitutions guarantee equal rights, permit polygamous marriage in accordance with personal or customary law. This violates the constitutional rights of women, and breaches the provisions of article 5 (a) of the Convention.

Article 16 (1) (a) and (b) 15. While most countries report that national constitutions and laws comply with the Convention, custom, tradition and failure to enforce these laws in reality contravene the Convention.

16. A woman's right to choose a spouse and enter freely into marriage is central to her life and to her dignity and equality as a human being. An examination of States parties' reports discloses that there are countries which, on the basis of custom, religious beliefs or the ethnic origins of particular groups of people, permit forced marriages or remarriages. Other countries allow a woman's marriage to be arranged for payment or preferment and in others women's poverty forces them to marry foreign nationals for financial security. Subject to reasonable restrictions based for example on a woman's youth or consanguinity with her partner, a woman's right to choose when, if, and whom she will marry must be protected and enforced at law.

* * *

18. Moreover, generally a de facto union is not given legal protection at all. Women living in such relationships should have their equality of status with men both in family life and in the sharing of income and assets protected by law. Such women should share equal rights and responsibilities with men for the care and raising of dependent children or family members.

* * *

6. Regional Conventions

The European Council has acknowledged the importance of recognizing divorce judgments in connection with the free movement of persons within the Community.

Council Regulation (EC) on jurisdiction and the recognition and enforcement of judgments in matrimonial matters and in matters of parental responsibility for children of both spouses[4]

1. The Member States have set themselves the objective of maintaining and developing the Union as an area of freedom, security and justice, in which the free movement of persons is assured. To establish such an area, the Community is to adopt, among others, the measures in the field of judicial cooperation in civil matter needed for the proper functioning of the internal market.
2. The proper functioning of the market entails the need to improve and simplify the movement of judgments in civil matters.
3. This is subject now falling within the ambit of Article 65 of the Treaty.
4. Differences between certain national rules governing jurisdiction and enforcement hamper the free movement of persons and the sound operation of the internal market. There are accordingly grounds for enacting provisions to unify the rules of conflict of jurisdiction in matrimonial matters and in matters of parental responsibility so as to simplify the formalities for rapid and automatic recognition and enforcement of judgments.

* * *

10. This Regulation should be confined to proceedings relating to divorce, legal separation or marriage annulment. The recognition of divorce and annulment rulings affects only the dissolution of matrimonial ties; despite the fact that they may be interrelation [sic], the Regulation does not affect issues such as the fault of the spouses, property consequences of the marriage, the maintenance obligation or any other ancillary measures.
11. This Regulation covers parental responsibility for children of both spouses on issues that are closely linked to proceedings for divorce, legal separation or marriage annulment.
12. The grounds of jurisdiction accepted in this Regulation are based on the rule that there must be a real link between the party concerned and the Member State exercising jurisdiction; the decision to include certain grounds corresponds to the fact that they exist in different national legal systems and are accepted by the other Member States.

* * *

16. The recognition and enforcement of judgments given in a Member State are based on the principle of mutual trust. The grounds for non-recognition are kept to the minimum required. Those proceedings should incorporate provisions to ensure observance of public policy in the State addressed and to safeguard the rights of the defence and those of the parties, including the individual rights of any child involved, and so as to withhold recognition of irreconcilable judgments.

* * *

Article 2 – Divorce, legal separation and marriage annulment
1. In matters relating to divorce, legal separation or marriage annulment, jurisdiction shall lie with the courts of the Member State:
   (a) in whose territory:
   - the spouses are habitually resident, or
   - the spouses were last habitually resident, in so far as one of them still resides there, or
   - the respondent is habitually resident, or
   - in the event of a joint application, either of the spouses is habitually resident, or
   - the applicant is habitually resident if he or she resided there for at least a year immediately before the application was made, or
   - the applicant is habitually resident if he or she resided there for at least six months immediately before the application was made and is either a national of the Member

State in question or, in the case of the United Kingdom and Ireland, has his 'domicile' there;

* * *

Article 15 – Grounds of non-recognition

1. A judgment relating to a divorce, legal separation or marriage annulment shall not be recognised:
   (a) if such recognition is manifestly contrary to the public policy of the Member State in which recognition is sought;
   (b) where it was given in default of appearance, if the respondent was not served with the document which instituted the proceedings or with an equivalent document in sufficient time and in such a way as to enable the respondent to arrange for his or her defence unless it is determined that the respondent has accepted the judgment unequivocally;
   (c) if it is irreconcilable with a judgment given in proceedings between the same parties in the Member State in which recognition is sought;

* * *

Relations with certain multilateral conventions. In relations between Member States, this Regulation shall take precedence over the following Conventions in so far as they concern matters by this Regulation: the Hague Convention of 5 October 1961 concerning the Powers of Authorities and the Law Applicable in respect of the Protection of Minors, the Luxembourg Convention of 8 September 1967 on the Recognition of Decisions Relating to the Validity of Marriages, the Hague Convention of 1 June 1970 on the Recognition of Divorces and Legal Separations, the European Convention of 20 May 1980 on Recognition and Enforcement of Decision concerning Custody of Children and on Restoration of Custody of Children, the Hague Convention of 19 October 1996 on Jurisdiction, Applicable law, Recognition, Enforcement and Cooperation in Respect of Parental Responsibility and Measures for the Protection of Children, provided that the child concerned is habitually resident in a Member State.

7. National Implementation

As the following examples indicate, divorce by mutual consent is now widely recognized, although fault grounds may also be available.

China/Marriage Law of the People's Republic of China[5]

Chapter Four/Divorce Article 31 Divorce shall be allowed if both husband and wife are willing to divorce. Both parties shall apply to the marriage registration authority for divorce. The marriage registration authority issues a certificate of divorce after confirming that both parties are indeed willing to divorce and have made proper arrangements for their children and have properly disposed of their property.

Article 32 Where either the husband or wife applies to get divorced, the departments concerned may make mediations, or he or she may file a suit at the peoples court for divorce. The peoples court shall make mediations in the process of hearing a divorce suit; divorce shall be granted if mediation fails because mutual affection no longer exists.

Divorce shall be granted if any of the following circumstances occurs and mediation fails:
a. either party is a bigamist or a person who has a spouse but co-habits with another person;
b. there is family violence or maltreatment or desertion of any family member;
c. either party is indulged in gambling, drug-abuse or has other vicious habits and refuses to mend his or her ways despite of repeated admonition;
d. both parties have lived separately due to lack of mutual affection for up to two years;
e. other circumstances that have led to the nonexistence of mutual affection as husband and wife.
If either party has been declared by court as to be missing and the other party applies to be divorced, divorce shall be granted.

Article 33 The application of the spouse of a soldier in active service for divorce shall be granted by the soldier unless the soldier is in grave fault.

Article 34 The husband may not apply for divorce when his wife is pregnant or within one year after giving birth to a child or within six months after terminating gestation. This restriction shall not apply to the case where the wife applies for divorce or the people's court deems it necessary to accept the application of the husband for divorce.

* * *

Article 36 The relationship between parents and children does not terminate due to the divorce of parents. After the divorce of the parents, the children remain the children of both parties no matter they are supported directly by either the father or mother. Both father and mother shall, after divorce, have the right and the obligation of upbringing their children.

It is the principle that the children during lactation shall be brought up by their mother after the divorce of the parents. If any dispute arises concerning which party shall bring up the children beyond lactation, such dispute shall be settled by the people's court according to the specific conditions of both parties and in light of protecting the rights and interests of the children.

Article 37 If, after the divorce of parents, the children are to be brought up by either party, the other party shall undertake a part or all of the necessary living and education expenses. The amount and term of payment shall be agreed upon by both parties; if no agreement is achieved, the amount and term shall be decided by the people's court. No agreement or judgment concerning the expenses for the living and education of the children may in no way prevent the children from making reasonable requests, where necessary, to either parent for an amount beyond the amount as determined in the said agreement or judgment.

French Divorce Law[6]

Divorce Divorce is pronounced:
- by mutual consent, upon a joint request, or upon the request of either party when accepted by the other one.
- by fault.
- by termination of common life.

In any case, the assistance of a lawyer is indispensable. In a joint request, both parties may request the assistance of the same lawyer. If your income is not sufficient to pay for the services of a lawyer, you may request, and be granted, judicial aid. Information on how to obtain legal aid is provided by the city hall.

When Your Spouse Consents to Divorce To sue for divorce by mutual agreement, there are two possibilities:

1. Divorce upon mutual consent:

The two of you file a joint request. You do not have to give the judge the reason why you want to divorce, because you are in agreement to settle the conditions of your divorce. You submit your written request for the judge's approval, one stating the mutual conditions for the duration of the divorce proceedings, and another request stating permanent conditions to be reached after the divorce is pronounced (child custody, visiting rights, alimony, allowance, lodging and partition of real property). If you confirm your desire to divorce in the presence of the judge, you will need to confirm your wish to divorce after the expiration of a probationary period of three to nine months. N.B.: This proceeding can be done only if you have been married for more than six months.

2. Divorce requested by one party and accepted by the other: Only one party files for divorce. The other party accepts it in principle. The divorcing spouse submits to the judge, through a lawyer, a request, accompanied by a statement of the facts which led him/her to decide to divorce. A copy of such request is given to the other party. If the other party recognizes the facts, the judge enters them into the record and sends the case to court for a final divorce decree.

When You and Your Spouse Are Not in Agreement to Divorce

1. Divorce requested for fault:

I- There are facts to be charged to one of spouses concerning violations of the duties and obligations of marital life, which render the marriage untenable: adultery or violence, for example. These facts are submitted for the judge's comment

2. Request to divorce because of breach of communal life:

I- When you have lived apart for at least six years.

II- When the mental faculties of your spouse have, for at least the past six years, become so altered that life together is no longer possible.

N.B.: The spouse who is requesting the divorce assumes responsibility for all fees involved, and must continue to meet his/her obligations to the children and the other spouse. The court will reject the request if either one of the spouses can prove that the divorce may result in severe moral or material consequences toward the other spouse or the children. In either case, the divorcing spouse must start the divorce proceedings with the judge, through an attorney. Such a request must specify how the spouse requesting the divorce will assure his/her obligations to the other spouse and children.

3. Consequences of Divorce for Ex-spouses

III- Ex-spouses may remarry once the final divorce is pronounced. A woman must, in principle, wait 300 days after the dissolution of the marriage or after the official decree authorizing spouses to reside separately (e.g ordonnance de non-conciliation) before remarrying. This waiting period can be waived in certain cases (such as by medical certificate stating non-pregnancy at the time of divorce).

IV- Each spouse assumes usage of his/her name before marriage unless:

a) both spouses agree otherwise;

b) there is a judge's authorization;

c) if in a case of breach of common life, the party that did not request the divorce is in accord.

V- If the divorce causes the 'innocent' spouse to suffer moral or material damages, he/she may sue for damages.

VI- If the termination of marital life has a negative effect on either of the ex-spouses, he/she may, if desired, request payment of a compensatory allowance (except in the event of breach of common life). Such an allowance should be equal to whatever it would have been if life together still existed. If one-time payment is not possible, the compensatory allowance may be paid as either a temporary or lifetime annuity. The amount of the compensatory allowance is fixed by the judge, and can be revised only in very exceptional cases.

VII- If the divorce is pronounced due to breach of common life, the ex-spouse may, if necessary, request alimony, in an amount to be determined in accordance with the financial situation of the ex-spouse.

VIII- Concerning the annulment of communal life and the settlement of accounts between husband and wife, the spouses must address themselves to the notary (notaire) appointed in the divorce decree. In the case of a joint request, a list of items belonging to the estate must be submitted to the judge with the final request.

In Case 93 - 325 DC,[7] the French Constitutional Court upheld the constitutionality of the ban on the issuance of residence cards to aliens living in France in polygamous marriages:

> Regarding section 9:
>
> 29. This section forbids the issuing of this residence card to aliens living in a situation of polygamy and to spouses of the same;
>
> 30. The Deputies, authors of the second referral, state that this section does not recognise the role of the judicial authority in guaranteeing the respect of individual freedom and that this is contrary to the principle of equality since this provision only applies to aliens and implies that children of the same father would be treated differently with regard to their right to reside in the same country as their father;
>
> 31. In the first place, a residence card is only issued to aliens; therefore, with regard to the regulations on the issuing of this card there can be no question of discrimination between nationals and aliens;
>
> 32. Secondly, the contested provision must be understood as applicable only to aliens living in France in a situation of polygamy; subject to this interpretation, the legislature acting in the public interest, as set out in the legislation, has not violated any constitutional principles or regulations

India/Hindu Marriage Act[8]

13. Divorce.
    1. Any marriage solemnized, whether before or after the commencement of this Act, may, on a petition presented by either the husband or the wife, be dissolved by a decree of divorce on the ground that the other party
        1. [Has, after the solemnization of the marriage, had voluntary sexual intercourse with any person other than his or her spouse; or
        2. Has, after the solemnization of the marriage, treated the petitioner with cruelty; or
        3. Has deserted the petitioner for a continuous period of not less than two years immediately preceding the presentation of the petition; or]
        4. Has ceased to be a Hindu by conversion to another religion; or
        5. [Has been incurably of unsound mind, or has been suffering continuously or

intermittently from mental disorder of such a kind and to such an extent that the petitioner cannot reasonably be expected to live with the respondent.

6. Has [* * *] been suffering from a virulent and incurable, form of leprosy; or
7. Has [* * *] been suffering from venereal disease in a communicable form; or
8. Has renounced the world by entering any religious order; or
9. Has not been heard of as being alive for a period of seven years or more by those persons who would naturally have heard of it, had that party been alive; [* * *]

* * *

2. A wife may also present a petition for the dissolution of her marriage by a decree of divorce on the ground,

1. In the case of any marriage solemnized before the commencement of this Act, that the husband had married again before such commencement or that any other wife of the husband married before such commencement was alive at the time of the solemnization of the marriage of the petitioner:

   Provided that in either case the other wife is alive at the time of the presentation of the petition; or

2. That the husband has, since the solemnization of the marriage, been guilty of rape, sodomy or [bestiality; or]

3. [That in a suit under section 18 of the Hindu Adoptions and Maintenance Act, 1956 (78 of 1956), or in a proceeding under section 125 of the Code of Criminal Procedure, 1973 (2 of 1974) (or under the corresponding section 488 of the Code of Criminal Procedure, 1898 (5 of 1898)), a decree or order, as the case may be, has been passed against the husband awarding maintenance to the wife not withstanding that she was living apart and that since the passing of such decree or order, cohabitation between the parties has not been resumed for one year or upwards;

4. That her marriage (whether consummated or not) was solemnized before she attained the age of fifteen years and she has repudiated the marriage after attaining that age but before attaining the age of eighteen years.

* * *

13B. Divorce by mutual consent.

Subject to the provisions of this Act a petition for dissolution of marriage by a decree of divorce may be presented to the district court by both the parties to a marriage together, whether such marriage was solemnized before or after the commencement of the Marriage Laws (Amendment) Act, 1976 (68 of 1976), on the ground that they have been living separately for a period of one year or more, that they have not been able to live together and that they have mutually agreed that the marriage should be dissolved.

On the motion of both the parties made not earlier than six months after the date of the presentation of the petition referred to in sub-section (1) and not later than eighteen months after the said date, if the petition is not withdrawn in the meantime, the court shall, on being satisfied, after hearing the parties and after making such inquiry as it thinks fit, that a marriage has been solemnized and that the averments in the petition are true, pass a decree of divorce declaring the marriage to be dissolved with effect from the date of the decree.]

14.   No petition for divorce to be presented within one year of marriage.

1.   Notwithstanding anything contained in this Act, it shall not be competent for any court to entertain any petition for dissolution of a marriage by a decree of divorce,[unless at the date of the presentation of the petition one year has elapsed] since the date of the marriage:

Provided that the court may, upon application made to it in accordance with such rules as may be made by the High Court in that behalf, allow a petition to be presented [before one year has elapsed] since the date of the marriage on the ground that the case is one of exceptional hardship to the petitioner or of exceptional depravity on the pail of the respondent, but if it appears to the court at the hearing of the petition that the petitioner obtained leave to present the petition by any misrepresentation or concealment of the nature of the case, the court may, if it pronounces a decree, do so subject to the condition that the decree shall not have effect until after the [expiry of one year] from the date of the marriage or may dismiss the petition without prejudice to any petition which may be brought after [expiration of the said one year] upon the same or substantially the same facts as those alleged in support of the petition so dismissed.

2.   In disposing of any application under this section for leave to present a petition for divorce before the [expiration of one year] from the date of the marriage, the court shall have regard to the interests of any children of the marriage and to the question whether there is a reasonable probability of a reconciliation between the parties before the expiration of the [said one year].

15. Divorced persons when may marry again.

When a marriage has been dissolved by a decree of divorce and either there is no right of appeal against the decree or, if there is such a right of appeal, the time for appealing has expired without an appeal having been presented, or an appeal has been presented but has been dismissed, it shall be lawful for either party to the marriage to marry again.

Russia

The Russian Family Code was adopted on December 25, 1995 and came in to force on March 1, 1996. These reforms were part of a comprehensive revision of Russian law undertaken to conform that law to the new Russian Federation Constitution (adopted in 1993), the U.N. Convention on the right of the child, and the new value of freedom and openness embodied in *Perestroika*.

An explicit objective was to simplify the procedure for obtaining a divorce, especially in cases of mutual consent. The new code provides in part: 'an agreement concerning the payment of alimony (amount, conditions, and procedure for payment of alimony), is made between the person obliged to pay alimony and the recipient thereof.'[9] It should be noted that the 'person obliged to pay alimony' refers very specifically to three basic, and very limited, contexts. Under Russian Law, the person is obliged to pay alimony only to: 1) a needy ex spouse who is unable to work, 2) a needy ex spouse during pregnancy and for three years after the birth of the common child; and 3) a needy ex spouse caring for a common disabled child. Except in these very limited circumstances, a spouse is not entitled to maintenance.

This is consistent with the underlying premise of gender equality, which has been a feature of Russian Law since 1917. In Russia, as in most states, the ideal of gender equality is quite different from the reality, in which women assume most responsibility for care of the home and the family. Since the end of the collapse of the Soviet Union, however, and the end of State supported social safety nets, including child care, many women have been unable to remain in the labor force. This is exacerbated by high unemployment. Thus, without maintenance, they are destitute.

8. IOs and NGOs

IOs

The Committee established by the Convention on the Elimination of All Forms of Discrimination Against Women has addressed the availability of divorce in its review of State party reports.

Consideration of reports submitted by States parties under article 18 of the Convention on the Elimination of All Forms of Discrimination against Women/Third and fourth periodic reports of States parties. New Zealand, Addendum/Status of women in New Zealand 1998: supplementary material[10]

> *Article 16. Marriage and family life/Property rights/Matrimonial property rights*
> 10. The De Facto Relationships (Property) Bill introduces a property regime to apply on the breakdown of a de facto relationship. There is currently no specific statute law for dividing property when a de facto relationship ends. The proposed property regime includes a presumption of equal sharing of the family home and chattels. The division of other relationship property will reflect both financial and non-financial contributions – unlike the Matrimonial Property Act where there is a presumption of equal sharing.

Consideration of reports submitted by States parties under Article 18 of the Convention on the Elimination of all Forms of Discrimination against Women/Fifth Periodic Reports of State Parties, Peru

* * *

328. At the initiative of the Commission on Women and Human Development, the Congress is currently holding a plenary session to mark up a bill ordering that physical separation of at least three years shall constitute grounds for divorce.

* * *

Consideration Of Reports Submitted By States Parties Under Article 18 of the Convention on the Elimination of All Forms of Discrimination Against Women/Second Periodic Reports of States Parties, Armenia

* * *

Article 16 115. In the Republic of Armenia, spouses have equal rights in entering into a marriage, during a marriage and at its dissolution. During a divorce, the interests of the children are considered paramount. Right and obligations concerning marriage and family relations are codified in the Marriage and Family Code of the Republic of Armenia.

116. According to article 1 of the Marriage and Family Code, the Code's purpose is to contribute to the building of family relations based on the free and full consent of the spouses, free of any financial motivation, and on love and respect. Marriages may be concluded only by mutual consent (art. 14).

According to article 15, the minimum legal age for marriage is 17 years, but in exceptional circumstances it may be lowered by one year for women.

117. The new Civil Code does not provide for punishment for polygamy, since this is not a current problem in Armenia.

118. Women have equal rights with men to initiate divorce proceedings, to remarry and have custody of children, and also to receive support from children.

* * *

NGOs

NGOs have focused on divorce from a range of perspectives. Some view it as crucial to women's independence and lobby for increased access to divorce. Others view the easy availability of divorce as a threat to family stability, the stability of the nation and morality in general. The first view is expressed in the excerpt from Human Rights Watch and the second in the excerpt from Focus on the Family – Malaysia.

Human Rights Watch World Report 2002: Women's Human Rights[11] Women's Status in the Family. The family remained one of the most contested sites for progress on women's rights. During Beijing + 5 at the U.N. in June, governments congratulated themselves on their efforts to ensure equality for women in all spheres of life. Some governments did, in fact, change national legislation to guarantee women's equality in the family. For example, according to a September 2000 United Nations Population Fund (unfpa) report, both the Czech Republic and Cape Verde enacted new family codes that guaranteed women equality. Nevertheless, many other governments were unyielding in their resistance to reform personal status laws that discriminated against women. Governments justified their inaction as preserving their societies' morals, unity, religion, culture, and tradition. Countries like Morocco, Rwanda, Algeria, Israel, and Egypt maintained laws and practices that blatantly discriminated against women in marriage, access to divorce, child custody, and inheritance, among other issues. These laws and practices relegated women to a subordinate status in the family and restricted their autonomy to make decisions about their lives.

In Morocco, the Family Code granted different rights to women and men and consistently rendered women's autonomy subject to male guardianship and authority. The introduction by Prime Minister El-Yousoufi of a national plan for the integration of women in development in March 1999 raised hopes that women's status would improve in critical areas. However, by late 2000, the government had made negligible progress toward implementing the plan, as a result of resistance by conservative and Islamist factions to the plan's section on reforming the Family Code. The section on the reform of the personal status code calls for, among other things, raising the age of marriage for girls and women from fifteen to eighteen, canceling the guardianship requirement for adult women, outlawing polygamy except in certain cases, giving women the right to half of their husbands' property after a divorce, and allowing divorced women to maintain custody of their children if they remarry. In March 2000, conservative and Islamist factions organized a march in Casablanca in opposition to the plan, while progressive factions organized a march in Rabat in support of it. In May 2000, in response to the intense public debate around the proposed legal reforms, the prime minister appointed a committee of scholars and religious authorities to consider the controversial aspects of the plan and make recommendations to King Mohamed VI. As of late October 2000, this committee had not met. Moroccan women's rights activists argued that, since the plan addresses only a minimum of their demands, a self-described progressive government should have no problem meeting them.

In Israel, an amendment to the Equal Rights for Women Law was passed in March 2000. The amendment deals with, inter alia, equal social rights for women in all spheres of life: the right of women over their bodies, protection against violence and trafficking, and representation for women in the public sector. The equality proposed by this law extended to all spheres of life except family life. Issues of marriage and divorce continued to be exclusively within the jurisdiction of the religious courts, be they Jewish, Christian, Muslim, or Druze. These courts controlled women's lives and their right to administer their lives. For example, under these religious courts, women did not have equal access to divorce. According to the Israel Women's Network, thousands of Jewish women continued to be a gunot, 'chained' women whose husbands refused to divorce them. Mevoi Satum (Impasse), an Israeli organization dedicated to helping a gunot, estimated that over 97 percent of men who deny their wives a divorce were physically abusive.

In January 2000, the Egyptian parliament passed a new law on divorce. The Khole' law opened the possibility for the first time for women unilaterally to request divorce on grounds of incompatibility, while requiring women to forgo alimony and to repay their husbands any dowry. Many women's rights activists acknowledged that the new law facilitated women's access to divorce, but noted that it is too early to assess its full impact.

In Uzbekistan, despite the constitutional guarantee of full legal equality between men and women, in practice, women continued to face discrimination in their access to divorce and to marital property. Privileging 'protection of the family,' over women's equality and autonomy, the Uzbek government erected legal and administrative barriers to divorce. Courts refused to grant women divorce without permission from local authorities. Also, a husband's refusal to divorce barred his wife's legal claim to marital property, although he, relying on the lax enforcement of laws against bigamy, could re-marry at will.

Focus on the Family Malaysia[12] Focus on the Family Malaysia was established in 1998 by Lee Wee Min out of concern for the deterioration of the family unit. Alarming police statistics show an increase in crime involving juveniles. Some 1,719 were arrested in 1997 for offences including murder, armed robbery, thefts and housebreaking, rape, and assault. In the year 2000, over 7,300 juvenile cases have been recorded. This is indeed a reason to worry for a small nation like Malaysia. This tip of the iceberg excludes unreported petty crimes, vandalism, sexual promiscuity, school gangsterism, truancy, drugs, smoking, gambling, and the infamous hanging out lepak culture around shopping complexes. Not only are juvenile crimes escalating, the delinquents are getting younger as well.

Many fingers are pointed in as many directions with many solutions proposed for this malaise in our society. However, from whichever angle we scrutinise this problem, there is no escaping the fact that the rapid breakdown of the family as the basic functional unit of our society is largely to be blamed.

Poor parenting skills, polygamous marriages, divorces, and the lack of or total abdication of parenting responsibilities arising from career and material pursuits have taken a heavy toll on family life. This, in concert with peer pressure, media influence and the invasion of technology like the Internet into homes have all contributed to the decline in the quality of family life.

Our Mission Focus on the Family Malaysia is a non-profit organisation with a clear mission. We believe that the family is the basic functional unit of our society, and that the well being of the family is essential to the stability, morale, security and prosperity of the nation. We are committed to strengthening families through education, training and support to help achieve this objective.

To do this, Focus on the Family Malaysia will be working through a network of professional counsellors, educationists, family support organisations, resource agencies and volunteers.

Our Activities Awareness Campaign Focus on the Family Malaysia has in place, a comprehensive programme to reach out to families and to train and equip people to help fulfil our mission. These include:

Raising public awareness on family issues and providing practical solutions through the mass media and corporations. Radio, television programmes and talk shows, feature articles in press and magazines, dedicated and regular columns in selected publications and newsletters of organisations are some of the planned activities.

With everything from wholesome entertainment and values-packed stories for children to character-builders for teenagers and adults, you can be assured of the very best family products from Focus on the Family.

Author Al Janssen, *The Marriage Masterpiece* takes a fresh look at the exquisite design God has for your marriage and brings to light the reasons your union was intended to last a lifetime.

Education and Training Seminars, Education and Training with the view to help families gain practical skills, information, support and assist them to be more affective in finding fulfilment in their roles. These seminars and workshops will be conducted at community centres, educational institutions and any organisation who wants to promote strong family values. Through these, we hope to tap into the people resource of the various bodies to eventually build up a network of people with the skills to help others. Retreats for families with on-site counselling are also being planned.

Counselling Referral Network Counselling forms an important part of our help programme. Counselling services are offered via telephone calls, letters and e-mails. A counselling referral network has also been set up through which we can refer people to a service that is nearer to, or will meet, a special need.

9. A Possible Approach to the Problem

Both women want divorces, so the first question is whether they are eligible for divorce under French or possibly Egyptian law. As explained in Section 2. Overview, divorce is not available unless the parties are married. Azizah, as the second wife in a polygamous marriage, is not legally married under French law. Rather, she (and Abu) are bigamists and their marriage is void. Indeed, as set out in Section 7, there is a ban on the issuance of residence cards to aliens living in France in polygamous marriages. (This might be an important factor for Abu, but additional facts regarding the family's legal status in France are necessary.)

As explained in Section 3, under the Egyptian version of no-fault divorce adopted in 2000, both women may be able to obtain divorces without actually proving adultery or any other ground. Assuming their applications are granted, after the mandatory court-supervised mediation, they would be required to return any property received under their respective marriage contracts. In addition, as set out in greater detail in Section 8, they would also forgo alimony. It is doubtful that this is a practical option for either.

Zahra may be able to obtain a divorce under French law, as indicated in Section 7, with or without Abu's consent. As emphasized in that Section, it will be necessary for her to retain French counsel. Since she wants to return to Egypt, however, she should be aware that a French divorce may not be recognized in Egypt. While Egypt is a party to the Convention on the Recognition of Divorces excerpted in Section 4, France is not and the Convention only requires recognition of divorces obtained in other Contracting States. Even if France were a party, moreover, Zahra has not been a habitual resident there for at least a year as required under Article 2. Whether Zahra's French divorce, including property settlement or maintenance provisions, would be recognized in Egypt, accordingly, would be a question of Egyptian law.

While Azizah cannot obtain a divorce in France, she does not need one. She can leave Abu whenever she likes, although this may be difficult as a practical matter unless she finds a job. She cannot obtain property or maintenance for herself from Abu, since she is not his wife under French law, but it is unlikely that she will be required to return any dowry either. She may also be able to obtain support for Nasr from Abu, as considered in greater detail in Chapter 10.

As explained in Section 5, under international human rights law, polygamy is generally viewed as harmful to women. As this problem illustrates, however, State refusal to recognize polygamous marriages may also present a dilemma for women like Azizah.

For Further Research

1. For detailed accounts of Shari'ah in connection with divorce, see Brown (1997), *The Rule of Law in the Arab World: Courts in Egypt and the Gulf*, Cambridge; El Alami and Hinchcliffe, *Islamic Marriage and Divorce Laws of the Arab World,*

London; Mahmood (1996), 'Egypt,' in *Statues of Personal Law in Islamic Countries*, 2nd ed., New Delhi.

2. In addition to the well-known Catholic prohibition against remarriage following divorce, Orthodox Jews, Muslims and fundamentalist Protestants often impose barriers to divorce. Orthodox Jews, for example, require the wife to obtain a *get* from her husband. Radafy (1992), 'Israel – The Incorporation of Religious Patriarchy in a Modern State,' in *Gender Bias and Family Law: Comparative Perspectives* (B. Stark ed.), pp. 209-226 (describing Jewish law, the *halacha*, under which divorce is the husband's prerogative, and Shara'ite Courts which apply Muslim Law, including the husband's right to unilateral divorce).

3. For discussions of recent divorce reforms in various States, see Ngwafor, E.N. (2000), 'Cameroon: Customary Law Versus Statutory Law: An Unresolved Second Millennium Moral Quagmire,' in A. Bainham (ed.), *The International Survey of Family Law: 2000 Edition*, Jordan, Bristol, p. 56; Palmer, M. (2000), 'China: Caring for Young and Old: Developments in the Family Law of the People's Republic of China, 1996-1998,' in ibid., p. 96; Haderka, J. (2000), 'Czech Republic: A Half-Hearted Family Law Reform of 1998,' in ibid., pp. 124-125; Copson, J. (2000) 'The Attitude of the English Court to Conflict of Jurisdiction in Divorce and Related Financial Proceedings,' *Family Law Quarterly*, Vol. 34, p. 177 (analysing English courts' approach to discretionary jurisdiction); Ali, S.S. (2002), 'Testing the Limits of Family Law Reform in Pakistan: A Critical Analysis of the Muslim Family Laws Ordinance 1961' (Bainham, A. ed.), *The International Survey of Family Law: 2002 edition*, Jordan, Bristol, pp. 317-337; Teshome, T. (2002), 'Ethiopia: Reflections on the Revised Family Code of 2000,' in ibid., pp. 153-170; Ekirikubinza, L.T. (2002), 'Family Relations and the Law in Uganda: Insights into Current Issues,' in pp. 433-437; Khazova, O.A. (2002), 'Five Years of the Russian Family Code: The First Results,' in ibid., pp. 347-356.

4. For accounts of recent efforts to legalize divorce in the Phillippines and in Chile, see Raquiza, M. (2001), 'Couplings and Uncouplings in a land without Divorce'; http://www.legmanila.com//22/article/1016.asp; Gallardo, E. (2003); 'Church speaks against Chile Divorce Law,' *Boston Globe*, 10 October 2003, p. A25.

5. The Nigerian law on adultery, described in Section 3, attracted an enormous amount of international media attention when young a mother was sentenced to death by stoning for allegedly violating it. See, e.g., Dowden, R. (2002); 'Death By Stoning,' *New York Times*.

Her sentence was ultimately invalidated by a Shariah Court of Appeals, but not before a coalition of lawyers and African feminists issued a plea to Westerners to stop their barrage of protests, which was producing a backlash. See, e.g., Koinange, J. (2003), 'Woman Sentenced to Stoning Freed'; CNN.Com/World, September, p.1.

Notes

[1] The following States are parties to this Convention: Australia, China, Hong Kong (Special Administrative Region only), Cyprus, Czech Republic, Denmark, Egypt, Estonia, Finland, Italy, Luxembourg, Netherlands, Norway, Poland, Portugal, Slovakia, Sweden, Switzerland, United Kingdom.

[2] G.A. res. 2200A (XXI), 21 U.N. GAOR Supp. (No. 16) at 52, U.N. Doc. A/6316 (1966), 999 U.N.T.S. 171, *entered into force* Mar. 23, 1976.

[3] http://www.un.org/womenwatch/daw/cedaw/committ.htm.

[4] No 1347/2000 of 29 May 2000.

[5] 1980 – amended according to the Decision on Amending the Marriage Law of the People's Republic of China made at the 21st meeting of the Standing Committee of the Ninth National People's Congress on April 28, 2001.

[6] Consular Section, U.S. Embassy, Paris
http://www.international-divorce.com/frenchdivorcelaw/ (last visited 11/11/2003).

[7] /laws/global_law/french-cases/constitutionnel/print_constitutionnel.shtml?13aug1993 Print Date 13 August 1993 Translated by Conseil Constitutionnel Copyright Conseil Constitutionnel.

[8] http://law.indiainfo.com/personal/hindu/nullity-div.htm (last visited Sept. 16, 2003).

[9] Russian Family Codes 99.

[10] 20 April, 1998.

[11] http://www.hrw.org/wr2k2/women/women.html (last visited 10/10/03).

[12] http://www.family.org.my.

Chapter 5

Divorce/Maintenance and Support

1. The Problem

Isabelle and Ferdinand were married in the Philippines in 1980. Isabelle was 20 and Ferdinand was 30. They have three children and the youngest, Gloria, is 17 and still lives at home. Isabelle took care of the home and the family and Ferdinand supported them through his government job. When her youngest daughter was in middle school, Isabelle decided that she would like to work as a legal secretary and told Ferdinand about a training program she had seen advertised on television. Ferdinand said that he was perfectly capable of providing for his family and that he would prefer if she did not work outside the home. She deferred to his wishes.

In 2000, Isabelle and Ferdinand moved to California. There they lived comfortably on income from Ferdinand's investments. Isabelle had a brief, torrid affair with the young man who installed their swimming pool. She confessed to Ferdinand, who immediately demanded a divorce.

Is Isabelle entitled to support? If so, how much? How long should she receive such support? What additional facts would be helpful in answering these questions?

2. Overview

As described in Chapter 4, *Divorce/Marital Status*, divorce remains problematic in many States. The extent to which a woman's role in society is determined by her role within the family is the major factor in determining the extent to which divorce will be viewed as a problem in that society. Where marriage determines a woman's social role, for example, divorce creates a social problem.

This chapter focuses on the termination of marriage as an economic relationship. Women everywhere in the world earn less than men. Marriage enables them to benefit from their husbands' higher incomes. Women who have not been employed outside the home (or who cannot be employed outside the home because of social restrictions), face a lower lifestyle at divorce, and sometimes destitution.

The question of maintenance or support is often a question of who is responsible for the support of divorced women? In many States, the answer depends on who was responsible for the divorce. An 'innocent' wife is entitled to support from her husband, while a wife whose adultery or 'disobedience' led to the divorce is not. In some States, if the divorce is the fault of the husband, the wife may be entitled to relatively generous maintenance until she remarries or dies.

As this brief summary has already indicated, there are many variables. These include: the parties' standard of living before the divorce, the length of the marriage, the parties' respective economic situations, property owned by either party, the contribution of each party to the marriage, including child care and home-making responsibilities, and the age and health of the parties at the time of the divorce. Because of the range of variables, and the similarly broad range of State approaches to each, different States are unlikely to reach the same results in a particular case. Whether a State will respect and enforce a decision of another tribunal depends on whether both States are parties to a treaty requiring recognition of such foreign judgments. States which have very different perspectives on these issues are unlikely to become parties to the same agreements.

3. Cultural Variations

As the examples below demonstrate, dependent spouses generally get little support at divorce. In some states, they get nothing.

United States

The modern consensus in the United States is that alimony should be awarded at the dissolution of a long marriage when the parties would otherwise have very different living standards. There is considerably less consensus when the specifics are addressed. *How* equal should the standard of living be after divorce? How long should a spousal maintenance award continue? If alimony is not based on gender roles or limited to fault cases, what is its justification?

The influential American Law Institute has proposed that alimony be reconceptualized as compensation for loss, rather than as relief in connection with need. This reflects the understanding that there may be need without any unfairness, or that there may be no need in a situation where a denial of alimony would be unfair. The ALI draft is limited to financial loss; emotional damages are not taken into account unless they rise to the level of a tort. Under the ALI proposal, a spouse is entitled to compensable loss where there has been a long marriage and a loss of living standard after divorce, where one spouse has taken more responsibility for childcare or other nurturing care, or where there has been a loss of earning capacity.

Compensable losses are also recognized in a short-term marriage when the marriage is dissolved before the spouse who has incurred the loss has not received a return on her investment or where there is an unfair disparity between the spouses' post-marital ability to recover the premarital standard of living. More specifically, compensable loss is recognized if one spouse has made significant expenditures from separate assets, or given up specific opportunities, to allow the other spouse to pursue opportunities or some other mutually agreed upon purpose and those assets are not recoverable at the time of divorce.

Rehabilitative alimony is a popular alternative to long-term or indefinite alimony. It is recognized in a growing number of U.S. jurisdictions. Rehabilitative alimony refers to a short-term award for an otherwise dependent spouse, the purpose of which is to enable her to become self-sufficient. Many commentators have noted the irony of the term 'rehabilitative alimony,' which suggests that a homemaker spouse is in need of 'rehabilitation.'

Islamic Family Law

In the Philippines, a wife is entitled to spousal support during *idda*, or her waiting period. A husband is also required to provide maintenance if a divorced mother is nursing for up to two years. A married woman may work in the Philippines with her husband's consent and may appeal to an arbitration council if he unreasonably withholds that consent.

In Malaysia, an innocent wife may apply for maintenance during her *idda* and she may also apply for a *mut'a* (consolatory gift). The amount of maintenance is set by a court. In Algeria, similarly, an innocent wife may seek 'damages' if the husband wrongfully exercised his right to divorce. The amount of maintenance is left to the discretion of the court. A divorced woman is often entitled to maintenance during her waiting period, as required by the Hanafi school.

United Kingdom

In some States, such as the United Kingdom, the factors taken into account in determining maintenance are inextricably bound up with those taken into account in determining property distribution. These factors are set out in Chapter 6, Section 7. This recognizes the reality that as a practical matter maintenance and property awards are basically fungible in most cases.

The Law relating to finances and divorce in a nutshell[1]

Maintenance Maintenance is often called 'periodical payments'. Interim Maintenance/This can be claimed as soon as the Petition has been issued and is intended to be an emergency measure to provide income before the final amount is settled or dealt with at a final hearing. A recent case in the Court of Appeal has said that the Court can order part of a spousal order to include payments in respect of children pending a CSA assessment. Dorney Kingdom-V-Dorney Kingdom 15/6/00. This overturned the previous thought that the court could only make a children order by consent.

Maintenance Pending Suit Similar to Interim Maintenance but will end upon Decree Absolute, so we would advise you apply for both. Maintenance can be for a fixed term (e.g. 2 years) to cover a period of training or to allow for children to reach school age and for the receiving party to obtain employment. It can also be for life and will usually end upon remarriage, cohabitation and death.

After Retirement Where a petition for divorce is sent to the court after 1st July 1996, the court can order maintenance or the lump sums that may be available on retirement to be paid direct from any pension scheme in which one or other spouse has a benefit. (This is called pension earmarking). This will only usually apply where the parties are fairly close to retirement age.

4. Private International Law Conventions

The question of international maintenance was addressed almost 50 years ago. Dramatic changes in domestic laws regarding maintenance, along with broader social and economic changes, have inspired an effort to draft a new instrument, as described in Section 8.

Convention on the Recovery Abroad of Maintenance[2]

Preamble Considering the urgency of solving the humanitarian problem resulting from the situation of persons in need dependent for their maintenance on persons abroad,

Considering that the prosecution or enforcement abroad of claims for maintenance gives rise to serious legal and practical difficulties, and

Determined to provide a means to solve such problems and to overcome such difficulties,

The Contracting Parties have agreed as follows:

Article 1 scope of the convention 1. The purpose of this Convention is to facilitate the recovery of maintenance to which a person, hereinafter referred to as claimant, who is in the territory of one of the Contracting Parties, claims to be entitled from another person, hereinafter referred to as respondent, who is subject to the jurisdiction of another Contracting Party. This purpose shall be effected through the offices of agencies which will hereinafter be referred to as Transmitting and Receiving Agencies.
2. The remedies provided for in this Convention are in addition to, and not in substitution for, any remedies available under municipal or international law.

Article 2 designation of agencies 1. Each Contracting Party shall, at the time when the instrument of ratification or accession is deposited, designate one or more judicial or administrative authorities which shall act in its territory as Transmitting Agencies.
2. Each Contracting Party shall, at the time when the instrument of ratification or accession is deposited, designate a public or private body which shall act in its territory as Receiving Agency.
3. Each Contracting Party shall promptly communicate to the Secretary-General of the United Nations the designations made under paragraphs 1 and 2 and any changes made in respect thereof.
4. Transmitting and Receiving Agencies may communicate directly with Transmitting and Receiving Agencies of other Contracting Parties.

Article 3 application to transmitting agency 1. Where a claimant is in the territory of one Contracting Party, hereinafter referred to as the State of the claimant, and the respondent is subject to the jurisdiction of another Contracting Party, hereinafter referred to as the State of the respondent, the claimant may make application to a Transmitting Agency in the State of the claimant for the recovery of maintenance from the respondent.
2. Each Contracting Party shall inform the Secretary-General as to the evidence normally

required under the law of the State of the Receiving Agency for the proof of maintenance claims, of the manner in which such evidence should be submitted, and of other requirements to be complied with under such law.

3. The application shall be accompanied by all relevant documents, including, where necessary, a power of attorney authorizing the Receiving Agency to act, or to appoint some other person to act, on behalf of the claimant. It shall also be accompanied by a photograph of the claimant and, where available, a photograph of the respondent.

4. The Transmitting Agency shall take all reasonable steps to ensure that the requirements of the law of the State of the Receiving Agency are complied with; and, subject to the requirements of such law, the application shall include:
   a. The full name, address, date of birth, nationality, and occupation of the claimant, and the name and address of any legal representative of the claimant;
   b. The full name of the respondent, and, so far as known to the claimant, his addresses during the preceding five years, date of birth, nationality, and occupation;
   c. Particulars of the grounds upon which the claim is based and of the relief sought, and any other relevant information such as the financial and family circumstances of the claimant and the respondent.

Article 4 transmission of documents 1. The Transmitting Agency shall transmit the documents to the Receiving Agency of the State of the respondent, unless satisfied that the application is not made in good faith.

2. Before transmitting such documents, the Transmitting Agency shall satisfy itself that they are regular as to form, in accordance with the law of the State of the claimant.

3. The Transmitting Agency may express to the Receiving Agency an opinion as to the merits of the case and may recommend that free legal aid and exemption from costs be given to the claimant.

* * *

Article 6 functions of the receiving agency 1. The Receiving Agency shall, subject always to the authority given by the claimant, take on behalf of the claimant, all appropriate steps for the recovery of maintenance, including the settlement of the claim and, where necessary, the institution and prosecution of an action for maintenance and the execution of any order or other judicial act for the payment of maintenance.

2. The Receiving Agency shall keep the Transmitting Agency currently informed. If it is unable to act, it shall inform the Transmitting Agency of its reasons and return the documents.

3. Notwithstanding anything in this Convention, the law applicable in the determination of all questions arising in any such action or proceedings shall be the law of the State of the respondent, including its private international law.

* * *

Article 18 reciprocity A Contracting Party shall not be entitled to avail itself of this Convention against other Contracting Parties except to the extent that it is itself bound by the Convention.

Convention on the Law Applicable to Maintenance Obligations (Concluded October 2nd, 1973)

The States signatory to this Convention,
Desiring to establish common provisions concerning the law applicable to maintenance obligations in respect of adults,

Desiring to coordinate these provisions and those of the Convention of the 24th of October 1956 on the Law Applicable to Maintenance Obligations in Respect of Children,

Have resolved to conclude a Convention for this purpose and have agreed upon the following provisions:

Chapter I – Scope of Convention

Article 1 This Convention shall apply to maintenance obligations arising from a family relationship, parentage, marriage or affinity, including a maintenance obligation in respect of a child who is not legitimate.

Article 2 This Convention shall govern only conflicts of laws in respect of maintenance obligations.

* * *

Article 8 Notwithstanding the provisions of Articles 4 to 6, the law applied to a divorce shall, in a Contracting State in which the divorce is granted or recognised, govern the maintenance obligations between the divorced spouses and the revision of decisions relating to these obligations.

The preceding paragraph shall apply also in the case of a legal separation and in the case of a marriage which has been declared void or annulled.

Article 9 The right of a public body to obtain reimbursement of benefits provided for the maintenance creditor shall be governed by the law to which the body is subject.

Article 10 The law applicable to a maintenance obligation shall determine inter alia –

1. whether, to what extent and from whom a creditor may claim maintenance;
2. who is entitled to institute maintenance proceedings and the time limits for their institution;
3. the extent of the obligation of a maintenance debtor, where a public body seeks reimbursement of benefits provided for a creditor.

Article 11 The application of the law designated by this Convention may be refused only if it is manifestly incompatible with public policy ('ordre public').

However, even if the applicable law provides otherwise, the needs of the creditor and the resources of the debtor shall be taken into account in determining the amount of maintenance.

* * *

Article 13 Any Contracting State may, in accordance with Article 24, reserve the right to apply this Convention only to maintenance obligations –

1. between spouses and former spouses;
2. in respect of a person who has not attained the age of twenty-one years and has not been married.

Article 14 Any Contracting State may, in accordance with Article 24, reserve the right not to apply this Convention to maintenance obligations –

1. between persons related collaterally;
2. between persons related by affinity;
3. between divorced or legally separated spouses or spouses whose marriage has been declared void or annulled if the decree of divorce, legal separation, nullity or annulment has been rendered by default in a State in which the defaulting party did not have his habitual residence.

* * *

Article 18 This Convention shall replace, in the relations between the States who are Parties to it, the Convention on the Law Applicable to Maintenance Obligations in Respect of Children, concluded at The Hague, the 24th of October 1956.

However, the preceding paragraph shall not apply to a State which, by virtue of the reservation provided for in Article 13, has excluded the application of this Convention to maintenance obligations in respect of a person who has not attained the age of twenty-one years and has not been married.

* * *

Article 24   Any State may, not later than the moment of its ratification, acceptance, approval or accession, make one or more of the reservations referred to in Articles 13 to 15. No other reservation shall be permitted.

Any State may also, when notifying an extension of the Convention in accordance with Article 22, make one or more of the said reservations applicable to all or some of the territories mentioned in the extension.

Any Contracting State may at any time withdraw a reservation it has made. Such a withdrawal shall be notified to the Ministry of Foreign Affairs of the Netherlands.

Such a reservation shall cease to have effect on the first day of the third calendar month after the notification referred to in the preceding paragraph.

5. Public International Law Conventions

Human rights instruments refer generally to equality within marriage and at its dissolution.

Convention on the Elimination of All Forms of Discrimination against Women[3]

Article 16   1. States Parties shall take all appropriate measures to eliminate discrimination against women in all matters relating to marriage and family relations and in particular shall ensure, on a basis of equality of men and women:
(a) The same right to enter into marriage;
(b) The same right freely to choose a spouse and to enter into marriage only with their free and full consent;
(c) The same rights and responsibilities during marriage and at its dissolution;

* * *

(g) The same personal rights as husband and wife, including the right to choose a family name, a profession and an occupation;

* * *

The following Report suggests how the CEDAW Committee actually shapes maintenance regimes.

Consideration of Reports Submitted by States Parties Under Article 18 of the CEDAW/ Luxembourg[4]   The divorce legislation was reformed in 1978 and a provision was introduced into article 300 of the Civil Code whereby one spouse may be required to pay alimony to the other, even when both parties were at fault. Before the Act of 15 March 1993, in such cases the court had to take into account the seriousness of the fault of the spouse requesting alimony. The Act eliminated the reference to the fault of the spouse requesting alimony, but it does prohibit the partner by whose sole fault the divorce is granted from receiving alimony. When one party is solely to blame for the divorce damages can be awarded to compensate for the material or moral injury the other partner will sustain due to the dissolution of the marriage. This is intended to protect a wife who is financially dependent on her husband because she was engaged in unpaid activity in the family home. Also with a view to protecting the wife, the Ministry of Social Security has drafted a bill providing for the sharing of contributory pensions in case of divorce, as well as certain measures intended to complement the pension coverage of a spouse who abandoned or cut back on her career during the marriage. Its purpose is to improve the pension coverage of a divorced spouse by granting her a part of the former spouse's pension proportional to the length of the marriage, and also to make it possible for a spouse – divorced or not – who interrupted her career to build up her own pension.

6. Regional Conventions

Council Regulation (EC) No 44/2001 of December 2000 on jurisdiction and the recognition and enforcement of judgments in civil and commercial matters

The Council of the European Union
Having regard to the Treaty establishing the European Community, and in particular Article 61(c) and Article 67(1) thereof, Having regard to the proposal from the Commission. Having regard to the opinion of the European Parliament. Having regard to the opinion of the Economic and Social Committee.
Whereas:
(1) The Community has set itself the objective of maintaining and developing an area of freedom, security and justice, in which the free movement of persons is ensured. In order to establish progressively such an area, the Community should adopt, amongst other things, the measures relating to judicial cooperation in civil matters which are necessary for the sound operation of the internal market.
(2) Certain differences between national rules governing jurisdiction and recognition of judgments hamper the sound operation of the internal market. Provisions to unify the rules of conflict of jurisdiction in civil and commercial matters and to simplify the formalities with a view to rapid and simple recognition and enforcement of judgments from Member States bound this Regulation are essential.
(3) This area is within the field of judicial cooperation in civil matters within the meaning of Article 65 of the Treaty.
(4) In accordance with the principles of subsidiary and proportionally as set out in Article 5 of the Treaty, the objectives of this regulation cannot be sufficiently achieved by the Member States and can therefore be better achieved by the Community. This Regulation confines itself to the minimum required in order to achieve those objectives and does not go beyond what is necessary for that purpose.

* * *

(6) In order to attain the objective of free movement of judgments in civil and commercial matter, it is necessary and appropriate that the rules governing jurisdiction and the recognition and enforcement of judgments be governed by a Community legal instrument which is binding and directly applicable.
(7) The scope of this Regulation must cover all the main civil and commercial matters apart from certain well-defined matters.
Article 1
1. This regulation shall apply in civil and commercial matters whatever the nature of the court of tribunal. It shall not extend, in particular, to revenue, customs or administrative matters.

* * *

2. In this Regulation, the term 'Member State' shall mean Member States with the exception of Denmark.

*Chapter II/Jurisdiction/Section I/General provision/*Article 2 1. Subject to this Regulation, persons domiciled in a Member State shall, whatever their nationality, be sued in the courts of that Member State.

2. Persons who are not nationals of the Member State in which they are domiciled shall be governed by the rules of jurisdiction applicable to national, of that State.

Article 3

1. Persons domiciled in a Member State may be sued in the courts of another Member only by virtue of the rules set out in Sections 2 to 7 of this Chapter.

2. In particular the rules of national jurisdiction set out in Annex I shall not be applicable as against them.

Article 4

1. If the defendant is not domiciled in a Member State, the jurisdiction of the courts of each Member State shall, subject to Articles 22 and 23, be determined by the law of that Member State.

2. As against such a defendant, any person domiciled in a Member State may, whatever his nationality, avail himself in that State of the rules of jurisdiction there in force, and in particular those specific in Annex I, in the same way as the nationals of that State.

*Section 2/Special jurisdiction/*Article 5 A person domiciled in a Member State, may be sued:

1. in matters relating to maintenance, in the courts for the place where the maintenance creditor is domiciled or habitually resident or, if the matter is ancillary to proceedings concerning the status of person, in the court which, according to its own law, has jurisdiction to entertain those proceedings, unless that jurisdiction is based solely on the nationality of one of the parties.

The United States has entered into a series of bilateral agreements, primarily with States in North and South America. These apply to child support as well as to spousal maintenance and are set forth in Chapter 10, Section 7.

7. National Implementation

United Kingdom
The Law relating to finances and divorce in a nutshell[5]

Maintenance Maintenance is often called 'periodical payments'. Interim Maintenance/This can be claimed as soon as the Petition has been issued and is intended to be an emergency measure to provide income before the final amount is settled or dealt with at a final hearing. A recent case in the Court of Appeal has said that the Court can order part of a spousal order to include payments in respect of children pending a CSA assessment. Dorney Kingdom-V-Dorney Kingdom 15/6/00. This overturned the previous thought that the court could only make a children order by consent.

Maintenance Pending Suit Similar to Interim Maintenance but will end upon Decree Absolute, so we would advise you apply for both. Maintenance can be for a fixed term (e.g. 2 years) to cover a period of training or to allow for children to reach school age and for the receiving party to obtain employment. It can also be for life and will usually end upon remarriage, cohabitation and death.

After Retirement Where a petition for divorce is sent to the court after 1st July 1996, the court can order maintenance or the lump sums that may be available on retirement to be paid direct from any pension scheme in which one or other spouse has a benefit. (This is called pension earmarking). This will only usually apply where the parties are fairly close to retirement age.

The following excerpts, from Indian and Californian law, reflect their very different approaches to this subject.

India/The Muslim Women (Protection of Rights on Divorce) Act [6]

1. Short title and extent. – (1) This Act may be called the Muslim Women (Protection of Rights on Divorce) Act, 1986.

(2) It extends to the whole of India except the State of Jammu and Kashmir.

2. Definition. – In this Act, unless the context otherwise requires, –

(a) 'divorced woman' means a Muslim woman who was married according to Muslim law, and has been divorced by, or has obtained divorce from her husband in accordance with Muslim law;

(b) 'iddat period' means, in the case of a divorced woman, –

(i) three menstrual courses after the date of divorce, if she is subject to menstruation;

(ii) three lunar months after her divorce, if she is not subject to menstruation;

(iii) if she is enceinte at the time of her divorce, the period between the divorce and the delivery of her child or the termination of her pregnancy whichever is earlier;

(c) 'Magistrate' means a Magistrate of of the First Class exercising jurisdiction under the Code of Criminal Procedure, 1973 in the area where the divorced woman resides.

(d) 'prescribed' means prescribed by rules made under this Act.

3. Mahr or other properties of Muslim woman to be given to her at the time of divorce. –

(1) Notwithstanding anything contained in any other law for the time being in force, a divorced woman shall be entitled to –

(a) a reasonable and fair provision and maintenance to be made and paid to her within the iddat period by her former husband;

(b) where she herself maintains the children born to before or after the divorce, a reasonable and fair provision and maintenance to be made and paid by her former husband for a period of two years from the respective date of birth of such children;

(c) an amount equal to the sum of mahr or dower agreed to be paid to her at the time of her marriage or at any time thereafter according to Muslim Law; and

(d) all the properties given to her before or at the time of marriage or after the marriage by her relatives or friends or the husband or any relatives of the husband or his friends.

(2) Where a reasonable and fair provision and maintenance or the amount of mahr or dower due had not been made or repaid or the properties referred to in clause (d) of sub-section (1) have not been delivered to a divorced woman on her divorce, she or anyone duly authorised by her may, on her behalf, make an application to a Magistrate for an order for payment of such provision and maintenance, mahr or dower or the delivery of properties, as the case may be.

(3) Where an application has been made under sub-section (2) by a divorced woman, the Magistrate may, if he is satisfied that –

(a) her husband having sufficient means, has failed or neglected to make or pay her within the iddat period a reasonable and fair provision and maintenance for her and the children; or

(b) the amount equal to the sum of mahr or dower has not been paid or that the properties referred to in clause (d) of sub-section (1) have not been paid or that the properties referred to in clause (d) of sub-section (1) have not been delivered to her, make an order, within one month of the date of the filing of the application, directing her former husband to pay such reasonable and fair provision and maintenance to the divorced woman as he may determine as fit and proper having regard to the needs of the divorced woman, the standard of life enjoyed by her during her marriage and the means of her former husband or, as the case may be, for the payment of such mahr or dower or the delivery of such properties referred to in clause (d) of sub-section (1) to the divorced woman:

Provided that if the Magistrate finds it impracticable to dispose of the application within the said period, he may, for reasons to be recorded by him, dispose of the application after the said period.

(4) If any person against whom an order has been made under sub-section (3) fails without sufficient cause to comply with the order, the Magistrate may issue a warrant for levying the amount of maintenance or mahr or dower due in the manner provided for levying fines under the Code of Criminal Procedure, 1973, and may sentence such person, for the whole or part of any amount remaining unpaid after the execution of the warrant, to imprisonment for a term which may extend to one year or until payment if sooner made, subject to such person being heard in defence and the said sentence being imposed according to the provisions of the said Code.

4. Order for payment of maintenance. – (1) Notwithstanding anything contained in the foregoing provisions of this Act or in any other law for the time being in force, where a Magistrate is satisfied that a divorced woman has not re-married and is not able to maintain herself after the iddat period, he may make an order directing such of her relatives as would be entitled to inherit her property on her death according to Muslim law to pay such reasonable and fair maintenance to her as he may determine fit and proper, having regard to the needs of the divorced woman, the standard of life enjoyed by her during her marriage and the means of such relatives and such maintenance shall be payable by such relatives in the proportions in which they would inherit her property and at such periods as he may specify in his order:

Provided that where such divorced woman has children, the Magistrate shall order only such children to pay maintenance to her, and in the event of any such children being unable to pay such maintenance, the Magistrate shall order the parents of such divorced woman to pay maintenance to her:

Provided further that if any of the parents is unable to pay his or her share of the maintenance ordered by the Magistrate on the ground of his or her not having the means to pay the same, the Magistrate, on proof of such inability being furnished to him, order that the share of such relatives in the maintenance ordered by him be paid by such of the other relatives as may appear to the Magistrate to have the means of paying the same in such proportions as the Magistrate may think fit to order.

(2) Where a divorced woman is unable to maintain herself and she has no relatives as mentioned in sub-section (1) or such relatives or any one of them have not enough means to pay the maintenance ordered by the Magistrate or the other relatives have not the means to pay the shares of those relatives whose shares have been ordered by the Magistrate to be paid by such other relatives under the second proviso to sub-section(1), the Magistrate may, by order direct the State of Wakf Board established under Section 9 of the Wakf Act, 1954, or under any other law for the time being in force in a State functioning in the area in which the woman resides, to pay such maintenance as determined by him under sub-section (1) or, as the case may be, to pay the shares of such of the relatives who are unable to pay, at such periods as he may specify in his order.

United States (California)

Cal. Fam. Code §4320 (a) The extent to which the earning capacity of each party is sufficient to maintain the standard of living established during the marriage ... ; (b) The extent to which the supported party contributed to the attainment of an education, training, a career position, or a license by the supporting party; (c) The ability to pay of the supporting party, taking into account the supporting party's earning capacity, earned and unearned income, assets, and standard of living; (d) The needs of each party based on the standard of living established during the marriage; (e) The obligations and assets, including the separate property, of each party; (f) The duration of the marriage; (g) The ability of the supported party to engage in gainful employment without unduly interfering with the interests of dependent children in the custody of the party; (h) The age and health of the parties, including, but not limited to, consideration of emotional distress resulting from domestic violence perpetrated against the supported party by the supporting party where the court finds documented evidence of a history of domestic violence, as defined in Section 6211, against the supported party by the supporting party; (i) The immediate and specific tax consequences to each party; (j) The balance of the hardships to each party; (k) The goal that the supported party shall be self-supporting within a reasonable period of time. Except in the case of a marriage of long duration as described in Section 4336, a 'reasonable period of time' for purposes of this section generally shall be one-half the length of the marriage. However, nothing in this section is intended to limit the court's discretion to order support for a greater or lesser length of time, based on any of the other factors listed in this section, Section 4336, and the circumstances of the parties; and (l) Any other factors the court determines are just and equitable.

8. IOs and NGOs

IOs

The Hague Conference on Private International law has addressed the problem of transnational maintenance in series of thoughtful studies. In 2003, in response to the results of an exhaustive questionnaire, excerpted below, it called for a new convention.

From Maintenance Obligations – Drawn up by Michel Pelichet, Deputy Secretary General, 9/95

* * *

16 The two Conventions drafted at the Eighth Session are restricted in their scope *ratione personae*, since they only apply to maintenance creditors who are *children*, the latter being defined in both Conventions as any legitimate, illegitimate or adopted child who is unmarried and under the age of twenty-one. On the other hand, the two Conventions of 1973 do not contain any limitation *ratione personae*, but on the contrary apply to any maintenance creditor, hence also to children. It should be borne in mind in this connection that initially, when the Member States of the Conference decided at the Tenth and Eleventh Sessions to resume work on maintenance obligations, such work was to be confined 'to maintenance obligations not governed by the Conventions of 1956 and 1958 (maintenance obligations in respect of adults)'. In the course of the discussions of the Special Commissions, at the proposal of several delegations, in particular that of Belgium, it was decided to revert to the subject-matter of maintenance obligations as a whole and to constitute two new treaties, one dealing with the determination of the applicable law, the other facilitating the recognition and enforcement of decisions in respect of all maintenance creditors, including children, who had already been covered by the Conventions drafted at the Eighth Session. However, the two Conventions of 1973 contain a series of reservations enabling the scope of the two Conventions to be exclusively restricted to certain categories of creditors.

30 b Article 8 of the 1973 Convention lays down an *exceptional rule* which is in derogation of the provisions of Articles 4-6 and which exclusively concerns maintenance obligations between divorced spouses, those who are legally separated or whose marriage has been declared void or annulled. The uncertain nature of the maintenance allowance to a divorced spouse (which, according to the State, may have the character of maintenance or of an indemnity, or a mixed character) justified the Convention containing a special solution for problems which could not readily be assimilated to the other maintenance obligations covered by the Convention. Hence maintenance obligations between divorced spouses are governed, under the terms of Article 8, by the law applied to the divorce. This rule may naturally confirm the one provided for under Articles 4-6 of the Convention, either if the judge applied to the divorce the law of the spouses' common nationality, or if he applied the *lex fori*. But the special feature of the rule in Article 8, which departs from the general principle of the Convention, is that for the revision of maintenance decisions in case of divorce, this rule confirms the so-called '*perpetuatio juris*' solution: the law applied to the divorce will remain applicable to variation of such decisions.

Information Note and Questionnaire Concerning A New Global Instrument on the International Recovery of Child Support and Other Forms of Family Maintenance – Drawn up by William Duncan, Deputy Secretary General

I Background

The Special Commission on Maintenance Obligations of the Hague Conference on Private International Law of April 1999 met '*to examine the operation of the Hague Conventions on maintenance obligations and the* New York Convention of 20 June 1956 on the Recovery Abroad of Maintenance *and to examine the desirability of revising those Hague Conventions, and the inclusion in a new instrument of judicial and administrative co-operation*'.

On the question of reform of the system, the Special Commission reached the following unanimous recommendation:

The Special Commission on the operation of the Hague Conventions relating to maintenance obligations and of the New York Convention on the Recovery Abroad of Maintenance,

– having examined the practical operation of these Conventions and having taken into account other regional and bilateral instruments and arrangements,

– recognising the need to modernise and improve the international system for the recovery of maintenance for children and other dependent persons,

– recommends that the Hague Conference should commence work on the elaboration of a new worldwide international instrument.

The new instrument should:

– contain as an essential element provisions relating to administrative co-operation,

– be comprehensive in nature, building upon the best features of the existing Conventions, including in particular those concerning the recognition and enforcement of maintenance obligations,

– take account of future needs, the developments occurring in national and international systems of maintenance recovery and the opportunities provided by advances in information technology,

– be structured to combine the maximum efficiency with the flexibility necessary to achieve widespread ratification.

The work should be carried out in co-operation with other relevant international organisations, in particular the United Nations.

* * *

II Plan of Action

The Permanent Bureau is currently carrying out research and consultations to prepare the ground for negotiations within the Hague Conference on the new global instrument on maintenance obligations. A report will be prepared by the Permanent Bureau to provide Member and other States with background information on developments at the national and international level, and to identify some of the issues which are likely to be the subject of debate when negotiations over the new instrument begin. It is planned that this report should be available to States before the end of 2002, and that a first Special Commission to begin the negotiations should be convened in the first part of the year 2003.

* * *

Form of maintenance decision

1. What form may a maintenance decision take in respect of (a) a child and (b) a spouse or other family member? In particular, are they confined to periodic payments of money? Are there any circumstances in which a lump sum, property transfer or similar order may be made to satisfy a maintenance obligation?

Eligibility

2. Who is eligible in your country to benefit from a maintenance decision? (e.g. child, spouse, other relative, etc).

* * *

4. Which is the law applicable to the question of eligibility of (a) child and (b) a spouse or other family member to obtain maintenance?

* * *

6. Is the process different where either the applicant or the respondent live abroad? If so, please give details.

7. Is the process different where the application is for maintenance for a spouse or other family member rather than a child? If so, can the two processes be joined?

* * *

10. Is the method different when the application is for maintenance in respect of a spouse or other family member rather than a child?

* * *

12. Are maintenance payments in respect of children or spouses or other family members subject to automatic reassessment, and if so, by whom and with what frequency?

13. Are such payments subject to automatic adjustment in accordance with an external marker, such as the cost of living index, and if so, by what mechanisms and with what frequency?

14. In what circumstances may a maintenance decision or assessment in respect of a child or a spouse or other family member be varied/modified upwards or downwards? Is this done by the same authority that made the original determination?

15. In what circumstances may a foreign decision or assessment be varied/modified on the application of a resident debtor?

Towards a New Global Instrument on the International recovery of Child Support and Other Forms of Family Maintenance Report drawn up by William Duncan, Deputy Secretary General

* * *

D) Some relevant developments in national systems

13. 'A quarter of a century has passed since the last two Hague Conventions on maintenance obligations were drawn up. It is worth noting certain trends in the development of domestic systems of family support which have been in evidence during the intervening years, and which may have some relevance in considering appropriate reforms at the international level. Some of the legal systems represented during the negotiations twenty-five years ago shared certain common features. Maintenance awards were for the most part determined by courts on an individualised basis, with the judge having a considerable degree of discretion in determining what constituted reasonable maintenance for a dependant having regard to the resources of the liable relative and the needs of the dependant. This system of individualised justice has come under increasing criticism in several jurisdictions on the basis that in its practical operation it tends to be very costly and ineffective. The amounts of maintenance awarded are often small, not justifying the expense of a detailed judicial inquiry, and problems of enforcement have tended to be chronic especially in the longer term. The burden on lone parents of instituting maintenance proceedings and taking measures to enforce judgements has been a heavy one, often undertaken with little prospect of obtaining an adequate or regular income in the long term. The problems of poverty surrounding single parent families has been met in part by increased public assistance. At the same time, many governments have become concerned by the consequent fiscal burden in so far as it arises from a failure by liable relatives to honour family commitments. The result has been the introduction of various reforms, some still at an experimental stage, designed on the one hand, to reduce the burden on individuals of pursuing maintenance claims and to secure a regular income for dependant family members, especially children, and on the other, to enforce more effectively and at lower cost private support obligations ... '

14. This passage taken from the 1999 Note, was followed by a description of more specific developments in national child support systems. These are recalled here with some additions and updates.

In some countries there has been a change in the way in which maintenance is assessed from a broad discretionary basis to one (which has a longer history in certain States) in which calculation proceeds on the basis of a more or less refined formula, designed to increase predictability and certainty (and indirectly encourage agreement) and to reduce the length and costs of hearings. The formulae differ from one country to another: they are often complex and sometimes difficult to understand. This is a matter of some relevance when considering whether it is desirable to adopt applicable law rules requiring authorities/judges in one country to apply the assessment criteria which are peculiar to another country.

In some countries the function of determining the amount of maintenance to be paid, at least in the first instance, has become an administrative rather than a judicial function, not necessarily involving a hearing, with the objective again of reducing costs and improving efficiency. Administrative procedures are sometimes limited to claims for maintenance at or below a subsistence level.

There has been a tendency in a number of countries for systems of child support, on the one hand, and systems for spousal support or the support of other family members, on the other, to diverge in terms of both procedure and substance. In particular, most of the newer administrative systems have been established primarily for child support purposes and, although there is sometimes provision for cases of child and spousal support to be joined, maintenance for spouses and other family members is usually left for determination judicially. These divergences can make international cooperation more complicated in that interaction may be required between a diversity of administrative and judicial authorities in respect of one family's maintenance needs.

There is a further complication in that it is not yet clear whether some of the newer administrative authorities will or will not play a role in respect of international cases. For example, the UK child support authorities deal only with domestic cases and international cases are dealt with by the courts. The Australian child support authority, on the other hand, handles international cases and there is a special agreement between Australia and New Zealand providing for co-operation between the support agencies in international cases.

Mechanisms for locating liable relatives, determining their resources, and enforcing maintenance orders have become more sophisticated. The use, for example, of orders providing for automatic deductions from wages at source has by now become commonplace. Government controlled databases (relating for example to revenue, social welfare or public licensing) are being employed more frequently both in gathering relevant information and in assisting with enforcement.

State involvement in securing private maintenance, motivated in part by a wish to reduce costs to the State, has intensified in certain jurisdictions. There is a tendency in some States towards the integration of public and private support systems, and an acceptance that the effective enforcement of private obligations often requires the initiative of the State in bringing and enforcing claims against the recalcitrant maintenance debtors. Systems of advance payment by the State of maintenance due to a maintenance creditor are sometimes used.

15. The system established by the New York Convention of 1956, though still providing the only global framework for administrative co-operation in the international recovery of maintenance, suffers from major operational problems. It remains clear that a large number of States Parties do not fulfil even their most basic obligations under the Convention. Among those that do, there exist divergences in interpretation and practice under the Convention relating to a wide range of issues which are described in more detail below. The system of co-operation set out in the Convention lacks specifics in areas such as documentation and translation requirements, time lines, progress reports, information exchange and paternity establishment. At the same time, other instruments, such as the *Hague Convention of 2 October 1973 on the Recognition and Enforcement of Decisions Relating to Maintenance Obligations,* suffer from the absence of an integrated system of administrative co-operation. It is obvious, both from the Conclusions and recommendations of the Special Commission of April 1999, as well more recently from the responses to the 2002 Questionnaire, that the establishment of an effective system of administrative co-operation will be an essential, and perhaps the most important, element in the new instrument on the international recovery of maintenance.

16. Our consultations suggest that, in devising a modern system of administrative cooperation, the following objectives should be kept to the fore –

1. The system should be capable of processing requests swiftly, in particular making full use of the new communication technologies;

2. The system should be cost effective. The costs involved should not be disproportionate, having regard to the relatively modest level of most maintenance orders. It should be seen to give good value for money when comparing administrative costs against the amounts of maintenance recovered;

3. The obligations imposed on co-operating States should not be too burdensome and should take into account differing levels of development and resource capacities. On the other hand, it has to be recognised that an efficient structure must involve some outlay of resources. No purpose is served by devising a cheap but ineffective system;

4. The system should be flexible enough to provide effective links between very different national systems, administrative or judicial, for the collection, assessment and enforcement of maintenance;

5. The system should be efficient in the sense of avoiding unnecessary or over complex formalities and procedures;

6. The system should be user-friendly – easy to understand and transparent.

NGOs

NGOs have mobilized support for destitute women, as shown in the excerpt from the Japanese NGO below. There are also organizations of disgruntled former spouses, as shown in the excerpt from the 'Alliance for Freedom from Alimony' which follows.

Poverty[7] There is a social security system in Japan, but the system does not work well for women and only a limited number of women are able to receive its benefits. Because of this, the system instead tends to create further poverty and discrimination against women. Women receive only half the amount of the employee pension of men, because the amount is based on wages and term of payment of premium. Women's wages are very low, and the systems of wages, taxes, pensions and social security are all based on a family that has a husband as a breadwinner and a wife as a dependent. If a woman gets divorced, she has to face poverty.

The social security system provides two kinds of services. One is public assistance. Even though this is based on the principle of giving support to anyone who needs it, this principle is not followed. There are many obstacles, such as a means test, a test of work eligibility, and an investigation into support responsibility, before people can receive the service. The feeling of stigmatization toward recipients is so strong that the application rate is under one third of people who are eligible to receive the service. (There was an incident in which a solo mother and her child died of starvation in Tokyo in 1996.) Undocumented foreign residents have no right to ask for assistance.

The other kind of service provides accommodation for women. Women can stay at facilities which are run under the Child Welfare Law, the Anti-Prostitution Law, the Daily Life Security Law, or at Women's Advice Centers. However, the number of facilities is very limited, and some are reluctant to accept foreigners.

Alliance for Freedom from Alimony[8] *What we are* The Alliance For Freedom From Alimony, Inc. is a non profit Florida Corporation formed exclusively to reform the current Alimony Laws. We will educate the general public on the way that the State imposes lifetime Alimony on, mostly men, requiring them to pay involuntarily against their will under threat of jail, for the rest of their natural life. We will provide assistance mentally, emotionally, and judicially to individuals that need our assistance to engage in the program to Reform Alimony Laws.

Alimony Today The forceful collection of lifetime Alimony is a form of involuntary servitude, prohibited by the 13th Amendment to the Constitution. It also violates the laws against 'Peonage' and the new 9th Amendment to Florida's Constitution.

Our organization is dedicated to eliminating this form of Involuntary Servitude called 'Alimony'. We are engaged in educational, political and judicial means to stop this abuse that presently exists.

Times Have Changed Both the State and Federal Constitutions have equal protection clauses that identifies that we are all equal in the eyes of the Law. However, there still exists laws on the books of statutes that make one class less equal than another and those are the laws of Alimony. Never before has a potential court challenge to those laws existed as they do today, in the State of Florida. Indeed in 1979 the U.S. Supreme Court struck down Alabama's law that provided Alimony only to women.

Women are no longer the property of men, non-voters, uneducated and whose only career options were to become school teachers or prostitutes, as the old men argued. We represent male voters and their second wives who in many cases live substandard to their first wives. We have heard too many horror stories from men, who have been horribly treated in matters of divorce. There are pretended financial 'dependents'. These will reduce a man to ruin through biased courts, and enemies in the increasingly venomous battle of the sexes.

Generally trial lawyers are in love with the current system of Alimony. We would expect they would consider Alimony Reform to be a major reduction in billable hours, however there may be exceptions.

9. A Possible Approach to the Problem

As set out in the Overview, maintenance is usually a function of many variables. In the U.S., as set out in Section 3, it is generally awarded at the end of a long marriage, like the twenty-four year marriage here, where the parties would otherwise have very different standards of living, as they would here because Isabelle is unemployed. Under the guidelines proposed by the ALI, Isabelle would also be entitled to some compensation for the years she presumably took care of her family and their home. Isabelle was not employed outside the home because Ferdinand preferred that she not be.

At the time of the divorce, Isabelle is only 44 years old and her youngest child is 17. At the very least, she is likely to be entitled to rehabilitative alimony, that is, short-term alimony intended to enable her to obtain the training or education necessary for her to support herself. Her affair would not be a bar.

If Isabelle is considering going back to the Phillippines, the situation would be very different, especially if she and Ferdinand are Muslims. As set out in Section 3, she would be entitled, at most, to support during her *idda*, or waiting period (defined in more detail in Section 7). If she had been more insistent about joining the labor force, and Ferdinand had refused to consent, however, she could have appealed to an arbitration council.

A list of the relevant factors for awarding maintenance under California law is set out in Section 7. Given the length of their marriage, Isabelle may be entitled to long term support, unless the court finds that she is able to support herself, or, with additional training or education, to become self-supporting. Additional facts necessary to determine the amount and duration would include: detailed budgets, net worth statements of both parties, and analyses of the specific tax consequences to each party.

For Further Research

1. The Hague Conference site includes an excellent bibliography on this topic. Some noteworthy examples follow: cited there follow Cavers, D.F. (1973), 'Draft Convention on the Recognition and Enforcement of Decisions Relating to Maintenance Obligations (Introductory Note),' *American Journal of Comparative Law*, Vol. 21, p. 154; Cavers, D.F. (1973), 'Recognition and Enforcement of Decisions Relating to Maintenance Obligations; Report of the United States Delegation to the Twelfth Session of the Hague Conference on Private International Law,' *International Legal Materials*, Vol. 12, p. 869; Cavers, D.F. (1973), 'Twelfth Session of the Hague Conference on Private International Law: Supplementary Report,' *American Journal of Comparative Law*, Vol. 21, p. 593; Cavers, D.F. (1981), 'International Enforcement of Family Support,' *Columbia Law Review*, Vol. 81, p. 994; DeHart, G.F. (Spring 1994), 'Comity, Conventions, and the Constitution: State and Federal Initiatives in International Support Enforcement,' *Family Law Quarterly*, Vol. 28, p. 89; Duncan, W. (2000), 'The Hague Conference on Private International Law and its Current Programme of Work Concerning the International Protection of Children and Other Aspects of Family Law', *Yearbook of Private International Law*, Vol. II, p. 41; Kikuchi, Y. (1987), 'Japan's acceptance of the Hague Convention on the Law Applicable to Maintenance Obligations', *The Japanese Annual of International Law*, p. 36; Raday, F. (1978), 'Transnational Maintenance Obligations', *Israel Law Review*, Vol. 13, p. 525;

2. On the economic status of women globally, see, e.g., U.N. Statistic Division, Indicators on Income and Economic Activity,
http://unstata.un.org/unsd/demographic/social/inc-eco.htm (last visited Nov. 11, 2003).

Notes

[1] http://www.divorce-online.co.uk/redirect.asp?goto=/process/applications/thelaw.htm
     U.N.T.S., Vol. 268, pp. 3-7, 1956.
[2] New York, 20 June 1956. (available at
     http://www.autlii.edu.au/au/other/dfat/treaties/1985/12.html.
[3] G.A. res. 34/180, 34 U.N. GAOR Supp. (No. 46) at 193, U.N. Doc. A/34/46, *entered into force* Sept. 3, 1981.
[4] http://www.un.org/documents/ga/cedaw/17/country/Luxembourg/cedawc-lux1en.HTM.
[5] http://www.divorce-online.co.uk/redirect.asp?goto=/process/applications/thelaw.htm
     7U.N.T.S., Vol. 268, pp. 3-7, 1956.
[6] http://www.vakilno1.com/bareacts/muslimwomenprotact/s1.htm.
[7] http://www.jca.apc.org/fem/bpfa/NGOreport/A_en_Poverty.html#1.
[8] http://www.alimonyreform.org/.

Chapter 6

Divorce/Property Distribution

1. The Problem

In Kenya, as in much of Africa, husbands and wives may choose among civil, religious and customary marriages. These choices determine the law governing the parties' marriage and divorce, including their respective property rights. As set out in considerable detail in the Report of Human Rights Watch, set out in Section 8, below, this has had grave consequences for Kenyan women who have opted for religious or customary marriages.

First, assume that you are a member of the CEDAW Committee. You have reviewed the pertinent section of Kenya's Report, also excerpted in Section 8, as well as the Human Rights Watch Report. How can the Committee respond constructively? Second, assume that you are a member of the Task Force referred to in Kenya's Report. What changes, if any, do you propose for your national law? What kinds of opposition do you anticipate? How should this opposition be addressed?

2. Overview

Property division refers to the law governing the division of property owned by the husband and wife, individually and both of them together, at the time of divorce. This is distinguished from alimony, or spousal support, which refers to an ongoing obligation from one spouse to the other. Property division is generally a one-time event and the distribution of property is usually final.

In the civil law tradition of countries such as France and Spain, all property acquired by the husband or wife during the marriage is the community property of both of them. The only property acquired by either which is exempt is that which is acquired by gift, devise, or descent. Community property does not require in-kind division; that is, each asset is not necessarily divided in half. Rather, the division is practical as well as equal. The crucial consideration is that the assets received by each spouse are equal in value.

The increase in value of an asset that one of the parties owned coming into the marriage may be community property if the increase is attributable to spousal labor. If the increase in value is a 'natural' increase, such as an increase in the market value of a piece of real estate, the increase remains the separate property of the spouse to whom it originally belonged.

In common law countries, such as the U.K. and the U.S., in contrast, the traditional rule was that each spouse owned the property he or she earned and everything derived from it. Thus, in the traditional breadwinner-breadmaker marriage, the breadwinner left the marriage with all the property acquired through his breadwinning activity during the marriage. The breadmaker got nothing, although some courts developed flexible doctrines to justify some award to the dependent spouse. Alimony was also a possibility.

Under traditional Islamic law, there was no provision for property division at divorce, except to the extent that the marriage contract so provided. If the marriage contract does not explicitly state when dower shall be paid to the wife, under the Hanafi school, half is due when the marriage contract is concluded and payment of the other half is to be made if the marriage ends by death or divorce. In some Islamic states, the traditional law has been codified. In Malaysia, for example, upon the granting of a judicial divorce, the court divides the assets of the parties that were acquired by joint effort during the marriage. Where one party has contributed to the acquisition of assets by the other, through housework or caring for the family, she may share in that property although she will always receive a smaller portion. The wife is entitled to reside in the marital home during the 'idda' (waiting period) or if there is a minor child and her former husband cannot provide another suitable residence.

Whether pension and retirement benefits are considered marital property or the sole property of the wage-earning spouse is an important question, especially when older couples separate. In the U.S., the general rule is that the amount invested in the pension during the marriage was earned during the marriage. The other spouse, accordingly, has a claim to that portion of the pension acquired during the marriage. In Japan, the Tokyo District Court held in 1999 that a court can take a husband's retirement pay into account in determining a property award if the husband is within 6 years of retirement. While Japanese courts generally refuse to award a wife any share of a pension at divorce, the Yokohama District Court in 1999 ordered the husband, who had already begun to collect his pension, to make periodic payments to his former wife.

3. Cultural Variations

Africa

> *Kenya/Marriage Laws and Practices.*[1] There are five separate legal systems for marriage in Kenya: civil (under the Marriage Act), Christian (under the African Christian Marriage and Divorce Act and the Marriage Act), Islamic (under the Mohammedan Marriage, Divorce ans Succession Act), Hindu (under the Hindu Marriage and Divorce Act), and customary (under customary laws). All types of marriages other than customary must be registered, but there are different and unconnected registries for each type, making it possible to have multiple marriages registered under different systems, in contravention of the law.
>
> Marriages under civil, Christian, and Hindu regimes are legally required to be monogamous. A spouse who enters into another marriage while married under these regimes commits bigamy under Kenya's criminal law, but this crime is rarely prosecuted. Marriages under the Islamic and Customary regimes are potentially polygamous. Islamic

law allows a man to have up to four wives; customary laws do not limit the number of wives.

Although cohabitation is not formally recognized under Kenya's statutes, courts have developed the common law principle of presumption of marriage, conferring some marital rights and duties on cohabiting couples meeting certain criteria. The exact criteria vary, but judges generally weigh the length of the cohabitation, whether there are children, and whether the man and woman held themselves out as husband and wife.

The existence of customary marriages can be difficult to prove since they are not registered, but are rather formed through a series of customary steps. The steps vary among the ethnic groups but generally include elements such as dowry payment by the man's family to the woman's family (not to the woman directly); consent of the parties and their families; the slaughter of a ram or goat; and cohabitation. Although women married under customary laws are considered part of their husband's clan, when it come to property ownership, they are regarded as neither full members of their natal nor their marital clans.

Namibia In Namibia, unless the parties explicitly agree otherwise, the distribution of property at the time of divorce depends on the race of the couple and the place where the marriage was entered into. Thus, while marital property is treated as community property for those in the South, 'natives' in the North are subject to a different property regime because they are still subject to the Native Administrative Proclamation of 1928. Under the Communal Land Reform Bill, men and women have equal rights with respect to customary land. If the land was acquired by the husband, however, which has historically been the case, the woman will have no claim to it upon divorce. Namibia is an agricultural country and most of the population depends upon the land for their livelihood. Since divorce will effectively deprive a woman of access to the land, it becomes economically impossible.

Marriage Law of the People's Republic of China[2]

Article 39 At the time of divorce, both husband and wife shall agree upon the disposal of the jointly owned property; if they fail to come to any agreement, the people's court shall decide the disposal thereof, taking into consideration the actual circumstances of the property and following the principle of favoring the children and the wife.

The rights and interests that both husband and wife enjoy in the contracted management of land shall be protected by law.

Article 40 In the case both husband and wife agree to separately own the property they respectively obtain during the existence of their marriage and if either of them has spent considerably more effort on supporting children, taking care of the old or assisting the other party in work, etc, this party shall be entitled to demand the other party to make compensations at the time of divorce, and the requested party shall make compensations.

Article 41 At the time of divorce, the debts jointly incurred by both husband and wife for the common life shall be paid out of the jointly owned property. If the jointly owned property is not enough to pay the debts or if the property is individually owned, both parties shall agree upon the payment of the debts. If both parties fail to reach any agreement, the people's court shall decide on the payment of the debts.

Article 42 If, at the time of divorce, either party has difficulties in life, the other party shall render appropriate assistance from his or her personal property like house, etc. Specific arrangements shall be agreed upon by both parties. In case no agreement is agreed upon, the people's court shall make a decision.

* * *

4. Private International Law Conventions

Convention on the Law Applicable to Matrimonial Property Regimes (concluded March 14, 1978)[3]

Chapter I – Scope of the Convention Article 1. This Convention determines the law applicable to matrimonial property regimes.

Chapter II – Applicable Law Article 3. The matrimonial property regime is governed by the internal law designated by the spouses before marriage.

The spouses may designate only one of the following laws –

(1) the law of any State of which either spouse is a national at the time of designation;

(2) the law of the State in which either spouse has his habitual residence at the time of designation;

(3) the law of the first State where one of the spouses establishes a new habitual residence after marriage.

The law thus designated applies to the whole of their property.

Nonetheless, the spouses, whether or not they have designated a law under the previous paragraphs, may designate with respect to all or some of the immovables, the law of the place where these immovables are situated. They may also provide that any immovables which may subsequently be acquired shall be governed by the law of the place where such immovables are situated.

Article 4. If the spouses, before marriage, have not designated the applicable law, their matrimonial property regime is governed by the internal law of the State in which both spouses establish their first habitual residence after marriage.

Nonetheless, in the following cases, the matrimonial property regime is governed by the internal law of the State of the common nationality of the spouses –

(1) where the declaration provided for in Article 5 has been made by that State and its application to the spouses is not excluded by the provisions of the second paragraph of that Article;

If the spouses do not have their habitual residence in the same State, nor have a common nationality, their matrimonial property regime is governed by the internal law of the State with which, taking all circumstances into account, it is most closely connected.

Article 5. Any State may, not later than the moment of ratification, acceptance, approval or accession, make a declaration requiring the application of its internal law according to sub-paragraph 1 of the second paragraph of Article 4.

This declaration shall not apply to spouses who both retain their habitual residence in the State in which they have both had their habitual residence at the time of marriage for a period of not less than five years, unless that State is a Contracting State which has made the declaration provided for in the first paragraph of this Article, or is a State which is not a Party to the Convention and whose rules of private international law require the application of the national law.

Article 6. During marriage the spouses may subject their matrimonial property regime to an internal law other than that previously applicable.

The spouses may designate only one of the following laws –

(1) the law of any State of which either spouse is a national at the time of designation;

(2) the law of the State in which either spouse has his habitual residence at the time of designation.

The law thus designated applies to the whole of their property.

Nonetheless, the spouses, whether or not they have designated a law under the previous paragraphs or under Article 3, may designate with respect to all or some of the immovables, the law of the place where these immovables are situated. They may also provide that any immovables which may subsequently be acquired shall be governed by the law of the place where such immovables are situated.

Article 7. The law applicable under the Convention continues to apply so long as the spouses have not designated a different applicable law and notwithstanding any change of their nationality or habitual residence.

5. Public International Law

As noted in earlier chapters, public international law requires that women and men be treated equally. What this requires in practical terms is often controversial in the family law context. Public international law also requires the State to respect minority cultures within the State. International law provides little guidance on reconciling these norms, which may be in tension with each other, or on which norm should prevail if they cannot be reconciled.

International Covenant on Civil and Political Rights[4]

Article 27. In those States in which ethnic, religious or linguistic minorities exist, persons belonging to such minorities shall not be denied the right, in community with the other members of their group, to enjoy their own culture, to profess and practise their own religion, or to use their own language.

CEDAW, General Recommendation No. 21 (13th session, 1994)[5]

Equality in marriage and family relations 1. The Convention on the Elimination of All Forms of Discrimination against Women (General Assembly resolution 34/180, annex) affirms the equality of human rights for women and men in society and in the family. The Convention has an important place among international treaties concerned with human rights.

* * *

Article 16 (1) (c) 17. An examination of States parties' reports discloses that many countries in their legal systems provide for the rights and responsibilities of married partners by relying on the application of common law principles, religious or customary law, rather than by complying with the principles contained in the Convention. These variations in law and practice relating to marriage have wide-ranging consequences for women, invariably restricting their rights to equal status and responsibility within marriage. Such limitations often result in the husband being accorded the status of head of household and primary decision-maker and therefore contravene the provisions of the Convention.

6. Regional Conventions

The European Communities have explicitly exempted property rights from the jurisdictional regime established in Council Regulation (EC) No. 44/2001, set out more fully in Chapter 5, Section 6.

Council Regulation (EC) No 44/2001of December 2000 on jurisdiction and the recognition and enforcement of judgments in civil and commercial matters

> The Regulation shall not apply to:
> (a) the status or legal capacity of natural persons, rights in property arising out of a matrimonial relationship, wills and succession.

7. National Implementation

Ethiopia

The 1960 Civil Code of Ethiopia governed property distribution until the enactment of the Revised Family Code of 2000 (RFC). In 1991, there was a change of government in Ethiopia. The new government sought to distinguish itself from the prior military regime by establishing laws that complied with international human rights law. The Charter enacted by the new government, for example, explicitly referred to the Universal Declaration of Human Rights. The government went on to ratify the International Bill of Rights, including the Civil and Economic Covenants, the Convention on the Rights of the Child and the Convention on the Elimination of All Forms of Discrimination Against Women. In 1995, the Constitution of the Federal Democratic Republic of Ethiopia was drafted, which explicitly provided for the equal rights of women in connection with marriage (Article 34).

Under the old Civil Code, fault was taken into the account in determining the allocation property in divorce. Thus, the innocent spouse could be awarded more than half or even all of the marital property. The arbitrators responsible for allocating property at divorce could go further; up to 1/3 of the property of the party responsible for the divorce could be awarded to the innocent spouse. Under the RFC, in contrast, the old Civil Code has been replaced by no-fault divorce. Only 'when justice requires' may a court award damages to the innocent spouse.

Singapore

In 1981, courts in Singapore were given the authority to divide marital property by an amendment to the Women's Charter.[6] This Act authorizes the court to 'order the division between the parties of the assets acquired by them during the marriage by their joint efforts [or] the sole effort of one party [and even of] assets owned before the marriage by one party which have been substantially improved by the marriage.' As of 2002, between 35% to 45% of the matrimonial property is typically awarded to a full-time homemaker spouse. In 1996, the law was again amended to allow courts the discretion to order property division 'in such proportions as the court thinks just and equitable.'[7]

In *Sherli Koo v. Kenneth Mok Kong Chua*, the high court of Singapore held in 1989 that all assets acquired during the marriage were matrimonial assets and subject to distribution. Where the wife has worked outside the home, the trend seems to be toward an equal division of matrimonial assets.

Uganda

In Uganda, women own only 7% of the land, although they comprise more than 80% of agricultural workers. Women's access to land is through marriage. An amendment to the Land Act was proposed which would give women 50% ownership of the matrimonial home upon marriage. The amendment was omitted from the final bill, however. Thus, upon divorce women are not entitled to any of the land.

United Kingdom

Section 25 of the Matrimonial Causes Act 1973

25. Matters to which court is to have regard in deciding how to exercise its powers under ss. 23, 24 and 24A.

(1) It shall be the duty of the court in deciding whether to exercise its powers under section 23, 24 or 24A above and, if so, in what manner, to have regard to all circumstances of the case, first consideration being given to the welfare while a minor of any child of the family who has not attained the age of eighteen.

(2) As regards the exercise of the powers of the court under section 23 (1) (a), (b) or (c), 24 or 24A above in relation to a party to the marriage, the court shall in particular have regard to the following matters

(a) the income, earning capacity, property and other financial resources which each of the parties to the marriage has or is likely to have in the foreseeable future, including in the case of earning capacity any increase in that capacity which it would in the opinion of the court be reasonable to expect a party to the marriage to take steps to acquire;

(b) the financial needs, obligations and responsibilities which each of the parties to the marriage has or is likely to have in the foreseeable future;

(c) the standard of living enjoyed by the family before the breakdown of the marriage;

(d) the age of each party to the marriage and the duration of the marriage;

(e) any physical or mental disability of either of the parties to the marriage;

(f) the contributions which each of the parties has made or is likely in the foreseeable future to make to the welfare of the family, including any contribution by looking after the home or caring for your family;

(g) the conduct of each of the parties, if that conduct is such that it would in the opinion of the court be inequitable to disregard it;

(h) in the case of proceedings for divorce or nullity of marriage, the value of each of the parties to the marriage of any benefit which, by reason of the dissolution or annulment of the marriage, that party will lose the chance of acquiring.

(3) As regards the exercise of the powers of the court under section 23 (1) (d), (e) or (f), (2) or (4), 24 or 24A above in relation to a child of the family, the court shall in particular have regard to the following matters

(a) the financial needs of the child;

(b) the income, earning capacity (if any), property and other financial resources of the child;

(c) any physical or mental disability of the child;

(d) the manner in which he was being and in which the parties to the marriage expected him to be educated or trained;

(e) the considerations mentioned in relation to the parties to the marriage in paragraphs (a), (b), (c) and (e) of subsection (2) above.

(4) As regards the exercise of the powers of the court under section 23(1) (d), (e) or (f), (2) or (4), 24 or 24A above against a party to a marriage in favour of a child of the family who is not the child of that party, the court shall also have regard

(a) to whether that party assumed any responsibility for the child's maintenance, and, if so, to the extent to which, and the basis upon which, that party assumed such responsibility and to the length of time for which that party discharged such responsibility;

(b) to whether in assuming and discharging such responsibility that party did so knowing that the child was not his or her own;

(c) to the liability of any other person to maintain the child.

* * *

Lump Sum Orders The court can only make one order dealing with capital. A lump sum order can be made by installments, and if it is, then it can be varied (although that is rare). If there is an ongoing order for maintenance, the court can be asked to make a capital order whenever the maintenance is varied to achieve a Clean Break. This is an exception to the general position set out above.

Maintenance can always be varied up or down as circumstances often change, maintenance rights can also be dismissed.

Lump sums can be payable in respect of savings, stocks and shares, investment policies such as endowments and ISA's.

Property Adjustment Orders The court can order that all or part of a party's share in privately owned property be transferred to the other party or to the children. This will usually either be for a fixed term such as to a child's 18th birthday or remarriage. The court can order that the other party's share be paid later on. Where the parties are in rented accommodation the courts can transfer the tenancy to the other party. If there is a potential to buy under the Right to Buy Scheme for council property this can be taken into account.

Orders for Sale The Court can order that any property owned by the parties is sold and can make orders for the division of the proceeds and payment of mortgage legal fees and other debts.

Property Protection The Court can hear emergency applications to protect property or money being disposed of before a final hearing. This is known as a Mareva Order or in Matrimonial matters a Section 37 order (s.37 Matrimonial Causes Act 1974).

If you believe the other side is hiding money or property you can apply to the High Court for an 'Anton Piller' order requiring the other side to allow your representatives to enter their premises to search for and seize documents or property. This order is rarely used except in High Value cases.

8. IOs and NGOs

IOs

The Committee on the Elimination of All Forms of Discrimination Against Women has encouraged States to report on reforms in their marital property regimes, as Guatemala and Kenya do below.

Combined third and fourth periodic reports of States parties: Guatemala[8]

With regard to the administration of the marital property, the Civil Code establishes the following:

Article 116. Marriage settlements. 'The economic regime governing the marriage shall be that specified in the marriage settlements concluded by the spouses before or during the celebration of the marriage.'

'Article 121. Marriage settlements must include: 1. A detailed description of the property owned by each of the spouses at the time of entering into marriage; 2. A statement of the debts owed by each spouse; 3. An express declaration by the spouses as to whether they are adopting the regime of absolute community of property, that of separation of acquisitions or such other procedures and conditions as they may choose for the administration of the marital property.'

Article 122. Absolute community of property. 'Under the regime of absolute community, all the property brought by the spouses to the marriage or acquired during it forms part of the marital property and shall be divided equally between them in the event of dissolution of the marriage.'

Article 123. Absolute separation of property. 'Under the regime of absolute separation, each spouse retains ownership and control of the property belonging to him/her and remains exclusive owner of the proceeds and acquisitions resulting therefrom.

Each spouse shall also retain ownership of any wages, salaries, emoluments or earnings obtained by providing personal services or engaging in trade or industry.'

Article 124. Community of acquisitions. 'Under the regime of community of acquisitions, the husband and the wife retain ownership of such property as they had upon entering into marriage and of such property as they acquire during marriage either without paying for it or by paying equal amounts, but the following shall be divided equally between them in the event of dissolution of the marital property: 1. The proceeds of the property owned by each of the spouses, after deduction of the corresponding production, repair and maintenance costs and taxes and municipal charges; 2. Property purchased with or exchanged for such proceeds, even if it was purchased in the name of only one of the spouses; 3. Property acquired by each spouse through his/her work, job, profession or industry.'

Article 125. Alteration of marriage settlements. The spouses have an inalienable right, during the marriage, to alter the marriage settlements and adopt another economic regime for the marital property.

The alteration of marriage settlements must be effected by means of a public deed which shall be recorded in the corresponding register; the alteration shall have a prejudicial effect on third parties only from the date on which it is recorded.

Article 126. Subsidiary regime. 'In the absence of property settlements, the marriage shall be understood to have been entered into under the regime of community of acquisitions.'

Article 127. Property of each spouse. 'Notwithstanding the provisions of the preceding articles, the following shall be considered the personal property of each spouse: property acquired by inheritance, gift or otherwise without payment; and accident compensation or personal injury or sickness insurance payments, after deduction of the premiums paid during the community property regime.'

With regard to the administration of the family property, article 131 of the Civil Code used to stipulate: 'Administration. The husband is the administrator of the marital property under the regime of absolute community or that of community of acquisitions, although his powers may not exceed the limits of normal administration. In order to be valid, the disposal or encumbrance of the community's immovable property must have the consent of both spouses.'

As amended by Decree No. 80-98, the article now reads: 'Under the regime of absolute community or that of community of acquisitions, both spouses shall administer the marital property, either jointly or separately. In order to be valid, the disposal or encumbrance of the community's immovable property must have the consent of both spouses.'

Article 141. 'Unjustified abandonment of the marital home by one of the spouses shall terminate for that spouse, as from the date of such abandonment, the effects of the community property regime that are favourable to him/her.'

In the draft preliminary amendments to the Civil Code, this article is expanded to include the obligation to report the abandonment to the competent judge and to notify the other party. This means that if one party is forced to leave the marital home for reasons not attributable to him/her, he or she will be able to request a family court judge to draw up a document stating the reasons which prompted the decision to leave, thereby ensuring that the effects of the community property regime that are favourable to him/her are not terminated.

Third and Fourth Periodic Reports of States Parties: Kenya[9]

Article 16

(i) Generally women have the same right to enter into marriage as men. Kenya however, has various laws governing marriage and divorce, based on the different major religions recognized in the country. This is one area where the administration does not strictly follow the letter of the law. For example the Mohammedan marriage and divorce Act, allows the marriage of minors where a school age girl is forcibly married under this Act, the administration interferes on the ground that the minor complete her education first. Under the said law however, both parties must give consent to the marriage.

(ii) Should a woman elect to get married under African Customary Law, then she has expressly given consent to possible polygamous union. Divorce also depends on the form of marriage law the couple celebrated. As regards custody of children both have equal rights and the courts decide the cases in accordance with the best interest of the children.

(iii) There are equal rights as provided for under the law regarding guardianship, wardship, trusteeship and adoption of the children.

(iv) The right to choose a family name is not legally provided for the law does not interfere in this area.

(v) Women whether married or not, have a right to choose a profession and an occupation. A woman may acquire or dispose of her property freely, however in some instances especially where the property is owned jointly with the husband the consent of the husband may be required.

(vi) Marriage of children is forbidden and the administration takes all possible measures to prevent this occurring.

Conclusion Article 24 provides that state parties undertake to adopt all the necessary measures at the National level aimed at achieving the full realization of the rights recognized in the present convention.

In realization of the above requirement, the Government set up a Task Force to review all laws relating to women as well as the on going Constitutional Review Process as a way of realizing this objective. The Task Force was mandated not just to review the laws and regulations but also to consider practices, customs and policies that should be put in place in order to give full effect to the CEDAW Conventions.

NGOs

The following case studies are drawn from the field work of Human Rights Watch. They illustrate the impact of the multiple legal systems, and the related lack of consistent enforcement, on Kenyan women and children.

Human Rights Watch, Double Standards: Women's Property Rights Violations in Kenya[10]

There is no one to go to if you want part of the family property. It's hard, because you won't get it back. Elders exist, but they would never give property to a woman. If I dare go back I would be tortured. My husband would beat me. As a wife, you don't own any property.
– Tipira Kamuye, divorced woman, Ngong, October 24, 2002

Divorced or Separated Women Divorced and separated women told Human Rights Watch of leaving their homes with nothing but clothing and never getting a share of the family property. Despite case law establishing that women can be awarded half of the family property, men typically keep the house and almost everything in it, and women leave with practically nothing. Women are expected to go 'home' and live with their parents, which is not always an option. Domestic violence victims are hardest hit, often staying in abusive relationships for years because they think it is hopeless to have their husbands leave, and the women have nowhere else to go. 'In most cases it's the women who leave the matrimonial home upon separation.... Lots of abused women are held back by that,' said a lawyer who handles domestic violence and property cases.

Human Rights Watch interviewed women whose husbands had significant property during the marriage, but the women got none of it upon separation or divorce. Many said they had no idea they could claim a share of the family property. Tipira Kamuye, a thirty-five-year-old Maasai woman, was abused by her husband for years before they divorced in 1999. 'My husband cut me on the head,' she said. 'He was going to kill me.... He told me, "I'll cut your neck," and tortured me.'

Kamuye and her three children fled to her parents' home, and her father returned the dowry to her husband. At the time, her husband owned at least two hundred sheep and cattle, but she got none of them. She explained: 'When I left my husband's home, I didn't try to take property.... In Maasai custom, women are not supposed to go back for property. A woman has to look for new livestock.... If a woman buys property during the marriage or brings it to the marriage, she would leave that with the husband upon divorce.... When I married, my parents-in-law gave me twenty sheep and twenty cattle. These were not really mine, even though they were given to me. I had to leave them.' Kamuye did not try to get a share of the matrimonial property: she believed elders would never allow a woman to keep family property and her husband would attack her if she tried to claim it. When asked whether she considered hiring a lawyer, she laughed. 'There's nothing like that here,' she said. 'Maasais don't have that.'

Some women who suffered domestic violence knew they were entitled to family property, but were so frightened of further attacks, they did not attempt to claim a share. Mary Atieno, a Luhya woman living in Nairobi, separated from her husband in 1998 after his beatings and rapes became life threatening. She had briefly left her husband and reported the violence to police in 1996, but they took no action. Having nowhere else to stay, Atieno went back to her husband: 'The police said this was a domestic issue. I went to my parents, but my father said that as an African woman, I should stay with my husband. I received no help from anyone, so I went back to my husband.... It made it worse that my husband knew no one would help me. I was at his mercy.... I had no money to look for a place of my own. If I had money, I would have moved out.' When Atieno left the marriage for good, she did not take property. 'I didn't try to get the property because I was trying to save my life. I don't even want to dream about getting the property. I want nothing to do with my husband. I won't bother.' The family property at the time consisted of a commercial plot, money in a bank, a pension fund, household goods, and furniture. Atieno purchased most of the household goods and furniture. The house she shared with her husband had a tile roof, brick walls, cement floor, electricity, and running water.

She and her children now live in Nairobi's Kibera slum in a one-room mud and iron shelter, where they initially slept on cardboard boxes. Her slum shelter has no electricity, water, or sanitation, and there are no public schools nearby. Atieno's parents would not let her live with them: 'To them it was not good that I left my husband and was spoiling tradition. Leaving a husband is like being a prostitute.'

Ellen Achieng, a Luo woman, left her violent husband and the matrimonial home in 2002. Achieng had separated from him for short periods in the past, once reporting his abuse to the local chief. 'In spite of all that was happening, I still wanted the house.... The chief said I should go back to my husband if he wanted me to.... So I went back to live with him.' The violence escalated when she returned, but she said she had no alternatives. 'I would have left years earlier if I could have,' she said, 'but the costs of setting up another home were beyond my reach.' When Achieng left her husband permanently, the matrimonial property included a house, furniture, cash, a pension fund, and rural land.

Achieng has none of that property. 'When I left home I didn't take anything – just the clothes I was wearing.... My husband had locked me out with nothing.'

Achieng filed for divorce with the assistance of a women's organization, but did not seek division of the matrimonial property. 'I just wanted to leave my husband.... He had said, "I'll kill you," even in front of our children.... My major concern is the children. I just want maintenance [child support] for them. I'm not interested in the other property.' Achieng did not realize that under Kenyan case law she could claim property on the basis of a non-monetary contribution. 'All the property belongs to my husband. I don't own anything,' she said. The house Achieng shared with her husband was of solid block construction with electricity, running water, sanitation, schools nearby, and convenient public transportation. Now she and her three children live in a one-room metal shanty with no bathroom, electricity, running water, or sanitation and no school nearby.

Maisy Wanjiku, a forty-six-year-old woman with a graduate-level education, lost her home and virtually all her property when she and her husband separated. After Wanjiku discovered her husband's infidelity in 1999, he became brutally violent and started threatening to kill her. One night, after Wanjiku's husband told her, 'This is the final threat – it's the last time I'll tell you I'm going to kill you,' she fled with her three children, their school clothes, and nothing for herself. She briefly stayed with her brother, who insisted that she return to her husband. She went back to her husband until the day he said, 'I hate you. I mean what I've told you – I'm going to kill you,' and punched her in the mouth so hard she lost all of her front teeth. She left again with no property. She stayed with her sister until she was pressured by her sister to return to her husband, at which point Wanjiku moved to a small hotel room with her children.

Wanjiku and her husband were well off, but she has none of the matrimonial property. When they separated in 2000, their property included rural land, a modern house on that land, a house in Nairobi, several cars, a beach plot, a commercial plot, shares in companies, money in a bank, a pension fund, furniture, and household goods. Wanjiku was formally employed throughout her marriage and bought most of the household goods and appliances. Her husband paid the mortgages and she paid school fees for the children.

Wanjiku sought help from traditional, governmental, and religious authorities to resolve her marital problems, get some protection from the violence, and obtain maintenance for her children. These attempts ended so disastrously, and her husband is so threatening, that Wanjiku has not dared to pursue this further. When Wanjiku told the police about her husband's death threats, an officer said, 'You women – I always tell you when your husband comes home you should smile and cook good food.' When she talked to a priest, he told her, 'God is punishing you for giving birth to only three children when you could have had more.' She went to a lawyer, who asked for a deposit of KSh30,000 (U.S.$377). Wanjiku paid the deposit, but could not afford to pay the lawyer to handle a legal separation. She also sought help from clan leaders in her husband's rural hometown. A clan meeting was organized, and the elders seemed sympathetic. Yet when Wanjiku asked if she could live in the rural home, her father-in-law left the decision to her husband, who refused. Wanjiku not only lacks the money to pursue a property claim, but also fears for her life if she tried. 'I can't go to the police, a lawyer, the church, or my family. There is no help. All doors are closed,' she said.

Even women who pay for property and have title solely in their name are not immune from property rights violations. Ndunge Ritah, a thirty-four-year-old Kamba woman, was separated from her husband on and off for several years. During one period of separation, she borrowed money, purchased land, and constructed a house, all in her name alone. When she reconciled with her husband in 2001, they moved into the house together.

He became violent again, and accused her of sleeping with everyone who helped her construct the house. He threatened to kill her, slashed her face with a knife, and beat her so severely she could not get out of bed for three days. Ritah fled to her mother's house. She obtained legal services from a women's organization and filed for legal separation. Ritah's lawyer sent her husband a letter demanding that he move out of the house, which he ignored. At a preliminary hearing, a judge refused to order Ritah's husband to vacate the house even though the judge knew that Ritah paid for it herself and had title to the house. Ritah still pays the mortgage while she stays with friends and family, and her husband pays nothing. The experience of losing her home has been demoralizing. 'Sometimes I cry until there are no more tears to cry,' she said.

Dowry also impedes women from getting a share of family property upon divorce. For the Maasai, payment of dowry even means that the woman and any children she has or property she acquires for the rest of her life belong to her husband. Unless the dowry is returned to the husband, he can even take children the woman has with other men. Divorced women in such communities do not get family property because the dowry is supposed to suffice, even if the woman does not benefit from the dowry. Naiyeso Samperu, a forty-five-year-old Maasai woman who was forced to marry at age ten, separated from her husband because of his savage beatings. 'I was tortured all over my body,' she said, and pointed out scars on her head, legs, and arms. Samperu's husband had more than one hundred cattle and sheep, but when she ran away from him, she took only the clothes she was wearing. Her husband asked her father to return the dowry, but her father refused. Later, her husband took a child Samperu had had with another man. She reported this to the chief and elders in her village. The elders told her to 'let the child stay with him to represent the dowry that was not repaid.... I just cried and left.' The child was two years old at the time, and Samperu has not seen him for the last seventeen years.

Of the sixteen divorced and separated women Human Rights Watch interviewed, only two were able to stay in their home from the time of separation. In one case, the woman was wealthy and thus had resources to afford an expensive court battle to keep her there. In the other, the woman was able to stay because her husband moved out of their dilapidated Nairobi shelter and into a modern Mombasa house. Gacoka Nyaga, a Kikuyu woman with three children, managed to stay in her home when she and her husband separated. 'We had lots of property,' she said. 'My concern was not to end up without a home. More than anything, I wanted shelter.' Nyaga filed in court for division of family property and later divorce. Although she initially sought half of the family property, she settled for about one-fourth but was able to stay in her home. All told, Nyaga spent approximately KSh8 million (U.S.$100,645) in legal fees.

Sophie Yusuf, a Muslim woman from the Luhya ethnic group, said her husband abandoned her in 1998. They lived in Nairobi in a two-room, semi-permanent house on her husband's employer's land. After they had children, they built a modern, six-room house in Mombasa with running water and electricity. They continued living in Nairobi but visited the Mombasa house on weekends. When Yusuf's husband left her and their six children, she stayed in the Nairobi dwelling (thanks to the largesse of her husband's employer) and he moved into the luxurious Mombasa house with a new wife, whom he married without Yusuf's consent. Yusuf asked for a divorce and hoped for some amount of maintenance. He refused the divorce and did not give her maintenance or any other property. Yusuf went to an imam for help. The imam summoned Yusuf's husband, but he did not appear. The imam said there was nothing more he could do, and Yusuf did not pursue this further. 'I was tired of the whole thing.... But if I die today, I don't know what will happen to my children.'

Some Kenyans say that divorced women should not get property because they can go back to their parents. With the transformation that community and family structures have undergone since pre-colonial days, this is not always an option or the desire of the woman.

Women who do turn to their families are often ordered to go back to their husbands, even when they are abusive. Women who have lost their property have a hard time contributing to costs in their families' homes and are considered an unwelcome economic burden.

Mary Abudo, a fifty-four-year-old Luo woman with eight children, said that when she and her husband separated, he kept all of the property, including vehicles, the land she cultivated, household goods, furniture, and bicycles, and she received nothing. Her violent husband forced her out of their home, and she went to her parents. They wanted her to return to her husband, but he would not take her back. Abudo stayed in her mother's hut, but was forced out when her mother died: 'A daughter is not supposed to stay in her parents' homestead [after the mother dies], so I became homeless.... . I wanted to stay there, but there was so much pressure from the clan that I should move out. My relatives set upon me and beat me viciously. I was afraid I'd die... I fled after the attack. I went to Nairobi, but even there I didn't have a place to stay... Now I'm thrown out by my husband and I'm landless.... . My major desire is to get a house of my own to live in.' Abudo did not try to claim any matrimonial property: 'I didn't dare to go back. My husband had issued threats.' He told Abudo's sister that if he saw Abudo he would 'kill her, and he was certain the government wouldn't do anything to him.' Abudo, who now has HIV, lives in a Nairobi slum and cannot afford medical treatment.

Divorced and separated women from all social classes and ethnic groups experience property rights violations. In several cases, educated, formally-employed women who married men with high salaries and ample property told Human Rights Watch that they were evicted and left empty-handed just like poorer women. These women had enough knowledge of their rights to pursue legal claims, but had only limited success. Ruth Odish, a forty-eight-year-old Luo woman, endured years of beatings and death threats from her husband. She often reported this to police and her local chief, but they did nothing. In 1997, she went to the only shelter in Nairobi for battered women. Odish's husband owned eight modern houses in Nairobi and had a high salary as a company manager. Odish obtained legal counsel from a women's organization, and her lawyer sent a letter to her husband demanding maintenance and a share of the property. Her husband did not respond, and no case was ever filed in court. Odish now lives in a dangerous part of Nairobi's Kayole slum.

Priscilla Echaria, a university-educated woman who worked as a teacher, lived in a modern house on a tea plantation that she and her diplomat husband purchased and operated together. Echaria said her husband was so physically and psychologically abusive that in 1987 she and her children moved to her father's house and she filed for divorce.

Echaria then rented a bare, simple house, and her husband continued to live in their modern home. Echaria hired lawyers to seek division of the property and a divorce. She wrangled in and out of court for years before regaining possession of her house and half the property. Even then, several years elapsed before the judgment was enforced. As of February 2003, fifteen years after filing the lawsuits, an appeal is still pending. Often on appointed hearing dates, her case would be missing from the court calendar and a new date would be set for a year later. The ordeal took a toll on Echaria:

'This was a very expensive case. I don't have running water because of paying lawyers. It cost five million shillings [U.S.$62,893].... . By the time the case is done, it may be three or four million more. I also wasted lots of time. It's like an obsession.... . I'd be abandoning myself if I abandoned this.... It's not in my nature to take nonsense.... . Most women would give up. It's so difficult to live this way. They talk about African traditions, but there is no tradition you can speak of – just double standards.'

My husband hits me if I say the property was mine and shouldn't be sold.
– Ndati Muita, Maasai woman, Ngong, October 24, 2002

Married Women's Lack of Control over Property Married women in Kenya often have little control over family property. According to the customary laws of some ethnic groups, all property a woman acquires before or during the marriage belongs to her husband, who can sell it without her consent. Kenyan law recognizes women's right to own separate property during marriage, but there is no legal presumption of co-ownership of matrimonial property. To stop a husband from disposing of family property, wives must rely on legal maneuvers (such as arguing that the property is held in an implied trust), which only help in limited circumstances.

Ndati Muita, a Maasai woman with seven children, said that her alcoholic husband sold cow after cow until they were gone and the family was destitute. Muita's husband did not ask her consent before selling the livestock, and beat her when she complained: 'My husband sold the livestock.... I didn't consent. He sold them when I wasn't there.... I didn't go to the elders or police. I fear my husband. If I report, maybe my husband will abuse me...My husband hits me if I say the property was mine and shouldn't be sold. He beats me – specifically when I talk about the sheep and the cattle.... As a woman, you have nothing.' Samperu, a Maasai woman with six children, explained how limited married women's rights are to livestock, an important asset in the Maasai community. 'Women don't have rights to cows or sheep during marriage – only the milk,' she said. 'We just take care of the sheep and cows.'

Gacoka Nyaga said that before she and her husband divorced, he sold family land and invested the proceeds in company shares in his name. 'I didn't have access to the property,' she said. 'I told him I wanted my name on the investment, but he refused.' When Nyaga initiated a division of property case, her husband threatened to sell everything. Nyaga says she was only able to prevent him from doing so because she had an attorney.

Consequences of Women's Property Rights Violations As the accounts above illustrate, when a woman's property rights are violated, the consequence is not just that she loses assets. The repercussions reverberate throughout women's lives, often resulting in poverty, inhuman living conditions, and vulnerability to violence and disease for women and their dependents. Each of these consequences is amplified by Kenya's high HIV/AIDS rates: with increasing AIDS deaths, there are more widows who face potential property grabbing and its consequences. HIV infected and affected women and their dependents experience the hardships of losing property all the more intensely.

Living in squalor is one common consequence of women's property rights violations. The housing women resort to when evicted by their relatives is often decayed, cramped, and unsafe. In the case of women with HIV/AIDS, these conditions can lead to earlier death. As reflected in many of the testimonies above, women whom Human Rights Watch interviewed consistently described being forced to live in substandard housing: the physical structures are dilapidated; services (including running water, energy, and sanitation) are unavailable; and the locations (in terms of schools, health-care facilities, and safety) are bad. For example, Mary Adhiambo was forced to leave her rural home and land in 1998 after her husband beat her and demolished her home. 'Where I live now is a bad place in the Kibera slums,' she said. 'It's a very small room. When it rains, water comes through the roof. I have no money for a better house. I have no electricity. I buy water from a stand pipe, but when I have no money, I have no water.'

Josephine Omuga, a widow from Siaya district, said that after her husband died in 1997, her in-laws took her land and other property, forced her to have sex with a jater, and evicted her from the homestead. Before her husband died, she lived in a solid three-room hut. Now she lives in a small barn that she shares with cows and goats.

Women who lose their property lose their economic base and often descend into abject poverty. Many of the women Human Rights Watch interviewed said the property rights violations left them poor and struggling to pay school fees, buy food and water, obtain medical treatment, and meet other subsistence needs. Some were poor before the property rights violations but became infinitely poorer when their possessions, and especially their land, were taken from them. The traditional solutions to this dilemma – being inherited by a male in-law, remaining with an abusive husband, or returning to a father's homestead – keep women economically dependent on men and preserve their inequality.

The poverty resulting from women's property rights abuses affects children, too. A teacher said: 'It's very common for children to drop out of school when their mothers are disinherited... . Some drop out because of general poverty, but when it comes to widows, it's even more serious.... I know a lady whose husband had built a house, but her mother-in-law came after the husband died and grabbed it. The child dropped out of school last week because the mother couldn't pay the school fees.'

Violence is another by-product. Some women said they stayed in violent relationships for years because they believed no court or other authority would give them a share of the family property or remove the abusive partner from the home. Some women were beaten, threatened, and harassed by husbands or relatives when they protested about property rights violations. Women are also abused for trying to learn about their property rights. A paralegal who offers trainings on property rights said, 'Husbands have threatened, "don't ever go [to a training] again or I'll kick you out... ." One woman was beaten senseless for coming to our meeting.'

Property rights violations also threaten women's health. Women who succumb to customary practices like wife inheritance and cleansing are vulnerable to all types of sexually transmitted diseases. An expert on HIV/AIDS and the law said women's property rights violations increase their vulnerability to HIV/AIDS: 'Because women do not own property as such, men have more say over them. They can't negotiate safer sex, and this increases infection.' Many women with HIV/AIDS are likely to die sooner because of their unequal property rights, depriving them of the resources and shelter they need to survive. Women who have lost their property often cannot afford medical treatment.

9. A Possible Approach to the Problem

This problem is unlike those in the previous chapters in that it requires a broad, policy-oriented response rather than a specific course of action for an individual. The major dilemma here is grounded in the tension between religious or cultural norms and human rights, which are effectively denied under certain regimes. As set out in Section 3, there are five separate legal systems for marriage in Kenya. Since the registries are unconnected, it is possible to have multiple marriages registered under different systems within Kenya.

Since all of the systems are subject to Kenyan law, resolution should be possible. As the Convention on the Law Applicable to Matrimonial Property Regimes set out in Section 4 indicates, moreover, the State obviously has an interest in assuring the fair and orderly disposition of property, especially immovables, or real property, within its territory. As set out in Section 5, religious and customary practices, including those regarding marriage, are protected under international human rights law. At the same time, as set out in the CEDAW General Recommendation No. 21, these practices may conflict with women's right to equality.

This would probably be the focus for a member of the CEDAW Committee. The Human Rights Watch Report, although anecdotal, persuasively documents the denial of Kenyan women's human rights at divorce. Despite case law to the contrary, women are routinely denied their share of marital property. Husbands routinely refuse to recognize their ex-wives' entitlements, and the courts and police routinely refuse to protect women's rights. A CEDAW member is likely to insist that Kenya take whatever measures are necessary to rectify this. The CEDAW Committee's comments, while not legally binding, may serve as leverage for those seeking to further women's rights within Kenya. While Kenya's submission of a Report to the CEDAW Committee indicates it is a party to the CEDAW, further research would be necessary to ascertain the precise status of the Convention under domestic law, i.e., whether its provisions (as opposed to the Committee's comments) are considered legally binding. If so, demands by the Committee are likely to be taken more seriously.

A member of the Kenyan Task Force has a very different mandate. As a threshold issue, it appears that law that should protect women is not in fact being enforced. Familiarity with local law and conditions is necessary to determine whether this may be most constructively addressed by a high-level directive, by fines or other sanctions (for officials or recalcitrant husbands), or by fee-shifting mechanisms assuring payment to wives' representatives. The potential for importing foreign enforcement mechanisms, such as those set out in Section 7, employed in the U.K. similarly requires an understanding of the local cultural and political context.

One possible change in domestic law would be to provide access to the civil courts for women who have been denied their human rights under customary or religious laws. The women denied their rights to their family homes, for example, would be allowed to sue in civil court. Traditional tribal and religious leaders are likely to object strenuously to such modifications as violative of Kenyan law and of the human right to culture. Pragmatic limits on such access to civil courts would be one way to respond to such objections. Access could be limited, for example, to those who would otherwise be destitute. Legal representation would need to be provided for such women.

For Further Research

1. Hubbard, D. and Cassidy, E. (2002), 'Family Law Reform in Namibia: Work in Progress,' in (Bainham, A. ed.), *The International Survey of Family Law: 2002 Edition*, Jordan, Bristol, pp. 255-275; Teshome, T. (2002), 'Ethiopia: Reflections of the Revised Family Code 2000,' in ibid., pp. 3-17; Minamikata, S. and Tamaki, T. (2000), 'Family Law in Japan during 2000,' in ibid., pp. 221-228; Leong, W.K. (2002), 'Singapore: Supporting Marriage through description as an equal partnership of efforts,' in ibid., pp. 379-391; Ekirikubinza, L.T. (2002), 'Family Relations and the Law in Uganda: Insights into Current Issues', in ibid., pp. 433-437. For a rigorous analysis of the reform of divorce law in South Africa, see Chambers, D. (2000), 'Civilizing the Natives: Marriage in Post-Apartheid South Africa,' *Daedalus*, Vol. 129, pp. 101-124.

2. The tension between human rights norms of non-discrimination, on one hand, and respect for minority cultures, on the other, has generated a substantial body of commentary. Noteworthy examples include: An-Na'im, A. (1987), 'Law, International Relations and Human Rights: Challenges and Response,' *Cornell International Law Journal*, Vol. 20, pp. 317-334; Sullivan, D. (1992), 'Gender Equality and Religious Freedom: Toward a Framework for Conflict Resolution,' *New York University Journal of International Law and Politics*, Vol. 24, pp. 795-823. In 1981, The Human Rights Committee finessed the issue in *Lovelace v. Canada*.[11]

Notes

[1] Human Rights Watch March 2003, Vol. 15, No. 5 (A) 25;
http://hrw.org/reports/2003/kenya0303.

[2] 1980 – amended according to the Decision on Amending the Marriage Law of the People's Republic of China made at the 21st meeting of the Standing Committee of the Ninth National People's Congress on April 28, 2001.

[3] http://www.hcch.net/e/conventions/text25e.html.

[4] G.A. res. 2200A (XXI), 21 U.N. GAOR Supp. (No. 16) at 52, U.N. Doc. A/6316 (1996), 999 U.N.T.S. 171, *entered into force* Mar. 23, 1976.

[5] http://www.un.org/womenwatch/daw/cedaw/committ.htm.

[6] Women's Charter (amendment) act (26/1980, s 100.

[7] Women's Charter PAC 353 1997, revised addition of the statues of the Republic of Singapore sec. 112.

[8] CEDAW/C/GUA/3-4 (State Party Report) 20 March 2001.

[9] CEDAW/C/KEN/3-4 (State Party Report) 14 February 2000.

[10] Human Rights Watch March 2003, Vol. 15, No.5(A) 25;
http://hrw.org/reports/2003/kenya0303.

[11] U.N. Doc. CCPR/C/OP/ 1 at 83.

Chapter 7

Reproductive Rights and Abortion

1. The Problem

You are a lawyer for Women on Waves (WOW), a group which travels on a medical ship (The Aurora) flying under the flag of the Netherlands. WOW provides counseling, contraceptives, and abortions for women whose countries do not. WOW anchors outside of the territorial sea of a country and women are ferried from the mainland to obtain its services. WOW plans to go to Ireland and has asked you to advise regarding the following legal issues:

1. *Whether Ireland can prohibit women from taking the ferry out to* The Aurora*?*
2. *Even if Irish women cannot be prevented from coming out to the boat, can Irish teenagers be prohibited from doing so?*
3. *If either Irish women or Irish teenagers return from the boat with instructions for follow-up care after taking the abortion pill, can they be arrested under Irish law?*

The Aurora *also plans to visit Morocco, and WOW would like you to consider the same questions with regard to that visit.*

2. Overview

Reproductive rights generally refer to the cluster of rights which enable an individual to decide on the number and spacing of children by preventing unwanted pregnancies. These rights, which include education about family planning, access to contraception, and freedom from gender discrimination, are widely recognized throughout the world. Almost every State allows access to contraception, and several States provide contraceptives as a free public health benefit. Abortion, the termination of an unwanted pregnancy, is more problematic.

Reproductive Rights

Access to information and education regarding contraception is the crucial first step. This includes the effects of spacing children on maternal health as well as on infant and child mortality. Second, equally crucial, families must have access to effective, dependable, and safe contraception. This includes sterilization, condoms, spermicides, diaphragms and other barrier methods, as well as intrauterine devices and oral contraceptives. Hormonal emergency contraception (EC), the 'morning-after pill,' prevents pregnancy by preventing a fertilized egg from becoming attached to the uterine wall. The morning-after pill, accordingly, is also properly considered a form of contraception.

Women's equality is increasingly recognized as a factor in their enjoyment of reproductive rights. If women do not enjoy equal rights within the family, the reproductive rights of the *couple* are apt to be exercised by the husband. If a woman cannot support herself, but is dependant on her husband for her sustenance, her reproductive rights may well be illusory. The Committee on the Elimination of Discrimination against Women has criticized rules requiring women to obtain spousal consent in order to undergo tubal ligation or abortions even when their health was in danger. In its General Comment No. 24 on Article 12 of the Women's Convention, the Committee recognizes that women's health issues are of central importance to the family as a whole but notes that an imbalance of power may effectively deprive women of access to health care. The General Comment concludes that in interpreting Article 12 of the Convention there should be 'no restrictions on the ground that women do not have the authority of husbands, partners, parents or health authorities.'

While the State should recognize the reproductive rights of individuals and couples, the State also has legitimate interests in promoting the use of contraceptives. The UK, for example, launched a national campaign to reduce teen pregnancy in the Spring of 2002. As part of this campaign, the Tesco supermarket chain began distributing free morning-after pills to teenagers. In order to combat the AIDS epidemic, States such as Brazil, in cooperation with international organizations and non-governmental organizations, have initiated widespread condom distribution programs.

Other States, confronted with burgeoning populations, have adopted comprehensive population policies in order to assure basic human rights, including rights to an adequate standard of living, education, and healthcare. The means adopted by the State in connection with such policies cannot be 'compulsory or discriminatory,' according to the Human Rights Committee. Thus, incentives, propaganda, and education are generally considered acceptable, while coerced sterilizations or abortions, criminal sanctions, and onerous fines are not. In China, for example, the infamous one-child policy was adopted in 1980, limiting each family to one or at most two children. This policy was enforced through a broad range of methods, including onerous fines on excess children, forced sterilizations and abortions, the refusal to register 'unauthorized' children, and oppressive campaigns in which committees would monitor women's menstrual cycles and pay unwelcome visits to women who became pregnant, sometimes harassing them for hours until they agreed to abortions.

Abortion

Abortion refers to the termination of a pregnancy after the fertilized egg has become attached to the uterine wall. Unlike reproductive rights in general, there is no international consensus on abortion in particular. The controversy is grounded in the belief in some States that abortion involves two lives, that of the fetus as well as that of the mother, unlike contraception, which only involves the decision by the mother (or the parents) whether or not to become pregnant. Among those States which recognize a State interest in the preservation of human life, moreover, there is a range of views as to when fetal life comes into being. The Inter-American Convention, for example, refers to 'a right to life from the moment of conception.' German law, in contrast, accepts as a matter of scientific fact that life begins fourteen days after conception. Under the Hanafi school of Islamic law, 'ensoulment' occurs at four months, before which abortion may be permitted.

Even where abortion is legal, moreover, there is growing condemnation of sex-selective abortions as a 'cleaner' form of female infanticide. In China, for example, almost one million baby girls are missing annually. That is, gender ratios predict that one million more baby girls will be born every year than appear on national registries. Approximately fifteen percent, or 191,089 of these baby girls are missing because of selective female mortality or infanticide, sex-selective abortions, or neglect.

3. Cultural Variations

Abortion includes a broad range of procedures, depending in part upon the stage of fetal development. Abortion includes a similarly broad range of social and political meanings. These vary as a function of several distinct but related factors, including the position of women in society, state population policy, what the UN calls the 'reproductive health context' in the country, including the availability of contraceptives, and the status of the fetus under national law, which may reflect the influence of religious groups in the country.

China, South Africa, and Germany have all reformed their abortion laws within the past ten years. In South Africa, the debate over the new abortion law became a microcosm of national politics, as Islamic, tribal, and other factions struggled with the rhetoric of equality and the bitter legacy of apartheid. In China, abortion is both a human rights rallying cry against the coerced abortions performed pursuant to the one-child policy (and a ground for asylum claims), and a privilege limited to those who can afford the sex-selective abortions that remain technically illegal. In Germany, unification forced a problematic synthesis between pro-natalists and those eager to exorcise any trace of the Nazi policies in the West, and the far more liberal abortion laws of the formerly socialist East.

Before the reforms in the 1990s, there were dual systems governing abortion for German, South African, and Chinese women. For German and South African women, this reflected the dual legal systems in which abortion laws were embedded. East and West Germany were separate political entities, with distinct laws and distinct conceptions of women's role in society. South Africa under apartheid had two similarly distinct legal systems, one for Blacks and one for whites. Although China had a unified legal system, that system functioned in two very distinct urban and rural contexts. Thus, the same one-child policy that allowed urban women to participate in economic life subjected rural women to forced abortions and sterilizations. The two-tiered systems in each state were serviceable for some women, and disastrous for others.

In each state, the abortion law reforms of the 1990s were shaped by the larger domestic political contexts from which they emerged. In China, globalization and the accompanying scrutiny from the international community resulted in a rhetorical nod to human rights. In South Africa, abortion was reconstructed within rhetorical frameworks of human rights and liberation to which the new government was authentically committed. In Germany, the Court (which actually set out the parameters of the new law), crafted an uneasy synthesis between women's rights and the recognition of fetal rights urged by Christian groups and grounded, like the First Abortion Decision, in recognition of the Basic Law's 'human dignity.'

China

Historically, large families were the ideal in China, especially for the vast majority of the population that lived in rural areas. As in most agrarian, pre-industrial societies, children were valued as laborers. Children were also valued as members of the family, the most important unit of social organization. In part because girls joined their husbands' families upon marriage, boys were more important to their parents. Sons were their parents' social security and old age insurance.

By 1980, however, China's Communist leadership viewed the burgeoning population as a major national crisis, putting all other national policies, including those regarding modernization and economic stability, at risk. Fertility rates of over five live births per woman would make it impossible to maintain, let alone improve, an already dismal standard of living. The country faced imminent disaster, including widespread famine (Greenhalgh, 2001).

Although the statistics compiled by the government were challenged by demographers outside of China at the time, and later by Chinese demographers, the State mobilized its vast bureaucracy to cope with the emergency, the government crafted a comprehensive population control policy. Local party cadres were ordered to 'grasp birth control work firmly,' to make it part of the 'fierce struggle between the two classes [and]' to reassert 'the dictatorship of the proletariat' in family planning work (Joint Economic Committee, 1982).

In terms of population, the one-child policy was an unprecedented success. Fertility rates fell dramatically. By 1990, the child-bearing rate had dropped to 2.31 from 5.81 in 1970. (2.1 is the rate at which the population does not grow, but merely replaces itself.) The one-child policy, however, was never formally rescinded. On the contrary, in a recent statement by the State Family Planning Commission, the government reiterated its commitment to family planning work. But the recent clarification of policy insists that 'family planning personnel ... perform their duties in accordance with the law and ... in a just and civilized way [so] that the legitimate rights and interests of the people are protected.' Rather, the focus is to be on education and publicity, to change public attitudes, especially in rural areas, and to explicitly draw women into the process (State Family Planning Commission, 2001).

South Africa

In 1975, South Africa enacted the Abortion and Sterilization Act which medicalized the abortion decision, basically leaving it to the woman's doctor. Only if he determined that the pregnancy posed a 'serious threat' or actually caused 'permanent damage' to the woman was abortion permitted, and then only following compliance with a rigid set of procedural requirements. Of those who applied for abortions 60% were denied. The 40% (approximately 800-1000 women annually) who were approved were overwhelmingly white. Of these, more than 70% were approved on psychiatric grounds. As Najma Moosa observes, 'Access was thus largely affected by class position and racial background. Very few black women who might have qualified had access to psychiatric assessment or knowledge of the qualifications.' In South Africa, as in West Germany, wealthy women also had the option of going abroad to obtain abortions.

Although the 1975 law had serious consequences for South African women, especially poor Black women unable to go abroad for safe, legal abortions, abortion remained a divisive issue. In part, this may be attributed to a range of Muslim and Christian religious beliefs. As Najma Moosa observes, neither the Qu'ran nor Sunna provide 'a clear directive on abortion. While classical jurists and religious authorities do deal with the subject, juristic rulings on abortion differ between the legal schools.' While most Muslim scholars agree that abortion is permitted in certain circumstances, 'they disagree as to the circumstances ... [and] when an abortion may be permitted.' According to one interpretation of Islamic law, for example, 'the period of gestation before which abortion can be allowed is deemed to be 120 days (16 weeks or 4 months) ... [after which] the fetus is considered to possess a soul or spirit (*ruh*), the possession of which sets human life above other life forms.' However, 'a second "authentic" Hadith relating to conception and also reported in Muslim texts ... [set the cutoff time for abortion at 7 weeks]' (Moosa, 2002).

While abortion will be allowed if it is necessary to preserve the life of the mother, rape or incest is not a ground for abortion under Islamic law. This is further complicated by the different positions on abortion taken by the four schools of Islamic law. For example, 'social abortions to protect the health of existing children or to ensure a better standard of living for the family during the first 40 days of pregnancy if it occurred by mistake and her husband consents thereto' is permitted by the Maliki school. The Hanafi school approves abortion 'before the 4th month of pregnancy, if the survival of an already nursing infant depends on it.' Christian pro-life groups similarly opposed liberalized abortion.

The ANC, in contrast, championed liberalized abortion as part of its comprehensive platform to promote human rights. This expressly included women's rights — women's equality rights in general and reproductive rights more particularly. It also explicitly included economic rights, such as the right to health.

Germany

During the Nazi regime, there were both state coerced abortions for those considered 'unfit' to procreate because of hereditary defects or 'racial inferiority,' and a pro-natalist policy, including strict laws prohibiting abortion for 'racially valuable' women. After World War II, the Allies partitioned Germany. East Germany joined the Soviet bloc and West Germany soon became part of the European Community. Although they shared a common culture and law before partition, their very different trajectories, toward capitalism and democracy in the West and toward socialism in the East, led to very different roles for women. These different roles were reflected in their respective abortion laws (Telman, 1998).

East Germany hoped to increase population after the war. In 1950, accordingly, a very restrictive abortion law was enacted. Under this law, abortion was permitted only 'if the life or health of the mother was endangered or if either parent suffered from a severe hereditary defect.' After five years, during which an estimated 20,000 to 100,000 illegal abortions were performed annually, the law was replaced by a much more liberal law (Zielinska, 1987).

Like women in China, women in East Germany were to be equal to men under communism. They were expected to join their husbands in building the socialist State. The government recognized that women workers had to have control over their own reproduction.

The government also recognized that motherhood had to be accommodated if women were to participate fully in the labor force. For example, in 1975 the East German government introduced the 'baby year,' which allowed 'women, [b]eginning with their second child, [to] take a year off with 65-90% pay and with a guaranteed right to return to their job with accumulated seniority. State-supported daycare was guaranteed at a [reasonable] cost' (Telman, 1998).

In West Germany, in contrast, women were relegated to the private sphere of the home and the family. At the same time West Germany was grappling with its shameful past. Strongly repudiating the eugenics laws and ethnic cleansing of the Nazis, the Basic Law (*Grundgesetz*) of the Federal Republic provides in Article 1(1) that: 'Human dignity shall be inviolable.' Article 2(2), similarly, guarantees that: 'Everyone shall have the right to life and inviolability of his person.' Abortion was strictly regulated.

As in East Germany in the 1950s, the difficulty of obtaining a legal abortion only increased the number of illegal abortions. In 1974, following energetic lobbying, the Reform Act, liberalizing abortion, was passed. It was soon challenged. Reimposing stringent limitations, the Federal Constitutional Court reiterated its commitment to 'human dignity' in the First Abortion Decision: '[T]he categorical inclusion of the inherently self-evident right to life in the Basic Law may be explained principally as a reaction to the "destruction of life unworthy to live", the "final solution", and "liquidations" that the National Socialist regime carried out as government measures.'

These two trends in West Germany; i.e., one, encouraging women to take care of their homes and families (and, as a corollary, discouraging the participation of married women in the labor force) and two, rejecting the Nazi past, resulted in a very restrictive abortion law. Rather, the emphasis was on providing single women with the support to raise children on their own. The proximity of the Netherlands, where abortion was readily available, provided a safety valve, an alternative to dangerous back street abortions (Miedel, 1993-1994).

By the time of reunification, women in East Germany had relied on unrestricted access to first trimester abortion for 20 years. Women in East Germany had no desire to relinquish the right to control their own reproduction that they had taken for granted for twenty years. At the same time, however, most East Germans were eager for reunification and the more liberal political climate, increased affluence, and restoration of German culture that it promised.

4. Private International Law Conventions

There are no private international law conventions on reproductive rights and abortion. This reflects both the absence of consensus on these issues and the recognition in many States that although their nationals, including women seeking abortion, regularly travel to neighboring States for medical services unavailable at home, they cannot exercise extraterritorial jurisdiction over these nationals while they are abroad. Some States prohibit traveling for such purposes, however, although enforcement of such prohibitions remains problematic.

5. Public International Law

International Covenant on Civil and Political Rights[1]

Reproductive rights are increasingly recognized as part of international human rights law. Article 3 of the ICCPR requires States parties to 'ensure the equal right of men and women to the enjoyment of all civil and political rights' set forth in the Covenant, although there is no explicit reference to reproductive rights. The right to privacy set out in Article 17 has not been interpreted to include the right to reproductive privacy, unlike the right to privacy in the U.S. Constitution. Although 'privacy' has been held to encompass reproductive rights under some national laws, such as the Constitution of the United States, this reading of 'privacy' has been explicitly rejected under other laws, including the European Convention on Human Rights.

Article 23 of the ICCPR assures the 'right of men and women of marriageable age to marry and to found a family' and requires the State to 'take appropriate steps to ensure equality of rights and responsibilities of spouses as to marriage, during marriage, and at its dissolution.' As the Human Rights Committee observed in its General Comment No. 19 in 1990, this implies protection for reproductive rights:

> The right to found a family implies, in principle, the possibility to procreate and live together. When States parties adopt family planning policies, they should be compatible

with the provisions of the Covenant and should, in particular, not be discriminatory or compulsory. . . .

But in times of 'public emergency' such as China's population crisis in the early 1980s, Article 4 allows States to derogate from, or abridge, certain rights, including reproductive rights. While forced abortions or sterilizations should be prohibited even under this standard, fines for unauthorized children might be acceptable, if they are not onerous.

Even in the absence of a 'public emergency,' international human rights law permits its States to limit some rights, if necessary to ensure 'the public welfare.' Such permissible limits might include incentives for families with only one child, such as preferred housing or bonuses.

International Covenant on Economic, Social and Cultural Rights[2]

Articles 2 and 3 of the ICESCR similarly require States to 'ensure the equal right of men and women to the enjoyment of all economic, social, and cultural rights.' Article 10 refers to 'family rights' and Article 12 refers to the 'right to health.' It has been argued that both necessarily include 'reproductive rights,' since without these rights, parents cannot determine the most fundamental issues of family membership; i.e., the spacing or number of children.

Convention on the Elimination of All Forms of Discrimination Against Women[3]

The Women's Convention is considerably more expansive. Article 1 begins by defining the term 'discrimination against women' to mean 'any distinction, exclusion or restriction made on the basis of sex, which has the effect or purpose of impairing or nullifying the recognition, enjoyment or exercise by women . . . of human rights and fundamental freedoms in the political, economic, social, cultural, civil or any other field.'

Article 2 of the Women's Convention further requires the State:

(d) to refrain from engaging in any act or practice of discrimination against women and to ensure that public authorities and institutions shall act in conformity with this obligation;

(e) to take all appropriate measures to eliminate discrimination against women by any person, organization or enterprise;

(f) to take all appropriate measures, including legislation, to modify or abolish existing laws, regulations, customs and practices which constitute discrimination against women.

The Women's Convention makes the State responsible for *all* discrimination on the basis of gender, whether through State policy or private prejudice. The Women's Convention arguably imposes an affirmative obligation on the State to counteract cultural bias which leads to sex-selection abortion.

Article 12 explicitly requires the State to 'ensure access to healthcare services, including those related to family planning' and, more specifically, to 'ensure to women appropriate services in connection with pregnancy, confinement in the postnatal period, granting free services when necessary, as well as adequate nutrition during pregnancy and lactation.' Article 14 reiterates the right to family planning services for rural women in particular and Article 16, relating generally to women's rights within marriage, again emphasizes that women have 'the same rights [as men] to decide freely and responsibly on the number and spacing of their children.'

6. Regional Conventions

Africa

The only regional convention that explicitly addresses abortion is the Protocol to the African Charter on Human and Peoples' Rights on the Rights of Women in Africa, adopted by the African Union Summit in Maputo, Mozambique on July 11, 2003. The Protocol requires fifteen signatories to come into force.

Protocol to the African Charter on Human and Peoples' Rights on the Rights of Women in Africa.

* * *

Article 14. Health and Reproductive Rights
1. State Parties shall ensure that the rights to health of women are respected and promoted. These rights include:
a) the right to control their fertility;
b) the right to decide whether to have children;
c) the right to space their children;
d) the right to choose any method of contraception;
e) the right to protect themselves against sexually transmitted diseases, including HIV/AIDs;
f) the right to be informed on one's health status and on the health status of one's partner.
2. State Parties shall take appropriate measures to:
a) provide adequate, affordable and accessible health services to women especially those in rural areas;
b) establish pre-and post-natal health and nutritional services for women during pregnancy and while they are breast-feeding;
c) protect the reproductive rights of women particularly by authorising medical abortion in cases of rape and incest.

Europe

The European Convention on Human Rights does not address abortion specifically, but the Commission has rejected arguments that abortion is either prohibited by Article 2,[4] or required by Article 8's guarantee of privacy. The European Court of Human Rights has held, however, that the right to freedom of information assured by Article

10 was violated when Ireland banned the provision of information on abortion abroad on the ground that such provision was contrary to public morals.

European Convention on Human Rights[5]

* * *

Article 2. Everyone's right to life shall be protected by law. No one shall be deprived of his life intentionally save in the execution of a sentence of a court following his conviction of a crime for which this penalty is provided by law.

* * *

Article 8. 1. Everyone has the right to respect for his private and family life, his home and his correspondence.

2. There shall be no interference by a public authority with the exercise of this right except such as in accordance with the law and is necessary in a democratic society in the interests of national security, public safety, or the economic well-being of the country, for the prevention of disorder or crime, for the protection of health or morals, or for the protection of the rights and freedoms of others.

* * *

Article 10. 1. Everyone has the right to freedom of expression. This right shall include freedom to hold opinions and to receive and impart information and ideas without interference by public authority and regardless of frontiers ...

2. The exercise of these freedoms, since it carries with it duties and responsibilities, may be subject to such formalities, conditions, restrictions or penalties as are prescribed by law and are necessary in a democratic society, in the interests of national security, territorial integrity or public safety, for the prevention of disorder or crime, for the protection of health or morals, for the protection of the reputation or rights of others ...

In *Bruggemann and Scheuten v. Federal Republic of Germany*, the Commission rejected the argument of the petitioners that German legislation restricting abortion contravened Article 8, noting that 'pregnancy cannot be said to pertain uniquely to the sphere of private life. Whenever a woman is pregnant, her private life becomes closely connected with the developing foetus.' In addition, the Commission pointed out that at the time the Convention entered into force in 1953, 'the law on abortion in all member States was as least as restrictive as the one now complained of.'

*Open Door Counselling Ltd v. Ireland (A/246)/Dublin Well Woman Centre v. Ireland (A/246)/Open Door Counselling Ltd v. Ireland (14234/88, 14253/88)/(ECHR) European Court of Human Rights 29 October 1992/*Abstract: On a complaint from the Society for the Protection of the Unborn Child, the Irish Attorney General applied for an injunction to prevent two counselling organizations from assisting clients to have abortions in England. Their actions, it was claimed, infringed the Irish constitution which protects the unborn's right to life. The counsellors challenged the injunction insofar as it specifically prevented them from giving information that might help clients contact abortion clinics. This, they claimed, infringed the European Convention on Human Rights 1950 Art. 10 which guaranteed freedom of expression. The government argued that the exception to Art. 10 applied in that the injunctions were necessary in a democratic society to protect morals. Summary: Held: The ban constituted an infringement of

Art. 10. The court accepted that because the constitutional protection reflected majority opinion about abortion, the legal basis of the injunctions was the protection of morals but although governments had a wide discretion in this area they could not necessarily take any actions they saw fit. Freedom of expression included information which offended the majority. The ban was too general, allowing no exception. The counsellors proposed to confine the information given to an explanation of available options, and as the information on abortion was available elsewhere in Ireland without supervision to protect women's health, the result of denying information could constitute a risk to health. For all these reasons the ban exceeded what could be described as 'necessary,' and so infringed Art. 10.

Americas

The American Declaration on the Rights and Duties of Man[6] provides, 'Every human being has the right to life, liberty and the security of his person.' The American Convention on Human Rights[7] is more specific:

Article 4.1 Every person has the right to have his life respected. This right shall be protected by law, and, in general, from the moment of conception. No one shall be arbitrarily deprived of his life. In *White and Potter v. United States*,[8] petitioners argued that the United States was in violation of the Declaration, which it had signed, and which should be interpreted in light of the American Convention, which the United States had not ratified. The Commission rejected this argument and refused to 'impose upon the United States Government, or that of any member State of the OAS, by means of "interpretation", an international obligation based upon a treaty that such State has not duly accepted or ratified.'

7. National Implementation

South Africa

African National Congress (ANC) had promised to decriminalize abortion and to eliminate the onerous procedures that effectively precluded legal abortion for the vast majority of South African women. After the ANC won the election, the old abortion law was discarded along with apartheid. Reproductive rights were explicitly assured in the new South African Constitution, which establishes the right 'to make decisions concerning reproduction' and the right to 'security in and control over [the] body'. (Moosa, 2002)

The Choice on Termination of Pregnancy Act (CTOP) was enacted in South Africa in 1997. It requires the state to provide abortion on request during the first 12 weeks of pregnancy. Women were deliberately made part of the drafting process. 15 women were on the 1995 parliamentary committee which reviewed the restrictive 1975 Act; 11 were men.

Germany

Under the terms of the German Reunification Treaty, West German law replaced inconsistent East German law. Abortion was treated differently, however. The Aid for Pregnant Women and Families Act of July 27, 1992 (the '1992 Act') represented a compromise between the very liberal abortion laws of the socialist East and the very restrictive abortion laws of the democratic West. Under the new law, extensive counseling was provided with the express goal of protecting the unborn fetus, and preventing future unwanted pregnancies. Like the 1974 Reform law before it, the new law was challenged before the Constitutional Court on the ground that it conflicted with the German Basic Law. The Court found that the law was indeed in conflict with the Basic Law and established a new model.

The core principle of the new law was to prevent abortion through counseling and, at the same time, to decriminalize abortion. Some features of the 1992 Act were retained by the Court. Abortions within the first twelve weeks, after counseling, for example, are not criminal. Since criminal sanctions have basically been eliminated in the new law, it is enforced for the most part by denial of state insurance benefits. Women will not be reimbursed for abortions unless they are authorized by a certificate of indication. An exception is made, however, for poor women who cannot otherwise afford an abortion. The new law is in continuing tension with other provisions of German law, however, because of its characterization of fetuses as legal persons and bearers of rights.

United Nations Population Division/Country Profiles[9]

Ireland Abortion is permitted in Ireland only if necessary to save the life of the woman. Abortion in Ireland has been illegal since the founding of the Republic. The major source of abortion law is the Offences against the Person Act, 1861, the same legislation that governs abortion in the United Kingdom of Great Britain and Northern Ireland, which remained in effect in Ireland after the country gained its independence from the United Kingdom. Under the Act, the performance or procuring of an abortion 'unlawfully' is a crime, with both the person performing the abortion and the pregnant woman subject to imprisonment. The Act does not provide which abortions, if any, will not be considered unlawful.

Although court decisions in the United Kingdom ... gradually developed an exception to this ban for abortions performed for medical purposes, including mental health purposes, in Ireland no such development occurred and it was presumed that almost all abortions were prohibited, with the possible exception of an abortion performed to save the life of the pregnant woman. Despite this fact, a constitutional amendment was approved by referendum in 1983 adding the following even stronger anti-abortion language to the Irish Constitution: 'The State acknowledges the right to life of the unborn and, with due regard to the equal right to life of the mother, guarantees in its laws to respect and, as far as practicable, by its laws to defend and vindicate that right.' In essence, this amendment placed the lives of the mother and the unborn child on an equal level and obligated the State to adopt measures to protect the latter.

Although under this amendment abortions were prohibited completely in Ireland and rarely if ever performed, an Irish woman who wanted to obtain one was not without recourse. After 1967, when England liberalized its abortion law by statute, women could easily travel to England to have an abortion performed legally and safely. Approximately 4,000 Irish women chose this approach each year, with a significant number of them aided by Irish family planning associations and other groups that provided abortion counseling, the names and addresses of abortion providers in England, and, in some cases, direct referral services. After the approval of the 1983 amendment, these services became the centre of an abortion controversy in Ireland, with critics charging that they were in violation of the 1983 amendment. At the request of the Government, in 1988 and 1990, the Supreme Court of Ireland issued permanent injunctions against the provision of these services by family planning groups and student groups. It based its decisions on the Government's duty to defend and vindicate the rights of the unborn.

The issue continued to generate controversy. In 1993 it was revealed that, in negotiations over the text of the Treaty of European Union, which the member States of the organization were drafting in order to create even closer economic, social, and political ties, language had been agreed upon that would exempt Ireland's abortion law from any oversight by the European Union and its laws. In addition, a lawsuit challenging the Supreme Court of Ireland's denial of the right to provide information on abortion was brought before the court of a larger European organization, the Council of Europe. One of the responsibilities of that organization is to monitor human rights in member States in the light of the provisions of the Convention for the Protection of Human Rights and Fundamental Freedoms. The court of the Council of Europe found that the denial violated the right to impart and receive information contained in the Convention. Under the Convention, Ireland was obligated to change its law to correct this violation.

The controversy over abortion took on a new dimension following a 1992 court case concerning a suicidal fourteen year-old girl who had been raped by an older man and whose parents wished to take her to England for an abortion. The attorney-general of Ireland, acting to defend the right of the unborn in furtherance of the 1983 constitutional amendment, sought an injunction prohibiting the family from leaving the country. In a landmark decision, the Supreme Court allowed the family to go to England, holding for the first time that there were exceptions in Ireland to the blanket prohibition of abortion and that, even under the 1983 amendment to the Constitution, an abortion could be legally performed if there was a real and substantial risk to a pregnant woman's life, including a risk of suicide.

The ongoing debate over both the right to impart and receive abortion information and the right to travel to obtain an abortion prompted the Government to enact legislation authorizing a constitutional referendum on the two issues, as well as on the broader issue of whether there should be constitutionally worded provisions allowing abortions in some circumstances. With respect to the latter issue, it proposed language that would have specifically allowed abortions to be performed to save the life of the mother in case of risk to physical, but not mental health. In the referendum, the Irish public approved the rights to information and to travel, but defeated the proposed wording on exceptions to the ban on abortions, thus allowing the decision of the Supreme Court on this issue to stand.

Owing to controversy over the issue, however, successive Governments delayed for over two years, until early 1995, to announce proposed legislation to implement the results of the referendum. As approved by the Irish Parliament in March 1995, the legislation was designed primarily to define the right to impart and receive information in Ireland on abortion and, as argued by its supporters, to reduce the need for abortions through counselling. The legislation authorizes the provision of information that would likely be needed by a woman desiring to obtain an abortion outside Ireland, such as information on the identity, location and method of communication with clinics for the termination of pregnancy. However, it places a number of restrictions on the way in which such information can be provided. This information must be about services that are lawful where provided, must be truthful and objective, and must not advocate or promote abortion. In addition, the manner in which it is provided must be lawful in the jurisdiction where the abortion services are provided. The information may not be displayed by notice in a public place and may not be provided in publications that are distributed without having been solicited by recipients.

Further restrictions apply if the information is provided by a person who engages in giving information, advice or counselling to the public on matters related to pregnancy. That person must not advocate or promote abortion; must also provide information, counselling, and advice on all courses of action open to the woman; must not provide the abortion service him- or herself or have an interest in a body providing such services; must not gain directly or indirectly any financial or other benefit from any person who provides the services or, with respect to the provision of information, from the woman; and must not make an appointment or any other arrangement for the woman for such services.

The legislation was opposed by both those who thought that it was too liberal and those who believed it to be too conservative. Because of this opposition and doubts about the law's constitutionality, the President of Ireland referred the law to the Supreme Court for review before it came into effect. Here the Court appointed lawyers to present opposing arguments to the Court, as well as letting the Government argue that the legislation was constitutional. Subsequently, in May 1995, in a unanimous opinion, the Court held that the legislation did not violate the Constitution. It concluded that the approval of the referendum on information in 1992 was clearly intended to modify the State's duty to defend the unborn in the area of information and that there was no natural law superior to the Constitution. On the other hand, it concluded that the amendment did not overly restrict the activities of a physician who was treating a pregnant woman whose life was endangered because, although the physician could not make a direct referral, he was free to provide the pregnant woman with full information on her state of health and with materials identifying an abortion clinic, discuss all aspects of the case with the clinic once the pregnant woman had made an appointment, and give the woman her medical records when she went to the clinic. The Court also rejected the argument that the legislation was unconstitutional because it did not take into consideration the rights of parents with respect to minors, and husbands with respect to wives, in the decision over abortion. The Court found these rights not to be affected by the legislation. Overall, the Court held that the legislation was a 'fair and reasonable balancing of conflicting rights.'

The decision was greeted with approval by most Irish political parties, including those that originally opposed it as being too conservative. Leaders of the family planning organizations involved in litigation were also pleased since it resulted in a consent agreement in the High Court to allow them to distribute information on abortion. Leaders of the pro-life movement and the Catholic Church, however, were seriously disappointed. The Church issued a detailed statement on the right to life that took exception, in particular, to the Supreme Court's rejection of the superiority of natural law over man-made law. They continued actively to oppose the idea that abortion could ever be permitted in Ireland.

* * *

The provision of contraceptives in Ireland has also aroused considerable controversy. For example, since contraception was forbidden by the law, the Irish Family Planning Association clinic that opened in Dublin in 1969 operated only semi-legally until a Supreme Court decision in 1973 ruled that, on the basis of a right to marital privacy, it was unconstitutional to ban the importation of contraceptives and allowed adults to import and possess contraceptives. Nonetheless, the decision did not nullify the sections of the law forbidding the sale of contraceptives. In 1979, the Health (Family Planning) Act was enacted by Parliament. It allowed the importation and sale of contraceptives only by pharmacists and by prescription. In 1985, an amendment to the Act enlarged the categories of persons allowed to sell contraceptives, also authorizing medical practitioners, employees of health boards and family planning services that were approved by the Department of Health (since 1997, the Department of Health and Children), as well as employees of hospitals that provided maternity services or services for the treatment of sexually transmitted diseases. The Act also allowed persons over 18 years of age to buy condoms and spermicides without prescription. Other contraceptives are still sold in Ireland only by prescription. Owing in part to the rise in the incidence of sexually transmitted diseases, new legislation removing further restrictions on the sale and distribution of contraceptives was enacted in 1992 and 1993.

Morocco In Morocco, abortion is available to save the life of the woman or to preserve her physical or mental health with the consent of her spouse. Morocco's abortion law was first liberalized in 1967. At that time, Article 453 of the Penal Code was amended by Royal Decree No. 181-66 (1 July 1967) to provide that the performance of an abortion shall not be punished when it is a necessary measure to safeguard the health of the mother and is openly performed by a physician or a surgeon with the consent of the spouse. If there is no husband or the husband refuses or is prevented from giving his consent, the physician or surgeon may not perform the abortion without the written opinion of the chief medical officer of the province or prefecture, certifying that the intervention is the only means of safeguarding the health of the woman. If the physician believes that the woman's life is in jeopardy, the consent of the spouse or opinion of the chief medical officer is not required. The physician or surgeon must, however, give his opinion to the chief medical officer of the province or prefecture.

In all other cases, abortion is illegal under the Penal Code, although some evidence exists that foetal impairment may be taken into account under medical indications. Any person performing an illegal abortion is subject to one to five years' imprisonment and payment of a fine of 120-500 Moroccan dirhams (DH). The penalty of imprisonment is doubled in the case of persons who regularly perform abortions. Medical and health personnel who perform an illegal abortion are subject to the same penalties, as well as to temporary or permanent suspension from exercising their profession. A woman who induces her own abortion or consents to it being induced is subject to six months' to two years' imprisonment and payment of a fine of DH 120-500.

Family planning in Morocco has encountered strong religious and political opposition. Consequently, moves to strengthen family planning efforts have been quite cautious. In the case of abortion, the issue has been complicated by the views of religious scholars concerning the beginnings of life. Some believe that abortion should be allowed only in exceptional circumstances and that the abortion law of Morocco should not be liberalized.

The Government of Morocco has supported family planning since independence in 1956 and has recognized the influence of demographic factors on national development. Royal Decree No. 181-66 of 1 July 1967, which modified the abortion law, also repealed the French law of 10 July 1939, which prohibited the advertisement and sale of contraceptives. Since then, contraceptives have been distributed free of charge in government family planning centres. Beginning with the development plan of 1968-1972, population issues, including family planning, have been accorded high priority in the planning process in Morocco. In 1971, the Association Marocaine de planification familiale, a private body, was established. Its role has evolved over the years, expanding its informational and educational activities to include clinical services.

Family planning activities in Morocco have been fully integrated into the overall health-care facilities, which has resulted in some financial difficulties and has actually hampered access to contraception by subsuming it under medical services. For these reasons, in the early 1980s, the Government assigned to the Ministry of Public Health the responsibility for undertaking a policy of 'de-medicalization' of family planning services in order to increase access to contraception. In addition, two innovative programmes were introduced, one involving mobile clinics providing maternal and child health and family planning services in remote rural areas and the other involving systematic home visits to encourage the use of contraception and to provide family planning and primary health-care services.

Illegal abortion appears to be quite widespread in Morocco, with many women resorting to abortion as a contraceptive method. In addition, it appears that the incidence of illegal abortion is underestimated, given the fact that many women obtaining an illegal abortion appear to be married women from the urban upper and middle classes who undergo an abortion in a private clinic. Surveys of public hospitals suggest that a significant number of admissions are of women from lower socio-economic groups suffering from complications due to septic abortion.

8. IOs and NGOs

In 1994, at the International Conference on Population and Development held in Cairo, the focus of international population policy shifted from demographic targets to the enhancement of women's sexual and reproductive health and rights. This has not percolated down to the national level in many states, however, and absent national legislation or adherence to the Optional Protocol to the Women's Convention there are no legal mechanisms through which this can be implemented. IOs and NGOs have nevertheless made significant advances.

IOs

The United Nations Population Fund (UNPF) sponsors a broad range of projects promoting reproductive rights, as described in the following press releases describing projects in Pakistan, Iraq, and Timor-Leste.

> *UNFPA and Partners Expand Family Planning in Pakistan*[10] To combat high levels of maternal mortality and meet people's needs for family planning, UNFPA and other partners have agreed to significantly expand the delivery of reproductive health commodities and services in Pakistan during the next five years. The agreement, signed earlier this month in Islamabad with the Government of Pakistan, is intended to save the lives of Pakistan's mothers and help stabilize its population growth.
>
> Under the agreement covering a five-year period, UNFPA will spend a total of $18 million for the procurement of contraceptives, $8 million from its own funds and $10 million from the United Kingdom Department for International Development. In addition, the United States Agency for International Development will provide $50 million to help communities purchase contraceptives and services. The Pakistan Government will seek to earmark a minimum of $7 million each year to procure contraceptives.

UNFPA will be responsible for international procurement of all contraceptives. It will also provide technical assistance to improve the distribution of contraceptives to public health centres around the country, with special attention to rural areas suffering from insufficient supplies.

Reproductive Health Supplies from UNFPA Arrive in Mosul[11] A shipment of much-needed reproductive health supplies and medications arrived last week in the northern Iraqi city of Mosul.

The supplies, sent by UNFPA, the United Nations Population Fund, included emergency obstetric care supplies, clean delivery equipment, contraceptives, essential drugs and other medical products. They also included equipment for blood transfusion and testing. The shipment is intended to serve a population of 400,000 people for a 3-month period.

Midwives Get Motorcycles to Save Mothers' Lives in Timor-Leste[12] Midwives in Timor-Leste will be able to better reach pregnant women across the country by moving around on motorcycles contributed by UNFPA, the United Nations Population Fund. The 80 new motorcycles, delivered to Timor-Leste's Ministry of Health yesterday, will help the midwives to widen their outreach to the communities they serve, especially in remote rural areas.

Expanding midwives services is among the main health objectives of the newly independent State. That is particularly crucial to reduce the country's high level of maternal deaths, which, at an estimated 850 per 100,000 live births, is the highest in Asia and the Pacific. It is estimated that only one quarter of all deliveries in Timor-Leste are currently attended by a trained midwife. Increasing the number of midwife-assisted deliveries will help lower maternal death rates.

NGOs

There are many active NGOs in this area, ranging from local groups to powerful international organizations. There was a major upheaval in 1984, however, when then U.S. President Ronald Reagan announced what came to be known as the Mexico City Policy. Under this policy, the U.S. refused to fund any organization that either provided abortions or provided counseling regarding abortions. Many NGOs took the position that they could not serve their clients without informing them that abortion was an option. Some NGOs reorganized; that part of the NGO that provided counseling, including counseling regarding abortion, became a separate entity. Some sought funds from other sources.

The examples below indicate the range of NGO activities in connection with reproductive rights and abortion.

International Planned Parenthood Federation, The Young Person's Guide to the UN Convention on the Rights of a Child and Sexual and Reproductive Health[13] This guide makes the links between the rights, as laid out in the Convention, and sexual and reproductive rights – traditionally one of the most controversial areas in UN discussions. The United Nations Convention on the Rights of the Child is the most powerful legal instrument available to all children for the protection and enforcement of their human rights. It has been ratified by every country in the world, with the exception of USA and

Somalia. By ratifying this instrument, national governments have committed themselves to protecting and ensuring children's rights and they have agreed to hold themselves accountable for this commitment before the international community. Despite this, there has been little progress in the protection and promotion of adolescent sexual and reproductive health. Written for young people, in a clear, youth-friendly language, the guide aims to highlight specific links between this legally binding international instrument and sexual and reproductive health.

Center for Reproductive Rights, Nepal's King Legalizes Abortion[14] Reversing 150 years of legal discrimination against women, today King Gyanendra of Nepal signed the 11th Amendment Bill, officially legalizing abortion and bringing about sweeping changes in many other discriminatory laws. Effective September 27, 2002, abortion will be legal under certain conditions, including upon request during the first 12 weeks of pregnancy, when a woman's life or health is in danger, and in cases of rape, incest, and fetal impairment.

While today is considered a landmark victory for women, the law does not address the rights of women who are currently in prison on charges of abortion and infanticide. Of additional concern is that abortion will remain out of reach for many Nepalese women as a function of the Bush Administration's Global Gag Rule, which prohibits non-governmental organizations receiving U.S. assistance from performing abortions or making necessary referrals. The Center for Reproductive Rights is working closely with local Nepalese advocacy groups to help address these particular issues.

Uganda to support youth initiative[15] The Family Planning Association of Uganda (FPAU) in collaboration with IPPF Africa Region plans to develop a comprehensive youth programme that will address sexual and reproductive health (SRH) issues and related concerns such as employment and the empowerment of young people in Uganda.

Uganda's Ministry of Gender, Labour and Social Development will also fully participate in the programme's development and implementation, according to the Minister, Mrs Zoe Bakoko. Other key actors from the private sector, civil society and donor community, will also be involved in the programme.

The Minister who was addressing IPPFAR staff in Nairobi on 4th June said the youth programme initiative was one of the outcomes of the visit to Uganda by the Regional Director, Mr. Tewodros Melesse, at the end of May. Mrs. Bakoko visited the Regional Office to share ideas and experiences with the staff.

Mrs. Bakoko, whose portfolio covers gender, culture, youth and children, elderly and disabled, labour and industrial relations, as well as economic and civic rights and micro-finance emphasized the urgent need to address SRH need of the youth, including the prevention of the spread of HIV/AIDS.

In traditional society there were established ways of communicating about sexuality, said the Minister who has vast experience in public health. 'Today, parents are embarrassed to talk to their children about sex. We are not counseling them and they are turning to the internet and TV for information'.

Mrs. Bakoko, a FPAU volunteer from the rural Arua, and a member of its national executive Council (NEC) also pledged to take a lead in organizing an Africa women ministers' caucus to champion SRH issues and concerns. She also lauded IPPFAR's efforts to integrate SRH and other social aspects into the NEPAD framework and assured the regional office of her support in pushing the initiative forward.

Vehicles Promoting Reproductive Health Tour China[16]   Special vehicles carrying reproductive health experts will be dispatched to China's vast rural areas starting this week, according to sources from the State Family Planning Commission (SFPC).

These vehicles, whose task is to educate people about pregnancy, reproduction and adult sexual life, will begin in north China's Hebei Province and in Beijing and Tianjin municipalities. According to Xiao Shaobo, director of the science and technology department of the SFPC, the experts will lecture local farmers on contraception, women's health and prenatal and postnatal care. They will also offer free consultations and provide free contraceptives.

'With the arrival of the Spring Festival, they will also hand out traditional new year paintings and verses written on scrolls to local residents for their celebrations,' Xiao said.

Initiated by China Population News (CPN), the promotional vehicles will tour the country for about a year. CPN's director Xi Xiaoping said that there is still widespread lack of knowledge about reproductive health mattters, relating to physiology, psychology, morality, emotions, ethics and other social aspects.

9. A Possible Approach to the Problem

The problem poses three related questions regarding 1) access to *The Aurora* in general, 2) access by teenagers in particular, and 3) potential sanctions by the State against women who avail themselves of certain services. First, in view of the history and resulting legislation regarding the right to travel and to receive information in connection with abortion, set out in Section 7, it seems unlikely that Ireland would attempt to prohibit women from taking the ferry out to *The Aurora*. As set out in Section 5, moreover, the European Court of Human Rights has already held that the right to freedom of information under Article 10 of the European Convention on Human Rights was violated when Ireland banned the provision of information on abortion abroad.

Additional information would be helpful to determine whether a bar might be imposed with respect to underage women. Teenagers' right to information received support in the May 1995 Supreme Court decision rejecting claims of parental rights with respect to such information. It is unclear, however, which restrictions on contraception were removed by the legislation in the 1990s and which, if any, remain in place for those under 18.

Since *The Aurora* would be outside the territorial sea of Ireland, in general, Irish law would not apply. (There may be a few exceptions. Laws regarding smuggling, for example, may well extend several nautical miles beyond the territorial sea.) Thus, Irish women could not be prosecuted for taking the abortion pill aboard *The Aurora*.

The same questions will have very different answers if *The Aurora* visits Morocco. Under the provisions of Moroccan criminal law, set out in Section 7, women as well as minors could be subject to fines and up to two years' imprisonment for 'inducing' or 'consenting to' their own abortions. Thus, any female who was pregnant when she went out to *The Aurora* and was no longer pregnant when she returned could face serious penalties.

For Further Research

1. Abortion has generated a considerable comparative jurisprudence. See, e.g., Wardle, L. (1983), '"Crying Stones": A Comparison of Abortion in Japan and the United States,' *New York Law School Journal of International and Comparative Law*, Vol. 14, pp. 183ff.; Savage, M. (1988), 'The Law of Abortion in the Union of Soviet Socialist Republics and the People's Republic of China: Women's Rights in Two Socialist Countries,' *Stanford Law Review*, Vol. 40, pp. 1027-1117; Schlegel, C.P. (1997), 'Landmark in German Abortion Law: The German 1995 Compromise Compared with English Law,' *International Journal of Law, Policy, and Family*, Vol. 11, p. 36. For a comparative analysis of sex-selection abortion in Korea and the United States, see Kim (2000), 'Breaking Free from Patriarchy: A Comparative Study of Sex-Selection Abortions in Korea and the United States,' *University of California at Los Angeles Pacific Basin Law Journal*, Vol. 17, p. 301.

2. For analyses of the German law, see Funk, N. (1996), 'Abortion Counseling in the 1995 German Abortion Law,' *Connecticut Journal of International Law*, Vol. 12, p. 33; Will, R. (1996), 'German Unification and the Reform of Abortion Law,' *Cardozo Women's Law Journal*, p. 399.

3. For an in-depth analysis of the WHO's efforts to promote reproductive rights, see Fuluss, S. (2000), 'The World Health Organization and Women,' in Askin, K. and Koenig, D. (eds), *Women in International Human Rights Law*.

4. For more information on China's population policy, see State Family Planning Commission, Population Planning for 1995-2000 www.unefcat.org/pop/database/law-china/ch-record015.htm (last visited 9/27/02); Joint Economic Committee, Congress of the United States (1982), China Under the Four Modernizations, Part I, U.S. Government Printing Office, Washington; Greenhalgh, S. (2001), 'Fresh Winds in Beijing: Chinese Feminists Speak Out on the One-Child Policy and Women's Lives,' *Signs*, Vol. 26, p. 847.

5. For more on abortion in Germany, see Telman, D.A.J. (1998), 'Abortion and Women's Legal Personhood in Germany: A Contribution to the Feminist Theory of the State,' *New York University Review of Law and Social Change*, Vol. 24, pp. 91-146; Bridenthal, R. (1984), *When Biology Becomes Destiny*; Meidel, F., 'Is West Germany's 1975 Abortion Decision a Solution to the American Abortion Debate?', *New York University Review of Law and Social Change*, Vol. 20, p. 471 (1993-1994).

6. For detailed accounts of the genesis of abortion law in South Africa, see Moosa, N. (2002), 'A Descriptive Analysis of South African and Islamic Abortion Legislation and Local Muslim Community Responses,' *Medicine and Law*, Vol. 21, pp. 257-276; Sarkin, J. (1998), 'Patriarchy and Discrimination in Apartheid South Africa's Abortion Law,' *Buffalo Human Rights Law Review*, Vol. 4, pp. 141-183.

7. For a comparative survey of reproductive rights, see Symposium, *Texas International Law Journal*, Vol. 35 (2000) (including: Dorner, D., 'Human Reproduction: Reflections on the Nachmani Case,' pp. 1-12; Gowry, A., 'Reproduction, Rights, and Public Policy: A Framework for Assessment,' pp. 13-30; Skene, L. 'An Overview of Assisted Reproductive Technology Regulation in Australia and New Zealand,' pp. 31-50; Ping, X., 'Population Policy and Program in China: Challenge and Prospective,' pp. 51-64; Marquez, C.L., 'Assisted Reproductive Technology (ART) in South America and the Effect on Adoption,' pp. 65-92; te Braake, T.A.M., 'Regulation of Assisted Reproductive Technology in the Netherlands,' p. 93.

Notes

[1] 1999 U.N.T.S. 171, 6I.L.M. 368 (1967). Adopted by the General Assembly of the United Nations on December 16, 1966; entered into force on March 23, 1976.

[2] 933 U.N.T.S. 3, 6 I.L.M. 360 (1967). Adopted by the General Assembly of the United Nations on December 16, 1966; entered into force on January 3, 1976.

[3] 19 I.L.M.33 (1980). Adopted by the General Assembly of the United Nations on December 19, 1979, entered into force on September 3, 1981.

[4] 8416/79 (U.K.) D.R.. 9.244, cited in Janis, M. and Kay, R. (1990), *European Human Rights Law.*

[5] 213 U.N.T.S. 221, E.S.T. 5. *Entered into force* September 3, 1953.

[6] O.A.S. Res. XXX, adopted by the Ninth International Conference of American States (March 30-May 2, 1948), Bogota, O.A.S. Off. Rec. OEA /Ser. L/V/I.4 Rev. (1965).

[7] 9 I.L.M. 101(1970).

[8] Case 2141, Inter-Am. C.H.R. 25, OEA ser.L/V/II.54, doc. 9 rev.1 (1981).

[9] http://www.un.org.esa/population/publications/abortion/profiles.htm.

[10] http://www.unfpa.org/news/news.cfm?ID=318 (May 22, 2003).

[11] http://www.unfpa.org/news/news.cfm?ID=316 (May 12, 2003).

[12] http://www.unfpa.org/news/news.cfm?ID=309 (April 25, 2003).

[13] http://www.ippf.org/youth/young_person.htm.

[14] http://www.crlp.org/pr_02_0926nepal.html (Sept. 26, 2002).

[15] http://ippfnet.ippf.org/pub/IPPF_News/News_Details.asp?ID=2727 (June 6, 2003).

[16] Xinhua General News Service (China), *at* http://ippfnet.ippf.org/pub/IPPF_News/News_Details_s.asp?ID=2541 (Jan. 15, 2003).

Chapter 8

Visitation

1. The Problem

Tessa and her son Jomo, age 8, have recently moved from Nairobi, Kenya to Brussels, Belgium. Jomo's biological father, Arnold, lives in Kenya. Tessa and Arnold never lived together, although Arnold visited his son at least twice a month, even after Tessa ended her relationship with him five years ago.

Tessa's former husband, Justin, lives in London. Tessa and Jomo lived with Justin until Tessa divorced him six years ago. Justin, too, has maintained ties with Jomo, visiting him weekly until he moved to London two years ago. Even after his move, he returned to Kenya twice a year (including the week of Jomo's birthday) and sent cards and little gifts to the boy he considered his son.

Arnold's mother, Gloria, who visited her son and her grandson every year at Christmas, now lives in Lieden, the Netherlands.

Gloria, Arnold and Justin all want to maintain contact with Jomo. Gloria and Justin would like to see him every other weekend – although not, of course, at the same time. Arnold would like Jomo to come stay with him for two weeks twice a year during winter and summer school breaks. In addition, he would like to see Jomo when he comes to Brussels every year for a few weeks. All of them want unrestricted telephone and email contact.

Tessa has no serious objections to any of them having contact with Jomo. She does not want Jomo to visit Arnold in Kenya, however, unless she can be certain that Arnold will not keep him there. She is happy for Jomo to maintain contact with Gloria and Justin, but she would like to have her son to herself some weekends. She is also reluctant to agree to a rigid schedule.

Tessa comes to you for advice. What are her rights with respect to determining the adults who have contact with her son? What are Jomo's rights? What are the rights of Gloria, Justin, and Arnold, respectively? What additional information if any, would you need before you can advise Tessa?

2. Overview

The right of visitation, or access of noncustodial parents to a child, is favored in many States. In the West, denial of visitation is rare and generally requires a finding of actual harm, such as physical violence to the child. In a 1988 U.S. case, *Suttles v. Suttles*, the father was convicted on four counts of assault with intent to murder. Even though two of these counts were against the wife and child, the father was allowed to phone and write to his child and possibly regain visitation if he underwent successful psychological counseling while in prison. In addition, drug addiction, sexual abuse, severe conflict or the child's absolute refusal to cooperate may result in the denial of visitation. More often, the court is likely to order supervised visitation, that is, visitation in a specified 'safe' place or in the presence of a neutral third party. The objective is to enable the noncustodial parent to maintain a relationship with the child while assuring the child's security.

The specific harm feared by the custodial parent may well be that the noncustodial parent will abduct the child. Under the Hague Convention on Abduction, discussed in Chapter 9, a parent may be found to have wrongfully retained or wrongfully removed the child if the parent neglects to return the child or retains her beyond the agreed-upon visitation. The concern in such situations is that the noncustodial parent will remove the child from her place of habitual residence and persuade a court in the new country to assume jurisdiction and rule in his favor. This is more appropriately considered in the context of custody, however, since that is the real issue.

3. Cultural Variations

Cultural approaches to contact with a child cover a broad range. In some Islamic States, for example, visitation is allowed only with the permission of the custodial father, and upon terms which he establishes. At the other extreme is the emerging trend in Northern Europe not only to encourage liberal visitation by non-custodial parents, but to allow the child to have contact with non-family members, even over the objection of a parent.

This reflects and reinforces fundamentally different conceptions of the child's place within the family and of 'children' themselves. Under the strict version of Islamic law, for example, the father is viewed as the child's protector and guardian and it would be a violation of religious law for the State to interfere in that relationship, or to substitute its assessment of the child's 'best interest' for the father's judgment. Deference to the father, moreover, does not necessarily mean the denial of visitation to the mother; as set forth below.

> *International Parental Child Abduction/Jordan*[1] *Right of Visitation* In cases where the father has custody of a child, the mother is guaranteed visitation rights. It has been the experience of the Embassy in Amman that the father and the paternal grandparents of the child are generally very open and accommodating in facilitating the right of the mother to visit and maintain contact with the child.

In the industrialized North, in contrast, the child is increasingly viewed as a rightsholder. Thus, the emphasis is on the child's right to contact, or to refuse contact, rather than the rights of the child's parents to determine what is best for the child.

4. Private International Law Conventions

The growing need for harmonization of national laws is reflected in the following convention.

Convention on Jurisdiction, Applicable Law, Recognition, Enforcement and Co-operation in Respect of Parental Responsibility and Measures for the Protection of Children (Concluded 19 October 1996)

The States signatory to the present Convention,
Considering the need to improve the protection of children in international situations,
Wishing to avoid conflicts between their legal systems in respect of jurisdiction, applicable law, recognition and enforcement of measures for the protection of children,
Recalling the importance of international co-operation for the protection of children,
Confirming that the best interests of the child are to be a primary consideration,
Noting that the Convention of 5 October 1961 concerning the powers of authorities and the law applicable in respect of the protection of minors is in need of revision,
Desiring to establish common provisions to this effect, taking into account the United Nations Convention on the Rights of the Child of 20 November 1989,
Have agreed on the following provisions –

Chapter I – scope of the convention

Article 1 1. The objects of the present Convention are –
a. to determine the State whose authorities have jurisdiction to take measures directed to the protection of the person or property of the child;
b. to determine which law is to be applied by such authorities in exercising their jurisdiction;
c. to determine the law applicable to parental responsibility;
d. to provide for the recognition and enforcement of such measures of protection in all Contracting States;
e. to establish such co-operation between the authorities of the Contracting States as may be necessary in order to achieve the purposes of this Convention.
2. For the purposes of this Convention, the term 'parental responsibility' includes parental authority, or any analogous relationship of authority determining the rights, powers and responsibilities of parents, guardians or other legal representatives in relation to the person or the property of the child.

Article 2 The Convention applies to children from the moment of their birth until they reach the age of 18 years.

Article 3 The measures referred to in Article 1 may deal in particular with –
a. the attribution, exercise, termination or restriction of parental responsibility, as well as its delegation;
b. rights of custody, including rights relating to the care of the person of the child and, in particular, the right to determine the child's place of residence, as well as rights of access including the right to take a child for a limited period of time to a place other than the child's habitual residence;
c. guardianship, curatorship and analogous institutions;

d.   the designation and functions of any person or body having charge of the child's person or property, representing or assisting the child;
e.   the placement of the child in a foster family or in institutional care, or the provision of care by kafala or an analogous institution;
f.   the supervision by a public authority of the care of a child by any person having charge of the child;
g.   the administration, conservation or disposal of the child's property.

* * *

Chapter II – Jurisdiction

Article 5   1.   The judicial or administrative authorities of the Contracting State of the habitual residence of the child have jurisdiction to take measures directed to the protection of the child's person or property.
2.   Subject to Article 7, in case of a change of the child's habitual residence to another Contracting State, the authorities of the State of the new habitual residence have jurisdiction.

Article 6   1.   For refugee children and children who, due to disturbances occurring in their country, are internationally displaced, the authorities of the Contracting State on the territory of which these children are present as a result of their displacement have the jurisdiction provided for in paragraph 1 of Article 5.
2.   The provisions of the preceding paragraph also apply to children whose habitual residence cannot be established.

* * *

Article 7   1.   In case of wrongful removal or retention of the child, the authorities of the Contracting State in which the child was habitually resident immediately before the removal or retention keep their jurisdiction until the child has acquired a habitual residence in another State, and
a.   each person, institution or other body having rights of custody has acquiesced in the removal or retention; or
b.   the child has resided in that other State for a period of at least one year after the person, institution or other body having rights of custody has or should have had knowledge of the whereabouts of the child, no request for return lodged within that period is still pending, and the child is settled in his or her new environment.
2.   The removal or the retention of a child is to be considered wrongful where –
a.   it is in breach of rights of custody attributed to a person, an institution or any other body, either jointly or alone, under the law of the State in which the child was habitually resident immediately before the removal or retention; and
b.   at the time of removal or retention those rights were actually exercised, either jointly or alone, or would have been so exercised but for the removal or retention.

* * *

Article 8   1.   By way of exception, the authority of a Contracting State having jurisdiction under Article 5 or 6, if it considers that the authority of another Contracting State would be better placed in the particular case to assess the best interests of the child, may either
   –   request that other authority, directly or with the assistance of the Central Authority of its State, to assume jurisdiction to take such measures of protection as it considers to be necessary, or
   –   suspend consideration of the case and invite the parties to introduce such a request before the authority of that other State.

* * *

Chapter III – applicable law

Article 15 1. In exercising their jurisdiction under the provisions of Chapter II, the authorities of the Contracting States shall apply their own law.

2. However, in so far as the protection of the person or the property of the child requires, they may exceptionally apply or take into consideration the law of another State with which the situation has a substantial connection.

* * *

Article 17 The exercise of parental responsibility is governed by the law of the State of the child's habitual residence. If the child's habitual residence changes, it is governed by the law of the State of the new habitual residence.

* * *

Chapter IV – recognition and enforcement

Article 23 1. The measures taken by the authorities of a Contracting State shall be recognised by operation of law in all other Contracting States.

2. Recognition may however be refused –

a. if the measure was taken by an authority whose jurisdiction was not based on one of the grounds provided for in Chapter II;

b. if the measure was taken, except in a case of urgency, in the context of a judicial or administrative proceeding, without the child having been provided the opportunity to be heard, in violation of fundamental principles of procedure of the requested State;

c. on the request of any person claiming that the measure infringes his or her parental responsibility, if such measure was taken, except in a case of urgency, without such person having been given an opportunity to be heard;

d. if such recognition is manifestly contrary to public policy of the requested State, taking into account the best interests of the child;

e. if the measure is incompatible with a later measure taken in the non-Contracting State of the habitual residence of the child, where this later measure fulfils the requirements for recognition in the requested State;

f. if the procedure provided in Article 33 has not been complied with.

* * *

Article 28 Measures taken in one Contracting State and declared enforceable, or registered for the purpose of enforcement, in another Contracting State shall be enforced in the latter State as if they had been taken by the authorities of that State. Enforcement takes place in accordance with the law of the requested State to the extent provided by such law, taking into consideration the best interests of the child.

* * *

Article 33 1. If an authority having jurisdiction under Articles 5 to 10 contemplates the placement of the child in a foster family or institutional care, or the provision of care by kafala or an analogous institution, and if such placement or such provision of care is to take place in another Contracting State, it shall first consult with the Central Authority or other competent authority of the latter State. To that effect it shall transmit a report on the child together with the reasons for the proposed placement or provision of care.

2. The decision on the placement or provision of care may be made in the requesting State only if the Central Authority or other competent authority of the requested State has consented to the placement or provision of care, taking into account the child's best interests.

* * *

Article 50 This Convention shall not affect the application of the Convention of 25 October 1980 on the Civil Aspects of International Child Abduction, as between Parties to both Conventions. Nothing, however, precludes provisions of this Convention from being invoked for the purposes of obtaining the return of a child who has been wrongfully removed or retained or of organising access rights.

* * *

5. Public International Law Conventions

The emerging focus on the best interests of the child is grounded in the Convention on the Rights of the Child, as set forth below.

Convention on the Rights of the Child[2]

Article 9 1. States Parties shall ensure that a child shall not be separated from his or her parents against their will, except when competent authorities subject to judicial review determine, in accordance with applicable law and procedures, that such separation is necessary for the best interests of the child. Such determination may be necessary in a particular case such as one involving abuse or neglect of the child by the parents, or one where the parents are living separately and a decision must be made as to the child's place of residence.
2. In any proceedings pursuant to paragraph 1 of the present article, all interested parties shall be given an opportunity to participate in the proceedings and make their views known.
3. States Parties shall respect the right of the child who is separated from one or both parents to maintain personal relations and direct contact with both parents on a regular basis, except if it is contrary to the child's best interests.
4. Where such separation results from any action initiated by a State Party, such as the detention, imprisonment, exile, deportation or death (including death arising from any cause while the person is in the custody of the State) of one or both parents or of the child, that State Party shall, upon request, provide the parents, the child or, if appropriate, another member of the family with the essential information concerning the whereabouts of the absent member(s) of the family unless the provision of the information would be detrimental to the well-being of the child. States Parties shall further ensure that the submission of such a request shall of itself entail no adverse consequences for the person(s) concerned.

Article 10 1. In accordance with the obligation of States Parties under article 9, paragraph 1, applications by a child or his or her parents to enter or leave a State Party for the purpose of family reunification shall be dealt with by States Parties in a positive, humane and expeditious manner. States Parties shall further ensure that the submission of such a request shall entail no adverse consequences for the applicants and for the members of their family.
2. A child whose parents reside in different States shall have the right to maintain on a regular basis, save in exceptional circumstances personal relations and direct contacts with both parents. Towards that end and in accordance with the obligation of States Parties under article 9, paragraph 1, States Parties shall respect the right of the child and his or her parents to leave any country, including their own, and to enter their own country. The right to leave any country shall be subject only to such restrictions as are prescribed by law and which are necessary to protect the national security, public order (order public), public health or

morals or the rights and freedoms of others and are consistent with the other rights recognized in the present Convention.

Article 11 1. States Parties shall take measures to combat the illicit transfer and non-return of children abroad.
2. To this end, States Parties shall promote the conclusion of bilateral or multilateral agreements or accession to existing agreements.

Article 12 1. States Parties shall assure to the child who is capable of forming his or her own views the right to express those views freely in all matters affecting the child, the views of the child being given due weight in accordance with the age and maturity of the child.
2. For this purpose, the child shall in particular be provided the opportunity to be heard in any judicial and administrative proceedings affecting the child, either directly, or through a representative or an appropriate body, in a manner consistent with the procedural rules of national law.

* * *

Article 18 1. States Parties shall use their best efforts to ensure recognition of the principle that both parents have common responsibilities for the upbringing and development of the child. Parents or, as the case may be, legal guardians, have the primary responsibility for the upbringing and development of the child. The best interests of the child will be their basic concern.
2. For the purpose of guaranteeing and promoting the rights set forth in the present Convention, States Parties shall render appropriate assistance to parents and legal guardians in the performance of their child-rearing responsibilities and shall ensure the development of institutions, facilities and services for the care of children.
3. States Parties shall take all appropriate measures to ensure that children of working parents have the right to benefit from child-care services and facilities for which they are eligible.

6. Regional Conventions

African Charter on the Rights and Welfare of the Child[3]

2. Every child who is separated from one or both parents shall have the right to maintain personal relations and direct contact with both parents on a regular basis.

See Chapter 9 for pertinent excerpts from the *1980 Council of Europe Convention on Recognition and Enforcement of Decisions Concerning Custody of Children and on Restoration of Custody of Children,*[4] and *Council Regulation (EC) on jurisdiction and the recognition and enforcement of judgments in matrimonial matters and in matters of parental responsibility for children of both spouses*[5]

Convention for the Protection of Human Rights and Fundamental Freedoms[6]

Article 8 right to respect for private and family life 1. Everyone has the right to respect for his private and family life, his home and his correspondence. 2. There shall be no interference by a public authority with the exercise of this right except such as is in accordance with the law and is necessary in a democratic society in their interest of national security, public safety or the economic well-being of the country, for the prevention of disorder or crime ...

Article 14 – Prohibition of discrimination The enjoyment of the rights and freedoms set forth in this Convention shall be secured without discrimination on any ground such as sex, race, colour, language, religion, political or other opinion, national or social origin, association with a national minority, property, birth or other status.

Explanatory Report to the Convention on contact concerning children[7]

Contact with children and the possible restrictions thereto, when these are considered necessary in the best interests of the child, is a major concern for the member States of the Council of Europe.

The inherent problems with respect to the exercise of contact give rise to significant disputes in many countries. Some parents – and sometimes rightly so – are reluctant to grant contact rights while others are deprived of the possibility of obtaining or of maintaining any type of contact at all with their child. Disputes relating to contact are often long and painful for the parties concerned and raise problems as regards making, modifying and enforcing court orders relating to contact. Furthermore, the internationalisation of family relations and the difficulties created by geographical separation, which brings with it the application of different legal systems, different languages as well as cultural differences, illustrate just some of the problems encountered in transfrontier contact.

However, according to the case-law of the European Court of Human Rights ' "respect" for a family life (...) implies an obligation for the State to act in a manner calculated to allow these ties to develop normally.' (Eur. Court HR, Scozzari and Giunta v. Italie of 13 July 2000, A, par. 221)

The aim of the Convention is to improve certain aspects of the right of national and transfrontier contact and, in particular, to specify and reinforce the basic right of children and their parents to maintain contact on a regular basis. This right may be extended, if necessary, to include contact between a child and other persons than his or her parents, in particular when the child has family ties with such a person.

In this respect, the object of the Convention is to determine the general principles to be applied to contact orders, as well as to fix appropriate safeguards and guarantees to ensure the proper exercise of such contact and the immediate return of children at the end of the period of contact. It establishes co-operation between all the bodies and authorities concerned with contact orders and reinforces the implementation of relevant existing international legal instruments in this field.

The Convention also addresses non-member States of the Council of Europe and will therefore also be open to their accession to this Convention. The Convention was opened for signature on 15 May 2003 and signed by 12 States: Austria, Belgium, Bulgaria, Croatia, Cyprus, Czech Republic, Italy, Malta, Moldova, Portugal, San Marino and Ukraine.

Convention on contact concerning children[8]

Preamble The member States of the Council of Europe and the other Signatories hereto, Taking into account the European Convention on Recognition and Enforcement of Decisions concerning Custody of Children and on Restoration of Custody of Children of 20 May 1980 (ETS No. 105);

Taking into account the Hague Convention of 25 October 1980 on the Civil Aspects of International Child Abduction and the Hague Convention of 19 October 1996 on Jurisdiction, Applicable Law, Recognition, Enforcement and Co-operation in respect of Parental Responsibility and Measures for the Protection of Children;

Taking into account the Council Regulation (EC) No. 1347/2000 of 29 May 2000 on jurisdiction and the recognition and enforcement of judgments in matrimonial matters and in matters of parental responsibility for children of both spouses;

Recognising that, as provided in the different international legal instruments of the Council of Europe as well as in Article 3 of the United Nations Convention on the Rights of the Child of 20 November 1989, the best interests of the child shall be a primary consideration;

Aware of the need for further provisions to safeguard contact between children and their parents and other persons having family ties with children, as protected by Article 8 of the Convention for the Protection of Human Rights and Fundamental Freedoms of 4 November 1950 (ETS No. 5);

Taking into account Article 9 of the United Nations Convention on the Rights of the Child which provides for the right of a child, who is separated from one or both parents, to maintain personal relations and direct contact with both parents on a regular basis, except when this is contrary to the child's best interests;

Taking into account paragraph 2 of Article 10 of the United Nations Convention on the Rights of the Child, which provides for the right of the child whose parents reside in different States to maintain on a regular basis, save in exceptional circumstances, personal relations and direct contacts with both parents;

Aware of the desirability of recognising not only parents but also children as holders of rights;

Agreeing consequently to replace the notion of 'access to children' with the notion of 'contact concerning children';

Taking into account the European Convention on the Exercise of Children's Rights (ETS No. 160) and the desirability of promoting measures to assist children in matters concerning contact with parents and other persons having family ties with children;

Agreeing on the need for children to have contact not only with both parents but also with certain other persons having family ties with children and the importance for parents and those other persons to remain in contact with children, subject to the best interests of the child;

Noting the need to promote the adoption by States of common principles with respect to contact concerning children, in particular in order to facilitate the application of international instruments in this field;

Realising that machinery set up to give effect to foreign orders relating to contact concerning children is more likely to provide satisfactory results where the principles on which these foreign orders are based are similar to the principles in the State giving effect to such foreign orders;

Recognising the need, when children and parents and other persons having family ties with children live in different States, to encourage judicial authorities to make more frequent use of transfrontier contact and to increase the confidence of all persons concerned that the children will be returned at the end of such contact;

Noting that the provision of efficient safeguards and additional guarantees is likely to ensure the return of children, in particular, at the end of transfrontier contact;

Noting that an additional international instrument is necessary to provide solutions relating in particular to transfrontier contact concerning children;

Desiring to establish co-operation between all central authorities and other bodies in order to promote and improve contact between children and their parents, and other persons having family ties with such children, and in particular to promote judicial co-operation in cases concerning transfrontier contact;

Have agreed as follows:

Chapter I – Objects of the Convention and definitions

Article 1 – Objects of the Convention The objects of this Convention are:

a.   to determine general principles to be applied to contact orders;

b.   to fix appropriate safeguards and guarantees to ensure the proper exercise of contact and the immediate return of children at the end of the period of contact;

c.   to establish co-operation between central authorities, judicial authorities and other bodies in order to promote and improve contact between children and their parents, and other persons having family ties with children.

Article 2 – Definitions For the purposes of this Convention:

a.   'contact' means:

i.   the child staying for a limited period of time with or meeting a person mentioned in Articles 4 or 5 with whom he or she is not usually living;

* * *

d.   'family ties' means a close relationship such as between a child and his or her grandparents or siblings, based on law or on a de facto family relationship;

* * *

Article 4 – Contact between a child and his or her parents

1.   A child and his or her parents shall have the right to obtain and maintain regular contact with each other.

2.   Such contact may be restricted or excluded only where necessary in the best interests of the child.

3.   Where it is not in the best interests of a child to maintain unsupervised contact with one of his or her parents the possibility of supervised personal contact or other forms of contact with this parent shall be considered.

Article 5 – Contact between a child and persons other than his or her parents

1.   Subject to his or her best interests, contact may be established between the child and persons other than his or her parents having family ties with the child.

2.   States Parties are free to extend this provision to persons other than those mentioned in paragraph 1, and where so extended, States may freely decide what aspects of contact, as defined in Article 2 letter a shall apply.

Article 6 – The right of a child to be informed, consulted and to express his or her views

1.   A child considered by internal law as having sufficient understanding shall have the right, unless this would be manifestly contrary to his or her best interests:

   –   to receive all relevant information;

   –   to be consulted;

   –   to express his or her views.

2.   Due weight shall be given to those views and to the ascertainable wishes and feelings of the child.

Article 7 – Resolving disputes concerning contact When resolving disputes concerning contact, the judicial authorities shall take all appropriate measures:

a.   to ensure that both parents are informed of the importance for their child and for both of them of establishing and maintaining regular contact with their child;

b.   to encourage parents and other persons having family ties with the child to reach amicable agreements with respect to contact, in particular through the use of family mediation and other processes for resolving disputes;

c. before taking a decision, to ensure that they have sufficient information at their disposal, in particular from the holders of parental responsibilities, in order to take a decision in the best interests of the child and, where necessary, obtain further information from other relevant bodies or persons.

Article 8 – Contact agreements

1. States Parties shall encourage, by means they consider appropriate, parents and other persons having family ties with the child to comply with the principles laid down in Articles 4 to 7 when making or modifying agreements on contact concerning a child. These agreements should preferably be in writing.

2. Upon request, judicial authorities shall, except where internal law otherwise provides, confirm an agreement on contact concerning a child, unless it is contrary to the best interests of the child.

Article 9 – The carrying into effect of contact orders States Parties shall take all appropriate measures to ensure that contact orders are carried into effect.

Article 10 – Safeguards and guarantees to be taken concerning contact

1. Each State Party shall provide for and promote the use of safeguards and guarantees. It shall communicate, through its central authorities, to the Secretary General of the Council of Europe, within three months after the entry into force of this Convention for that State Party, at least three categories of safeguards and guarantees available in its internal law in addition to the safeguards and guarantees referred to in paragraph 3 of Article 4 and in letter b of paragraph 1 of Article 14 of this Convention. Changes of available safeguards and guarantees shall be communicated as soon as possible.

2. Where the circumstances of the case so require, judicial authorities may, at any time, make a contact order subject to any safeguards and guarantees both for the purpose of ensuring that the order is carried into effect and that either the child is returned at the end of the period of contact to the place where he or she usually lives or that he or she is not improperly removed.

a. Safeguards and guarantees for ensuring that the order is carried into effect, may in particular include:
    – supervision of contact;
    – the obligation for a person to provide for the travel and accommodation expenses of the child and, as may be appropriate, of any other person accompanying the child;
    – a security to be deposited by the person with whom the child is usually living to ensure that the person seeking contact with the child is not prevented from having such contact;
    – a fine to be imposed on the person with whom the child is usually living, should this person refuse to comply with the contact order.

b. Safeguards and guarantees for ensuring the return of the child or preventing an improper removal, may in particular include:
    – the surrender of passports or identity documents and, where appropriate, a document indicating that the person seeking contact has notified the competent consular authority about such a surrender during the period of contact;
    – financial guarantees;
    – charges on property;
    – undertakings or stipulations to the court;
    – the obligation of the person having contact with the child to present himself or herself, with the child regularly before a competent body such as a youth welfare authority or a police station, in the place where contact is to be exercised;
    – the obligation of the person seeking contact to present a document issued by the

State where contact is to take place, certifying the recognition and declaration of enforceability of a custody or a contact order or both either before a contact order is made or before contact takes place;

- the imposition of conditions in relation to the place where contact is to be exercised and, where appropriate, the registration, in any national or transfrontier information system, of a prohibition preventing the child from leaving the State where contact is to take place.

3. Any such safeguards and guarantees shall be in writing or evidenced in writing and shall form part of the contact order or the confirmed agreement.

4. If safeguards or guarantees are to be implemented in another State Party, the judicial authority shall preferably order such safeguards or guarantees as are capable of implementation in that State Party.

* * *

Article 16 – Return of a child

1. Where a child at the end of a period of transfrontier contact based on a contact order is not returned, the competent authorities shall, upon request, ensure the child's immediate return, where applicable, by applying the relevant provisions of international instruments, of internal law and by implementing, where appropriate, such safeguards and guarantees as may be provided in the contact order.

2. A decision on the return of the child shall be made, whenever possible, within six weeks of the date of an application for the return.

* * *

Chapter IV – Relationship with other instruments

Article 19 – Relationship with the European Convention on Recognition and Enforcement of Decisions concerning Custody of Children and on Restoration of Custody of Children Paragraphs 2 and 3 of Article 11 of the European Convention of 20 May 1980 (ETS N° 105) on Recognition and Enforcement of Decisions concerning Custody of Children and on Restoration of Custody of Children shall not be applied in relations between States Parties which are also States Parties of the present Convention.

Article 20 – Relationships with other instruments 1. This Convention shall not affect any international instrument to which States Parties to the present Convention are Parties or shall become Parties and which contains provisions on matters governed by this Convention. In particular, this Convention shall not prejudice the application of the following legal instruments:

a. the Hague Convention of 5 October 1961 on the competence of authorities and the applicable law concerning the protection of minors,

b. the European Convention on the recognition and enforcement of decisions concerning custody of children and on restoration of custody of children of 20 May 1980, subject to Article 19 above,

c. the Hague Convention of 25 October 1980 on the civil aspects of international child abduction,

d. the Hague Convention of 19 October 1996 on jurisdiction, applicable law, recognition, enforcement and co-operation in respect of parental responsibility and measures for the protection of children.

7. National Implementation

Many courts, in keeping with the emphasis in the Convention on the Rights of the Child on the child's best interest, have held that visitation rights run to the child rather than to the parent. In Argentina, for example, the applications of mothers seeking to have visitation suspended for failure of the fathers to meet their support obligation have been denied based on the ground that:

> Visitation rights belong to the minor, so their suspension or denial based on maintenance arrears amounts to a violation of the rights of children and a failure to take account of their interests, whereas they are not responsible for the father's conduct. To interrupt any regime of visits in view of the conduct of a parent towards a child or children is a measure to be used sparingly, even though the right is not absolute, to the extent that the exercise of the right should only be blocked for reasons so serious as to pose a threat to the children's safety or to their physical or mental health.

In Australia, similarly, a court refused the mother's petition to relocate to her native Scotland. Three of the four children also hoped to relocate to Scotland but the application was rejected because of the risk of emotional harm to the youngest child presented by depriving him of visitation with his father. *R. v. R.*

In Botswana, the courts have recently affirmed that the right to parental visitation belongs to non-marital as well as marital children. In *Langbaecher v. Chipe*, the father had lived with the mother and the two extra-marital children, aged 7 and 2. In granting the father access to the child every weekend, the court held that,

> Access should be regarded as a basic right of the child rather than a basic right of the parent, and save in exceptional circumstances, to deprive the parent of access is to deprive a child of an important contribution to his emotional and material growing up in the long term. In my view, for the purpose of access, 'parents' includes the biological father of an illegitimate child.

Following its ratification of the Convention on the Rights of the Child in 1990, Argentina sought to bring family law into compliance with the norms of the Convention. The emphasis on the overriding interest of the child in Article 3 has been interpreted to make the child's interest in maintaining a relationship with both parents the most important factor in visitation. Thus, where a custodial mother has restricted a visiting father's access to the child, courts have ordered family therapy. Failure to cooperate may result in a change of custody.

Under the Dutch Civil Code, in addition to parents, a person who has developed a relationship with a child that amounts to 'family life' as understood in Article 8 of the European Convention on Human Rights may also be granted visitation, or 'access' to the child (Sumner and Forder, 2002). Under this standard, access has been granted to grandparents, foster parents and unmarried fathers.

Hoppe v. Germany[9]

> Peter Hoppe is a German national, born in 1957 and living in Herne. In April 1990 a daughter, Svenja, was born to the applicant and his wife and in December 1992 the applicant and his wife separated. Svenja stayed with her mother who instituted divorce proceedings against her husband. On 19 October 1994 Wuppertal District Court, following

two hearings, decided that the applicant was entitled to see Svenja every second Saturday as well as St Stephens day, Easter Monday and Whit Monday. All the experts heard in the proceedings gave evidence that four-year-old Svenja was exposed to a conflict of loyalty and that she could not cope with the situation. The applicant was incapable of accepting restrictions on access and did not show concern for the child's psychological health. Svenja's mother had not yet managed to give Svenja such a feeling of security as to permit her to visit the applicant without feelings of fear. Svenja therefore needed the intervals of two weeks as times of rest in her mother's home. The applicant appealed. On 9 March 1995 Düsseldorf Court of Appeal increased the applicant's right of access by ruling that every first visiting weekend a month the applicant was entitled to see Svenja from Saturday morning until Sunday evening. The remainder of his appeal was dismissed. The court found that, as long as there was no agreement between the parents, any visit was an emotional strain for the child. The applicant's right of access had therefore to be assessed in the context of the continuing conflict between the parents. The applicant referred the case to the Federal Constitutional Court, which considered that the applicant's complaint did not raise any issue of fundamental importance. The applicant's visiting rights were later extended to every weekend. On 24 October 1994 Wuppertal District Court granted the divorce and gave Svenja's mother parental authority, as being in Svenja's best interests. She educated and looked after her daughter in an atmosphere of love and understanding and took an intense interest in ensuring her well-being. Svenja needed a stable life without being torn between different apartments and different styles of education. The Court noted that the applicant failed to see that his wishes obstructed Svenja's psychological development. The applicant appealed unsuccessfully to the Court of Appeal, which had considered that an oral hearing with the parties was not necessary, the relevant facts being clear from the case-file. The Federal Constitutional Court also refused to entertain the applicant's constitutional complaint as not raising any issue of fundamental importance. The applicant alleged, in particular, that the German courts' decisions concerning his right of access to his daughter and the awarding of parental authority breached his right to respect for his family life, that he was denied a fair hearing in the relevant proceedings and that he had been subjected to discrimination. He relied on Articles 6 (right to a fair hearing), 8 (right to respect for private and family life) and 14 (prohibition of discrimination).

Concerning Article 8, the European Court of Human Rights found that the domestic courts carefully considered the questions of access and of awarding parental authority. The District Court relied on expert reports and on the evidence given by the parents at hearings and was thus in a better position than the European judges to strike a fair balance between the competing interests involved. Furthermore, the District Court judgments were upheld by the Court of Appeal. The Court was therefore satisfied that when reducing the applicant's rights of access and awarding parental authority to the child's mother, the national authorities acted within the margin of appreciation afforded to them in such matters. The Court further noted, in particular in the first-instance proceedings, that the applicant, assisted by counsel, had the opportunity to present his arguments in writing and orally. The Court was satisfied that no hearing before the Court of Appeal appeared necessary, however. The Court further considered that the case was decided with special diligence, as required in cases concerning a person's relationship with his or her child, in view of the risk that the passage of time might result in a de facto determination of the matter. The Court was therefore satisfied that the procedural requirements implicit in Article 8 were complied with and that the applicant was involved in the decision-making process to a degree sufficient to provide him with the requisite protection of his interests. Accordingly, the Court held unanimously that there had been no violation of Article 8.

Judgment in the Case of Salgueiro da Silva Mouta v. Portugal[10]

In a judgment delivered at Strasbourg on 21 December 1999 in the case of Salgueiro da Silva Mouta v. Portugal, the European Court of Human Rights held unanimously that there had been a violation of Article 8 (right to respect for private and family life) taken together with Article 14 (prohibition of discrimination) of the European Convention on Human Rights, and that it was unnecessary to rule on the complaints made under Article 8 taken alone. Under Article 41 (just satisfaction) of the Convention, the Court held that the judgment constituted of itself sufficient just satisfaction for the damage alleged by the applicant; it awarded him 1,800,000 Portuguese escudos (PTE) for costs and PTE 350,000 for expenses.

1. Principal facts The applicant, João Manuel Salgueiro da Silva Mouta, a Portuguese national, was born in 1961 and lives in Queluz (Portugal).

He was prevented by his ex-wife from visiting his daughter M., in breach of an agreement reached at the time of their divorce. He sought an order giving him parental responsibility for the child, which was granted by the Lisbon Family Affairs Court in 1994. M. lived with the applicant until 1995 when, he alleges, she was abducted by her mother. On appeal, the mother was given parental responsibility whereas the applicant was granted a contact order which, he maintained, he was unable to exercise. The Lisbon Court of Appeal gave two reasons in its judgment for granting parental responsibility for M. to her mother, namely the interest of the child and the fact that the applicant was a homosexual and living with another man.

3. Summary of the judgment/Complaints The applicant complained of an unjustified interference with his right to respect for his private and family life, as guaranteed by Article 8 of the Convention and discrimination contrary to Article 14 of the Convention. He maintained, too, that contrary to Article 8 he had been forced by the court of appeal to hide his homosexuality when seeing his daughter.

Decision of the Court Article 8 taken together with Article 14 of the Convention The Court noted at the outset that under the case-law of the Convention institutions Article 8 applied to decisions concerning granting parental responsibility for a child to one of the parents on a divorce or separation. The judgment of the Lisbon Court of Appeal constituted an interference with the applicant's right to respect for his family life in that it had reversed the judgment of the Lisbon Family Affairs Court granting parental responsibility to the applicant.

The Court went on to observe that although the court of appeal had considered the interest of the child in deciding to reverse the judgment of the Lisbon Family Affairs Court and, consequently, to grant parental responsibility to the mother rather than the father, it had had regard to a new factor, namely the fact that the applicant was a homosexual and living with another man. There had therefore been a difference in treatment between the applicant and M.'s mother based on the applicant's sexual orientation, a notion that fell within Article 14 of the Convention. Such a difference in treatment was discriminatory under that provision if it had no objective or reasonable justification, that is if it did not pursue a legitimate aim or if there was not a reasonable relationship of proportionality between the means employed and the aim sought to be realised.

The court of appeal had pursued a legitimate aim in reaching its decision, namely the protection of the child's health and rights. In order to decide whether there was no reasonable basis for the decision that was finally made, the Court examined whether the new factor taken into account by the Lisbon Court of Appeal – the applicant's homosexuality – was a mere obiter dictum with no direct impact on the final decision, or whether, on the contrary, it was a decisive factor. To that end, the Court reviewed the Lisbon Court of Appeal's judgment and noted that after finding that there were no sufficient reasons for depriving the mother of parental responsibility – which the parents had agreed she should exercise – it had gone on to say: '... even if that had not been so, we consider that the mother should be granted custody of the child'. In so doing the court of appeal had noted that the applicant was a homosexual and living with another man and had stated: 'the child must live in ... a traditional Portuguese family' and 'it is unnecessary to examine whether or not homosexuality is an illness or a sexual orientation towards people of the same sex. Either way, it is an abnormality and children must not grow up in the shadow of abnormal situations'.

The Court was of the view that those passages from the judgment of the Lisbon Court of Appeal were not simply clumsy or unfortunate, or mere obiter dicta; they suggested that the applicant's homosexuality had been decisive in the final decision and thus amounted to a distinction dictated by factors relating to the applicant's sexual orientation that it was not permissible to draw under the Convention. That conclusion was supported by the fact that, when ruling on the applicant's contact rights, the court of appeal had discouraged the applicant from behaving during visits in a way that would make the child aware that he was living with another man 'as if they were spouses'.

The Court therefore held that there had been a violation of Article 8 taken together with Article 14.

8. IOs and NGOs

IOs

The Committee on the Rights of the Child has published Guidelines for States Parties in preparing the self-monitoring reports required under Article 44 of the CRC. Pertinent excerpts from the Guidelines for initial and periodic reports are set out below.

Committee on the Rights of the Child, general guidelines regarding the form and content of initial reports to be submitted by States Parties[11] *CRC/C/5.*

Family environment and alternative care
16. Under this section, States parties are requested to provide relevant information, including the principal legislative, judicial, administrative or other measures in force, particularly how the principles of the 'best interests of the child' and 'respect for the views of the child' are reflected therein;
factors and difficulties encountered and progress achieved in implementing the relevant provisions of the Convention; and implementation priorities and specific goals for the future in respect of:

* * *

(b) Parental responsibilities (art. 18, paras. 1-2);
(c) Separation from parents (art. 9);
(d) Family reunification (art. 10);

* * *

(h) Illicit transfer and non-return (art. 11);

Committee on the rights of the child, general guidelines for periodic reports CRC/C/58. 20/11/96.

C. Separation from parents (art. 9)

68. Please indicate the measures adopted, including of a legislative and judicial nature, to ensure that the child is not separated from his or her parents except when such separation is necessary for the best interests of the child, as in cases of abuse or neglect of the child or when the parents live separately and a decision must be made as to the child's place of residence. Please identify the competent authorities intervening in these decisions, the applicable law and procedure and the role of judicial review.

69. Please provide information on the measures taken pursuant to article 9, paragraph 2 to ensure to all interested parties, including the child, an opportunity to participate in any proceedings and to make their views known.

70. Please indicate the measures adopted, including of a legislative, judicial and administrative nature, to ensure that the child who is separated from one or both parents has the right to maintain personal relations and direct contacts with both parents on a regular basis, except if it is contrary to the best interests of the child. Please further indicate the extent to which the views of the child are taken into consideration in this regard.

71. Please indicate the measures adopted pursuant to article 9, paragraph 4 to ensure that in the case of the child's separation from one or both of his or her parents as a result of any action initiated by the State, essential information on the whereabouts of the absent member(s) of the family is provided, upon request, to the child, to the parents or, if appropriate, to another member of the family, unless the provision of the information would be detrimental to the well-being of the child. Also indicate the measures undertaken to ensure that the submission of such a request entails no adverse consequences for the person(s) concerned.

72. Relevant disaggregated information (for example, by age, gender and national, ethnic and social origin) should be provided inter alia in relation to situations of detention, imprisonment, exile, deportation or death, together with an assessment of progress achieved in the implementation of article 9, difficulties encountered and targets set for the future.

NGOs

NGOs focusing on the problems of transnational visitation have begun to establish websites and international networks. Some, such as Children's Rights Council/Japan, are basically lobbying efforts by non-custodial parents stymied by local laws which effectively deny them contact with their children. Others, such as the Supervised Visitation Network, attempt to facilitate transnational visitation by reducing the risks of violence, confrontation, or abduction.

Children's Rights Council/Japan

About CRC Japan[12] The Japan chapter of Children's Rights Council (CRC) was initially established on May 5, 1996, 'Children's Day' in Japan, by David Brian Thomas (British citizen) and Walter Benda (U.S. citizen) in response to our own difficulties obtaining access to our children in Japan. Both of us are the 'left behind parent' victims of parental abductions committed in Japan. The Children's Rights Council of Japan is a 501(c)(3) IRS nonprofit under the group exemption of the United States national Children's Rights Council headquartered in Hyattsville, Maryland. Our Motto is: 'The Best Parent is Both Parents.'

Japan Visitation Rights Nearly Non-Existent; Non-Enforceable Once custody is awarded to a Japanese parent, or in the case of unmarried parents where custody goes to the mother by default, the same allegedly biased Family Court gets to decide on visitation rights. Court ordered visitation is typically a maximum of only several hours per month and usually does not allow the child to leave the country to see other relatives. Even then, the custodial parent often seeks to cut off all contact with the other parent for traditional cultural reasons, and so actively denies visitation.

The only recourse is to return to the Family Courts. But the court processes take years, and neither courts nor the police will enforce court ordered visitation. So the offending parent can easily continue to be uncooperative. This is another common form of Japanese government sanctioned separation from one parent, and hence legalized parental child abduction. The responsibility to ensure regular visitation is a direct consequence of the United Nations Convention on the Rights of the Child, which was ratified by Japan in its entirety on May 22nd 1994.

The poster child for this 'uniquely Japanese' practice is none other than Prime Minister Junichiro Koizumi, who as reported by the Washington Post and LA Times, has denied his ex-wife any contact with their two children in his custody.

Supervised Visitation Network[13]

Mission The mission of SVN is to facilitate opportunities for children to have safe and conflict-free access to both parents through a continuum of child access services delivered by competent providers.

Purpose 1. To develop and disseminate standards for practice of child access services.
2. To maintain a directory of supervised child access providers. This is a large (615K) file. Please be patient while it loads.
3. To provide public education regarding the importance of children having safe conflict-free contact with both parents and other family members.
4. To provide public education regarding the role of child access programs in the continuum of services for divorced and separated families and for children in out-of-home placement.
5. To collect and make available research relevant to safe child access.
6. To gather and disseminate training and program materials for child access providers.
7. To provide professional conferences and forums for networking and sharing of information.
8. To educate public and private decision-makers regarding the importance of funding for child access services and provide information on funding to courts and service providers.

Functions 1. Our members throughout the world provide direct services to children and their families designed to keep families in safe contact.
2. We help families find services that are convenient to them and will meet their needs by

maintaining a directory of services nationwide.

We receive many calls from parents, attorneys, social workers, judges, and others looking for services in their area. Our goal is to have a comprehensive directory so services can easily be found by the families that need them. You can access this directory by clicking on the Service Providers Directory link in the navigation bar on this page.

3. We collect and disseminate research information relevant to safe child access and provide public education regarding the importance of children having access to their parents.

4. We work to improve the quality of services. This is accomplished in several ways:

- We develop and disseminate standards for practice.
- We provide opportunities for members to network with each other and exchange information that will help them in their practice.
- We hold an annual Conference that provides outstanding training for service providers.
- We disseminate resources and helpful information to members through our Newsletter and on our web site.
- We maintain a library of training and program materials.

5. We encourage the development of new programs in under-served areas and provide support through our members for new and developing programs.

6. We share information with each other about funding sources that will help provide affordable services.

9. A Possible Approach to the Problem

There are as many legal systems with a potential interest in Jomo's future as there are concerned adults. The first question is which laws apply. Tessa and Jomo have 'recently moved from Nairobi, Kenya to Brussels, Belgium' and it is not clear whether Brussels would qualify at this point as Jomo's 'habitual residence' under Chapter II, Article 5 of the Convention on Jurisdiction set out in Section 4, although presumably it will become his 'habitual residence' in the future. If Kenya and Belgium are both parties to the Convention, they are both likely to consider Belgium the new habitual residence and Belgian law applicable under Article 17.

While Tessa will obviously want to consult a Belgian lawyer, the Explanatory Report and the accompanying Convention on contact concerning children set out in Section 6 provides a useful introduction to the European perspective. It is noteworthy that the Convention explicitly adopts the international human rights standard, the 'best interest of the child,' as its 'primary consideration.' It further recognizes the child's right, under the Children's Convention, to maintain contact with both parents, the recognition of children as 'rightholders,' and the 'need for children to have contact ... with certain other persons having family ties ... subject to the best interests of the child.' Thus, Jomo's interests are the focus of the inquiry. He is only 8, however, and is not mature enough to make the final decision, although his wishes should be taken into account.

As the custodial parent, Tessa can arrange for Jomo to visit with all of the adults in his life. If she decides to prevent contact, however, Gloria, Justin, and Arnold have very different bases for their claims to contact with Jomo.

Gloria, Jomo's grandmother, lives nearby in Lieden, and travel should not be a problem. While the Convention on contact recognizes the rights of non-parents, like Gloria, her visitation rights are subject to the other demands on Jomo's time, consistent with his best interests. Tessa might suggest a flexible, modified schedule, in which Gloria sees Jomo every third or fourth week. Gloria could come to Brussels for every third or fourth Sunday afternoon, for example, subject to confirmation with Tessa, while Jomo could visit her in Lieden twice a year. If Jomo had a similar arrangement with Justin, Tessa would have her son at home most weekends, while Jomo would have contact with two people who have always been a part of his life. While Justin is not Jomo's biological father, since the boy was born into an extant marriage between Justin and his mother, Justin may well be his legal father. This would be determined, in the first instance, under Kenyan law.

Visitation with Arnold in Kenya is the most problematic issue here because of Tessa's concern that Arnold might try to keep him. While abduction (including abduction of a biological child) is the subject of Chapter 9, whether Kenya is a party to the Convention on Jurisdiction set out in Section 4, or the Abduction Convention, set out in Chapter 9, is pertinent here. Even if Kenya is a party to both, moreover, enforcement may be difficult. The safest course, especially while Jomo is so young, is to limit Arnold's visitation to Brussels. If Tessa wants Jomo to retain ties with his country of origin, and the biological father who still lives there, another alternative would be to arrange supervised visitation in Kenya, perhaps annually, though a trusted intermediary.

While everyone wants unrestricted telephone and email contract with Jomo, Tessa, as the custodial parent, certainly has the authority to impose reasonable restrictions on the amount of time Jomo spends on the phone or on email. Again, the adults' interests should be subordinated to those of the child, as determined by his mother at this point.

For Further Research

1. For discussion of visitation in Argentina, see Grossman, C.P. and Iñigo, D. (2000), 'Argentina: The "Overriding Interest of the Child" in Legislative Policy and in Judicial Decisions in Argentina,' in Bainham, A. (ed.), *The International Survey of Family Law: 2000 Edition*, Jordan, Bristol, pp. 9-18; in Australia, see Bates, F. (2000) '"Fast Fold Thy Child" – Australian Family Law in 1998,' in Bainham, A. (ed.) *The International Survey of Family Law: 2000 Edition*, Jordan, Bristol, pp. 29-34; in Canada, see Bailey, M. and Bala, N. (2000), 'Canada: Reforming the Definition of Spouse and Child-Related Laws,' in Bainham, A. (ed.), *The International Survey of Family Law: 2000 Edition Edition*, Jordan, Bristol, pp. 65-83; in Botswana, see Molokomme, A. (2000), 'Overview of Family Law in Botswana,' in Bainham, A. (ed.), *The International Survey of Family Law: 2000 Edition*, Jordan, Bristol, pp. 43-54.

2. For a description of the Dutch approach to contact, see FFR/9, 8 Sumner, I. and Forder, C. (2000), 'Bumper Issue: All You Ever Wanted to Know about Dutch Family

Law (and Were Afraid to Ask),' in A. Bainham (ed.), *The International Survey of Family Law: 2003 Edition.* Jordon, Bristol, pp. 263-321.

Notes

1. Http://www/internationa-divorce.com/jordan1childabduction/ (Last visited 12/11/2003).
2. G.A. res 44/25, annex, 44 U.N. GAOR Supp. (No. 49) at 167, U.N. Doc. A/44/49 (1989), *entered into force* Sept. 2, 1990.
3. OAU Doc. CBA/LEG/24.9/49 (1990), *entered into force* Nov. 29, 1999.
4. http://conventions.coe.int/Treaty/EN/Treaties/Html/105.htm.
5. No 1347/2000 of 29 May 2000.
6. 213 U.N.T.S. 222, entered into force Sept. 3, 1953, as amended by Protocols Nos 3, 5, 8, and 11 which entered into force on 21 September 1970, 20 December 1971, 1 January 1990, and 1 November 998 respectively.
7. ETS 192.
8. Strasbourg, 15. V. 2003.
9. (no. 28422/95) Press release issued by the Registrar, available at: http://www/coe.int/T/E/Legal_affairs/Legal_co-operation/Family_law_and_children's_rights/Press%20release%20 Hoppe.asp (last visited 12/7/2003).
10. Press release issued by the Registrar, available at: http://www/coe.int/T/E/Legal_affairs/Legal_co-operation/Family_law_and_children's_rights/Press%20release%20 Salgueiro_da_Silva_PRJ_Eng.asp (last visited 12/7/2003).
11. CRC/C/5 30 October 1991.
12. http//www.crcjapan.com.com/about/en (last visited 12/10/2003).
13. http://www/svnetwork.net/AboutSVN.htm (last visited 12/10/2003).

Chapter 9

Child Custody and Abduction

1. The Problems

Maria

Lisa, who was born in South Africa, and Arturo, who was born in Italy, were married in South Africa in 1989. They lived in Italy for a few years, where their daughter, Maria, was born in 1996. In 1997, the family emigrated to Canada and in 1998 Lisa and Arturo separated. In 1999, a consent order was entered into before the Supreme Court of British Columbia. It granted the mother sole custody of Maria and the father rights of access.

The order further provided that the child was not to be removed from British Columbia in the absence of a further court order or written permission, with the exception that the child would be permitted to travel outside the jurisdiction between her parents for a period not to exceed 30 days. If either party took Maria out of Canada for more than 30 days, sole custody would be awarded to the other party.

Lisa and Maria left for South Africa on June 1, 2002. By July 21, 2002, Arturo realized that they would not be coming back and he filed an application with the central authorities of Canada demanding the return of Maria. Lisa argued that the South African Constitution prohibited such return, which would not be in the best interest of Maria.

You are a clerk to a justice on the South African Constitutional Court. What do you advise?

Anwar

Mahmout left his home in Cairo to work as a surgeon in Los Angeles, California. There he met Nora, who was also a surgeon. They fell in love and in 1996 they married. In 1999, Nora gave birth to a baby boy, Anwar, who is now 5. In 2000, Mahmout was offered a top post in a teaching hospital in Cairo. After much soul-searching, Mahmout told Nora that he felt compelled to return to Egypt, in part to be closer to his large family, especially his ageing parents. Nora said that she would never move to Egypt or raise her son there. They have agreed to obtain a no-fault divorce in California.

Mahmout comes to see you because he is concerned about custody of Anwar. Under Egyptian law, the divorced mother is entitled to custody of boys until 7 years, after which the father becomes the child's legal custodian. After speaking with her *lawyer, Nora has told Mahmout that this is not the law in the United States and that she would not voluntarily agree to transfer custody of her son in two years. Mahmout has dual U.S./Egyptian citizenship and Nora and Anwar are citizens of the United States. Mahmout is willing to agree to allow Nora custody now, if she will agree to transfer custody when Anwar becomes 7.*

Is there any reason for Nora to agree to Mahmout's request? What are Mahmout's prospects for convincing a U.S. court to apply Egyptian law here? Does he have any other options for legally acquiring custody of Anwar?

2. Overview

Custody refers to the post-divorce or post-separation living arrangements of the minor child. The parent who has custody typically has responsibility for supervision of the child and for meeting the child's daily needs. Custody is not necessarily exclusive. The other parent may have input into decision-making regarding the child's education or religious training, for example. The non-custodial parent may also have actual physical custody of the child for agreed-upon periods of time. Whether this is characterized as visitation or joint custody depends on the laws of the jurisdiction in which it is ordered and on the intention of the parties. Visitation generally refers to briefer periods of time (during summer vacations, for example), while joint custody refers to a more equal balance of responsibility.

It should be noted that custody is generally distinct from child support. That is, where a parent has a legal obligation to support a child, that obligation applies regardless of the child's living arrangements. It can be argued, accordingly, that the parent's relative wealth should not be a factor in determining custody. Rather, if custody is awarded to the less well-off parent, the child will still have access to the resources of the better-off parent through child support (see Chapter 10).

In some States, custody may be claimed by either legal parent, whether married or not. 'Legal' parents include biological parents, the mother's husband, adoptive parents, or fathers who have acknowledged paternity on a birth certificate or on a putative father's registry. Custody proceedings typically take place in the context of divorce, but claims for custody may also be made in the context of a contested adoption or if a court has jurisdiction over the parties and either party seeks a change in the custody arrangements. There is often a threshold requirement that a substantial change in circumstances has occurred, warranting a change in custody. Such a requirement is intended to limit frivolous applications.

Some States determine custody by the age of the child. Under Islamic law, for example, a divorced mother is typically entitled to custody of boys until 7 years and girls until 9 years, subject to classical conditions. The father is generally considered the custodian of older children. In some Islamic States, such as Malaysia, a child who has reached the 'age of discernment may choose with which parent to live', unless otherwise ordered by a court. In Algeria, a divorced wife may be granted custody of boys until the age of 16 years (or 10 if she remarries) and retain girls until 18 years, as long as the mother does not remarry or marry someone within a prohibited degree of relation to the daughter. Under Egyptian law, a father has custody of sons over the age of 7 and daughters over the age of 9.

In most States in the West, in contrast, custody is to be determined according to the 'best interest of the child'. This standard encourages a detailed case-by-case analysis, ultimately depending on the discretion of the trial court. Because custody is such an emotional issue, and because it is often difficult to predict how a court will rule, the less risk-averse spouse has considerable leverage in a contested proceeding. In the overwhelming majority of cases, however, custody is not disputed. In most of these cases, the mother becomes the custodial parent.

Different states have adopted different presumptions regarding the best interest of the child. These presumptions vary from State to State and may change over time. In the United States, for example, under the 'tender years' presumption the mother was presumed to be the better caretaker for children of 'tender years,' generally children under 10. This has been replaced by a gender-neutral standard, at least formally.

The Hague Convention applies where a child physically resides in one contracting State and then is taken to another by the noncustodial parent. The purpose of the Convention is to restore the status quo: that is, to return the child to the place of habitual residence for the determination of custody by a court there. The Hague Convention does not apply unless both States are contracting parties to the Convention. (For a list of present contracting parties, see Status Sheet convention number 28, http://www.htch.nt/e/status/abdshte.html.) The point of the Hague Convention is to return the child to the jurisdiction of habitual residence so as not to reward the abducting parent. The Convention does not address the merits of the underlying dispute, but only decides which court has jurisdiction to do so.

When the Hague Convention was drafted, it was expected that it would be used against fathers exercising visitation rights and absconding with their children. In fact, it is frequently used against custodial mothers who want to return to their home country with their children after a divorce from a foreign spouse.

In order to do so legally, such mothers are generally required to file a petition with the court in which custody was originally awarded. Thus, the petitioner is in the often awkward position of arguing why it is in the child's best interest to leave the State in which that court is located, and of which its judges are nationals.

3. Cultural Variations

Joint custody, under which the parents share custody of the minor child after divorce or after the child's birth in the case of unmarried parents, illustrates the range of cultural variations in this area. The trend in the West is increasingly toward recognizing both the ability and the responsibility of the father to parent. In Germany, for example, joint custody was not allowed until 1982, when it was ordered by the German Constitutional Court. The parent had to explicitly request joint custody and aver that sole custody was not in the best interest of the child. The Parentage Law

Reform Act of 1998 established a presumption in favor of joint custody when the parents are separated or divorced. Sole custody is awarded only if it is specifically requested and if the other parent agrees or the court finds that sole custody is in the best interest of the child. Even if both parents oppose joint custody, it may nevertheless be ordered if the judge believes that they can cooperate.

In Sweden, similarly, joint custody has become the norm. In 1982, parents could acquire joint custody by notifying the Population Registration Authority. In 1991, unmarried parents were able to acquire joint custody by completing an acknowledgment of paternity form. In 1998, it was proposed that unmarried parents be granted joint custody automatically after 3 months from an acknowledgment of paternity, unless either parent objected. If there is an objection, the mother remains the sole custodian. A father can initiate proceedings to challenge this. Fifty-four percent of Swedish children are born of unmarried parents. Ninety-five percent of parents who cohabit file an acknowledgment of paternity, establishing joint custody. Only fifty percent of non-cohabitating parents file such an acknowledgment.

In the Netherlands, joint custody is automatic after divorce unless either or both parents explicitly ask for sole custody on the ground that it is in the child's interest (Sumner and Forder, 2002). The presumption that joint custody is best for the child is quite strong, and is not rebutted by the parents' inability to cooperate, unless there is an 'unacceptable risk that the child will be caught between warring parents' (ibid.).

In Islamic States, in contrast, custody is determined by the age and sex of the child, in accordance with Islamic law, as set out below:

U.S. Dept. of State, International Parental Child Abduction/Islamic Family Law[1]

Note: The information contained in this flyer is intended as an introduction to the basic elements of Islamic family law. It is not intended as a legal reference.

It is designed to make clear the basic rights and restrictions resulting from marriages sanctioned by Islamic law between Muslim and non-Muslim partners. For Americans, the most troubling of these restrictions have been:

– the inability of wives to leave an Islamic country without permission of their husbands;
– the wives' inability to take their children from these countries without such permission; and
– the fact that fathers have ultimate custody of children.

* * *

Mixed Marriages With few exceptions, a Christian or Jew who marries a Muslim and resides in an Islamic country will be subject to provisions of Islamic family law in that country. In these circumstances:

– Any children born to the wife will be considered Muslim. They will usually also be considered citizens of the father's country.
– The husband's permission is always needed for the children to leave an Islamic country despite the fact that the children will also have, for example, American citizenship. Foreign immigration authorities can be expected to enforce these regulations. The ability of U.S. consular officers to aid an American woman who wishes to leave the country with her children is very limited.
– The wife may be divorced by her husband at any time with little difficulty and without a court hearing.

- At a certain point in age, the children will come under the custody of the father or his family.
- In Islamic countries, the wife will need the permission of her husband to leave the country.

Children's Rights There are three types of guardianship which are fixed for a child from the time of its birth;

- The first is guardianship of upbringing, which is overseen by women during the age of dependence. The age at which this period of dependence terminates varies: anywhere from 7 years for a son and 9 for a daughter to 9 and 11, respectively. In the case of divorced parents, it is permissible for a daughter to remain with her mother if the parents agree. But such an agreement cannot be made for a son.
- The second is the child's spiritual guardianship. The spiritual guardian may be the father or a fullblooded male relative of the father.
- The third is guardianship over the child's property which usually is carried out by the father.

4. Private International Law Conventions

Convention on the Civil Aspects of International Child Abduction (concluded October 25, 1980)

The States signatory to the present Convention,

Firmly convinced that the interests of children are of paramount importance in matters relating to their custody.

Desiring to protect children internationally from the harmful effects of their wrongful removal or retention and to establish procedures to ensure their prompt return to the State of their habitual residence, as well as to secure protection for rights of access,

Have resolved to conclude a Convention to this effect, and have agreed upon the following provisions

Chapter I B scope of the convention *Article 1* The objects of the present Convention are –
a. to secure the prompt return of children wrongfully removed to or retained in any Contracting State; and
b. to ensure that rights of custody and of access under the law of one Contracting State are effectively respected in the other Contracting States.

* * *

Article 3 The removal or the retention of a child is to be considered wrongful where –
a. it is in breach of rights of custody attributed to a person, an institution or any other body, either jointly or alone, under the law of the State in which the child was habitually resident immediately before the removal or retention; and
b. at the time of removal or retention those rights were actually exercised, either jointly or alone, or would have been so exercised but for the removal or retention.

The rights of custody mentioned in sub-paragraph a) above, may arise in particular by operation of law or by reason of a judicial or administrative decision, or by reason of an agreement having legal effect under the law of the State.

Article 4 The Convention shall apply to any child who was habitually resident in a Contracting State immediately before any breach of custody or access rights. The Convention shall cease to apply when the child attains the age of 16 years.

* * *

Article 12 Where a child has been wrongfully removed or retained in terms of Article 3 and, at the date of the commencement of the proceedings before the judicial or administrative authority of the Contracting State where the child is, a period of less than one year has elapsed from the date of the wrongful removal or retention, the authority concerned shall order the return of the child forthwith.

The judicial or administrative authority, even where the proceedings have been commenced after the expiration of the period of one year referred to in the preceding paragraph, shall also order the return of the child, unless it is demonstrated that the child is now settled in its new environment.

* * *

Article 13 Notwithstanding the provisions of the preceding Article, the judicial or administrative authority of the requested State is not bound to order the return of the child if the person, institution or other body which opposes its return establishes that –

a. the person, institution or other body having the care of the person or the child was not actually exercising the custody rights at the time of removal or retention, or had consented to or subsequently acquiesced in the removal or retention; or

b. there is a grave risk that his or her return would expose the child to physical or psychological harm or otherwise place the child in an intolerable situation.

The judicial or administrative authority may also refuse to order the return of the child if it finds that the child objects to being returned and has attained an age and degree of maturity at which it is appropriate to take account of its views.

* * *

Article 16 After receiving notice of a wrongful removal or retention of a child in the sense of Article 3, the judicial or administrative authorities of the Contracting State to which the child has been removed or in which it has been retained shall not decide on the merits of rights of custody until it has been determined that the child is not to be returned under this Convention or unless an application under this Convention is not lodged within a reasonable time following receipt of the notice.

* * *

Article 20 The return of the child under the provisions of Article 12 may be refused if this would not be permitted by the fundamental principles of the requested State relating to the protection of human rights and fundamental freedoms.

* * *

Article 29 This Convention shall not preclude any person, institution or body who claims that there has been a breach of custody or access rights within the meaning of Article 3 or 21 from applying directly to the judicial or administrative authorities of a Contracting State, whether or not under the provisions of this Convention.

* * *

5. Public International Law Conventions

The Convention on the Rights of the Child explicitly incorporates the 'best interests of the child' standard developed in Western custody law. It also requires States to deter the non-return of children abroad. As the Committee makes clear in its guidelines for States, excerpted below, States are expected to explain how their domestic laws comports with this standard.

Convention on the Rights of the Child[2]

> *Article 3* 1. In all actions concerning children, whether undertaken by public or private social welfare institutions, courts of law, administrative authorities or legislative bodies, the best interests of the child shall be a primary consideration.
>
> 2. States Parties undertake to ensure the child such protection and care as is necessary for his or her well-being, taking into account the rights and duties of his or her parents, legal guardians, or other individuals legally responsible for him or her, and, to this end, shall take all appropriate legislative and administrative measures.
>
> 3. States Parties shall ensure that the institutions, services and facilities responsible for the care or protection of children shall conform with the standards established by competent authorities, particularly in the areas of safety, health, in the number and suitability of their staff, as well as competent supervision.
>
> * * *
>
> *Article 11* 1. States Parties shall take measures to combat the illicit transfer and non-return of children abroad.
>
> 2. To this end, States Parties shall promote the conclusion of bilateral or multilateral agreements or accession to existing agreements.

Committee on the Rights of the Child, General guidelines regarding the form and content of initial reports[3]

> *Family environment and alternative care* 16. Under this section, States parties are requested to provide relevant information, including the principal legislative, judicial, administrative or other measures in force, particularly how the principles of the 'best interests of the child' and 'respect for the views of the child' are reflected therein; factors and difficulties encountered and progress achieved in implementing the relevant provisions of the Convention; and implementation priorities and specific goals for the future in respect of:
>
> (a) Parental guidance (art. 5);
> (b) Parental responsibilities (art. 18, paras. 1-2);
> (c) Separation from parents (art. 9);
> (d) Family reunification (art. 10);
> (e) Recovery of maintenance for the child (art. 27, para. 4);
> (f) Children deprived of a family environment (art. 20);
> (g) Adoption (art. 21);
> (h) Illicit transfer and non-return (art. 11).

6. Regional Conventions

The *1980 Council of Europe Convention on Recognition and Enforcement of Decisions Concerning Custody of Children and on Restoration of Custody of Children*, attempted to confine recognition of foreign judgments and enforcement with the automatic termination of custody of children removed in violation of the Convention. In May 2000, *Council Regulation (EC) NO 1347/2000*, excerpted below, entered into force. The basis is that the free movement of people, required under Community instruments, would be facilitated by a Community instrument dealing with the recognition of matrimonial judgments. It has been argued, however, that an international solution would be more appropriate (this has been called 'inverted' or 'reverse' subsidiarity).

Council Regulation (EC) on jurisdiction and the recognition and enforcement of judgments in matrimonial matters and in matters of parental responsibility for children of both spouses[4]

1. The Member States have set themselves the objective of maintaining and developing the Union as an area of freedom, security and justice, in which the free movement of persons is assured. To establish such an area, the Community is to adopt, among others, the measures in the field of judicial cooperation in civil matters needed for the proper functioning of the internal market.
2. The proper functioning of the internal market entails the need to improve and simplify the free movement of judgments in civil matters.
3. This is a subject now falling within the ambit of Article 65 of the Treaty.
                              * * *
7. In order to attain the objective of free movement of judgments in matrimonial matters and in matters of parental responsibility within the Community, it is necessary and appropriate that the cross-border recognition of jurisdiction and judgments in relation to the dissolution of matrimonial ties and to parental responsibility for the children of both spouses be governed by a mandatory, and directly applicable, Community legal instrument.
                              * * *
11. This Regulation covers parental responsibility for children of both spouses on issues that are closely linked to proceedings for divorce, legal separation or marriage annulment.
                              * * *

Article 3 Parental responsibility
1. The Courts of a Member State exercising jurisdiction by virtue of Article 2 on an application for divorce, legal separation or marriage annulment shall have jurisdiction in a matter relating to parental responsibility over a child of both spouses where the child is habitually resident in that Member State.
2. Where the child is not habitually resident in the Member State referred to in paragraph 1, the courts of that State shall have jurisdiction in such a matter if the child is habitually resident in one of the Member States and:
   (a) at least one of the spouses has parental responsibility in relation to the child; and
   (b) the jurisdiction of the courts has been accepted by the spouses and is in the best interests of the child.
3. The jurisdiction conferred by paragraphs 1 and 2 shall cease as soon as:

(a) the judgment allowing or refusing the application for divorce, legal separation or marriage annulment has become final; or

(b) in those cases where proceedings in relation to parental responsibility are still pending on the date referred to in (a), a judgment in these proceedings has become final; or

(c) the proceedings referred to in (a) and (b) have come to an end for another reason.

Article 4 Child abduction The courts with jurisdiction within the meaning of Article 3 shall exercise their jurisdiction in conformity with the Hague Convention of 25 October 1980 on the Civil Aspects of International Child Abduction, and in particular Articles 3 and 16 thereof.

Article 5 Counterclaim The court in which proceedings are pending on the basis of Articles 2 to 4 shall also have jurisdiction to examine a counterclaim, in so far as the latter comes within the scope of this Regulation.

* * *

2. A judgment relating to the parental responsibility of the spouses given on the occasion of matrimonial proceedings as referred to in Article 13 shall not be recognised:

(a) if such recognition is manifestly contrary to the public policy of the Member State in which recognition is sought taking into account the best interests of the child;

(b) if it was given, except in case of urgency, without the child having been given an opportunity to be heard, in violation of fundamental principles of procedure of the Member State in which recognition is sought;

(c) where it was given in default of appearance if the person in default was not served with the document which instituted the proceedings or with an equivalent document in sufficient time and in such a way as to enable that person to arrange for his or her defence unless it is determined that such person has accepted the judgment unequivocally;

(d) on the request of any person claiming that the judgment infringes his or her parental responsibility, if it was given without such person having been given an opportunity to be heard;

(e) if it is irreconcilable with a later judgment relating to parental responsibility given in the Member State in which recognition is sought; or

(f) if it is irreconcilable with a later judgment relating to parental responsibility given in another Member State or in the non-member State of the habitual residence of the child provided that the later judgment fulfils the conditions necessary for its recognition in the Member State in which recognition is sought.

* * *

European Convention on Recognition and Enforcement of Decisions concerning Custody of Children and on Restoration of Custody of Children[5]

The member States of the Council of Europe, signatory hereto,

Recognizing that in the member States of the Council of Europe the welfare of the child is of overriding importance in reaching decisions concerning his custody;

Considering that the making of arrangements to ensure that decisions concerning the custody of a child can be more widely recognized and enforced will provide greater protection of the welfare of children;

Considering it desirable, with this end in view, to emphasize that the right of access of parents is a normal corollary to the right of custody;

Noting the increasing number of cases where children have been improperly removed across an international frontier and the difficulties of securing adequate solutions to the problems caused by such cases;

Desirous of making suitable provision to enable the custody of children which has been arbitrarily interrupted to be restored;

Convinced of the desirability of making arrangements for this purpose answering to different needs and different circumstances;

Desiring to establish legal co-operation between their authorities,

Have agreed as follows:

* * *

Part 1 – Central authorities

Article 2   1. Each Contracting State shall appoint a central authority to carry out the functions provided for by this Convention.

2. Federal States and States with more than one legal system shall be free to appoint more than one central authority and shall determine the extent of their competence.

3. The Secretary General of the Council of Europe shall be notified of any appointment under this Article.

* * *

Part II – Recognition and enforcement of decisions and restoration of custody of children

Article 7 A decision relating to custody given in a Contracting State shall be recognized and, where it is enforceable in the State of origin, made enforceable in every other Contracting State.

Article 8 1. In the case of an improper removal, the central authority of the State addressed shall cause steps to be taken forthwith to restore the custody of the child where:

2. at the time of the institution of the proceedings in the State where the decision was given or at the time of the improper removal, if earlier, the child and his parents had as their sole nationality the nationality of that State and the child had his habitual residence in the territory of that State, and

3. a request for the restoration was made to a central authority within a period of six months from the date of the improper removal.

4. If, in accordance with the law of the State addressed, the requirements of paragraph 1 of this Article cannot be complied with without recourse to a judicial authority, none of the grounds of refusal specified in this Convention shall apply to the judicial proceedings.

5. Where there is an agreement officially confirmed by a competent authority between the person having the custody of the child and another person to allow the other person a right of access, and the child, having been taken abroad, has not been restored at the end of the agreed period to the person having the custody, custody of the child shall be restored in accordance with paragraphs 1.b and 2 of this Article. The same shall apply in the case of a decision of the competent authority granting such a right to a person who has not the custody of the child.

Article 9 1. In cases of improper removal, other than those dealt with in Article 8, in which an application has been made to a central authority within a period of six months from the date of the removal, recognition and enforcement may be refused only if:

a. in the case of a decision given in the absence of the defendant or his legal representative, the defendant was not duly served with the document which instituted the proceedings or an equivalent document in sufficient time to enable him to arrange his defence; but such a failure to effect service cannot constitute a ground for refusing recognition or enforcement where service was not effected because the defendant had concealed his whereabouts from the person who instituted the proceedings in the State of origin;

b. in the case of a decision given in the absence of the defendant or his legal representative, the competence of the authority giving the decision was not founded:

   i. on the habitual residence of the defendant, or

   ii. on the last common habitual residence of the child's parents, at least one parent being still habitually resident there, or

   iii. on the habitual residence of the child;

c. the decision is incompatible with a decision relating to custody which became enforceable in the State addressed before the removal of the child, unless the child has had his habitual residence in the territory of the requesting State for one year before his removal.

2. Where no application has been made to a central authority, the provisions of paragraph 1 of this Article shall apply equally, if recognition and enforcement are requested within six months from the date of the improper removal.

3. In no circumstances may the foreign decision be reviewed as to its substance.

* * *

Article 14   Each Contracting State shall apply a simple and expeditious procedure for recognition and enforcement of decisions relating to the custody of a child. To that end it shall ensure that a request for enforcement may be lodged by simple application.

* * *

Part V – Other instruments

Article 19   This Convention shall not exclude the possibility of relying on any other international instrument in force between the State of origin and the State addressed or on any other law of the State addressed not derived from an international agreement for the purpose of obtaining recognition or enforcement of a decision.

Common Law Countries

Although the Common Law countries are not located in the same geographical region, the following joint statement represents a significant consensus among a group of States.

The Common Law Judicial Conference on International Child Custody[6] *Best practices*
Judges representing the six delegations (Australia, Canada, Ireland, New Zealand, United Kingdom and the United States) attending the Common Law Judicial Conference on International Child Custody hosted by the U.S. Department of State (Washington, D.C., September 17-21, 2000) propose the following 'best practices' to improve operation of the Convention of 25 October 1980 on the Civil Aspects of International Child Abduction ('Hague Child Abduction Convention'). The views expressed are those of the judicial members of the delegations, and do not necessarily reflect the official views of their countries or judiciaries.

1. This Conference supports the conclusions adopted at the analogous Judicial Seminar on the International Protection of Children at the Conference Centre De Ruwenberg, June 3-6 2000, and adopts parallel resolutions, as follows:

    a. Such conferences are important events in emphasizing mutual understanding, respect and trust between the judges from different countries – factors which are essential to the effective operation of international instruments concerned with the protection of children, and in particular, the Hague Child Abduction Convention.

    b. The format adopted, involving intensive discussion among judges, administrators, academics and practitioners from six common law countries (two of which are bi-jural) around a number of selected topics, has been a success and is a model for such conferences in the future. Differences of approach, where they exist, have been revealed and the way has been opened to greater consistency in interpretation and practice under the Hague Child Abduction Convention.

    c. The judges participating in the conference will endeavor to inform their colleagues in their respective jurisdictions about the conference and its outcome, and will in particular make available information about the International Child Abduction Database (http://www.incadat.com) and about the Special Commission on the practical operation of the Hague Child Abduction Convention, which is to be held at the Hague in March 2001.

    d. It is recognized that, in cases involving the international abduction of children, considerable advantages are to be gained from a concentration of jurisdiction in a limited number of courts/tribunals. These advantages include accumulation of experience among the judges and practitioners concerned and the development of greater mutual confidence between legal systems.

    e. The need for more effective methods of international judicial cooperation in the field of child abduction is emphasized, as well as the necessity for direct communication between judges in different jurisdictions in certain cases. The idea of the appointment of liaison judges in the different jurisdictions, to act as channels of communication in international cases, is supported. Further exploration of the administrative and legal aspects of this concept should be carried out. The continued development of an international network of judges in the field of international child abduction to promote personal contacts and the exchange of information is also supported.

2. Prompt decision-making under the Hague Child Abduction Convention serves the best interests of children. It is the responsibility of the judiciary at both the trial and appellate levels firmly to manage the progress of return cases under the Convention. Trial and appellate courts should set and adhere to timetables that ensure the expeditious determination of Hague applications.

3. Central Authorities likewise have a responsibility to process Hague applications expeditiously. Delays in the administrative process can adversely affect judicial return proceedings.

4. It is recommended that State parties ensure that there are simple and effective mechanisms to enforce orders for the return of children.

5. The Article 13b 'grave risk' defense has generally been narrowly construed by courts in member states. It is in keeping with the objectives of the Hague Child Abduction Convention to construe the Article 13b grave risk defense narrowly.

6. Courts in many jurisdictions regard the use of orders with varying names, e.g., stipulations, conditions, undertakings, as a useful tool to facilitate arrangements for return and/or alleviate Article 13b concerns. Such orders, limited in scope and duration, addressing short-term issues and remaining in effect only until such time as a court in

the country to which the child is returned takes control, are in keeping with the spirit of the Hague Child Abduction Convention.

7. Left-behind parents who seek a child's return under the Hague Child Abduction Convention need speedy and effective access to the courts. Lack of legal representation is a significant obstacle to invoking the Convention's remedies. To overcome this obstacle, left-behind parents should be provided promptly with experienced legal representation, where possible at the expense of the requested state.

8. It is widely agreed that the problem of enforcing access rights internationally, though intertwined with international child abduction cases, is not adequately addressed by the Hague Child Abduction Convention. Other legal and judicial solutions should be pursued, including prompt consideration of the 1996 Hague Convention on the Protection of Children (which provides, inter alia, a mechanism for handling international access cases), and court-referred mediation in appropriate cases (to help parents make their own arrangements for international access).

9. Courts take significantly different approaches to relocation cases, which are occurring with a frequency not contemplated in 1980 when the Hague Child Abduction Convention was drafted. Courts should be aware that highly restrictive approaches to relocation can adversely affect the operation of the Hague Child Abduction Convention.

10. Judges need to be alert to the possibility of international child abduction, and can be instrumental in preventing abductions by entering and enforcing orders for appropriate safeguards.

11. Abductions to countries which are not parties to the Hague Child Abduction Convention pose serious obstacles for left-behind parents who seek return of, or access to, their children. Those government bodies responsible for foreign affairs might usefully explore the possibilities of treaty and bilateral approaches to resolve these cases, which approaches have already met with some success.

12. Given the vital role of judges in the operation of the Hague Child Abduction Convention, each country participating in this conference should endeavor to have at least one judge expert in the Convention in its delegation at the Fourth Special Commission meeting at the Hague in March 2001.

13. The support of the activities of the Permanent Bureau of the Hague Conference on Private International Law is critical to its role in coordinating and disseminating information to the international community. This support should extend to special projects and services provided by the Permanent Bureau, including the International Child Abduction Database ('Incadat') developed by the Permanent Bureau, which will be of significant assistance to the judiciary, Central Authorities, legal profession, and the parties. The judges at this Conference recognize the importance of the Permanent Bureau being adequately funded.

7. National Implementation

The U.S. State Department publishes brief summaries of the applicable custody laws in various jurisdictions. While each is accompanied by an explicit disclaimer, these remain useful references, especially for States in which the relevant law is not readily available in English.

U.S. Department of State, International Parental Child Abduction/Egypt[7]

NOTE: The information contained in this flyer is intended as an introduction to the basic elements of children's issues in Egypt. It is not intended as a legal reference. Currently there are no international or bilateral treaties in force between Egypt and the United States dealing with international parental child abduction. The Hague Convention on the Civil Aspects of International Child Abduction cannot be invoked if a child is taken from the United States to Egypt, or vice versa, by one parent against the wishes of the other parent or in violation of a U.S. custody order.

Parental Kidnapping The removal of a child by the non-custodial parent within Egypt, is not a crime in Egypt. However, the custodial parent can approach police authorities for the enforcement of a custody decree, or request that the court imposes a penalty.

Dual Nationality Under Egyptian law, children born to an Egyptian father are considered citizens of Egypt, while children born to an Egyptian mother and a non-Egyptian father may be Egyptian citizens under limited circumstances.

Enforcement of Foreign Court Orders A parent can request that a foreign custody order be recognized in Egypt, but enforcement will result only if the order does not contravene Sharia law and 'paternal rights.' Therefore, as a practical matter, foreign custody orders are not generally automatically recognized in Egypt, and the parent must seek legal representation in Egypt and file for custody in Egypt.

Jurisdiction and Right of Custody Egyptian Civil Courts have 'legal jurisdiction' to hear child custody petitions. However, Egyptian courts base their decisions on 'Islamic Sharia Law' when a custody dispute concerns a Muslim child. Thus, an Egyptian Civil Court considers a Fatwa, i.e., a ruling from an Islamic Institution, but the court in not bound by it.

Presumptive Custody Under Egyptian law, the mother is favored, which means that the mother is considered to be the appropriate custodian of children; this is based on the age and religion of the child. The criteria are as follows: Muslim children: ten years (up to 15) for boys and twelve years (or their marriage) for girls. Non-Muslim children: the age of seven years for boys and nine years for girls. Normally, if disputes arise between the parents, Egyptian courts uphold presumptive custody.

Conditions for 'Presumptive Custody' The Egyptian Courts uphold this custody for the mother if she is a person of the 'Book (Muslim, Christian or Jewish)' and if she is deemed to be a 'fit' mother. If the father is Muslim, the mother must commit herself to raise the child as Muslims in Egypt. It is important to note that 'the right of the father to control his children's travel outside of Egypt is inviolable.' Thus, a U.S. citizen mother can have custody, but be prohibited from taking her children to the U.S. Also, under Egyptian law, if the mother (Muslim or non-Muslim) remarries she will lose her claim to custody. However, this law does not apply to the father who retains custody rights if he re-marries.

Order of Preference for Non-parental Custody When the mother loses presumptive custody due to remarriage, death or inability to counter court findings that she is deemed to be an 'unfit mother,' the courts recognize an established order of preferences of another adult custodian. This order is from first to last based upon the child's religion. For a Muslim child: maternal grandmother or great-grandmother, paternal grandmother or great-grandmother, maternal aunt, paternal aunt, maternal niece, paternal niece, and finally to a male in either the father's or mother's family. For a non-Muslim child: maternal grandmother, paternal grandmother, sister (adult), maternal aunt, paternal aunt, and finally other nieces and aunts.

Right of Visitation In law as well as in practice, visitation depends on the willingness of the custodial parent. If a father has custody and does not voluntarily agree to visitation, the local authorities will not force the issue. The parent will have to seek a court order to enforce visitation.

Father's Permission Children under a certain age (generally, 18 years for boys and 21 years for girls) cannot depart Egypt without the permission of the father. If the child's name indicates an Egyptian father, even if the child is traveling on an U.S. passport, Egyptian Immigration officials require 'explicit' permission from the father before permitting departure. At times, when the name is Egyptian, a mother and child going to the United States for an ordinary visit, Egyptian authorities can require the father to go the airport to give his permission to immigration officials. In contrast, if the child's name is not noticeably Egyptian, and the passport does not indicate otherwise, an American citizen mother and child could depart without airport officials questioning citizenship or requesting the father's approval.

Travel Restrictions (child) Egyptian Immigration Officials allow a father to put a travel 'hold' on his wife and/or children. This requires no court order or legal determination. A simple administrative procedure, which takes ten days to two weeks to institute, authorizes a 'blacklist' entry that expires after six months if not renewed. However, this entry can be extended 'indefinitely' by the father or by anyone acting on a father's power of attorney.

Travel Restrictions (wife) An Egyptian wife requires the permission of her Egyptian husband to obtain a passport and depart the county. Although this law also extends to a non-Egyptian wife, we are not aware of any cases where a U.S. citizen wife with a U.S. passport was prohibited by her Egyptian husband from departing. Immigration authorities have not asked an American woman, married to an Egyptian, to produce permission from her husband.

Visa Stamps Departure Immigration officials will prevent departure of any individual whose passport lacks a valid entry stamp and residency visa. Egyptian procedures to obtain valid entry stamps and residencies must be followed by the bearer when the U.S. Embassy issues a parent or a child a new passport.

Residency Visa Often a parent will declare the first passport stolen or lost; the new passport plus a police report of loss or theft is generally sufficient for issuance of a tourist visa. However, if the immigration authority's records indicate the bearer's 'real' status in Egypt, issuance will halt pending the husband's permission. As with departure, extension of residency requires the father's explicit agreement.

Issuance of Egyptian Passports Under Egyptian Law, no child under 21 years of age can obtain an Egyptian passport without the written permission of the father. Therefore, if ordered by a foreign court, Egyptian Immigration authorities would accept a request from an Egyptian father not to issue a passport to a dual national child.

American citizens who travel to Egypt place themselves under the jurisdiction of Egyptian courts. If an Egyptian parent chooses to remain in Egypt or leave a child behind in Egypt, the U.S. Embassy cannot force either that parent or the Egyptian Government to return the child to the U.S. Additionally, it is not possible to extradite an Egyptian parent to the U.S. for parental child abduction. American citizens planning a trip to Egypt with dual national children should bear this in mind.

South Africa

Sonderup v. Tondelli and another[8] This appeal concerns a child, Sofia, who was brought to South Africa from Canada by her mother and kept here in violation of an order of the Supreme Court of British Columbia and against the wishes of her father.

In the High Court, the Family Advocate brought an urgent application seeking an order for the return of Sofia to British Columbia in terms of Article 12 of the Hague Convention on the Civil Aspects of International Child Abduction (the Convention).

In the High Court, the mother challenged the constitutionality of the Convention. The judge held that there is no conflict between the Convention and section 28(2) of the Constitution since both instruments consider the child's best interests. He determined that the best interests of the child would be to allow the court in the best position to dispose of the case, here the Supreme Court of British Columbia, to do so. He also decided that it was not inconsistent with Sofia's best interests to return her to the jurisdiction of that court and thus ordered her return.

Writing for a unanimous Constitutional Court, Goldstone J first determined that the Hague Convention applies to the facts of the case. He held that the mother's actions fell within the scope of the Convention because she had breached an agreement that had been made an order of court that Sofia would be returned to Canada by a certain date.

Goldstone J then considered the constitutionality of the Convention and held that even if the Convention were assumed to be inconsistent with section 28(2) of the Constitution which requires that the best interest of the child be paramount in every matter concerning the child, the inconsistency would be justified under a limitations analysis in terms of section 36 of the Constitution. The Court decided that the Convention has the important purpose of ensuring appropriate jurisdiction for custody matters, encouraging comity between countries, and discouraging unilateral parental self-help and giving some finality to custodial disputes.

The Court also found that the Convention is carefully tailored to achieve its ends with consideration given to the interests of the child since the Convention gives a requested state discretion to refuse to return a child under the 'grave risk' exception in Article 13. The Court found that courts applying the Convention within the spirit of the Constitution could take steps to protect the interests of the child by expansively interpreting what harms fell within 'grave risk' and by crafting court orders to protect the child.

Finally, the Court evaluated the evidence before it and determined, within the parameters of the Convention, that the return of Sofia posed no grave risk of harm to her. Accordingly, the Court ordered she be returned to British Columbia. The Court made efforts to assure that the mother and child would not be returned to Canada before the authorities there could guarantee the mother would not be arrested for her actions. In addition, the Court satisfied itself that on return, the custody matter would be heard by the Canadian court on an expedited basis and the needs of Sofia and her mother would be properly catered for in the interim.

Several States have launched public education campaigns urging parents to take sensible precautions, such as the entry of a court order prohibiting the issuance of a passport for a child upon the application of the other parent or person claiming responsibility. The objective of these brochures and other sources of information is to prevent abductions, especially to States which are unlikely to cooperate in the child's return.

Canada, Department of Foreign Affairs and International Trade, International Child Abductions: A Manual for Parents[9]

Other Actions In the event that your child has been abducted to a country that is not a party to the Hague Convention, it is possible for you to take other actions both in Canada and abroad that could lead to the return of your child. (Some of these actions may also be relevant if the abduction has been to a Hague Convention country.) In Canada, the civil justice system can be used to reinforce your custody rights and, if appropriate, the criminal justice system can be used to initiate criminal action against the abductor. It may be possible to take similar actions in the other country. As every situation is unique, it is important for you to seek legal and other professional advice and guidance before taking specific action.

Using the Civil Justice System Once you have obtained a custody order from the appropriate Canadian court, the next step is to decide whether you wish to use the justice system in the country to which your child has been abducted.

The Consular Affairs Bureau can provide you with general information on the legal system of that country, customs and practices of that country related to parental rights, and the experience of other people in seeking to use that country's justice system to have an abducted child returned.

Consular officers in Ottawa and overseas can provide advice and guidance on the laws of a foreign country or on what might be the most appropriate action to take. However, for authoritative information, you will need to retain a lawyer in that country who is knowledgeable and experienced in dealing with custody cases involving foreigners. Canadian officials in Ottawa and at Canadian government offices abroad can provide you with a list of lawyers who speak English or French, who may be experienced in parental child abduction or family law and who may have represented Canadians in circumstances similar to yours. However, as this lawyer will be working for you, it is most important that you, and only you, make the selection. If you decide to undertake legal action in the other country, it may be necessary for you to be there in person at some stage of the proceedings. Lawyers' fees vary widely from country to country and could be in excess of what would be paid in Canada. Therefore, you should be very direct when making arrangements for legal representation in another country: ensure that the arrangements are in writing and that you fully understand what the lawyer will and will not do, when it will be done and at what cost. If necessary, Canadian consular officials can assist with translation and provide guidance. They can also maintain contact with your lawyer to obtain status reports and to verify that your rights, as provided for by the laws of that country, are respected.

Your lawyer will advise you on the information and documentation that will be required in order to represent you within that country's justice system. In addition to providing a certified copy of your custody order, it may be necessary to supply copies of your marriage and / or separation or divorce documents, along with copies of the relevant provincial / territorial and federal laws relating to custody and child abductions. The Department of Foreign Affairs and International Trade in Ottawa can authenticate these documents before they are sent. For information, contact the Authentication and Service of Documents Section, tel.: (613) 995-0119; fax: (613) 944-7078; e-mail: jlac@dfait-maeci.gc.ca. Your Canadian lawyer can assist you in gathering this material and having it delivered to your lawyer in the foreign country.

A custody order issued by a Canadian court has no automatic binding legal force beyond the borders of Canada. Nevertheless, there may be procedures and laws in place in the foreign country to have that order recognized and enforced there. In addition, such an order could be persuasive in support of any legal action that you undertake. Courts in other countries, like those in Canada, must decide child custody cases on the basis of their own domestic laws. This may give an advantage to the person who has abducted your child, if the abduction is to the country of his or her nationality or origin. You could also be disadvantaged if the country has a legal tradition in deciding custody cases on the basis of gender. If custody is given to the abducting parent in another country, you should make every effort to have the court specify your access rights. Some countries, even if they award custody to you or provide for access for you, will not permit the child to leave without the consent of the other parent.

Your chances of having your Canadian custody order recognized and enforced in another country are subject to all these factors and conditions. While it may appear that the deck is stacked against you, it is important to accept that recourse to the courts of another country may be the only hope for the safe return of your child. Each country is unique, and it is up to you to decide whether to proceed with legal action.

Using the Criminal Justice System Parental abduction is a criminal offence under sections 281, 282 and 283 of the Canadian Criminal Code. In many situations, the criminal justice system can prove to be a very useful instrument in locating and recovering a child, especially when the person suspected of perpetrating the abduction has not yet left Canadian soil.

Since the administration of criminal justice is a provincial / territorial responsibility, criminal justice may be administered in a slightly different way from one province / territory to another. Thus, in the abduction of children, some provinces / territories require authorization from the Crown Attorney before proceedings can be set in motion, while in others proceedings can be initiated by the police themselves.

Use of the Criminal Code makes it easier for the police to search for and locate a child. An arrest warrant is generally issued, often improving co-operation among police forces both nationally and internationally. If necessary, an extradition request may be made if there is an extradition treaty with the country in which the alleged abductor is located.

Extradition Extradition may be worth considering in some cases of international abduction, but may be of no value in others. There is no guarantee that the child will be returned by foreign authorities even if they should permit the extradition of the alleged abductor. When threatened with extradition, some abducting parents have hidden the child or have gone into hiding themselves with the child.

In addition, not all countries regard child abduction by one of the parents as a criminal act. The Consular Affairs Bureau can provide information on the criminal justice system, in the country in question, and on whether it is likely to co-operate in parental child abduction cases.

Other reasons why extradition is not frequently used in connection with parental child abductions include:

Very few extradition treaties between Canada and other countries include parental child abduction or custodial interference as extraditable offences. In recent treaties, efforts have been made to include the concept of 'dual criminality' as the basis for extradition. However, this requires that parental child abduction be considered a crime in both the countries that have signed the treaty.

Many civil law countries (in contrast with common law countries such as Canada, Australia, the United States and the United Kingdom) will not extradite their own nationals. Nearly all the countries of Latin America and Europe are civil law countries. Experience has shown that foreign governments are often unwilling to extradite anyone for parental child abduction.

While it is important to report the abduction of your child to the police as soon as possible, your complaint will not necessarily result in child abduction charges. Whether at the level of the police, the Crown Attorney's office or the federal Department of Justice, which is responsible for extradition questions, such decisions are made in accordance with the particular circumstances of each situation and the possible repercussions on the return of the child. Protection of the child is the primary objective.

The United Kingdom Passport Service, Prevention of Child Abduction[10]

General The Child Abduction Act 1984 makes it a criminal offence for anyone connected with a child under the age of sixteen to take or send that child out of the United Kingdom without appropriate consent.

Persons connected with a child are parents, guardians and persons with a residence order or who have parental responsibility.

The appropriate consent is the consent of the mother, the father (if he has parental responsibility), guardian and anyone with a residence order or parental responsibility, or the leave of the court.

In general, a child's father only has automatic parental responsibility if he is or has been married to the child's mother. A person with a residence order may take or send the child out of the United Kingdom without the appropriate consent for up to a month at a time.

UKPS Scheme Normally the Passport Service will issue a passport for a child at the request of either parent or person with parental responsibility.

You can ask the Passport Service not to issue a passport for the child, should the Agency receive an application from another person claiming to have responsibility, if you have a UK court order as follows:

(i) a prohibited steps order made under the Children Act 1989 or the Children (Northern Ireland) Order 1995;

(ii) an interdict made under the Children (Scotland) Act 1995;

(iii) an order confirming that the child's removal from the jurisdiction is contrary to the wishes of the court;

(iv) a residence order made under (i) to (iii) above, and the objector is the person in whose favour the order has been made;

(v) an order awarding the objector custody of the child or care and control over the child;

(vi) an order specifying that the objector's consent to the removal of the child from the jurisdiction is necessary;

(vii) an order upholding the objector's objections to the child having a passport or leaving the country.

(viii) The mother of a child will not need a court order if she has not been married to the child's father.

8. IOs and NGOs

IOs

Hague Conference on Private International Law – The International Child Abduction Database (INCADAT)[11] Several thousand children are the victims of international parental child abduction each year. The *Hague Convention of 25 October 1980 on the Civil Aspects of International Child Abduction* is a multilateral treaty which seeks to protect children from the harmful effects of parental abduction and retention across international boundaries by providing a procedure to bring about their prompt return.

The International Child Abduction Database (INCADAT) has been established by the Permanent Bureau of the Hague Conference on Private International Law with the object of making accessible many of the leading decisions rendered by national courts in respect of the [Hague Convention] of 25 October 1980 on the Civil Aspects of International Child Abduction.

INCADAT is used by judges, Central Authorities, legal practitioners, researchers and others interested in this rapidly developing branch of law. INCADAT has already contributed to the promotion of mutual understanding and good practice among the 73 States Parties, essential elements in the effective operation of the 1980 Convention.

To achieve maximum accessibility, INCADAT is available free of charge. A password however is needed to access the information. Donations, while not obligatory, are indeed appreciated.

NGOs

Reunite[12]   We are the leading UK charity specialising in international parental child abduction. Reunite was formed in 1986 and registered as a charity in 1990. We provide advice, information and support to parents, family members and guardians who have had a child abducted or who fear child abduction. We also provide advice to parents who may have abducted their child as well as advising on international custody disputes.

We are part-funded by the Department of Constitutional Affairs, the Foreign & Commonwealth Office and the Home Office. We also receive funding for specific projects from charities and trusts as well as raising independent funds.

Our philosophy is one that firmly believes any child abduction, whether or not a criminal offence, is wrong. However, acting strictly within the law, Reunite will do all it can to assist parents who may have abducted their child. Emphasis is placed on helping parents to come out of hiding and to regulate the child's position within the law. This often entails assisting the abducting parent, guardian or family member to come to terms with the fact that the child must be returned. Then, focusing all the time on the best interests of the child, help return take place with minimum disturbance and trauma.

The Committee for Missing Children, Inc./Missing Children Europe[13]   The Committee for Missing Children, USA is one of the largest distributors of missing and abducted children's photos, and is a leader in the area of family abductions and parent advocacy. The CMC, Along with its photo partners has distributed several billion images of missing and abducted children worldwide. In 1998 the CMC opened a branch in Germany to assist parents who have had their children abducted across international borders.

The primary mission of the European branch will be to council victim parents. We want to help parents of missing and abducted children receive the help they deserve and direct their requests, applications and questions to the appropriate agencies. The CMC Europe maintains contact with other groups and organizations throughout Europe and the United States that have the same or similar objectives. We are collaborating with groups, organizations, and agencies associated with missing and abducted children.

The European branch is working with committed lawyers who have had experience dealing with child abduction and have litigated under the Hague Convention on the Civil Aspects of International Child Abduction. The CMC Europe is working to gather information, legal papers, court papers, judgments and statistics that will help a parent understand what they will face when forced to apply for the return of their children from a foreign country.

The CMC Europe will work closely with law enforcement in order to assist in the recovery and return of missing or abducted children.

Advice to Parents by the Association for Abducted Children[14] An association for abducted children (Kaapatut Lapsetry) has been formed in order to support and advise parents of abducted children. According to the experiences of the association parents should pay particular attention to the following:

- Find out about the culture and religion as well as about family law and the concept of the family in the country of your spouse.
- For instance the right of the father to decide on matters concerning the children may be regarded as natural in some countries. In other countries, a child is thought to belong to its mother, and she is thought to be the natural custodian of the child.
- The memorandum on the management of international child abduction prepared by the Ministry for Foreign Affairs and the Ministry of Justice on 31 August 1998 may be of use.

Try to Identify Risk Situations
The talk and behaviour of your spouse may indicate that everything is not in order. Such indications may come up in quarrels, discussions about upbringing and in disputes about child custody and rights of access. The other parent may voice a wish to return with the child to his or her native country or threaten with abduction. Perhaps this parent no longer works. A close relative to your spouse has moved in with you or to the home of the child, and supports a move to the native country. Friends of your spouse may assist in organizing the abduction. Your spouse sells personal property in your common apartment or in his or her own apartment. These signs have to be taken seriously.

The risk of abduction may increase in connection with custody disputes. A divorce between you and your spouse or a new relationship formed by you may also heighten the risk. Your former spouse may feel hurt and fear replacement by your new partner. Both the mother and the father may abduct the child, and the abductor may be Finnish just as well as a foreigner.

Find out about the Services of the Association for Abducted Children
The association for abducted children may provide you with contact information about parents whose children have been abducted to the same country as your child or to a neighbouring country.

Find out What the Authorities Can Do
Passports and Visas Inform the diplomatic Mission of your spouse's native country that you have not agreed to apply for a visa or passport for your child. More information about dual citizenship and about issuing a passport is available at the diplomatic Mission of your spouse's native country.

The police may be contacted as regards issuing and revoking the child's Finnish passport.

Precautionary Measures Find out about the possibilities of precautionary measures, for instance an emergency care order.

Supervised Meetings Advice and instructions are available at the child welfare authorities of the municipality of residence and at shelters.

Informing the Day-care Centre and School Inform the day-care centre and school that the child may not be given to the other parent or to some other person without your permission.

Informing the Police and Child Welfare Authorities Inform the police and child welfare authorities of the threat of abduction.

Try to Reach an Amicable Solution Your child has the right to both its parents. Therefore it makes sense to try to settle your differences and reach an amicable solution about child custody and rights of access. A settlement is probably the best preventive measure. Willingness to co-operate and amicability are also in the best interests of the child. In addition, they establish you as a responsible and good custodian of the child in possible future trials.

Retain a Good Lawyer If an amicable solution is impossible, consult a lawyer. You will need a counsellor in your legal proceedings and if you apply for e.g. precautionary measures, supervised meetings or a restraining order.

9. Possible Approaches to the Problems

Maria

As a judicial clerk for the same Court, you will have noted that the facts of Maria's case are very similar to the facts in the *Sonderup* case, set out in Section 7. There, like here, a child was brought to South Africa from Canada by her mother and kept in violation of an order of the Canadian court, against the wishes of the father. The major difference is that in Maria's case the Canadian order expressly provides for a transfer of custody following the child's wrongful removal. In *Sonderup*, in contrast, the return of the child was predicated, in part, by assurances that the custody determination would be made by the Canadian court, presumably based on the best interests of the child. While the Court is not bound by its holding in *Sonderup*, which is distinguishable on its facts, it may well reach a similar result in view of the Court's recognition of the importance of both the Abduction Convention and the constitutional stature of the best interests of the child under South African law. That is, it should probably order Maria's return, especially if counsel for Arturo will stipulate to a 'best interests' determination by the Canadian Court.

Anwar

As set out in Section 1, in most Western States, including the U.S., custody is determined under the best interests of the child standard. Since Anwar has always lived in the U.S., and presumably his friends, school, doctors, and home are there, it is unlikely that a U.S. Court would make a custody determination which would result in the child's relocation to Egypt. It is especially unlikely given the warnings of the U.S. Department of State regarding the difficulty, if not the impossibility, of securing the return of a child from Islamic States. Thus, since Nora faces little risk of an adverse decision, she is not likely to accede to Mahmout's request for a transfer of custody in two years.

At the same time, she may not want to leave Mahmout without any legal options for maintaining a relationship with his son, which might lead to desperation and illegal options. In addition she might consider it important for her son to have an ongoing relationship with his father and his father's culture. Mahmout may be able to obtain joint legal custody, with liberal visitation within the U.S., if he reassures Nora that he will not try to take the child to Egypt, and, as a token of his good faith, allows her to keep the child's passport. As explained in Section 7, Nora would have extremely limited rights if Mahmout takes Anwar to Egypt.

For Further Research

1. For an analysis of applications under the Hague Convention, see Lowe, N. et al. (2001), 'A Statistical Analysis of Applications made in 1999 Under the Hague Convention,' Preliminary Doc. No. 3 of March 2001 (available http://wwwhcch.net/e/conventions/reports28e.html) (last visited March 1, 2003).

2. For discussions of joint custody in national jurisdiction, see Frank, R. (2001), 'Civil Law Marriages Without Legal Consequences,' Bainham, A. (ed.), *The International Survey of Family Law: 2001 Edition*, pp. 111, 114 (Germany), and Saldeed, A., 'Joint Custody, Special Representation for Children and Cohabitees' Property,' ibid. at pp. 405-410.

3. June Carbone argues that custody disputes have become 'ground zero in the gender wars because they are among the few remaining family law disputes where courts judge adult behavior.' Carbone, J. (2000), *From Partners to Parents: The Second Revolution in Family Law*. For a comprehensive history of custody law in the United States, see Mason, M.A. (1994), *From Father's Property to Children's Rights: The History of Child Custody in the United States*. On the tender years doctrine in the U.S., under which maternal custody of children under 10 is presumed to be in the child's best interest, see *Pusey v. Pusey*, 72 P.2d 177 (Utah 1986) (tender years presumptions is based on outdated stereotypes); *Ex parte Devine*, 398 So. 2d 686 (Ala. 1981) (holding the doctrine unconstitutional); *Bazemore v. Davis*, 394 A.2d 1377 (D.C. 1977) (doctrine violates best interest standard).

4. For an excellent overview of the regional conventions contemplated in the European Community, see McEleavy, P. (2002), 'The Brussels II Regulation: How the European Union has moved into Family Law,' *International and Comparative Law Quarterly*, Vol. 51, October 2002, pp. 883-908.

5. Two American law professors, Linda Silberman and Merle Weiner, have written extensively on the Hague Conventions. For examples of their insightful and scholarly critiques, see, e.g., Silberman, L. (2003), 'Patching Up the Abduction Convention: A Call for a New International Protocol and a Suggestion for Amendments to ICARA,' *Texas International Law Journal*, Vol. 38, pp. 41-62; Weiner, M. (2001), 'International Child Abduction and the Escape from Domestic Violence,' *Fordham Law Review*, Vol. 69, p. 593.

Notes

1   [http://travel.state.gov/islamic_family_law.html (last visited 12/9/2003). Disclaimer: The information in this circular relating to the legal requirements of specific foreign countries is provided for general information only. Questions involving interpretation of specific foreign laws should be addressed to foreign counsel.

2   G.A. res. 44/25, annex, 44 U.N. GAOR Supp. (No. 49) at 167, U.N. Doc. A/44/49 (1989), *entered into force* Sept. 2, 1990.

3   CRC/C/5 30 October 1991.

4   http://www.kkinder-nach-hause.de/english/infos/eeeurop.htm.

5   http://conventions.coe.int/Treaty/EN/Treaties/Html/105.htm.

6   http://travel.state.gov/best_practices.html.

7   Disclaimer: the information in this circular relating to the legal requirements of specific foreign countries is provided for general information only. Questions involving interpretation of specific foreign laws should be addressed to foreign counsel. http://travel.state.gov/abduction_egypt.html (last visited 12/9/03).

8   Constitutional Court – CCT53/00 4 December 2000 http://www.concourt.gov.za/cases/2000/sonderupsum.shtml.

9   http://www.voyage.gc.ca/main/pubs/child_abduction-en.asp (last visited 12/9/03).

10   http://www.ukpa.gov.uk/_1_applications/1_abduction.asp (last visited 12/9/03).

11   http://212.206.44.26/index.cfm?fuseaction=stdtext.showtext_&lng=1(last visited July 22, 2003).

12   http://www.reunite.org/page.php?alias=newabout00.

13   http://www.kinder-nach-hause.de/english/mission.html (last visited 7/22/03).

14   http://www.om.fi/18263.htm (last visited 7/22/03).

Chapter 10

Child Support

1. The Problem

Astrid, who is Swedish, and Fumio, who is Japanese, lived together in Sweden for eight years, during which they had a daughter, Yuri, who is now six. Astrid and Fumio decided to part amicably two years ago. Yuri lives with Astrid and Fumio visits at least weekly. Yuri often sleeps at his flat, where she has a small loft. Fumio is a fabric designer and Astrid illustrates children's books. Fumio earns a very good living; Astrid's income is more sporadic.

Fumio has recently decided to return to Japan. He has been trying to persuade Astrid and Yuri to relocate also. Although he does not want custody of Yuri, he would like her to get to know her Japanese grandparents and aunts. He tells Astrid that he is certain that she will find lucrative work in Japan. Even if she does not, he promises that he will provide enough child support to keep her and Yuri as comfortable as they are in Sweden.

Astrid is seriously considering the move, which she thinks will be good for her career and for her daughter. She is concerned, however, about losing the considerable benefits she and Yuri enjoy in Sweden. She does not think that Fumio would deliberately mislead her, but she is reluctant to depend solely on his good will.

Astrid comes to see you for legal advice. How will relocation from Sweden to Japan change her situation with regard to child support? If she does decide to move, how can she protect herself and her daughter?

2. Overview

In general, parents have a duty to support their minor children whether or not the parents are married, and whether or not they have custody of the children. State laws differ, however, with respect to the amount of support to be paid, the process through which this amount is determined, the duration of support, the mechanisms for its enforcement and collection, and the responsibility of the State, or society at large, to make up the difference when the noncustodial parent is either unable to provide adequate support or cannot be compelled to do so.

In some States, such as Japan, child support is agreed to by the parties. If they are unable to do so by themselves, they must go to mediation, where a trained third party will help them resolve the matter. Other States leave the amount of child support to the discretion of a tribunal. Factors considered typically include: the financial resources of the child, the financial resources of the noncustodial and custodial parents, respectively, and the standard of living the child would have enjoyed had the parents remained married. The lack of specific guidelines often produces unpredictable and widely ranging results, which in turn make it difficult to negotiate support. The custodial parent usually incurs a disproportionate share of responsibility because she must actually meet the child's expenses on a day-to-day basis.

In general, the child is not entitled to what she would have had, had the parties remained married because that would impose disproportionate costs on the noncustodial parent. This becomes particularly sensitive when the non-custodial parents' support benefits the custodial parent as well as the child, as in the case of a housing subsidy. Although it is virtually impossible to insulate the child from the consequences of divorce or separation without also insulating the custodial parent at the other parent's expense, support that does not directly benefit the custodial parent, such as payment of school fees, may be more palatable. In addition, the child is entitled to a decent standard of living. The custodial parent is interested in being treated fairly regarding child-based expenditures and in being compensated for lost labor force opportunity.

In response to these problems, most western industrialized States have enacted guidelines. Establishing guidelines requires balancing the interests of the State, the child, and the parents. The State is interested in minimizing State expenditures and making sure that the next generation of citizens is adequately nurtured and educated. Some States, emphasizing the latter, provide relatively generous benefits to sole parents as well as State health and childcare programs which benefit all children, regardless of their parents' circumstances. In others, responsibility for the child's well- being is left almost entirely to the parents.

In the United States, for example, in 1984 Congress passed the Child Support Enforcement Amendment, which required all States to create guidelines in order to receive federal welfare funding. While all decision makers were required to have access to these guidelines, they were not mandatory. In 1987, the Family Support Act required the States to implement mandatory guidelines. These could be established legislatively, administratively, or judicially. They were to act as rebuttable presumptions in all support proceedings.

Other industrialized States have enacted laws requiring 'advanced maintenance' or 'child support assurance.' This is a public guarantee of a specific level of payment made by a government agency, which then attempts to collect it from the parent.

The amount of child support and its duration varies widely among States. There is no official mechanism for keeping track of these amounts, but a recent survey conducted under the auspices of the Hague Conference on Private International Law has compiled substantial information in connection with the proposed draft of a global convention. (See Section 2 below.)

Mechanisms for determining the amount of child support, similarly, vary considerably. They include: a percentage of the obligor's income, which sets a flat or varying percentage based solely on the noncustodial income. This model assumes that the noncustodial parent will contribute what she can. Another model is based on the parents' combined income. This assumes that support should represent the same proportion of parental income a child would receive if the parents lived together. A third model begins by assuring the ability of the noncustodial to meet his own subsistence needs. Thus, only when his income exceeds a certain minimal amount is any obligation imposed.

The needs of children change as they get older. Other factors may also require a change in child support. An unanticipated increase in health care needs, for example, may justify a modification. The substantive rules governing modification, as well as the procedural rules governing the jurisdiction in which such applications may be brought, also vary. This has resulted in conflicting judgments of different State courts, and the refusal of States to recognize the judgments or the jurisdiction of other States. This results in confusion, inconsistency, animosity, and often an inability to collect support due.

Where States are parties to a bilateral agreement regarding child support or parties to a multilateral agreement under which they recognize each other's judgments, a judgment of child support is entitled to enforcement like any other judgment. Like other judgments, however, it may be subject to challenge in the foreign court on grounds of that court's public policy. Examples of such challenges are set out in Section 8, below (see excerpt by Michel Pelichet, Deputy Secretary General). Failure to comply with the support judgment subjects the obligor to civil or criminal sanctions. In some States, these may include income withholding, income tax interception or licence revocation. Licences which may be revoked may include professional, trade, business, hunting, fishing, and driving licences.

3. Cultural Variations

In 2003, the Nineteenth Diplomatic Session of the Hague Conference on Private International Law decided that a global Convention on the Recovery of Maintenance should be a priority for the Twentieth Session. In preparation, a comprehensive questionnaire was distributed to the Member States of the Conference as well as other interested States as to their current laws and policies regarding such obligations. Excerpts from their responses are included below.[1] These suggest the range of approaches to child support. The second excerpt, more specifically, summarizes the mechanisms adopted by various States for determining the actual amount of the award.

Japan Preliminary Document No 2 (Responses to the 2002 Questionnaire)

The Answer By The Japanese Government A spouse who has the custody of an 'immature' child (see infra, 3) is entitled to receive child support from the other spouse as the share of the expenses of marriage life (Article 760 of the Civil Code), and a parent not married is entitled to receive it from the other parent as the expenses of the care and custody of children (Articles 766, 749, 771 and 788 of the Civil Code).

A child may obtain support from his / her parents when he / she is in need (Article 877 of the Civil Code), and we have no clear definition of a 'dependent child.' It is considered, however, that parents are under heavier duty of support to an 'immature' child (i.e. a child who cannot maintain his / her economic life without the care and custody of parents) than to a 'mature' child.

* * *

Child support is ultimately determined through judicial process.

Child support can be paid either a) by a parent to the child as the performance of maintenance obligation, or b) by a parent to the other as the payment of expenses for the care and custody of their child. Whatever the legal ground is, the amount can be determined by the agreement between the parties concerned. If no agreement is reached or possible, the Family Court shall determine the matter by the procedure provided by the Law for Determination of Family Affairs (Articles 766, 749, 771, 788 and 879 of the Civil Code and Paragraph 1, Article 9 of the Law for Determination of Family Affairs). The District Court may determine child support in the latter sense (i.e. the payment of expenses for the care and custody of the child) in conjunction with the declaration of divorce or annulment of marriage (Article 15 of the Law of Procedure in Actions Relating to Personal Status).

The question of international jurisdiction will be decided on the basis of case law where one of the parties lives abroad. Apart from that, the same process will apply regardless of the parties' residence.

* * *

We don't have any formula, guidelines, or other criteria in making the assessment of child support. The child support award may be determined at the discretion of the Family Court mainly based on the best interest of the child and the following considerations:
a. gross and net income of the parents
b. income taxes, health insurance payments etc. of the parents
c. business expenses of the parents
d. age of the child
e. educational expenses for the child
f. any other factors the court may deem relevant

* * *

There have been some reported court cases in which a Family Court of Japan rendered a decision which in effect altered the preceding foreign judgement by applying the applicable law designated by *Horei* (Law Concerning the Applicable Law in General) in a situation where there had been substantial change of circumstances after the foreign judgement and the court found that it had international jurisdiction over the case. However, there is no established precedent with respect to the modification of foreign maintenance decisions as such.

Sweden

In Sweden, child support guidelines are promulgated by the Department of Social Welfare. The starting point is the standard monthly amount established for dependant adults. The amount of maintenance for children is pro-rated, depending upon their age as follows: 0-6 years, 65%; 7-12 years, 80%; 13 years until majority, 95%. Parents are expected to support the child according to their respective incomes. If the parents stipulate an amount of child support, the courts will generally affirm it. Sweden has a child support assurance program; that is, there is a public guarantee of the basic payment which will be made to a lone mother if the father does not contribute. The Swedish government attempts to collect from the father, as set out more specifically in Sweden's response to the question below.

Sweden a) Maintenance payments shall be determined by a judgment or by agreement. Payments shall be made in advance for each calendar month. However, the court may decide on another mode of payment if there are special reasons for doing so. An agreement under which future maintenance is to be paid by means of a lump sum or for periods exceeding three months is valid only if it is in writing and is witnessed by two persons. If the child is under eighteen years of age, the agreement must also be approved by the Social Welfare Committee. Maintenance in the form of a lump sum shall be paid to the Social Welfare Committee if the child is under eighteen years of age. The sum paid to the committee shall be used to purchase from an insurance company an annuity for the child appropriate to the obligation to maintain the child, unless the agreement prevents this or the Committee finds that the sum can be used in some other appropriate manner for the maintenance of the child. An application for maintenance payments to be determined may not be granted for a retroactive period of more than three years prior to the date of which proceedings were commenced, unless the person liable to pay maintenance agrees. b) If the spouses cannot agree on the issue of maintenance, a court can determine the dispute. After a divorce, the maintenance allowance shall be periodic. However, payment of a lump sum can be ordered if there are special reasons, e.g. that the spouse needs to make a pension contribution. An application for maintenance payments to be determined may not be granted for a retroactive period of more than three years prior to the date of which proceedings were commenced, unless the person liable to pay maintenance agrees.

* * *

Children, spouses and divorced spouses are eligible to benefit from maintenance decisions.

What is your definition of a dependent child for support purposes? a) A child under eighteen years of age; b) A child over eighteen, but under twenty-one years of age, if the child's basic education is not concluded.

Which is the law applicable to the question of eligibility of (a) a child and (b) a spouse or other family member to obtain maintenance? The law of the State where the dependent has his or her habitual residence is applicable if the parties do not agree otherwise.

Procedures for the initial assessment of maintenance

Is child support determined through an administrative or a judicial process?

Maintenance support for a child with parents who are separated is paid to the custodial parent by the local Social Insurance Office at a rate of SEK 1173/month. The parent liable for maintenance must repay the State, related to income and total number of children. If the allowance instead is paid directly to the custodial parent, the Social Insurance Office pays an equally reduced support. The obligation to repay is initially determined through an administrative process. There is no reason for a child or a parent to ask a court for a maintenance order unless the liable parent should pay more than SEK 1173/month and neglects this obligation.

Is the process different where either the applicant or the respondent live abroad? If so, please give details.

Children living abroad are not entitled to maintenance support from the Social Insurance Office. In those cases the maintenance allowances are decided through an agreement or a judicial process.

If the liable parent lives abroad, the Social Insurance Office can order the custodial parent to take steps to get the maintenance obligation determined through a judicial process. The Social Insurance Office takes over the child's right to maintenance allowance up to the sum paid out by the office as maintenance support.

* * *

Methods of calculating maintenance

Is the assessment of child support based on a formula, guidelines, or other criteria? Please outline the principal elements involved in making an assessment.

It is based on legal criteria. A parent is entitled to retain from his or her incomes net of tax an amount for his or her own maintenance. Housing expenses are generally calculated. In addition to this, there are other living expenses, which are computed with the guidance of an index-linked standard amount. He or she can also reserve an amount for maintenance of a spouse at home if there are special reasons. Finally the liable parent can make a reservation for an amount for the support of children at home. How much of the excess that should be claimed for maintenance allowance depends, among other things, on the needs of the child and the other parent's capacity to bear the maintenance expenses. To some extent deductions can be made for expenses for contact.

Are there any differences in the assessment criteria employed when (a) the applicant or (b) the respondent live abroad?

No (if the same law still is applicable).

* * *

Responses of the Czech Republic to the Questionnaire

Form of maintenance decision Maintenance decisions concerning obligations toward child, spouse or parent are issued by Czech courts as judgments. In the judgment, the court specifies regular alimony payments and/or in what manner the due alimony debt is to be paid (by one-time amount paid or in several installments at due dates stipulated by the court). Parents may agree on the alimony for a minor child. The parents' written agreement is examined by the court in respect to its being in compliance with minor child's interest and needs and shall be approved by the same; the court approval is released as a judgment. The court judgment regarding the maintenance obligation satisfaction by means of a one-time amount settlement or property transfer is not governed by Czech Laws. Only spouses being parties of divorce proceedings may, pursuant to Family Act #94/1963 Coll. Sec. 94 para 2 in its current version, enter into a written agreement concerning a one-time maintenance settlement in an agreed amount once for ever.

Eligibility Pursuant to Family Act #94/1963 Coll. in its current version are eligible for maintenance in the Czech Republic children, spouses and parents. A maintenance allocation is due, under Sec. 95 of said Act, to unmarried mother of the child, for a period of 2 years. Under Sec. 85 para 1 of the Act, children are entitled to maintenance as long as they are incapable of earning their own living (e.g. until they complete a study preparing for performing certain occupation).

Procedures for the initial assessment of maintenance As stated hereabove, maintenance is established in court proceedings. The procedure in a Czech court in such proceedings is not affected by circumstances that the applicant or the respondent live abroad or that the application for maintenance judgment pertains to a spouse or a parent, to the difference to a child. Proceedings for maintenance of a child or a person specified here may not be combined.

Methods of calculating maintenance The calculation of maintenance for a child/spouse/parent is not being made on the basis of a formula, directions or firmly defined criteria. The Family Act #94/1963 Coll. in its current version sets forth that, in determining the alimony amount, the court shall take into consideration the justified needs of the beneficiary (i.e. the person entitled to maintenance) and the liable persons (i.e. person liable to provide for maintenance) abilities, capacity and property as well. This method shall be used for determining the maintenance also in cases when the beneficiary or the liable person is living abroad.

Reassessment (adjustment) modification of maintenance decisions or assessments If the material standing of the beneficiary or the liable person, being the basis for determining the maintenance for a minor child, change, the court may, even without a motion modify the original court judgment or parents' agreement on the maintenance. However, if the child is of lawful age already, a motion for change or revocation of a judgment on the maintenance must be filed. Maintenance is not automatically valorized in the Czech Republic.

Maintenance may be modified up or down due to reasons quoted hereabove (change of material standing on beneficiary's or liable person's part) only. A decision concerning maintenance or maintenance amount made by a foreign authority may be changed following a motion filed by liable person abroad (in the country where the liable person has his/her residence), however, the beneficiary must not be deprived of his/her rights as a part to the proceedings in such proceedings (any and all documents must be duly delivered to him/her or his/her legal counsel, he/she must have the opportunity to take position in the proceedings etc.), a decision of a foreign court must not collide with the public order of the Czech Republic. The enforcement of a foreign decision concerning maintenance is possible in the Czech Republic based on reciprocity, usually warranted by a bilateral or multilateral international treaty.

William Duncan, First Secretary, Note on the desirability of revising the Hague Conventions on Maintenance Obligations[2]

Generally speaking, child support formulae, whether judicially or legislatively established, involve a balance between the child's needs and the liable parent's ability to pay, but precise formulae differ from country to country and between states within certain federal systems. The following are examples.

In the United Kingdom, the *Child Support Act 1991* introduced a complicated formula, contained in algebraic form in the schedule to the Act, under which the liable parent could be required to pay at the rate of 50% of disposable income after tax and various allowances.

Under the new German law on child maintenance (*Kindesunterhaltsgesetz*), which came into force on 1 July 1998 (BGBl [*Bundesgesetzblatt*/Official Gazette] 1998 I 666), maintenance may be requested either in the form of a *fixed amount* (*Individualunterhalt*), or a *percentage of the relevant standard amount* (*Regelbetrag*). A fixed amount is usually claimed on the basis of one of the various tables established by the courts in the past (the best known being the *Düsseldorfer Tabelle*) and which continue to be used. The standard amounts are determined in a statutory instrument (*Regelbetrag-Verordnung*) which is annexed to the new law so as to enable amendment by the executive (presumably on a two-yearly basis). The statutory instrument distinguishes three different age categories of the maintenance creditor; it also establishes specific amounts applicable to the Eastern part of

Germany (the former GDR). The standard amounts serve essentially as an assessment basis for the issuing of a so-called dynamic maintenance title (*Unterhaltstitel in dynamisierter Form*). *Example*: Let us assume the maintenance debtor has a net income of 4500 DM and the child is 15 years old; according to the *Düsseldorfer Tabelle*, the fixed amount of maintenance would be 713 DM, which equals to 142% of the relevant standard amount determined by the statutory instrument (*i.e.* 502 DM); since this is below the limit of 150% fixed by the law, the maintenance debtor is entitled to a dynamic maintenance title. The particular benefit of a dynamic maintenance title lies in the fact that the amount to be paid by the maintenance debtor is *automatically adjusted* if the standard amounts are changed or if the maintenance creditor moves into the next age category. Furthermore, a dynamic maintenance title is *immediately enforceable*. The standard amounts also serve as a decisive marker for the possibility of a simplified maintenance procedure (see footnote 13).

In the United States, in order to be eligible for Federal funding of child support enforcement programmes, individual states must adopt guidelines for child support. (See the Child Support Enforcement Program under Title IV-D of the *Social Security Act*.) Some states employ percentage tables based on the liable parent's net or gross income. Another formula begins with an assessment of the minimum needs of the liable parent.

In Sweden, maintenance support is based on a percentage of the annual income of the liable parent reduced by a basic allowance. The percentage rate depends on the number of children for whom the liable parent is responsible.

In Canada, judicially established formulae (see *Paras v. Paras* [1971] 1 *OR* 130 (Ont. C.A.) and *Levesque v. Levesque* [1994], 4 *R.F.L.* (4th) 373 (Alta C.A.)) have recently been replaced by federal Guidelines, based on Tables which establish monthly child support payments by reference to the liable parent's income, with the percentage increased for the number of children and modified slightly by income levels. The tables differ for each Province in accordance with different tax rates. The Guidelines are in the form of regulations made pursuant to legislation amending the *Federal Divorce Act 1985*. In Austria, where maintenance payments continue to be assessed by the courts, guidelines established by the courts operate based on the statistically calculated average needs for children of a certain age and a certain percentage of the net income of the maintenance debtor.

4. Private International Law Conventions

There are four Hague Conventions dealing with maintenance obligation. English translations of two are set out below. As explained in the excerpt by William Duncan, set out in Section 8, these conventions are out of date, ineffective, and many States have never become parties to them. Until a new convention is drafted, however, they remain the only alternative in many cases.

Convention on the Law Applicable to Maintenance Obligations towards Children (24 October 1956)

The States signatory to the present convention;
    Desiring to establish common provisions concerning the law applicable to obligations to support minor children;

Have resolved to conclude a Convention for this purpose and have agreed to the following provisions:

Article 1 The law of the habitual residence of the minor child determines whether, to what extent, and from whom the minor child may claim support.

In case of change of the habitual residence of the minor child, the law of the new habitual residence is applicable as of the moment when the change occurs.

Said law equally controls in ascertaining who is qualified to institute the action for support and what periods limit its institution.

* * *

Article 2 In derogation of the provisions of article one each of the contracting States may declare its own law applicable, if

a. the claim is made before an authority of such State,
b. the person against whom support is claimed as well as the minor child have the nationality of such State, and
c. the person against whom support is claimed has his habitual residence in such State.

* * *

Article 4 The law declared applicable by the present Convention may be disregarded only if its application is manifestly incompatible with the public policy of the State to which the authority concerned pertains.

Article 5 The present Convention does not apply to relations concerning support between collaterals.

It governs only conflicts of laws respecting obligations of support.

* * *

Convention on the Recognition and Enforcement of Decisions Relating to Maintenance Obligations (2 October 1973)

The States signatory to the present Convention;

Desiring to establish common provisions to regulate the recognition and enforcement of decisions involving obligations to support minor children;

Have resolved to conclude a Convention for this purpose and have agreed to the following provisions:

Article 1 The purpose of the present Convention is to ensure reciprocal recognition and execution, by the contracting States, of decisions rendered pursuant to petitions, international or internal in character, involving claims for support by a legitimate, not legitimate, or adopted minor child, not married and less than twenty-one years of age.

If the decision contains provisions on a matter other than the obligation of support, the effect of the Convention is limited to the latter.

The Convention does not apply to decisions concerning support between collaterals.

Article 2 Decisions rendered concerning support in one of the contracting States shall be recognized and declared executory, without review of the merits (révision au fond) in the other contracting States, if

1. the deciding authority had jurisdiction under the present Convention;
2. the respondent party was duly cited or represented in accordance with the law of the State to which the deciding authority pertains; nevertheless, in case of decision by default, recognition and enforcement may be refused if, in view of the circumstances of the case, the executing authority deems that, without his fault, the defaulting party did not have knowledge of, or was not able to defend himself in, the proceeding;

3. the decision has become res judicata (chose jugée) in the State where it was rendered; nevertheless, decisions which are provisionally enforceable and interlocutory measures, although subject to review, shall be declared executory by the executing authority if like decisions may be rendered and enforced in the State to which such authority pertains;

4. the decision is not contrary to a decision rendered on the same subject matter and between the same parties in the State where it is invoked; recognition and enforcement may be refused if, before the decision was pronounced, the matter had been pending in the State where it is invoked;

5. the decision is not manifestly incompatible with the public policy of the State where it is invoked.

Article 3 For the purposes of the present Convention, the following authorities have jurisdiction to render decisions involving support:

1. the authorities of the State in the territory of which the party liable for support had his habitual residence at the moment when suit was instituted;

2. the authorities of the State in the territory of which the party entitled to support had his habitual residence at the moment when suit was instituted;

3. the authority to whose jurisdiction the party liable for support has submitted either expressly, or by pleading to the merits without reservations as respects the jurisdiction.

Article 4 A party who relies on a decision or who demands enforcement thereof must produce:

1. a transcript of the decision satisfying the conditions necessary for its authenticity;

2. documents serving to establish that the decision is executory;

3. in case of decision by default, an authentic copy of the process instituting the suit and documents serving to establish that such process has been duly served.

Article 5 Examination by the executing authority shall confine itself to the conditions contemplated in article 2 and the documents enumerated in article 4.

* * *

Article 7 If the decision of which enforcement is sought, has ordered support to be provided by periodical payments, enforcement shall be granted for both payments already due and future payments.

5. Public International Law

Child support has been recognized as a human right.

Convention on the Rights of the Child[3]

Article 27 1. States Parties recognized the right of every child to a standard of living adequate for the child's physical, mental, spiritual, moral and social development.

2. The parent(s) or others responsible for the child have primary responsible to secure, within their abilities and financial capacities, the condition of living necessary for the child's development.

3. States Parties, in accordance with national condition and within their mean, shall appropriate measures to assist parents and others responsible for the child to implement this right and shall in case of need provide material assistance and support programmes, particularly with regard to nutrition, clothing and housing.

4. States Parties shall take all appropriate measures to secure the recovery of maintenance for the child from the parents or other persons having financial responsibility for the child, both within the State Party and from abroad. In particular, where the person having financial responsibility for the child lives in a State different from that of the child, States shall promote the accession to international agreements or the conclusion of such agreement, as well as the making of other appropriate arrangements.

6. Regional Conventions

The following example suggests some of the difficulties, including language, in international child support, even where the States Parties have similar cultural norms.

Inter-American Convention on Support Obligations[4]

Scope

Article 1 The purpose of this Convention is to establish the law applicable to support litigations and to jurisdiction and international procedural cooperation when the support creditor is domiciled or habitually resides in one State Party and the debtor is domiciled or habitually resides or has property or income in another State Party.

This Convention shall apply to child support obligations owed because of the child's minority and to spousal support obligations arising from the matrimonial relationship between spouses or former spouses.

When signing, ratifying, or acceding to this Convention, a State may declare that it restricts the scope of the Convention to child support obligations.

Article 2 For the purposes of this Convent ion, a child shall be any person below the age of eighteen years. However, the benefits of this Convention shall also apply to those who, having attained that age, continue to be entitled to support under the applicable Iaw prescribed by Articles 6 and 7.

* * *

Article 5 Decisions rendered pursuant to this Convention shall be without prejudice to questions of parentage and family relationships between support creditors and debtors. Where relevant, however, such decisions may be used as evidence.

Applicable law

Article 6 Support obligations, as well as the definition of support creditor and debtor, shall be governed by whichever of the following laws the competent authority finds the most favorable to the creditor:

    a.   That of the State of domicile or habitual residence of the creditor;

    b.   That of the State of domicile or habitual residence of the debtor.

Article 7 The applicable law pursuant to Article 6 shall determine:

    a.   The amount of support due and the timing of and conditions for payment ;

    b.   Who may bring a support claim on behalf of the creditor; and

    c.   Any other condition necessary for enjoyment of the right to support.

Jurisdiction

Article 8 At the option of the creditor, support claims may be heard by the following judicial or administrative authorities:

    a.   Those of the State of domicile or habitual residence of the creditor;

    b.   Those of the State of domicile or habitual residence of the debtor; or

c. Those of the State to which the debtor is connected by personal links such as possessing property, receiving income or obtaining financial benefits.

Notwithstanding the provisions of this article, a judicial or administrative authority of another State shall also have jurisdiction if the defendant appears before it without challenging its jurisdiction.

Article 9 Actions to increase the amount of support may be heard by any of the authorities mentioned in Article 8. Actions to discontinue or reduce support shall be heard by the authorities of the State that set the amount of support.

Article 10 Support shall be commensurate with both the need of the creditor and the financial resources of the debtor.

Should a judicial or administrative authority responsible for enforcing or securing the effectiveness of a judgment order provisional measures or provide for execution of judgment in an amount lower than requested, the rights of the creditor shall not thereby be impaired.

International procedural cooperation

Article 11 Support orders of one State Party shall be enforced in other States Parties if they meet the following requirements:

a. The judicial or administrative authority issuing the order had jurisdiction under Articles 8 and 9 of this Convention to hear and decide the matter;

b. The order and the documents attached thereto required under this Convention have been duly translated into the official language of the State in which the order is to be enforced;

c. As necessary, the order and the documents attached thereto have been certified in accordance with the law of the State in which the order is to be enforced;

d. They have been certified in accordance with the law of the State of origin;

e. The defendant was served with notice or was summoned to appear in due legal form substantially equivalent to that established by the law of the State in which the order is to be enforced;

f. The parties had the opportunity to present their defense;

g. The orders are final in the State in which they were rendered. A pending appeal from such order shall not delay its enforcement.

Article 12 A request for enforcement of an order shall include the following;

a. A certified copy of the order;

b. Certified copies of the documents needed to prove compliance with Article 11.e and 11.f;

c. A certified copy of a document showing that the support order is final or is being appealed.

* * *

7. National Implementation

The following examples compare child support in two Asian societies. Both China and Japan expect the parties to reach agreement on this question. In addition, it sets forth the U.S. approach to problems involving international child support, which strongly favors bilateral agreements.

Marriage Law of the People's Republic of China[5]

Article 36 The relationship between parents and children does not terminate due to the divorce of parents. After the divorce of the parents, the children remain the children of both parties no matter they are supported directly by either the father or mother.

Both father and mother shall, after divorce, have the right and the obligation of upbringing their children.

It is the principle that the children during lactation shall be brought up by their mother after the divorce of the parents. If any dispute arises concerning which party shall bring up the children beyond lactation, such dispute shall be settled by the people's court according to the specific conditions of both parties and in light of protecting the rights and interests of the children.

Article 37 If, after the divorce of parents, the children are to be brought up by either party, the other party shall undertake a part or all of the necessary living and education expenses. The amount and term of payment shall be agreed upon by both parties; if no agreement is achieved, the amount and term shall be decided by the people's court. No agreement or judgment concerning the expenses for the living and education of the children may in no way prevent the children from making reasonable requests, where necessary, to either parent for an amount beyond the amount as determined in the said agreement or judgment.

Japan[6]

Since the nineties, the number of Japanese children living in families headed by divorced, separated, widowed or unmarried mothers has been on a sharp upward trajectory. The 1998 lone-mother national survey recorded 954,900 such families, representing a 20.9% increase from the previous 1993 survey. The ranks of such families continue to grow with the divorce rate hitting a record 2.27 per thousand people in 2001. In a comparison with European countries, this figure places Japan in the middle band of divorce rates. However, unlike most European countries, Japan has no system for the collection of child support (maintenance) payments from non-compliant fathers. This unsatisfactory situation is causing very serious hardship for many Japanese mother-headed families and puts Japan behind in this very important area of social legislation.

Non-payment of child support (Youikuhi in Japanese) by absent fathers is one of the three primary causes of child poverty in Japan. The other two are low wages and inadequate social transfers. According to the Citizen's Basic Living Survey (Kokumin seikatsu kiso chosa) released in August 2002, lone-mother families are now some of the poorest in Japan. Their average annual income was just 2.52 million yen compared with the average household of about 6.17 million yen.

Japan is deficient in several areas of child support (Youikuhi), most importantly having no mechanism in place for enforcing payment or collecting arrears. There is also no system for tracking down non-compliant fathers, no requirement to conduct DNA-paternity tests and no means for deducting money from the delinquent father's salary. The courts normally do not take action if a spouse does not meet their obligations. To make matters worse, the legal framework for solving child support disputes is totally inadequate and requires an inordinate amount of time and money.

Considering the high cost of raising a child in Japan, child support (maintenance) payments are relatively low. This is even the case if such payments are awarded by the family court. In normal divorce proceedings, the level of child support is usually mutually agreed. However, if a husband reneges on the agreement, the wife can do little unless she has the financial resources to pursue the matter legally. Even then, she will not be able to obtain full redress.

For example, a couple sign an official divorce arbitration document in which the husband agrees to pays 20,000 yen in child support per month. If he subsequently doesn't pay, the wife only has the option of taking the matter to the courts. However, even if she eventually wins, the husband can only be forced to pay up to a quarter of the agreed monthly amount. This makes the entire exercise rather fruitless. Furthermore, the legal option takes between six months and two years and is an expensive process. Compounding the problem is the acute shortage of lawyers in many prefectures, which makes a legal solution even more unrealistic. Since the overwhelming majority of lone-mothers do not have the financial resources required to go to court, they just have to accept non-payment when it occurs. Additionally, it is very difficult to repeatedly go to court with children, especially if the mother is working. The few women who take the legal avenue complain that nearly all the judges and lawyers are men and the entire process is conducted from a male's perspective.

Attempts to amend the law have been made, but conservative lawmakers have always managed to derail or castrate enforcement measures. For example, a 1985 amendment to the child maintenance law had a provision that legally required fathers who could pay to pay. However, when this item came before the Diet, the concrete measures required to implement the policy were deleted from the final draft. This rendered the legislation next to worthless as a father was merely obliged rather than forced to pay child support. Some conservative lawmakers argued that making men liable to pay for divorced children would go against Japanese traditions. The extremely low number of female politicians may also be a factor in the inability of Japanese lawmakers to pass meaningful legislation.

In comparison to other countries, Japan has been very slow to respond to the changes in family structures. Despite the dramatic increase in mother-headed families, the only policy the government has consistently pursued is to reduce the welfare budget for such families.

At present, government policy only stipulates that divorced fathers have an obligation to contribute to the cost of raising their children, but there are still no legal measures to make them do so. This ineffectual policy was reaffirmed by the Koizumi Cabinet in June 2002. Currently, there are no plans on the horizon to introduce a law to force delinquent fathers to pay child support.

Non-payment or the failure to pay the correct amount of child maintenance has been, and is, a major problem in most OECD countries. Research indicates that when a father is not legally obliged to pay child support, default of these payments is very common. For example, most American fathers did not comply with child support orders in the early eighties. For this reason, the US passed a series of laws starting in 1984 to increase the amount of compliance. A similar pattern occurred in most European countries. In 1993, Ontario introduced a scheme for deducting maintenance payments directly from a father's salary. At the same time, a similar arrangement was also functioning in Australia and Wisconsin State. In 1993, the British government set up the Child Support Agency to collect support payments from absent fathers. Germany, France, the Netherlands, Sweden, Denmark and Norway all took varying approaches to ensure that non-compliant fathers paid child support. Only Japanese fathers have been able to escape their obligations with impunity.

Consequently, in the nineties various surveys showed that only between 10% to 20% of fathers paid the correct level of child support. There was a great deal of regional variation with a 1999 Okinawa survey showing only 10% of fathers there paid child support.

It can be seen that child support legislation is an area where Japan is completely out of sync with other industrially advanced nations. The present payment system is unsatisfactory for a number of reasons. Primarily, many fathers simply do not pay, even if they are high income earners. Unlike in most other developed nations, the law has not been amended to take into account the rise in the divorce rate and the increase in the number of children living in single-parent families.

One of the primary reasons for lone-mother poverty in Japan is that fathers do not financially support their children. Research conducted in other countries clearly shows that this is largely due to the lack of an adequate system for the collection of child support payments from non-compliant fathers. Since the number of divorces continues to climb, there is a pressing need for lawmakers to overhaul the current system. Without adequate provision, both Japanese mothers and children will continue to suffer. Despite this critical situation, legislators still appear to be reluctant to act.

United States

The United States has historically been reluctant to become a party to any multilateral treaty regarding maintenance obligations, in part because the states, rather than the federal government, assume responsibility for such obligations. Instead, the United States has entered into a series of bilateral agreements.

Agreement Between the Government of the United States of America and the Government of _____ for the Enforcement of Maintenance (Support) Obligations

The Government of the United States of America and the Government of _____
(hereinafter referred to as the Parties),
Resolved to establish a uniform and effective framework for the enforcement of maintenance obligations and the recognition of maintenance decisions, and the determination of parentage,

* * *

Have agreed as follows:

Article 1 Objective
1. Subject to the provisions of this Agreement, the Parties hereby seek to provide for:
   a. the recovery of maintenance or the reimbursement of maintenance to which a maintenance creditor or a public body having provided benefits for a maintenance creditor subject to the jurisdiction of one Party (hereinafter referred to as the claimant) is entitled from a maintenance debtor who is subject to the jurisdiction of the other Party (hereinafter referred to as the respondent), and
   b. the recognition and enforcement of maintenance orders, reimbursement orders and settlements (hereinafter referred to as maintenance decisions) made or recognized within the jurisdiction of either Party.

Article 2 Scope
1. This Agreement shall apply to maintenance obligations arising from a family relationship or parentage, including a maintenance obligation towards a child born out of wedlock. However, a maintenance obligation towards a spouse or former spouse where there are no minor children will be enforced in the United States under this Agreement only in those States and other jurisdictions of the United States that elect to do so.

2. This Agreement applies to the collection of payment arrears on a valid maintenance obligation and any applicable interest on arrears and to the modification or other official change in amounts due under an existing maintenance decision.

3. The remedies provided for in this Agreement are not exclusive and do not affect the availability of any other remedies for the enforcement of a valid maintenance obligation.

Article 3 Central Authorities

1. The Parties shall each designate a body as Central Authority which shall facilitate compliance with the provisions of this agreement.

* * *

Article 5 Functions of the Central Authority of the Requested Party

The Central Authority or other designated public body of the Requested Party shall take on behalf of the claimant all appropriate steps for the recovery or reimbursement of maintenance, including the institution and prosecution of proceedings for maintenance, the determination of parentage where necessary, the execution of any judicial or administrative decision and the collection and distribution of payments collected.

Article 6 Cost of services

All procedures described in this Agreement, including services of the Central Authority, and necessary legal and administrative assistance, shall be provided by the Requested Party without cost to the claimant.

* * *

Article 7 Recognition and enforcement of maintenance decisions

1. Maintenance decisions, including maintenance decisions arising from a determination of parentage, from one Party shall be recognized and enforced in the other Party to the extent that the facts in the case support recognition and enforcement under the applicable laws and procedures of the latter Party.

* * *

Article 8 Applicable Law

1. All actions and proceedings under this Agreement by either Party shall be carried out pursuant to the law including choice of law provisions and procedures of that Party.

2. The physical presence of the child or custodial parent shall not be required in proceedings under this Agreement within the jurisdiction of the Requested Party.

8. NGOs and IOs

NGOs

The Poverty of Families Headed by Solo Mothers[7]   The number of families headed by solo mothers (solo mothers with children under 20 years old) is about 789,000. The number of divorces has been increasing recently. The average income of these families is about 2.15 million yen (1993), only one third of that of general families. About 87% of solo mothers have jobs, but only 50% have full time jobs, while 30% are part-timers. Only 15% of the fathers pay for the cost of bringing up children. Solo mothers do not get a sufficient share of property in the case of divorce and a very low percentage of them own their own homes.

Because of the recent downturn in the economy, many solo mothers, who are in a weak position in the labor market, are forced to face sudden dismissal, bankruptcy, a change in the type of contract, bullying, and sexual harassment. One solo mother pays 80,000 yen out of her monthly income of 150,000 yen, to rent a small private room. Her family has to survive on the remaining 70,000 yen, paying all other expenses out of this.

In Japan, families headed by solo mothers caused by the death of fathers can receive a survivor's pension and others can receive a child-rearing allowance. The amount of the former is twice as much as that of the latter.

In 1998, as part of a governmental economic restructuring policy, the upper limit of the annual income permitted to get the benefit of the child-rearing allowance was lowered from 4.07 million yen to 3 million yen and as a result, about 74,000 mothers lost the benefit. At the same time, local government bodies carried out the same kind of policies, such as lowering the annual income limit for free medical services for solo mothers' families. If children need constant medical care such as for asthma, solo mothers face even more difficulties.

The Japanese government has partly amended its discriminatory treatment of the child-rearing allowance for unmarried mothers. This is the government's only positive move. We demand that the government lowers the upper limit of the income permitted for solo mothers to receive the allowance, and takes more positive initiatives to help solo mothers to find jobs.

* * *

IOs

As noted in Section 3, the Hague Conference on Private International Law has long recognized the importance of transnational maintenance and the difficulties in enforcing it. In 1995, a study sponsored by the Conference concluded that the multiple conventions in effect functioned adequately. To the extent that they did not, it was felt that deep underlying differences among the States precluded reform. An excerpt from that study, focusing on the different public policy objectives of various States in connection with out of wedlock births, is set forth below.

In 1999, the subject was revisited and the conclusion was very different. An excerpt from the report of First Secretary William Duncan follows.

From Maintenance Obligations – Drawn up by Michel Pelichet, Deputy Secretary General, 9/95

87 A large number of decisions concern public policy invoked against maintenance allowances which have to be paid to a child born out of wedlock and are founded on the existence of intimate relations between the defendant and the mother, established solely on the basis of a statement by the latter. In this connection, an important judgment of the Court of Cassation of 25 January 1977 sanctions a well-established trend in French case law. The judgment first of all ascertains that in the light of Article 2, paragraph 5, of the Hague Convention of 1958, the French concept of international public policy cannot impede the enforcement, unless the foreign decision is manifestly incompatible with this concept; it subsequently asserts that this is not the case, as the mother's statements are corroborated by other factors, *the evidential force of which is sovereignly appraised by the foreign judge.* In this case, the Court of Appeal had found that, in the light of the German decision, not only was there no indication that the mother had lied under oath, but also the defendant, who had raised an objection on the grounds of *plurium concubentium,* had failed to provide any evidence of the plurality of lovers; nor had he invoked any other ground in support of his non-paternity. In another judgment of the French Court of Cassation delivered on 7 March 1978, it is equally clearly established that the French concept of international public policy does not stand in the way of the enforcement of a foreign judgment, which based the order to pay maintenance on the existence of sexual relations between the defendant and the mother of the child, established on the basis of a statement by the latter, provided that such a statement is corroborated by other factors, the evidential force of which is sovereignly appraised by the foreign judge.

88 A decision of the Italian Court of Cassation goes even further: in fact, the Court of Appeal of Brescia had refused to enforce a German judgment, on the grounds that the ascertainment of paternity under German law had been based exclusively on evidence taken from a statement by the child's official guardian, in the absence of any objective evidence. The Italian Court of Cassation set aside this decision, drawing a distinction between recognition of the part of the judgment dealing solely with maintenance, which had to be distinguished from the decision concerning the relationships under family law. With regard more specifically to the possibility of a partial recognition of the foreign judgment – the maintenance obligations alone – it considered that in the case of such a partial recognition, the verification of its compatibility with Italian public policy had to be confined to the operative clause and ought not to include the merits and evidence, in accordance with Italian private international law.

89 A decision of the Belgian Court of Cassation of 25 October 1979 reaches the same conclusion: the defendant maintained that the judgment ordering him to pay a maintenance allowance was based solely on a statement made under oath by the mother of the child and that was contrary to Article 340 of the Belgian Civil Code, a provision of public policy. The Belgian Court of Cassation considered that Article 340 of the Civil Code was a provision of *internal* public policy and would only be contrary to international public policy in the event that by this limitation, the legislator had intended to establish a fundamental principle of the political, economic and moral system in Belgium. However, the provision of Article 340 did not constitute such a limitation; the public policy referred to in Article 2, paragraph 5, of the 1958 Convention was not the internal public policy of the State in which the enforcement was applied for, but the international public policy of that State.

William Duncan, First Secretary, Note on the desirability of revising the Hague Conventions on Maintenance Obligations[8]

9 A quarter of a century has passed since the last two Hague Conventions on maintenance obligations were drawn up. It is worth noting certain trends in the development of domestic systems of family support which have been in evidence during the intervening years, and which may have some relevance in considering appropriate reforms at the international level. Some of the legal systems represented during the negotiations twenty-five years ago shared certain common features. Maintenance awards were for the most part determined by courts on an individualised basis, with the judge having a considerable degree of discretion in determining what constituted reasonable maintenance for a dependant having regard to the resources of the liable relative and the needs of the dependant. This system of individualised justice has come under increasing criticism in several jurisdictions on the basis that in its practical operation it tends to be very costly and ineffective. The amounts of maintenance awarded are often small, not justifying the expense of a detailed judicial inquiry, and problems of enforcement have tended to be chronic especially in the longer term. The burden on lone parents of instituting maintenance proceedings and taking measures to enforce judgements has been a heavy one, often undertaken with little prospect of obtaining an adequate or regular income in the long term. The problems of poverty surrounding single parent families has been met in part by increased public assistance. At the same time, many governments have become concerned by the consequent fiscal burden in so far as it arises from a failure by liable relatives to honour family commitments. The result has been the introduction of various reforms, some still at an experimental stage, designed on the one hand, to reduce the burden on individuals of pursuing maintenance claims and to secure a regular income for dependant family members, especially children, and on the other, to enforce more effectively and at lower cost private support obligations. Such measures, which tend to concentrate particularly on child support, may be roughly categorised as follows:

a. In some countries there has been a change in the way in which maintenance is assessed from a broad discretionary basis to one (which has a longer history in certain States) in which calculation proceeds on the basis of a more or less refined formula, designed to increase predictability and certainty (and indirectly encourage agreement) and to reduce the length and costs of hearings.

b. In some countries the function of determining the amount of maintenance to be paid, at least in the first instance, has become an administrative rather than a judicial function, not necessarily involving a hearing, with the objective again of reducing costs and improving efficiency. Administrative procedures are sometimes limited to claims for maintenance at or below a subsistence level.

c. Mechanisms for locating liable relatives, determining their resources, and enforcing maintenance orders have become more sophisticated. The use, for example, of orders providing for automatic deductions from wages at source have by now become common place. Government controlled databases (relating for example to revenue, social welfare or public licensing) are being employed more frequently both in gathering relevant information and in assisting with enforcement.

d. State involvement in securing private maintenance, motivated in part by a wish to reduce costs to the State, has in fact intensified in certain jurisdictions. There is a tendency in some States towards the integration of public and private support systems, and an acceptance that the effective enforcement of private obligations often requires the initiative of the State in bringing and enforcing claims against the recalcitrant maintenance debtors. Systems of advance payment by the State of maintenance due to a maintenance creditor are sometimes used.

10 These trends prompt certain questions concerning the existing rules of private international law, especially those embodied in the international instruments, and concerning the existing systems of administrative and judicial co-operation at the international level. For example, does the trend towards simplification in the procedures and the basis for assessing maintenance, especially in respect of children, have any implications for applicable law rules? Is the increasing involvement of public authorities in the process of claiming and enforcing maintenance adequately reflected in current systems of administrative and judicial co-operation? Do the existing provisions concerning recognition and enforcement of decisions, as well as those concerning co-operation, take sufficiently into account the possibilities opened up by the new information technology? It is not easy to predict where current trends in the reform of domestic systems will eventually lead. However, it may be safe to assume that in any new international arrangements, governments will be concerned in particular with questions of cost effectiveness, as well as with the importance of making maximum use of the new technology.

Summary The potential advantages of working towards a new integrated international instrument concerning maintenance obligations may be summarised as follows:
(1) the development of a set of uniform rules of direct jurisdiction specifying which State's authorities have jurisdiction to decide upon a question of maintenance or to modify an existing decision;

(2) the revision of certain of the provisions concerning the law applicable to maintenance obligations contained in the Hague Conventions of 1956 and 1973;

(3) the reinforcement of the Hague Conventions of 1958 and 1973 on recognition and enforcement, by the addition (inter alia) of fast track enforcement procedures, integrated provisions concerning administrative co-operation, and provision to encourage the use of automated databases and electronic means of communication;

(4) the improvement of existing machinery for administrative co-operation, by giving more precision to the role and functions of responsible national organs;

(5) the development of a more uniform approach to the provision of assistance in proceedings initiated in the State where the debtor has his or her habitual residence.

81 The Special Commission may therefore wish to consider –

a   whether these are appropriate goals;

b   to what extent any of these goals are likely to be achievable through the development of a new international instrument;

c   whether the improvements which appear to be feasible would justify the efforts necessary to develop any new instrument.

82 If a view does emerge that a new instrument is needed, many of the matters which have been addressed only in outline above will need to be explored in more detail. The Permanent Bureau would then embark on the preparation of a more detailed report. Various matters which have not been mentioned in this Note may also need to be addressed. For example, is there need for a definition of maintenance to ensure the inclusion of all financial orders (i.e. not solely periodical payment orders) whose purpose is to provide for the support of dependent family members? Should the scope ratione personae of any new instrument take account of changes in the national laws of certain countries extending the range of partnerships which give rise to maintenance obligations? The Special Commission may wish to identify other areas which may require further study.

9. A Possible Approach to the Problem

Fumio is not subsidizing Astrid in Sweden, but in order for Astrid and Yuri to maintain their standard of living in Japan, he may have to, because Sweden is subsidizing them now. Healthcare and education, for example, may well be more expensive in Japan because the government assumes less of the cost. The descriptions of child support in Japan and Sweden set out in Section 3, suggests some important differences between Japanese and Swedish approaches to this issue. Japan does not have guidelines, for example, while Sweden not only has guidelines but a 'child support assurance program,' under which Sweden guarantees a payment to Astrid if Fumio does not contribute. If Astrid decides to move, she should not assume that legal process will be available in Japan to assure child support. Indeed, given the very low (15%) percentage of Japanese fathers paying support, she should probably expect nothing. Even if Fumio is sincere in his assurances in Sweden, he may feel very differently when he is back in Japan.

Thus, it might be advisable for Astrid to request a lump sum to cover her anticipated expenses, especially given the sporadic nature of her income. If Fumio does not have the money to give her up front, she should at the very least demand that he pay for a Japanese lawyer to advise her regarding the enforceability of an Agreement in which Fumio promises to pay her a certain sum every month. In addition, perhaps, she might seek a provision under which he assumes direct responsibility for Yuri's medical expenses and school fees. In view of the difficulties of collecting child support in Japan, described in Section 7, Astrid should be skeptical regarding any arrangement that is likely to require her to seek court enforcement. Finally, Astrid should consider making any move contingent upon the prior receipt of exit costs; i.e., the cost of tickets for Yuri and Astrid back to Sweden, and living expenses, including rent, while she re-establishes herself.

For Further Research

1. In response to an increasing divorce rate, Japan has sought to limit aid to single mothers to discourage divorce by mothers with young children. For an account of Japan's recent adoption of measures to further restrict eligibility for childcare benefits for single mothers, see Curtin, J.S. (2002), 'Poorest Japanese Families Getting Poorer'; at http:www.glocom.org/specialt_topics/social_trends/2002_trends_04/index.html.

2. For a detailed description of the problems in collecting child support in Argentina, and mechanisms adopted to remedy them, see Grossman, C. and Iñigo, D. (2000), 'Argentina: The Overriding Interest of the Child in Legislative Policy and in Judicial Decision in Argentina,' in A. Bainham (ed.), *The International Survey of Family Law: 2000 Edition*, Jordan, Bristol, pp. 15-16. For an explanation of Canada's requiring support from psychological as well as biological parents, see Bailey, M. and Bala, N. (2000), 'Canada: Reforming the Definition of Spouse and Child Related Laws,' in ibid. at 71. For a discussion of child support in the Czech Republic, see Gaderjam, J.F. (2002), 'Czech Republic: A Half-Hearted Family Law Reform of 1998,' in ibid. at 128. For a description of the Affiliation Proceedings Bill of 1999 in Botswana, see Molokomme, A., 'Overview of Family Law in Botswana,' in ibid.

3. For a comprehensive and rigorous update, see Hague Conference, William Duncan, First Secretary, *Note on the desirability of revising the Hague Convention on Maintenance Obligations.* (Excerpted in Sections 7 and 8, above.)

Notes

[1]   These all may be found at: http://www.hcch.net/e/workprog/maint.html.
[2]   Hague Conference on Private International Law, January 1999.
[3]   G.A. res. 44/25, annex 44 U.N. GAOR Supp. (No.49) at 167, U.N. Doc.A/44/49 (1989), *entered into force* Sept. 2 1990.
[4]   The parties to the Convention are: Argentina, Belize, Bolivia, Brazil, Costa Rica, Ecuador, Guatemala, Mexico, Panama, Paraguay, Uruguay.
[5]   1980 – amended according to the Decision on Amending the Marriage Law of the People's Republic of China made at the 21st meeting of the Standing Committee of the Ninth National People's Congress on April 28, 2001.
[6]   http://www.glocom.org/special_topics/social_trends/20020909_trends_s6/.
[7]   http://www.jca.apc.org/fem/bpfa/NGOreport/A_en_Poverty.html.
[8]   Hague Conference on Private International Law, January 1999.

Chapter 11

Domestic Violence

1. Problem

Naseen is a fifteen year-old girl who grew up in Pakistan. She has dated a married man and her brothers have sworn to kill her. She has been declared a kari, a 'black woman' and is serving as a maid in a home of a tribal leader for her own protection.

You are a lawyer with an aid agency in the region. Naseen comes to see you and explains that she has cousins in the U.K., the U.S., and Canada and that she can live with any of them while she finishes high school. Assuming she can get out of the country, where does she have the best chance of being granted asylum as a refugee?

2. Overview

Domestic violence refers to a broad range of actions, from verbal abuse, including threats, to spousal rape and murder, that take place within the privacy of an intimate relationship, often within the marital home. Domestic violence has been a part of marriage and other domestic relationships for millions of women throughout the world. Even if a husband did not beat his wife, both knew that he could do so if he so chose. Even if there are domestic laws prohibiting spouse abuse, as there are in the U.S., women are often ashamed or afraid to report it. Within the past ten years, however, domestic violence has been internationally recognized as a crime against women. It is a global problem and international family law deals with it in three specific contexts.

First, domestic violence is an issue in the enforcement of several 'private' international treaties, such as the Hague Convention on the Civil Aspects of International Child Abduction (see Chapter 9). These treaties resolve conflicts of law issues by coordinating the national laws of States Parties. Although domestic violence is not explicitly referred to in treaties, it is often a relevant issue in the underlying domestic law, which must be taken into account under the treaty.

Second, as part of public international law, domestic violence has recently been recognized as a violation of women's human rights. At the World Conference of the U.N. Decade for Women in 1980, domestic violence was explicitly condemned. In 1993 the U.N. General Assembly passed the Declaration on the Elimination of Violence Against Women. Recognition of domestic violence as a violation of women's human rights reflects and reinforces the growing numbers of national laws that criminalize domestic violence, recognize it as a form of persecution for purposes of asylum claims, and provide domestic civil remedies, including damage awards.

Since domestic violence is now considered a human rights violation, moreover, the State may be held accountable under international treaty monitoring bodies.

Third, domestic violence has been the subject of several important initiatives, as well as sustained efforts at education and intervention, by a number of IOs and NGOs. This includes growing networks of private as well as State-sponsored shelters for battered women.

At the same time, there is ongoing resistance to these developments and there are new backlashes against them. Some States, such as Bangladesh and the Sudan, for example, have enacted religious laws or Shariah, interpretations of Islam that severely limit the rights of women. This is often presented as a defense of local norms, including the traditional prerogative of the patriarch within the home, and resistance to Western cultural imperialism.

Cultures may vary within a State as well. In the United States, for example, a comprehensive study was done to determine the effectiveness of mandatory arrest policies in connection with domestic violence. Under such policies, adopted on the municipal level, a city would require its police force to arrest the defendant whenever a domestic violence complaint was made. In the absence of such policies, in contrast, when the police appeared in response to a domestic violence complaint, the complainant would often recant and withdraw her complaint.

The study showed mixed results. In some cities, mandatory arrests were effective in reducing domestic violence (or at least, domestic violence complaints) over time. In others, however, mandatory arrest policies produced an apparent *increase* in domestic violence complaints. The researchers determined that the different results correlated to the racial makeup of the cities studied. In predominately black cities, mandatory arrests produced a backlash, while in predominately white cities, mandatory arrest policies were an effective deterrent. Where the arrest had negative consequences for the defendant (in addition to those directly attributable to the arrest itself), such as shame, loss of status in the community, or loss of a job, such policies were apt to be effective. Where the defendants did not have an image to protect in the community, and may even have regarded the complaint against them as a betrayal, there was more likely to be retaliatory violence once the defendant was released. Thus, the promulgation of laws and policies to address domestic violence, as set forth below, may show a good faith effort on the part of State officials to address the problem. Unless such measures are carefully tailored to the culture in which they are expected to operate, however, they may be futile or even counterproductive.

3. Cultural Variations

Pakistan – Killings in the Name of Honor[1]

> In August 1998, Zarina and her alleged paramour, Suleiman, were killed in village Gul Mohammad Brohi, Larkana district, by Zarina's three brothers.
> In April 1998, a young man in the Punjab village Chak NO. 65, axed his mother, Ghulam Bibi, to death after she was traced by her family and brought back home following

her supposed elopement with a man.

In Kot Addu, near Multan, Naziran, a mother of six was axed to death by her brother on suspicion of an illicit relationship in November 1997.

On 29 April 1999, Shama Bib, 16, wife of Saif Khan, living in Kahuta, Punjab, was shot by her husband on suspicion of her having an illicit relationship. She received bullet injuries in her abdomen and her condition was stated to be critical; it is not known if she survived.

On 6 January 1999, Ghazala was set on fire by her brother in Joharabad, Punjab province on suspicion of illicit relations with a neighbour. The burned and naked body reportedly lay unattended on the street for two hours as nobody wanted to have anything to do with it.

In Pakistan, hundreds of women, of all ages, in all parts of the country and for a variety of reasons connected with perceptions of honour are killed every year. The number of such killings appears to be steadily increasing as the perception of what constitutes honour – and what damages it – steadily widens. Often honour killings are carried out on the flimsiest of grounds, for instance when a wife does not serve a meal quickly enough or when a man dreams that his wife betrays him (see below). As state institutions – the law enforcement apparatus and the judiciary – have dealt with such crimes against women with extraordinary leniency, and as the law provides many loopholes for murderers in the name of honour to get away, the tradition remains unbroken. In fact, more and more killings committed for other motives take on the guise of honour killings on the correct assumption that they are rarely – and if so, only lightly – punished.

Originally a Baloch and Pashtun tribal custom, honour killings are now reported not only in Balochistan, the North West Frontier Providence (NWFP) and Upper Sindh which has a strong Baloch influx, but in Punjab province as well. Honour killings are no longer only reported from remote rural areas but also – though less frequently – from towns and cities. The modes of killing vary somewhat. In Sindh, a *kari* (literally 'a black woman') and a *karo* ('a black man') are more ritualistically killed and hacked to pieces, often in view of and with the implicit or explicit sanction of the community. In Punjab, such killings usually take place by shooting and appear more often based on individual decisions, occurring in an urban context and not always perpetrated in public.

The victims include young pre-pubescent girls, unmarried young girls and women, old women, including grandmothers, married women and widows. The mere allegation of girls and women having entered illicit sexual relationships usually suffices for their male relatives to take the law into their own hands and to kill them. The women are usually not given an opportunity to respond to such allegation. An allegation is enough to defile a man's honour, and therefore enough to kill a woman – and the man with whom she is alleged to have behaved 'improperly', if he can be found.

According to the non-governmental Human Rights Commission of Pakistan (HRCP), 888 women were reported deliberately killed in 1998 in Punjab alone. Of these, 595 killings were carried out by relatives: of these 286 were reportedly killed for reasons of honour. The Sindh Graduates Association said that in the first three months of 1999 alone, 132 honour killings had been reported in Sindh. Everyone contacted by Amnesty International about the incidence of honour killings in Pakistan held that the real number of such killings is vastly greater than the number reported.

An analysis of data on *karo-kari* killings collected by the Special Task Force for Sindh of the HRCP during 1998 highlights several remarkable features of honour killings in that province: In a total of 196 cases reported in Sindh, 255 persons were killed, including 158 women and 97 men. The data does not in all cases include information about the perpetrators, but of 154 persons killed for reasons of honour where the relation of the perpetrators to the killed person is given:

- in 46 instances when both a *kara* and a *kari* were killed, exactly one half of the killings were carried out by the husband of the *kari* and the other half by male relatives of the women concerned;
- of the 81 women killed alone as *kari*, 40 were killed by their husbands, 36 by male relatives, including, brothers, fathers, uncles or sons, five by others including their fathers-in-law or brothers-in-law;
- of the 27 men killed as *karo*, three were killed by the husbands of the alleged *kari*, and 21 by other male relatives of the women, with three killed by others, including the husband's relatives.

The fact that male relatives of the women concerned are so frequently perpetrators of the killings reflects the conviction that marriage and fidelity are not a matter between husband and wife but relate to the family and that a woman's assumed infidelity reflects on the honour of the entire family. While in the majority of cases, husbands, fathers or brothers commit the killings of girls and women in the name of honour alone or together with male relatives, in some cases, tribal councils or *jirgas* decide that they should be killed and send out men to carry out the deed. A *jirga* of members of the Afridi tribe living in Karachi decided that Riffat Afridi and Kunwar Ahsan were to be killed when they got married against Riffat Afridi's family's wishes. In March 1998, the husband, Kunwar Ahsan, was shot at by his wife's relatives. He remains permanently disabled. While the couple are still seeking a way to settle in another country, the *jirga* has vowed to find and kill them wherever they go.

* * *

Honour killings are by no means confined to remote rural areas. They have been reported, though less frequently, in urban settings, sometimes among the urban elite. Samia Sarwar was killed on the grounds of honour in April 1999 in Lahore; Riffat Afridi and Kunwar Ahsan were attacked in Karachi for having defiled Riffat's family's honour by marrying against their wishes. A Faisalabad-based film producer on 16 February 1999 allegedly strangled his 28-year-old wife and mother of a small child at his rented studio office at Allama Iqbal Town on suspicion of her illicit relationship with another man.

The frequency and randomness of *karo-kari* incidents contribute to an atmosphere of fear among young women in Pakistan. Human rights activists in Balochistan told Amnesty International that women facing the danger of being branded *siahkari* [black women] by the merest chance contact with a man not belonging to their families, are driven into ever more profound seclusion.

* * *

International support for women fleeing abroad when they fear for their lives from their families' death threats has been hesitant. The threat to the lives of women who refuse to accept their fathers' decisions relating to their marriages has only recently been recognized as a ground for granting asylum to such women.

In a landmark decision, the UK House of Lords in March 1999 ruled that two women who had come to Britain after rumours about their having illicit relationships were spread in Pakistan, had a well-founded fear of persecution as members of a particular social group, namely women, who experience discrimination and oppression because they occupy a lower status than men in Pakistani society. They were consequently granted refugee status in the UK.

* * *

The judgment can be found on the web site www.parliament.uk under House of Lords, judgments.

'Ms. A's Story' (Jordan)[2]

The term 'honor killing' refers to the practice in Jordan and other Middle Eastern and South Asian countries in which male members of the family are duty-bound to kill a female family member whom they think has brought dishonor and shame to their family. The male members of the family believe they can only regain their honor by murdering the woman for her alleged sexual transgressions.

* * *

Ms. A fled to the United States in 1991 because she feared being the victim of an 'honor killing' in her home country of Jordan.

If returned to Jordan, A faces death by the hands of the male members of her family because of her alleged sexual transgressions. In the summer of 1991, A and her now-husband, H., secretly started spending time together. In August, they had premarital sex, and in September H. proposed marriage. However, A's father forbade the marriage because H. is Palestinian and had a low paying job. A feared that she would be killed if her family found out she had lost her virginity, and she decided to flee Jordan with H. and to get married abroad. The airport police told A's father that she had left the country.

Since A lost her virginity to H. prior to marriage, left Jordan without her family's permission and married against her family's wishes, her father has ordered the male members to kill her on sight. A has learned through letters from her sister that her father is enraged and has declared that the shame she has brought on the family can only be removed by 'blood'. He has made her brothers swear to kill her at any place and time they find her, and he has also demanded that all her male relatives – including uncles and cousins – kill her if they ever come in contact with her. In the most recent letter, A learned that her father said that he cannot rest in peace even if he dies, and if he dies before he can kill her, he will only rest in peace if her male relatives carry out the killings.

Honor killings are prevalent in Jordan and have been recognized as a gross human rights violation that is inadequately dealt with by the Jordanian government. According to the 1998 U.S. State Department Report on Human Rights Practices, more than 20 'honor killings' were reported in Jordan that year. The report points out, however, that most honor killings go unreported and the actual number is believed to be four times as high. Fully 25% of the murders in the country are estimated to be honor killings. The only form of protection offered by the Jordanian government for women who fear becoming victims of honor crimes is their own imprisonment. In 1998, there were up to 50 women involuntarily detained in this form of 'protective custody'.

* * *

Article 340 of the Jordanian Penal Code provides that men accused of honor killings are not prosecuted for murder but instead for 'crimes of honor,' which carry lenient sentences, averaging three months to a year. (The penalty for murder under the Jordanian Penal Code, by comparison, is death.) Recently there was a governmental proposal to abolish Article 340. Despite being supported by a worldwide campaign, the proposal was defeated in Parliament in November 1999. Members of Parliament stated that abolishing Article 340 would amount to 'legislating obscenity' and that the efforts in support of the proposal 'are attempts by the West to infiltrate Jordanian society and demoralize women.'

A applied for asylum in the U.S., but an immigration judge in California denied her claim on January 8, 1998. The immigration judge ruled that A did not have a well-founded fear of persecution because there was no evidence that her father had been violent towards her in the past, and because she had not directly spoken with her father to confirm his threats. The judge ignored the three letters from A's sister, received over a five-year period, that explicitly state her father's orders to the male members of the family to kill A on sight. Although the judge acknowledged that honor killings do occur in Jordan, the judge stated that they are violent episodes in specific families and not a pattern or practice against Jordanian women in general. The judge rejected the claim that A's fear of persecution was on account of her membership in a social group defined in part by her gender, and instead ruled that A's fear of becoming a victim of an honor killing was a 'personal problem' that 'without more, cannot be the basis of an asylum claim.'

The BIA upheld the judge's decision on August 20, 1999, ruling that A's fear of being the victim of an honor killing was speculative, and that such harm would not be persecution on account of social group membership, but, rather the unfortunate consequences of a 'personal family dispute.'

On February 14, 2000, [seven U.S. Senators] sent a letter to Attorney General Janet Reno asking her to reverse the BIA's decision in Ms. A's case, expressing concern that 'the BIA lacks sufficient understanding of current standards in both United States asylum law and policy and international human rights law.'

On April 10, 2000, [18 Congress people] wrote a letter to Reno, . . . asking her 'to consider withdrawing U.S. government opposition to Ms. A's application for asylum.'

In May 2002, after the INS withdrew its opposition to her case, the Board of Immigration on Appeals granted Ms. A asylum.

4. Private International Law Conventions

The Hague Convention on Abduction

The Hague Convention on Abduction creates a previously unavailable civil remedy for the return of abducted children (see Chapter 9). Under the Convention, the 'left-behind parent can request the designated Central Authority of the State in which the abducted child is being held to locate the child, institute proceedings to effect its return, assist in administrative formalities, and generally help to restore the status quo. The only purpose of the Hague Convention is 'to restore the actual situation that existed prior to a child's removal or retention.'

Article 13b of the Hague Convention is triggered in domestic violence cases. It provides:

> Notwithstanding the provisions of the preceding Article, the judicial or administrative authority of the requested State is not bound to order the return of the child if the person, institution or other body which opposes its return establishes that there is a grave risk that his or her return would expose the child to physical or psychological harm or otherwise place the child in an intolerable situation.

In *Thomson v. Thomson*, the Supreme Court of Canada held that 'the physical or psychological harm contemplated by the first clause of Article 13 is harm to a degree that also amounts to an intolerable situation.' The United States Court of Appeals for the First Circuit, in contrast, has rejected such a narrow reading. Rather, in *Walsh v. Walsh*, the Court held that the district court erroneously required a showing of an 'immediate, serious threat' to the children under Article 13b. The Court found that respondent mother had proven by clear and convincing evidence that the children faced a grave risk of exposure to physical or psychological harm should they be returned to Ireland. In reaching this conclusion, the Court relied on testimony establishing the father's 'clear and long history of spousal abuse, and of fights with and threats against persons other than his wife.'

The Court of Appeals held that the district court's failure to take John's attacks against others into account was reversible error:

> John has demonstrated an uncontrollably violent temper, and his assaults have been bloody and severe. His temper and assaults are not in the least lessened by the presence of his two youngest children, who have witnessed his assaults – indeed [his 8-year-old daughter] was forced by him to witness the aftermath of his assault on Michael. Second, John has demonstrated that his violence knows not the bonds between parent and child or husband and wife, which should restrain such behavior.

The Court explicitly noted 'credible social science literature' showing that serial spousal abusers are also likely to be child abusers. The Court further noted that 'both state and federal law have recognized that children are at increased risk of physical and psychological injury themselves when they are in contact with a spousal abuser.' Thus, the Court concluded that the requisite 'threshold showing of grave risk of exposure to physical or psychological harm'[3] had been made. In *In re F.* (a minor) Abduction: Rights of Custody Abroad, an English court reached a similar decision in a case involving abuse.

In *Condon v. Cooper*,[4] even though the mother had secretly taken the children to Australia and kept them there without allowing the father any access until the Australian courts ordered their return under the Convention, the California court allowed the mother to move to Australia with her two children on the condition that California courts retained jurisdiction. The court took into account 'such factors as [the ex-husband's] physical violence, their mutual verbal violence, her drug-taking and the amount of time the children spent with their father.'

The Hague Convention on Adoption

The Hague Convention on the Protection of Children and Cooperation in Respect of Intercountry Adoption (see Chapter 3) seeks to end abuses of intercountry adoption, which vary from State to State. Domestic violence is an issue under the Hague Convention on Adoption in at least two distinct contexts. First, the Convention requires that the birth parents voluntarily relinquish the child. Thus, it must be asked whether the mother's relinquishment is effectively coerced by domestic violence or the threat of domestic violence. Second, the Convention requires a determination as to the suitability of the adoptive parents. Thus, it must be asked whether the adoptive parents have been screened for domestic violence.

In the early 1990s, the prosecution of lawyer Joel Steinberg and his live-in-partner Hedda Nusbaum for the death of their adopted daughter, Lisa, made front page headlines throughout the United States. The six-year old child had been viciously abused, apparently for years, and beaten unconscious and left to die one night while her parents smoked crack cocaine in the next room. While Steinberg was prosecuted for actually beating the child, Nusbaum was prosecuted for failing to stop him. At the trial, evidence of the years of abuse that Nusbaum herself had suffered at Steinberg's hands was admitted to show that she had little capacity to protect herself, let alone anyone else. As the murder of Lisa Steinberg made so brutally clear, a child being adopted into an abusive relationship is at risk not only of witnessing abuse, but of being abused herself.

5. Public International Law

Historically, domestic violence was not viewed as a violation of women's human rights because it is not perpetuated by the State. Rather, it was considered 'private,' 'natural,' or cultural. International consciousness has been raised in the last decade, however. The three World Conferences on Women that the UN organized in connection with the UN Decade for Women between 1975 and 1985 (Mexico City 1975, Copenhagen 1980 and Nairobi 1985) provided opportunities to bring the issue of violence against women to international attention. After the Nairobi Conference, gender violence was placed on the agenda by the Commission on the Status of Women, a subsidiary body of the UN Economic and Social Council.

This raised consciousness is grounded in the work of women's groups on several fronts. Some groups lobbied for recognition of rape as a war crime before the *ad hoc* criminal tribunals in Rwanda and the former Yugoslavia. Others urged the international community to mobilize against female genital surgeries. Still others explicitly focused on violence within families. On virtually every issue, women's groups worked on the regional and national as well as the international level, as discussed in greater detail below.

Their work led to the appointment of the Special Rapporteur on Violence Against Women, Radhika Coomaraswamy. The Special Rapporteur, through a series of fact-finding missions and over two dozen reports prepared by her office on the topic of violence against women, brought international consciousness to a new level. A State's acquiescence, or failure to take effective measures to combat domestic violence, is now broadly recognized as a violation of women's human rights.

Declaration on the Elimination of Violence Against Women[5]

With the unanimous adoption of the Declaration on the Elimination of Violence Against Women in 1993, 180 States recognized that violence against women 'both violates and impairs or nullifies the enjoyment by women of human rights and fundamental freedoms.' The issue of state responsibility is explicitly addressed in Article 4: 'States should condemn violence against women and . . . pursue by all appropriate means and without delay a policy of eliminating violence against women.' Such measures should include: ratifying the Women's Convention (or withdrawing reservations), preventing, investigating and punishing violence against women, whether on the part of the state or private persons, and modifying social and cultural conduct based on stereotyped roles. Finally, the State should document its efforts in self-monitoring reports submitted to existing treaty bodies.

Although the Declaration was aspirational, prohibition of violence against women can be characterized as emerging customary international law. The requisite State practice and *opinio juris* can be found in its unanimous adoption in conjunction with the proliferation of domestic legislation, executive action, and national judicial decisions which followed, along with the repeated references to state responsibility for domestic violence in reports of the Human Rights Commission, the Special Rapporteur on Violence Against Women, and other international instruments as well as regional human rights instruments.

The Declaration explicitly recognizes that violence against women violates their 'human rights and fundamental freedoms.' 'Violence against women' has been defined by the Committee on Human Rights as 'any act of gender-based violence that results in, or is likely to result in, physical, sexual or psychological harm or suffering to women, including threats, domestic violence, crimes committed in the name of honor.' Paragraph 15d reiterates State obligations, including the State's obligations to pass domestic legislation prohibiting violence against women.

As the Special Rapporteur explains in her Report of 21 January 1999, the 'fundamental human rights to be free from torture, gender discrimination and the inherent right to life are directly applicable to ... violence against women.' These rights, i.e., to be free from torture, gender discrimination and the right to life, are well established in customary international law. Indeed, their lineage is cited in the Declaration itself. Thus, in a general sense, the rights set out in the Declaration are already customary international law. The Declaration, accordingly, represents the codification and clarification of general rights already recognized in customary international law in the specific context of domestic violence.

The Convention on the Elimination of All Forms of Discrimination Against Women[6]

The Women's Convention does not explicitly prohibit violence against women. The Committee on the Elimination of Discrimination Against Women (CEDAW) has attempted to retroactively fill in the gaps through 'creative interpretation' of the Women's Convention. In General Recommendation No. 19, for example, CEDAW explained that 'gender-based violence is a *form* of discrimination' and thus included in the Women's Convention's bar against gender discrimination in general.

In addition, the Women's Convention requires all parties to 'take all appropriate measures to eliminate discrimination against women by *any* person, organization or enterprise.' CEDAW reads this as making States responsible for private acts if they fail to 'act with due diligence to prevent violations of rights, or to investigate and punish acts of violence, and to provide compensation.'

The Convention Against Torture ('CAT')[7]

'Torture' is defined in Article 1 as the 'intentional infliction of severe pain and of suffering' with a view to achieving a wide range of purposes, by, or with the acquiescence of, a person acting in an official capacity. As Rhonda Copelon and others have argued, and as the Special Rapporteur has confirmed, domestic violence may be torture.

In addition, Article 3 of the CAT expressly provides 'No State Party shall expel, return (*refouler*) or extradite a person to another State where there are substantial grounds for believing that he would be in danger of being subjected to torture.' Thus, the CAT offers what one commentator characterizes as a 'viable alternative legal remedy' for immigrant women fleeing domestic violence.

6. Regional Conventions

Inter-American Convention on Violence Against Women[8]

The Inter-American Convention on the Prevention, Punishment, and Eradication of Violence Against Women (Convention of Belém Do Pará) was open for ratification in 1995. This Convention explicitly bars violence against women. Article 6 affirms women's right to be free from all forms of discrimination, including 'stereotyped patterns of behavior and social practices based on concepts of inferiority or subordination.'

Article 8 requires the State to support educational and training programs, to change attitudes that contribute to violence against women, to provide specialized services for women who are the victims of violence, to develop guidelines for the media to promote more positive images of women, to support research on the causes, consequences, and frequency of violence against women, and to foster 'international cooperation for the exchange of ideas and experiences and the execution of programs aimed at protecting women.' Article 10 defines violence against women as 'any act of conduct, based on gender, which causes death or physical, sexual or psychological harm or suffering to women, whether in the public or private sphere.' Article 11 authorizes the Inter-American Court of Human Rights to give advisory opinions on its interpretation at the request of the State signatories and the Inter-American Commission on Human Rights. Article 12 permits individuals as well as NGOs to file petitions with the Commission regarding violations of Article 7, which requires the State to 'pursue policies to prevent, punish, and eradicate ... violence.' Chapter IV of the Inter-American Convention sets out additional enforcement mechanisms, including self-monitoring.

European Council on Refugees and Exiles, Position on Asylum Seeking and Refugee Women[9]

Executive Summary In this position paper, the European Council on Refugees and Exiles (ECRE) has compiled the views of its member agencies, consisting of some 60 organisations throughout 22 European countries, with regard to how the claims of female asylum seekers should be determined and how female asylum seekers and refugees should be received and settled in European countries of asylum.

Statement of the Problem Female asylum seekers and refugees are unable to benefit equitably from current legal protection and social assistance measures for a number of reasons which this paper examines.

ECRE notes that the difficulty of assessing the problems facing refugee and asylum seeking women is increased by a lack of gender-differentiated data in European countries. This perpetuates the invisibility of refugee women and gender issues, and inhibits the development of policy and planning.

The legal obstacles faced by women in asylum determination fall into two broad categories: substantive and procedural. International refugee instruments – most notably the 1951 Refugee Convention – are based upon the assumption that all refugees, irrespective of their gender, face the same problems and will be treated equally. However, while there is nothing which explicitly precludes a woman from being recognised as a refugee, the current interpretation of these instruments by European States both reflects and reinforces gender biases.

Women are frequently persecuted for reasons similar to those of their male counterparts. However, the persecution of women may differ, both in terms of its form and its motivation, from that commonly experienced by men. Many women are targeted because they are community organisers or because they persist in demanding that their rights or those of their relatives are respected. Others are targeted because they are vulnerable – young women who can easily be sexually abused or mothers who will do anything to protect their children. In addition the authorities in some countries have exploited family relationships to intensify torture and ill-treatment. An attack on a woman may also represent an attack on her ethnic group; because they have a reproductive role, women may be viewed as the embodiment of the identity and future survival of a given ethnic group.

In many parts of the world, women who do not live according to the standards imposed on them by their societies can suffer cruel or inhuman treatment. Refusing arranged marriages, having sexual relations outside marriage, failing to provide a satisfactory dowry or wearing certain forms of dress can result in persecution. Due to social and economic constraints, relatively few of these women manage to flee to other countries for protection, yet when they do, their experiences tend to be interpreted as discriminatory rather than persecutory.

The substantive problems facing asylum seeking women stem from the failure of decision-makers to incorporate the gender-related claims of women into their interpretation of the existing grounds enumerated in the 1951 Convention. Decision-makers have largely failed to recognise the political nature of seemingly 'private' acts of harm to women. This paper argues that the interpretation of the 1951 Convention refugee definition should be reconsidered so that the claims of women are not precluded. It argues that both political opinion and membership of a particular social group can and should provide a legal basis for recognition of women fleeing persecution as Convention refugees. It proposes that European guidelines on gender issues in asylum cases should be developed and urges European States to follow Canada, the United States and Australia in developing and implementing such guidelines.

The procedures for determining asylum are also critical. Current procedures are based on the widespread assumption that asylum seekers are politically active men who have been persecuted by the State authorities as a result of those activities, and these procedures therefore need to be reviewed and amended through guidelines or legislation. It is particularly notable that information on the human rights situation of women in countries of origin is often lacking or inadequate, despite the fact that such information is essential for a fair evaluation of a claim.

This paper also examines the social aspects of women's needs both as asylum seekers and refugees in Europe, and the question of why they do not benefit equitably from social service provision. Particular problems concerning the physical safety of women arise in collective refugee reception centres, and this is as true in Europe as in other regions of the world. Such communal accommodation is usually overcrowded and lacks privacy for women. These factors increase the risk of sexual or other violence against them.

This paper highlights the most important recommendations concerning protection, social assistance, and voluntary return of women. It aims to raise awareness and improve standards among European NGOs, lawyers, judiciaries and the governmental sectors. ECRE believes that if harmonisation is possible at the level of best practice it would bring many improvements to the treatment of female asylum seekers and refugees in Europe.

Summary of Key Conclusions 1. European States should develop best practice guidelines on the determination of asylum claims from women, at the regional and at the national level, and should ensure that the content of such guidelines is widely known and implemented at all levels.

2. Any of the five enumerated grounds can and should provide a legal basis for the recognition of women fleeing persecution as Convention refugees, in particular many claims from women can be determined on the grounds of religion or political opinion. This should be reflected in the practice of European asylum States, who should no longer grant secondary or 'de facto' statuses to women who are refugees within the meaning of the Convention.

3. European decision-makers should not evaluate gender-specific forms of harm according to a standard different from that applied to other forms of harm which may amount to persecution. Human rights instruments should be used as the basis for assessing the risk of persecution.

4. Where a woman was unwilling to seek protection from State authorities, for example where it would have put her at further risk of abuse by a male relative, this fact should not prejudice her claim to asylum. European receiving States should not exclude persecution by non-State agents from their common understanding of 'persecution', and should regard State authorities in the country of origin as bearing responsibility for any persecution by private individuals where those authorities have failed in their duty to protect the victim.

5. Country of origin information should be collected that has relevance as evidence in gender-related claims, and this information should be routinely utilised by decision-makers. A gender perspective should always be incorporated into decision-making regarding the 'safety' of a country of origin; conditions justifying use of the cessation clause; and the existence of an 'internal flight alternative'.

6. When a female asylum seeker arrives accompanied by family members, she should be informed in private of her right to make an independent application and to be interviewed without the presence of other family members. Female interpreters and interviewers should be made available.

7. Specific measures to address the physical safety of asylum seeking and refugee women in European asylum States should be introduced, particularly where collective accommodation is provided.

8. All asylum seeking and refugee women should be given direct and equal access to advice, information and services in the host State, and all refugee women should receive a legal status, and set of personal identity documents, independent of their male relatives.

9. Asylum seeking and refugee women should be consulted at all stages of policy and planning, and should participate proportionately in whatever systems exist to consult residents in places of collective accommodation. They should also be fully consulted to ensure that any 'voluntary return' of refugees to a country of origin is truly voluntary in nature.

10. All asylum statistics provided by European States (including recognition rates, figures for refugees resettled from overseas, and asylum seekers in detention) should include a breakdown by gender.

7. National Implementation

Canada

Through its *Gender Guidelines for Asylum Adjudications*, originally issued in March 1993 and reissued in 1996, 'Canada became the first government to recognize formally that a woman fleeing persecution on gender-specific grounds can claim to 'fear persecution on account of her membership in a particular social group.'[10] The following Guideline establishes the parameters for immigration officials dealing with these issues.

Guideline 4 Women Refugee Claimants Fearing Gender-Related Persecution: Framework of Analysis[11] Assess the harm feared by the claimant. Does the harm feared constitute persecution? (a) For the treatment to likely amount to persecution, it must be a serious form of harm which detracts from the claimant's fundamental human rights. (b) To assist decision-makers in determining what kinds of treatment are considered persecution, an objective standard is provided by international human rights instruments. The following instruments, among others, may be considered:

> Universal Declaration of Human Rights
> International Covenant on Civil and Political Rights
> International Covenant on Economic, Social and Cultural Right
> Convention on the Elimination of All Forms of Discrimination Against Women
> Convention on the Political Rights of Women
> Convention on the Nationality of Married Women
> Convention Against Torture and other Cruel, Inhuman or Degrading Treatment or Punishment
> Declaration on the Elimination of Violence Against Women

Ascertain whether the claimant's fear of persecution is based on any of the grounds, singly or in combination, enumerated in the Convention refugee definition. Considerations: It is necessary to ascertain the characteristic of the claimant which places her or members of her group at risk, and to ascertain the linkage of that characteristic to a Convention ground. Gender is an innate characteristic and it may form a particular social group.

A subgroup of women may also form a particular social group. Women in these particular social groups have characteristics (possibly innate or unchangeable) additional to gender, which make them fear persecution.

The gender-defined group cannot be defined solely by the fact that its members share common persecution.

Determine whether the claimant's fear of persecution is well-founded. This includes assessment of the evidence related to the ability or willingness of the state to protect the claimant and, more generally, the objective basis of the claim.
Considerations:

There may be little or no documentary evidence of similarly situated women and the claimant's own experiences.

The claimant need not have approached non-state organizations for protection. Factors including the social, cultural, religious, and economic context in which the claimant finds herself should be considered in determining whether it was objectively unreasonable for the claimant not to have sought state protection. Where a woman's fear relates to personal-status laws or where her human rights are being violated by private citizens, an otherwise positive change in country conditions may have no impact, or even a negative impact, on a woman's fear of gender-related persecution.

If required, determine whether there is a possibility of an internal flight alternative.
Considerations:

Whether there would be undue hardship for the claimant, both in reaching the location of the IFA and in establishing residence there.

Religious, economic, social and cultural factors, among others, may be relevant in determining the reasonableness of an IFA for a woman fearing gender-related persecution.

* * *

A. Determining the Nature and the Grounds of the Persecution
    I. General Proposition

Although gender is not specifically enumerated as one of the grounds for establishing Convention refugee status, the definition of Convention refugee may properly be interpreted as providing protection for women who demonstrate a well-founded fear of gender-related persecution by reason of any one, or a combination of, the enumerated grounds.

* * *

Women who fear persecution resulting from certain circumstances of severe discrimination on grounds of gender or acts of violence either by public authorities or at the hands of private citizens from whose actions the state is unwilling or unable to adequately protect the concerned persons. In the refugee law context, such discrimination may amount to persecution if it leads to consequences of a substantially prejudicial nature for the claimant and if it is imposed on account of any one, or a combination, of the statutory grounds for persecution. The acts of violence which a woman may fear include violence inflicted in situations of domestic violence and situations of civil war.

Women who fear persecution as the consequence of failing to conform to, or for transgressing, certain gender-discriminating religious or customary laws and practices in their country of origin. Such laws and practices, by singling out women and placing them in a more vulnerable position than men, may create conditions for the existence of a gender-defined social group. The religious precepts, social traditions or cultural norms which women may be accused of violating can range from choosing their own spouses instead of accepting an arranged marriage, to such matters as the wearing of make-up, the visibility or length of hair, or the type of clothing a woman chooses to wear.

* * *

The United States

Considerations for Asylum Officers Adjudicating Asylum Claims From Women[12] This memorandum is written to provide the INS Asylum Officer Corps (AOC) with guidance and background on adjudicating cases of women having asylum claims based wholly or in part on their gender.

Recent international initiatives have increased awareness and suggested approaches to gender-related asylum claims. Enhancing understanding of and sensitivity to gender-related issues will improve U.S. asylum adjudications while keeping pace with these international concerns. This guidance will serve as a useful tool for new Asylum Officers, and will help to ensure uniformity and consistency in procedures and decisions. In-Service training at all Asylum Offices will be critical to using this guidance effectively.

Despite the increased attention given to this type of claim during the past decade, gender-based asylum adjudications are still relatively new developments in refugee protection. This 'Considerations' memorandum is a natural and multi-faceted outgrowth of a set of gender guidelines issued by the UNHCR in 1991, the 1993 Canadian gender guidelines, a proposed set of guidelines submitted by the Women Refugees Project (WRP) of the Harvard Immigration and Refugee Program, Cambridge and Somerville Legal Service, in 1994, and recent (and still developing) U.S. caselaw. It is similar in approach to the Haiti 'Considerations' memorandum of March 9, 1993 and other memoranda issued to maintain consistency among Offices and Officers. Additionally, this memorandum seeks to enhance the ability of U.S. Asylum Officers to more sensitively deal with substantive and procedural aspects of gender-related claims, irrespective of country or origin.

* * *

The United States' *Gender Guidelines for Overseas Refugee Processing,* drafted in 2000, explicitly recognizes domestic violence as a form of gender-related persecution. In the Matter of M.K., a woman from Sierra Leone requested asylum in the United States on the grounds of persecution based on domestic violence. The court found that there was in fact persecution, relying on evidence showing that 'violence against women, especially wife beating, is common ... [since] disobedience on the part of the wife is considered a justification for punitive measures ... by the husband, police are unlikely to intervene except in cases of severe injury or death, and few cases of violence go to court.'

The United Kingdom

In the United Kingdom, in contrast, such claims have been denied. In *R. v. The Immigrant Appeal Tribunal and the Secretary of State for the Home Department, ex parte Syede Kahatoon Shah,* a claim for asylum by a Pakistani woman who had suffered domestic violence and faced the death penalty for alleged adultery under Sharia law was denied. The special adjudicator held that,

> There is no accepted definition of social group and it is no more possible for a woman who has suffered domestic violence to be herself within the meaning of social group . . . than it is for anyone who has been divorced to say that she or he is a member of a social group within the purposes of (the) convention.

In 2000, the United Kingdom established a comprehensive set of guidelines for addressing gender-based asylum claims.

> *Asylum gender guidelines*[13] These Guidelines aim to assist the Immigration Appellate Authority in fully considering all aspects of asylum seekers' claims to international protection under United Kingdom law.
>
> * * *
>
> *Harm Within Family Life* Physical and mental violence and ill-treatment within the family is a wide-spread and often gender-specific form of harm. The fact that such treatment occurs within the family context does not mean that it will not constitute 'serious harm' – treatment which would constitute 'serious harm' if it occurred outside the family will also constitute 'serious harm' if it occurs within a family context. As with other forms of harm whether it constitutes 'serious harm' within the meaning of the Refugee Convention should be assessed on the basis of internationally recognized human rights standards.
> Harm within family life and marriage-related harm includes, *but is not limited to*:
> *Forced marriage* – marriage of a person without their free consent.
> domestic violence.
> *'Dowry death'* or *bride burning* – where a woman is subject to bullying, mental and physical harm and may be murdered or driven to suicide by her husband and/or in-laws who are dissatisfied with the dowry given by the bride's family or in order to obtain further payments of dowry from the bride's family
> * * *
> *'Honour killings'* – where a woman is killed in order to retain the 'honour' of her family; for example, this may occur where a woman has a sexual relationship , including a marriage relationship, with someone not approved of by the family, or is in some other manner considered to have affected the honour of the family.[14]

8. IOs and NGOs

IOs and NGOs have played important roles in advocacy as well as in public education. The Special Rapporteur considers them crucial allies. As she notes, for example,

> Very little effort has been undertaken at the international level to provide for a 'clearinghouse' on domestic violence. . . it is, therefore, proposed that a clearinghouse for information, perhaps located within UNIFEM or the Division for the Advancement of Women at headquarters, be established to ensure that information on ways and means of combating domestic violence at the national level is shared and accessible to all countries.

IOs

UNIFEM's Internet Working Group to End Violence Against Women is an example of an IO exploiting technology to develop effective working relationships among a broad range of women's groups. The Internet Working Group has considered strategies involving education, training, mobilization, changing male behavior, roles of NGOs and governments. In addition, the Working Group has considered strategies relating to the role of the media. The Working Group has also analyzed the factors contributing to the success of anti-violence strategies.

For women in refugee camps, domestic violence remains a fact of life. In 1990, however, the UN High Commissioner for Refugees recognized that women refugees had specific needs, including needs for safety, that were not being addressed. A new policy was adopted, accordingly, to explicitly address those needs. UNHCR Policy on Refugee Women, U.N. Doc.A/AC.96.754 (1990). The UNHCR and the Executive Committee of the High Commissioners Programme has promulgated Guidelines on the Protection of Refugee Women and Gender Based Violence as a Form of Persecution in a 1985 policy statement of the Executive Committee as well as in new guidelines with respect to female asylum seekers.

NGOs

The NGOs have been similarly proactive. OXFAM is an example of a major international NGO with a broad development-focused mandate which has recognized the impact of domestic violence in its projects. OXFAM seeks to address domestic violence within the development context. It recently sponsored a conference focusing on the factors contributing to the success of various anti-violence strategies. These included: sustained work by the women's movement, increased political participation of women, and alliances among local common national and international NGOs. The Conference also noted the obstacles to those strategies, including splits in the women's movement, social and political backlash, and threats against service providers and survivors.

An NGO focused on women in the developed world, the European Women's Lobby, has recently published an extensive report, *Unveiling the Hidden Data on Domestic Violence in the European Union*. This report notes that violence crosses class and cultural boundaries; that violence is the norm rather than the exception; and that violence is independent of poverty, education, alcohol or drug use. In addition, *Unveiling the Hidden Data* notes that women are particularly vulnerable when they are pregnant and during the post-natal period, during periods of separation and when their children are very young.

Amnesty International has specifically focused on the problems of women seeking asylum from domestic violence, as set forth in the excerpt below.

Amnesty International Canada, the right to find safety[15] The governments of Canada and the US are currently negotiating an agreement on refugee claims that could lead to violations of the basic rights of refugee claimants who pass through the US on their way to Canada.

Under the proposed agreement – known as a 'safe third country' agreement – the majority of asylum-seekers who come to Canada via the US will not be allowed to claim protection in Canada (save for a few exceptions). This is based on the premise that the Canadian Government considers the US a safe third country, and thus asylum-seekers who land there first should be required to make their claim there. However, Amnesty International has documented that the treatment of asylum-seekers in the US falls short of international standards, and has called upon the Canadian government to reconsider entering into this agreement. Serious shortcomings in the US asylum system mean asylum-seekers could be exposed to the following serious violations of their human rights:

- The very real likelihood that they would face arbitrary and lengthy imprisonment, often in isolated detention centres alongside criminal detainees.
- Women asylum-seekers fleeing honour killings or domestic violence, along with other categories of people in need of protection, could be denied based on an overly narrow interpretation of the Refugee Convention used in the US.
- Individuals without proper identity documents, a frequent reality for refugees, could be summarily removed, based on the decision of a US immigration officer, without access to legal counsel or advice from nongovernmental organizations.

It is vital that this agreement be reviewed by Parliament. Amnesty International is calling for the agreement to be referred to the parliamentary Standing Committee on Citizenship and Immigration. Canada and the US are moving quickly to finalize this agreement, so it is important to speak out now.

The recognition of domestic violence as a human issue reflects and reinforces the recognition of other forms of violence against women as human rights issues, as set forth in the excerpt below.

Human rights watch world report 1999, women's human rights – the role of the international community[16] The recent commitment of the international community to recognize violence against women as a human rights issue, to challenge de jure and de facto discrimination against women, and to end impunity for the widespread use of sexual violence in war and armed conflict, faced many challenges in 1998. After gaining momentum following the 1993 World Conference on Human Rights in Vienna, the 1994 World Conference on Population and Development in Cairo, and the 1995 Fourth World Conference on Women in Beijing, the significant progress made by the women's international human rights movement threatened to stall as attacks on women's human rights persisted in 1998.

Despite these attacks, the presence and impact of women's human rights activists contributed substantially in 1998 to strengthening standards protecting women's rights and to ensuring that policy makers felt obliged to acknowledge and even respond to violations of women's rights. For example, the Treaty of Rome for the creation of a permanent international criminal court (ICC) defines rape, sexual slavery, enforced prostitution, forced pregnancy, and enforced sterilization as war crimes and crimes against humanity. The same treaty condemns gender-based persecutions first.

As a direct result of the breadth and effectiveness of the women's human rights movement, countries throughout the world as well as intergovernmental organizations and international financial institutions appeared to understand that women's human rights could no longer be ignored. Nonetheless, significant financial resources were not consistently allocated to the advancement of women's human rights in 1998, nor was redress for violations of rights readily available to most women. However, it was clear that some governments and institutions were beginning to integrate the women's movements' analysis of the interrelatedness of economic development, non-discrimination, and access to justice into both their rhetoric and policies, if not always their actions.

United Nations From negotiations to create an international criminal court, to slow-moving work to give victims of sexual discrimination the right to seek redress by petitioning the Committee on the Elimination of Discrimination Against Women (CEDAW), to the U.N.'s failure to stand firm on women's rights in negotiations with the Taliban, U.N. member states showed their reluctance to deliver on the promise of human rights for women. Even instances of progress were hard-won.

At the June-July diplomatic conference in Rome to create a permanent international criminal court, member states were asked to ensure an end to impunity for crimes of gender and sexual violence as a basic principle of the treaty. This straightforward proposition, however, was under siege from the beginning as a small group of nations worked with the Holy See to undermine the potential for the ICC effectively to provide justice for victims of sexual and gender violence. Their attack sought to exclude from the treaty a list specifying the crimes of sexual violence that would be covered, particularly any reference to the crime of forced pregnancy. These efforts were rebuffed when governments acted to end the historical failure to prosecute crimes of sexual violence, by listing such crimes.

In the final days of the negotiation, due in large measure to the tireless advocacy of the Women's Caucus for Gender Justice and the stalwart support of Canada, Bosnia, and Australia, three major goals were achieved: rape and other crimes of sexual violence were included in the definition of war crimes and crimes against humanity; gender-based persecution was included in the definition of war crimes and crimes against humanity; and the term 'gender,' which had been under attack by the Vatican and a group of Arab League countries, was preserved. Despite widespread usage of the term 'gender' by the United Nations for at least fifteen years, the Syrian delegate, speaking on behalf of this group of states, insisted that the concept of gender threatened the very existence of civilization by challenging the concept that disparate treatment was not justified based on biological differences. Despite serious flaws in the statute, particularly in limits on jurisdiction and an opt-out provision for war crimes, the treaty represented a significant milestone in the struggle to end impunity for crimes of sexual and gender violence.

9. A Possible Approach to the Problem

Nareen should probably consider seeking asylum in Canada, the U.K. and the U.S., in that order. As set out in Section 7, in 1993 Canada became the first government to officially recognize gender specific grounds for asylum. Guideline 4 explicitly directs immigration officials to consider the pertinent human rights instruments and specifically considers threats posed by non-State actors, such as Naseen's brothers.

Since 2000, the U.K. has similarly adopted Guidelines, under which 'honour killings' are explicitly recognized as a 'harm' within the meaning of the Refugee Convention. The U.S. also adopted Gender Guidelines in 2000 and has in fact granted asylum on the ground of domestic violence. As Amnesty International contends, in Section 8, however, the U.S. falls short of international standards in its treatment of asylum-seekers. More specifically, AI accuses the U.S. of denying asylum to women fleeing honour killings based on 'overly narrow' interpretations of the Refugee Convention.

For Further Research

1. Domestic violence takes different forms in different cultures. For an excellent early exploration, see Eekebar, J. and Katz, S. (eds. 1978), *Family Violence: An International and Interdisciplinary Study*. See also, e.g., Yasmeen Hassan, 'Stove Burning, Acid Throwing and Honor Killings,' in *2 Women and International Human Rights Law*.

2. For U.N.-compiled data and analyses, see, e.g., United Nations, (2002) *The World's Women's 2000: Trends and Statistics*; United Nations, *Strategies for Confronting Domestic Violence: A Resource Manual* (describing national and international cooperation in developing strategies for responding to victims and working with perpetrators); United Nations (1999), *Violence Against Women in the Family* (discussing violence against women in the family as a global issue).

3. For discussions of domestic violence as human rights violations, see Thomas, D. and Beasley, M. (1995), 'Domestic Violence as a Human Rights Issue,' *Albany Law Review*, Vol. 58, p. 1119; Meyer, M. (1999), 'Negotiating International Norms: "The Inter-American Commission of Women and the Convention on Violence Against Women",' in M. Myer and E. Perügel (eds), *Gender Politics in Global Governance*; Jutta Joachim, 'Shaping the Human Rights Agenda: The Case of Violence Against Women,' in *Gender Politics in Global Governance*; Joan Fitzpatrick, 'The Use of International Rights Norms to Combat Violence Against Women,' in R. Cook (ed., 1994), *Human Rights of Women: National and International Perspectives*, p. 532; Sullivan, D. (1994), 'Women's Human Rights and the 1993 World Converence on Human Rights,' *American Journal of International Law*, Vol. 88, p. 152 (describing consideration of gender specific violence at the conference); Roth, 'Domestic Violence as an International Human Rights Issue,' in *Human Rights of Women*, supra, p. 326 (discussing some of the methodological problems that the Human Rights Watch Women Rights Project has encountered in addressing domestic violence against women).

4. For a compelling analysis of domestic violence as torture, see Copelon, R. (1994), 'Intimate Terror: Understanding Domestic Violence as Torture,' in ibid., p. 116; Copelon, R. (1994), 'Recognizing the Egregious in the Everyday: Domestic Violence as Torture,' *Columbia Human Rights Law Review*, Vol. 25, p. 291. For a description of other forms of gender-specific torture, see Report of the Special Rapporteur, Mr. Nigal S. Rodley, submitted pursuant to Commission on Human Rights Resolution 1992/32, U.N. Doc. E/CN.4 1995/34 (1995).

5. For accounts of the process through which rape was recognized as a war crime before the *ad hoc* criminal tribunals, see Askin, K. (1997), *War Crimes Against Women: Prosecution in International War Crimes Tribunals*; Askin, K. (1999), 'Sexual Violence in Decisions and Indictments of the Yugoslav and Rwandan

Tribunals: Current Status,' *American Journal of International Law*, Vol. 93, p. 97.

6. For a practical training model, see Bowman, H. 'Getting the Message Abroad: An International Training Model for Judges and Prosecutors', in *Integrating Responses to Domestic Violence*.

7. For additional discussions of national implementation of norms against domestic violence see Palmer, M., 'Caring for Young and Old: Developments in the Family Law of the People's Republic of China, 1996-98,' in A. Bainham (ed.), *The International Survey of Family Law: 2000 Edition* at 95. See also Minamikatas and Tamaki, 'Developments in Japanese Family Law During 1998 – Domestic Violence Reforms,' in ibid. at p. 231 (describing the recent emergence of law addressing domestic violence in Japan). See generally Paul, S. (1999), 'Combating Domestic Violence Through Positive International Action in the International Community and in the United Kingdom, India, and Africa'; *Cardozo Journal of International and Comparative Law*, Vol. 7, p. 227.

Notes

[1] Amnesty International – USA, http://www.amnestyusa.org/countries/pakistan/reports/honour/honour-2html.

[2] Center for Gender and Refugee Studies, http://www.uchastings.edu/cgrs/campaigns/honor.htm.

[3] *Walsh v. Walsh*, 221 F.3d 204, 2000 U.S. App. LEXIS (1st Cir. 2000).

[4] *Condon v. Cooper*, 62 Cal. App. 4th 533; 1998 Cal. App. LEXIS 231 (Cal. App. 2d. Dist. 1998).

[5] G.A. Declaration 48/104 of 20 Dec. 1993.

[6] G.A. Res. 34/180, 1249 U.N.T.S. 13 (1980).

[7] 465 U.N.T.S. 113 (1988).

[8] Entered into force March 5, 1995.

[9] http://www.ecre.org/positions/women.shtml, last visited Sept. 2, 2003.

[10] Further Promoting and Encouragement of Human Rights, Report of the Special Rapporteur on Violence Against Women, E/CN.4/1998/54 at 29.

[11] Immigration and Refugee Board/Canada, http://www.lrb.gc.ca/en/about/legal/guidline/women/GD4_F_I.htm.

[12] INS, Considerations for Asylum Officers Adjudicating Claims From Women, http://www.uchastings.edu/cgrs/law/intl.html. US (last visited Sept. 16, 2003).

[13] Crown Copyright – November 2000 Nathalia Berkowitz, Senior Legal and Research Officer Catriona Jarvis, Immigration Adjudicator.

[14] In Brazil '[m]en who commit crimes against women, including sexual assault and murder, are unlikely to be brought to trial. Although the Supreme Court in 1991 struck down the archaic concept of "defence of honour" as a justification for killing one's wife, courts are still reluctant to prosecute and convict men who claim that they attacked their wives for infidelity.' – U.S. Department of State, *1999 Country Report on Human Rights Practices in Brazil* (February 2000). With reference to honour killings in Pakistan see Amnesty Report September 1999, *Pakistan, Honour killings of girls and women*. The report states that,

according to the non-governmental Human Rights Commission of Pakistan, 286 women were reported to have been killed for reasons of honour in 1998 in Punjab province alone (pages 3-4 of the report). In Iran the killing will normally be carried out by the family of the women herself, rather than that of her husband. See Sana al-Khayyat, *Honour and Shame: Women in Modern Iraq* (1990) pp. 21-22 quoted in *Re MN* Refugee Appeal no 2039/93, 12 February 1996, Chairman: R. Haines, New Zealand Refugee Status Appeals Authority.

[15] http://www.amnesty.ca/actnow/righttosafety.htm (last visited 7/22/03).

[16] http://www.hrw.org/worldreport99/women/women4.html (last visited 7/22/03).

Chapter 12

Human Rights of the Family and Human Rights of Individuals within the Family

1. Problem

Miriam is a single mother of two children, Rebecca, age 4, and Ari, age 10. They live in a small apartment in Tel Aviv, Israel. Miriam describes herself as a strict disciplinarian and smacks her children when they disobey her. She hits them with her hand, or sometimes a slipper. The children have suffered no injury as a result of their mother's sometimes harsh treatment and in other respects she appears to be a responsible and loving parent.

Ari's teacher has noticed minor bruises on his shoulders and legs. She has reported this to the principal. You are an attorney with a prominent children's rights NGO. The principal asks for your advice.

2. Overview

Human rights are a recurring theme in international family law (see Section 5, *Public International Law*, in Chapters 1-11). A cluster of human rights are implicated in the formation of the family, for example. These range from the requirement that the parties freely consent to enter into marriage (see Chapter 1, Section 3), to the exercise of their reproductive rights by the married couple, as well as the exercise of these rights by the individuals within the couple, and by individuals who are not married. The human rights of the biological and adoptive parents in connection with adoption (Chapter 3), as well as the open issue of the extension of all of these rights to homosexuals (Chapter 2), have been addressed in the preceding chapters.

This Chapter addresses the rights of the family unit itself. First, the family is entitled to affirmative assistance from the State with respect to support, social security, and health care. Second, the family is entitled to privacy, to be left alone. That is, the State cannot interfere with the private life of the family. This right may conflict with human rights of individuals within the family, however, especially women and children.

Other human rights issues are related to the family less directly. Child labour, for example, often reflects both the composition of the family and the allocation of decision-making authority within it. A greater proportion of adult females in the family corresponds to lower rates of child labour, while a greater proportion of adult males corresponds to lower rates of child labour for boys only (Van Bueren and Wanduragala, 2000).

Claims of the Family Upon the State

Under the Universal Declaration of Human Rights, States parties recognized that, 'The family is the natural and fundamental group unit of society and is entitled to protection by society and the State' (Article 16.3.). More specifically, the Universal Declaration requires States to assure a family wage (Article 23.3) and an adequate standard of living, including food, clothing, shelter, and medical care (Article 25). The Universal Declaration was originally aspirational; that is, it was not legally binding.

The rights and obligations set out in the Universal Declaration were defined with greater specificity in the legally-binding international treaties which followed, i.e., the International Covenant on Civil and Political Rights and the International Covenant on Economic, Social, and Cultural Rights. The Economic Covenant basically addresses affirmative obligations of the State, including welfare and social security benefits. In Article 10 of the Economic Covenant, for example, the States parties recognize that mothers are entitled to 'special protection' before and after childbirth, including paid leave. Thus, a State party would be required to incorporate into domestic law either welfare provisions assuring compensation or a requirement that private employers do so.

Claims of the Family Against the State

There is some overlap between the two conventions. For example, the Civil Covenant expressly reiterates the State's obligation to protect the family as 'the natural and fundamental group unit of society' as set out in the Universal Declaration. This arguably requires the State to enact laws protecting vulnerable parties, especially women and children, upon dissolution of marriage, for example (see Chapter 5, Section 5 and Chapter 10, Section 5). For the most part, however, the Civil Covenant addresses negative obligations of the State; that is, it imposes limits on State interference with individuals. The Economic Covenant, in contrast, requires the State to affirmatively assure its people an adequate standard of living, healthcare, education, and employment.

In addition to the rights assured the family, human rights law protects the rights of individuals within the family from interference by other family members. This includes, controversially, the right of the minor child to freedom of religion and freedom of expression. As the Committee charged with the administration of the Convention on the Rights of the Children has made clear, while the exercise of such rights must always be age-appropriate, these are nonetheless rights of the child and the State is under a legal duty to safeguard them.

3. Cultural Variations

International family law is at the center of a major faultline in international human rights law; that is, the ongoing debate between universalism and cultural relativism. Put simply, the argument of the universalists is that human rights are basically the same everywhere. While there may be some variation in the ways in which these rights are expressed or enjoyed, the prohibition against torture, for example, applies everywhere. Freedom of expression, similarly, cannot be interpreted to mean 'freedom of expression as consistent with Islamic law' or 'freedom of expression as understood in the U.S. Constitution.' While freedom of religion may require the State to allow religious authorities some leeway (in sanctioning violations of religious law, for example) this cannot amount to abdication of the State in favor of those authorities.

Cultural relativists, on the other hand, insist that any conception of 'human rights' is necessarily determined by the cultural context in which it is defined. It has been argued, for example, that a Muslim cannot truly practice his religion in a secular State. The right to practice one's religion, under this view, may well require a State which affirmatively supports that religion.

A well-known and contentious example may clarify the universalist/relativist debate. Human rights advocates have long demanded an end to female genital mutilation (FGM) or circumcision of girls as a rite of passage. It has been condemned as a violation of children's rights and as a form of torture. Cultural relativists, in contrast, first point out that FGM encompasses a range of practices, from removal of the external genitalia to more symbolic and less invasive procedures. They have argued that it is a rite of passage through which a girl becomes a member of her social group. In addition, they have pointed out that within some groups, a girl is considered unclean and thus ineligible for marriage unless she has undergone FGM. Finally, they point out that sanctions against the practice, including its criminalization in many Western States, merely drives it underground and deters women who have undergone the procedure from seeking medical attention. Rather, they argue for a coordinated approach, including grassroots education and respectful consultation with those who actually perform the surgeries.

The cultural relativism/universalism debate is particularly sharp in the context of international family law because in many States, including Israel and South Africa, primary responsibility for marriage and divorce has been left with religious authorities. This reflects and enforces the paradox of family law as both below the political radar of national leaders and essential in shaping the basic constituent unit of the polity itself. Thus, family law may be given as a sop to religious authorities when power is divided during the formative years of a new State, even as some recognize that family law in fact carries with it an enormous amount of normative authority. While many Islamic States have ratified most of the international human rights conventions, for example, they have taken explicit reservations to the effect that their obligations under these instruments are to be interpreted in light of Sharia, or Islamic personal law.

4. Private International Law Conventions

Convention on the Civil Aspects of International Child Abduction
(Concluded October 25, 1980)

> *Article 20*
> The return of the child under the provisions of Article 12 may be refused if this would not
> be permitted by the fundamental principles of the requested State relating to the protection
> of human rights and fundamental freedoms.

5. Public International Law

Universal Declaration of Human Rights[1]

> *Article 16* 3. The family is the natural and fundamental group unit of society and is entitled
> to protection by society and the State.
> * * *
> *Article 23* 3. Everyone who works has the right to just and favourable remuneration
> ensuring for himself and his family an existence worthy of human dignity, and
> supplemented, if necessary, by other means of social protection.
> * * *
> *Article 25* 1. Everyone has the right to a standard of living adequate for the health and
> well-being of himself and of his family, including food, clothing, housing and medical care
> and necessary social services, and the right to security in the event of unemployment,
> sickness, disability, widowhood, old age or other lack of livelihood in circumstances
> beyond his control.
> 2. Motherhood and childhood are entitled to special care and assistance. All children,
> whether born in or out of wedlock, shall enjoy the same social protection.
> * * *
> *Article 26* 3. Parents have a prior right to choose the kind of education that shall be given
> to their children.

International Covenant on Economic, Social and Cultural Rights[2]

> *Article 10* The States Parties to the present Covenant recognize that:
> 1. The widest possible protection and assistance should be accorded to the family, which is
> the natural and fundamental group unit of society, particularly for its establishment and
> while it is responsible for the care and education of dependent children. Marriage must be
> entered into with the free consent of the intending spouses.
> 2. Special protection should be accorded to mothers during a reasonable period before and
> after childbirth. During such period working mothers should be accorded paid leave or
> leave with adequate social security benefits.
> 3. Special measures of protection and assistance should be taken on behalf of all children
> and young persons without any discrimination for reasons of parentage or other conditions.
> Children and young persons should be protected from economic and social exploitation.
> Their employment in work harmful to their morals or health or dangerous to life or likely to
> hamper their normal development should be punishable by law. States should also set age

limits below which the paid employment of child labour should be prohibited and punishable by law.

* * *

Article 11 1. The States Parties to the present Covenant recognize the right of everyone to an adequate standard of living for himself and his family, including adequate food, clothing and housing, and to the continuous improvement of living conditions. The States Parties will take appropriate steps to ensure the realization of this right, recognizing to this effect the essential importance of international co-operation based on free consent.

2. The States Parties to the present Covenant, recognizing the fundamental right of everyone to be free from hunger, shall take, individually and through international co-operation, the measures, including specific programmes, which are needed:

(a) To improve methods of production, conservation and distribution of food by making full use of technical and scientific knowledge, by disseminating knowledge of the principles of nutrition and by developing or reforming agrarian systems in such a way as to achieve the most efficient development and utilization of natural resources;

(b) Taking into account the problems of both food-importing and food-exporting countries, to ensure an equitable distribution of world food supplies in relation to need.

* * *

Article 12 1. The States Parties to the present Covenant recognize the right of everyone to the enjoyment of the highest attainable standard of physical and mental health.

2. The steps to be taken by the States Parties to the present Covenant to achieve the full realization of this right shall include those necessary for:

(a) The provision for the reduction of the stillbirth-rate and of infant mortality and for the healthy development of the child;

(b) The improvement of all aspects of environmental and industrial hygiene;

(c) The prevention, treatment and control of epidemic, endemic, occupational and other diseases;

(d) The creation of conditions which would assure to all medical service and medical attention in the event of sickness.

* * *

Article 13 1. The States Parties to the present Covenant recognize the right of everyone to education. They agree that education shall be directed to the full development of the human personality and the sense of its dignity, and shall strengthen the respect for human rights and fundamental freedoms. They further agree that education shall enable all persons to participate effectively in a free society, promote understanding, tolerance and friendship among all nations and all racial, ethnic or religious groups, and further the activities of the United Nations for the maintenance of peace.

2. The States Parties to the present Covenant recognize that, with a view to achieving the full realization of this right:

(a) Primary education shall be compulsory and available free to all;

(b) Secondary education in its different forms, including technical and vocational secondary education, shall be made generally available and accessible to all by every appropriate means, and in particular by the progressive introduction of free education;

(c) Higher education shall be made equally accessible to all, on the basis of capacity, by every appropriate means, and in particular by the progressive introduction of free education;

(d) Fundamental education shall be encouraged or intensified as far as possible for those persons who have not received or completed the whole period of their primary education;

(e) The development of a system of schools at all levels shall be actively pursued, an adequate fellowship system shall be established, and the material conditions of teaching staff shall be continuously improved.

3. The States Parties to the present Covenant undertake to have respect for the liberty of parents and, when applicable, legal guardians to choose for their children schools, other than those established by the public authorities, which conform to such minimum educational standards as may be laid down or approved by the State and to ensure the religious and moral education of their children in conformity with their own convictions.
4. No part of this article shall be construed so as to interfere with the liberty of individuals and bodies to establish and direct educational institutions, subject always to the observance of the principles set forth in paragraph I of this article and to the requirement that the education given in such institutions shall conform to such minimum standards as may be laid down by the State.

* * *

Article 17 1. No one shall be subjected to arbitrary or unlawful interference with his privacy, family, home or correspondence, nor to unlawful attacks on his honour and reputation.
2. Everyone has the right to the protection of the law against such interference or attacks.

* * *

Article 23 1. The family is the natural and fundamental group unit of society and is entitled to protection by society and the State.
2. The right of men and women of marriageable age to marry and to found a family shall be recognized.
3. No marriage shall be entered into without the free and full consent of the intending spouses.
4. States Parties to the present Covenant shall take appropriate steps to ensure equality of rights and responsibilities of spouses as to marriage, during marriage and at its dissolution. In the case of dissolution, provision shall be made for the necessary protection of any children.

Convention on the Rights of the Child[3]

Preamble The States Parties to the present Convention,

* * *

Recalling that, in the Universal Declaration of Human Rights, the United Nations has proclaimed that childhood is entitled to special care and assistance,

Convinced that the family, as the fundamental group of society and the natural environment for the growth and well-being of all its members and particularly children, should be afforded the necessary protection and assistance so that it can fully assume its responsibilities within the community,

Recognizing that the child, for the full and harmonious development of his or her personality, should grow up in a family environment, in an atmosphere of happiness, love and understanding,

Considering that the child should be fully prepared to live an individual life in society, and brought up in the spirit of the ideals proclaimed in the Charter of the United Nations, and in particular in the spirit of peace, dignity, tolerance, freedom, equality and solidarity,

* * *

Recognizing that, in all countries in the world, there are children living in exceptionally difficult conditions, and that such children need special consideration,

Taking due account of the importance of the traditions and cultural values of each people for the protection and harmonious development of the child,

Recognizing the importance of international co-operation for improving the living conditions of children in every country, in particular in the developing countries,
Have agreed as follows:
Article 11 1. States Parties shall take measures to combat the illicit transfer and non-return of children abroad.
2. To this end, States Parties shall promote the conclusion of bilateral or multilateral agreements or accession to existing agreements
Article 12 1. States Parties shall assure to the child who is capable of forming his or her own views the right to express those views freely in all matters affecting the child, the views of the child being given due weight in accordance with the age and maturity of the child.
* * *
Article 19 1. States Parties shall take all appropriate legislative, administrative, social and educational measures to protect the child from all forms of physical or mental violence, injury or abuse, neglect or negligent treatment, maltreatment or exploitation, including sexual abuse, while in the care of parent(s), legal guardian(s) or any other person who has the care of a child.
2. Such protective measures should, as appropriate, include effective procedures for the establishment of social programmes to provide necessary support for the child and for those who have the care of the child, as well as for other forms of prevention and for identification, reporting, referral, investigation, treatment and follow-up of instances of child maltreatment described heretofore, and, as appropriate, for judicial involvement.
* * *
Article 23 1. States Parties recognize that a mentally or physically disabled child should enjoy a full and decent life, in conditions which ensure dignity, promote self-reliance and facilitate the child's active participation in the community.
* * *
Article 27 1. States Parties recognize the right of every child to a standard of living adequate for the child's physical, mental, spiritual, moral and social development.

6. Regional Conventions

Arab Charter on Human Rights[4]

Article 38 (a) The family is the basic unit of society, whose protection it shall enjoy.
(b) The State undertakes to provide outstanding care and special protection for the family, mothers, children and the aged.
Article 39
Young persons have the right to be afforded the most ample opportunities for physical and mental development.

African Charter on the Rights and Welfare of the Child[5]

5. States Parties to the present Charter shall take all appropriate measures to ensure that a child who is subjected to schools or parental discipline shall be treated with humanity and with respect for the inherent dignity of the child and in conformity with the present Charter.
* * *
Article 16: Protection Against Child Abuse and Torture
1. States Parties to the present Charter shall take specific legislative, administrative, social

and educational measures to protect the child from all forms of torture, inhuman or degrading treatment and especially physical or mental injury or abuse, neglect or maltreatment including sexual abuse, while in the care of the child.

2. Protective measures under this Article shall include effective procedures for the establishment of special monitoring units to provide necessary support for the child and for those who have the care of the child, as well as other forms of prevention and for identification, reporting referral investigation, treatment, and follow-up of instances of child abuse and neglect.

* * *

1. Parents or other persons responsible for the child shall have the primary responsibility of the upbringing and development of the child and shall have the duty:

(a) to ensure that the best interests of the child are their basic concern at all times –

(b) to secure, within their abilities and financial capacities, conditions of living necessary to the child's development; and

(c) to ensure that domestic discipline is administered with humanity and in a manner consistent with the inherent dignity of the child.

7. National Implementation

Argentina

Laws against domestic violence, including violence against children, have been enacted in Buenos Aires and provinces throughout Argentina. In addition, a national campaign to increase public awareness and thereby deter such violence has been launched. This includes daily radio broadcasts advising victims or witness how to register complaints (Grossman and Iñigo 2000).

Israel

In *State of Israel v. Plonit*,[6] the District Court convicted a mother of assault and abuse, sentencing her to 12 months' imprisonment suspended and 18 months probation. The mother was a strict disciplinarian who smacked her children regularly. The court overruled an earlier decision upholding parents' right to use 'reasonable and moderate' physical punishment on the ground that norms had changed (Schulz 2001).

Japan

The Prevention of Child Abuse Act was enacted in Japan in 2000, resulting in dramatically increased visibility of the problem of violence against children. During its first year, for example, advice was sought from Child Welfare Offices regarding suspected abuse in 17,725 cases, 1.5 times the number of queries the year before and sixteen times the number of queries ten years earlier (Tamaki, 2002).

Scotland

In some states, corporal punishment remains legal. As of 2003, for example, it was still legal for Scottish parents to subject their children to 'reasonable chastisement' (Sutherland, 2002).

Second Periodic Reports of States Parties due in 1999: Canada[7]

I. Abuse and Neglect – Article 19 Measures in Force 192. In its Concluding Observations on Canada's First Report, the UN Committee on the Rights of the Child stated that further measures need to be considered to effectively prevent and combat all forms of corporal punishment and ill-treatment of children in schools or institutions where children may be placed. The Committee also referenced the existence of child abuse and violence within the family and insufficient protection afforded by existing legislation in that regard.

193. The Criminal Code of Canada contains several provisions to protect children and youth from all forms of sexual abuse, including: sections 151 (sexual interference), 152 (invitation to sexual touching), and 153 (sexual exploitation). Specific offenses in the Criminal Code concerning parents, guardians and householders include: sections 170 (parent or guardian procuring sexual activity), 171 (householder permitting sexual activity) and 172 (corrupting children).

194. The Family Violence Initiative (1991-1996) supported a wide range of activities including research, program development, demonstration projects, evaluation studies on existing programs, professional training, and public awareness and education. The current Family Violence Initiative (1997-2002) continues these activities through the funding of numerous information, training and evaluation projects.

195. Two components of the initiative are The National Clearinghouse on Family Violence and the Family Violence Prevention Unit. The National Clearinghouse on Family Violence provides support to front-line workers, health professionals, educators, law enforcement officials and others in the prevention and treatment of all forms of child abuse and neglect. Health Canada is the lead department on this initiative, and provides leadership in the prevention of family violence through the coordination of federal action and collaboration with voluntary and corporate sectors, national professional associations and provincial and territorial governments.

196. Since the 1970s, the Canada Mortgage and Housing Corporation (CMHC) has financed the building or renovation of shelters for women and children fleeing domestic violence. In 1992, in partnership with the Family Violence Initiative, CMHC launched the Next Step Program to provide capital funding for non-profit organizations to build second stage housing, provide transitional housing with more security, support services, and to permit longer stays than first stage emergency shelters for women who have left abusive domestic situations. During the five-year program, 174 second-stage units were developed.

197. A national consultation hosted by CMHC in 1994 indicated a need to ensure that existing shelters are safe and secure and that they address the special needs of children, persons with disabilities and older Canadians. In addition, a lack of shelters was identified in northern and remote regions. In response, the Shelter Enhancement Initiative (SEI) was established to renovate and upgrade existing shelters and to develop a limited number of new emergency and second stage units. Between 1995 and 1997, CMHC directed the enhancement of 4,448 bed/units and the development of 61 emergency beds and 22 second stage units. Additional federal funding extended the SEI project to March 31, 1998.

198. The Department of Indian Affairs and Northern Development (DIAND) and Health

Canada provide funding for First Nations family violence prevention projects on reserves.

In 1996-97, DIAND funded 321 projects in this area.

Factors, difficulties and progress 199. In its Concluding Observations, the UN Committee on the Rights of the Child asserted that existing Canadian legislation does not adequately protect children from abuse and neglect. The Government of Canada's view is that in addition to the protection provided in criminal legislation, all provinces and territories have child welfare legislation that permits authorities to remove a child from a home when in danger of physical or emotional abuse, including neglect. The Government of Canada has been seeking to reinforce and clarify protection under the Criminal Code.

200. The Criminal Code applies to actions taken against children as well as adults. However, s. 43 of the Criminal Code permits a parent, teacher or person acting in the place of parent to invoke a defence to a criminal charge where the parent, teacher or adult acting in place of the parent uses reasonable force against a child by way of correction. A non-government organization, Canadian Foundation for Children, Youth and the Law, has received funding from the government-funded Court Challenges program to apply to a Canadian court for a determination as to whether s. 43 of the Criminal Code infringes children's constitutional rights under the Canadian Charter of Rights and Freedoms.

Priorities and Goals 201. Health Canada continues to promote research on alternative methods of punishment and also works, through various media, to increase public awareness of family violence. A current example of the latter function is the Family Violence Prevention Unit's funding of a music video for children and adults on the subject of alternatives to corporal punishment.

202. Health Canada is also supporting the development of the Canadian Incidence Study of Reported Child Abuse and Neglect (CIS), which studies the incidence of several types of abuse. Also, through the Reporting and Classification of Child Abuse in Health Care Settings Project, the department has supported research on the ways in which selected Canadian pediatric hospitals classify and report child abuse.

203. In June 1997, DIAND and CMHC announced they would jointly fund the capital costs of building 10 new family violence emergency shelters across the country. They expect the centres to be in operation by the end of 1999.

Government and NGO Cooperation 204. The Child Welfare League of Canada, with financial support from Canadian Heritage and Health Canada, has developed resources to promote healthy parenting and disseminate information on child abuse in 11 languages. The brochures were distributed to organizations that provide family services to ethnocultural communities as a way of helping parents better understand the Canadian system to protect children from abuse.

205. Status of Women Canada, a federal agency, provides funding assistance to organizations in support of advancing gender equality, including those which support actions and strategies that address the impact of family violence on girls. These initiatives include public education activities and the development of action plans aimed at preventing sexual abuse, workshops in schools to address issues such as dating violence and sexual harassment and protocols to improve community responses to the needs of girls. For example, the agency has provided financial support under the Family Violence Initiative to an alliance of 5 research centres on family violence and violence against women. The funding supports the alliance in its development of recommendations for a national strategy for the prevention of violence to female children.

206. The Government of Canada is allocating $2.75 million per year to a non-governmental group to cover legal costs associated with cases of national

significance in further defining the nature and extent of constitutionally-based rights contained in the Canadian Charter of Rights and Freedoms. Cases encompass issues such as the aforementioned issue of corporal punishment of children, the right to education in a minority official language, and protection of children with disabilities, among others. The government's objective is to contribute to an up-to-date body of legally-protected individual rights, with special attention being paid to traditionally disadvantaged segments of our society.

207. Health Canada supports a range of activities to improve understanding of child abuse and its health consequences, to identify best practices through research, data gathering and evaluation activities. Moreover, Health Canada promotes increased public and professional awareness, particularly in the health field, about the causes and consequences of child abuse. Participation in these activities is ongoing with a number of advisory groups.

Committee on the Rights of the Child[8]

Written Replies by the Government of Singapore[9]

(ii) Declaration in respect of Articles 19 and 37 of the Convention

Upon accession, Singapore made the following Declaration:

The Republic of Singapore considers that articles 19 and 37 of the Convention do not prohibit –

(a) the application of any prevailing measures prescribed by law for maintaining law and order in the Republic of Singapore;

(b) measures and restrictions which are prescribed by law and which are necessary in the interests of national security, public safety, public order, the protection of public health or the protection of the rights and freedoms of others; or

(c) the judicious application of corporal punishment in the best interest of the child.

Singapore subscribes to the concept of the family being responsible for raising children and having responsibilities in matters of discipline. Schools, having the welfare of the children in mind, are also permitted to take disciplinary action against errant students. Caning as a judicial sentence by the High Court and the Subordinate Courts (for males only) is only statutorily permitted for a short list of very serious criminal offences which generally includes physical violence to the victims. Under the Children and Young Persons Act, it is expressly provided that notwithstanding the provisions of any other written law, no child (defined as a person who is below 14 years old) or young person (a person who is 14 years of age or above and below the age of 16 years) shall be sentenced by any court other than the High Court to corporal punishment. In the case of a youthful offender (defined as between 7 to 16 years old), caning shall be inflicted with a light rattan. In all circumstances, caning is imposed under medical supervision. A prisoner undergoing reformative training or a young offender who is found guilty of an aggravated prison offence as stated in the Prisons Act may also be ordered to undergo corporal punishment as prescribed in the aforementioned Act. Accordingly, Singapore entered this declaration to clarify that these Articles do not prohibit the application of any measures prescribed by Singapore law for maintaining law and order.

8. IOs and NGOs

IOs

The UN has recently undertaken a study on Violence Against Children, described in the first excerpt, below. In addition, like the CEDAW, the Economic Covenant, and the Civil Covenant, the Convention on the Rights of the Child ('CRC') seeks to promote State compliance by establishing a Committee to examine the progress made by States Parties in achieving the realization of the obligations undertaken in the convention. Like the other human rights treaties, the CRC requires States Parties to submit reports documenting their progress to the Committee. Upon review of these reports, the Committee 'may make suggestions and general recommendations' to the State. The following excerpts are examples of such suggestions and general recommendations from the Committee to the indicated States Parties in connection with two of the rights protected under the CRC: 1). Children's freedom of expression and 2) the prohibition on violence against children, including corporal punishment.

The United Nations Study on Violence against Children

On 12 February 2003, United Nations Secretary-General Kofi Annan appointed Paulo Sergio Pinheiro of Brazil as the independent expert to lead a global study on violence against children. The purpose of the study is to provide an in-depth picture of the prevalence, nature and causes of violence against children. It will put forward recommendations for consideration by Member States, the UN System and civil society for appropriate action, including effective remedies at the national and international levels.

The study will be guided by the Convention on the Rights of the Child which emphasizes children's rights to physical and personal integrity, and outlines States parties obligations to protect then from 'all forms of physical or mental violence, including sexual and other forms of exploitation, abduction, armed conflict, and inhuman or degrading treatment or punishment.' It also obliges the State to enact preventive measures and ensure that all child victims of violence receive the support and assistance they require.

The UN General Assembly called for the study in 2001 acting on the recommendation of the Committee on the Rights of the Child. In overseeing the implementation of the Convention on the Right of the Child, the Committee held two days of general discussion on the issue of state violence against children within the family and in school (2001) and state violence against children (2000). The request for an international study on the question of violence against children was an outcome of these days of discussion.

Letter date 12 October 2001 from the Chairperson of the Committee on the Rights of the Child addressed to the Secretary-General[10]

(7) In accordance with the provisions of article 45 (c) of the Convention on the Rights of the Child, the Committee recommends that the Secretary-General be requested, through the General Assembly, to conduct an in-depth international study on violence against children. The study should be as thorough and influential as the report of the expert of the Secretary-General, Mrs. Graca Machel, on the impact of armed conflict on children (see a/51/306/). Such a study should:

(a) Be guided by the Convention on the Rights of the Child and other relevant international standards and take full account of the recommendations adopted by the Committee on its days of general discussion, held in 2000 and 2001;

(b) Document the different types of violence of which children are victims, the prevalence of such violence and its impact on children, adults and societies. Areas of study should include violence within the family and home, in schools and care or residential institutions both State and private, in work situations and in the streets, in detention facilities and prisons, violence by the police and the use of capital and physical punishment. Violence should include all forms of physical or mental violence, injury or abuse, neglect or negligent treatment, including sexual abuse, bullying in schools and corporal punishment. Attention should be paid to the impact of discrimination based on gender, race, economic status etc. and on the patterns of violence and vulnerability experienced by children.

(c) Seek to identify the causes of and contributing factors to violence against children, including factors – such as the role of legislation, public education and training of professionals – that contribute to or obstruct prevention, protection and recovery, and explore the links between different provisions of the Convention on the Rights of the Child and other international human rights treaties in relation to violence against children;

(d) Draw primarily on existing research and documentation, including reports to and of the Committee on the Rights of the Child, special rapporteurs and other United Nations and United Nations-related bodies, including the United Nations Educational, Scientific and Cultural Organization, The United Nations Children's Fund, the United Nations Development Fund for Women, the United Nations Population Fund and the World Health Organization, and studies conducted by academic, research institutions and non-governmental organizations. The study should collect information on different human rights mechanism and United Nations bodies and agencies and the extent to which the problem of violence against children is addressed in those activities from a human rights perspective;

(e) Be conducted in collaboration with all United Nations agencies and bodies, and particularly the Committee on the Rights of the Child, the Office of the United Nations High Commissioner for Human Rights and the United Nations human rights mechanisms, the United Nations Children's Fund, the World Health Organization, and the United Nations Educational, Scientific and Cultural Organization, as well as with relevant non-governmental organizations, academic institutions and international professional organizations, and involved children themselves.

On this basis, and taking into account information on the effectiveness of existing approaches, the study should lead to the development of strategies aimed at effectively preventing and combating all forms of violence against children, outlining steps to be taken at the international level and by States to provide effective prevention, protection, intervention, treatment, recovery and reintegration.

Committee on the Rights of the Child[11]

Concluding Observations: Republic of Korea[12]

Respect for the views of the child 34. The Committee is concerned that traditional attitudes towards children in society still limit respect for their views within the family, schools, other institutions and society at large.

35. The Committee recommends that the State party, in accordance with article 12 of the Convention:

(a)   Ensure that the Child Welfare Act, amended in 2000, be revised to include the right of children to express their views freely in all matters affecting them, and take effective measures, including legislation, to promote respect for the views of children and facilitate their participation in all matters affecting them, by courts, administrative bodies, schools and disciplinary proceedings in the education system;

(b)   Provide educational information to, inter alia, parents, educators, government administrative officials, the judiciary and society at large on children's right to have their views taken into account and to participate in all matters affecting them;

(c)   Undertake a regular review of the extent to which children's views are taken into consideration and of the impact this has on policies, programmes and children themselves.

* * *

Corporal punishment 38.   The Committee notes with great concern that corporal punishment is officially permitted in schools. The Committee is of the opinion that corporal punishment does not conform with the principles and provisions of the Convention, particularly since it constitutes a serious violation of the dignity of the child (see similar observations of the Committee on Economic, Social and Cultural Rights, E/C.12/1/Add.79, para. 36). The fact that the Ministry of Education guidelines leave the decision on whether to use corporal punishment in schools to the individual school administrators suggests that some forms of corporal punishment are acceptable and therefore undermines educational measures to promote positive, non-violent forms of discipline.

39. The Committee recommends that the State party:

(a)   Implement the recommendation of the National Human Rights Commission that the relevant legislation and regulations be amended to expressly prohibit corporal punishment in the home, schools and all other institutions;

(b)   Carry out public education campaigns about the negative consequences of ill treatment of children in order to change attitudes to corporal punishment, and promote positive, non-violent forms of discipline in schools and at home as an alternative to such punishment.

Concluding Observations: Italy[13]

Respect for the views of the child 25. The Committee is concerned that the general principle, as laid down in article 12 of the Convention, is not fully applied in practice. In this regard, the Committee is concerned that the right of children to be heard is insufficiently guaranteed in proceedings affecting them, in particular in cases of the separation of parents, divorce, adoption or foster care, or within education.

26. The Committee recommends that:

(a) Legislation governing procedure in courts and administrative proceedings ensure that a child capable of forming his or her own views has the right to express those views and that they be given due weight;

(b) Particular emphasis be placed on the right of every child to participate in the family, at school, within other institutions and bodies and in society at large, with special attention to vulnerable groups;

(c) Awareness-raising among the public at large, as well as education and training of professionals on the implementation of this principle, be reinforced

Concluding Observations: Viet Nam[14]

Respect for the views of the child 29. The Committee is concerned that traditional attitudes towards children in society still limit the respect for their views, within the family, schools and society at large. In addition, administrative and judicial proceedings are not always required to take the views of the child into account, for instance in the case of divorce hearings.

30. The Committee recommends that the State party:

(a) Carry out awareness-raising campaigns aimed at, inter alia, parents, teachers, government administrative officials, the judiciary and society at large on children's right to have their views taken into account and to participate in all matters affecting them;

(b) Take legislative measures to guarantee that in all court and administrative proceedings affecting them, children have the right to express their views and have those views taken into account regarding children;

(c) Promote and facilitate, within the courts and all administrative bodies, respect for the views of children and their participation in all matters affecting them, in accordance with article 12 of the Convention.

* * *

Ill-treatment and violence 33. The Committee is concerned that children in the State party are subject to various forms of violence and ill-treatment, including child abuse and neglect, and corporal punishment.

34. The Committee recommends that the State party:

* * *

(e) Explicitly prohibit corporal punishment in the home, schools and all other institutions;

(f) Carry out public education campaigns about the negative consequences of ill treatment of children, and promote positive, non-violent forms of discipline as an alternative to corporal punishment.

Concluding Observations: Czech Republic[15]

Violence/abuse/maltreatment However, the Committee is concerned by the ill treatment and abuse committed against children in the family, the school and other institutions as well as by public officials in the streets and in places of detention, particularly in the context of a form of popular justice for an alleged crime such as theft. The Committee is further concerned that certain groups of children, such as Roma, are specifically targeted, and that a very small portion of reported cases of suspicion of abuse and neglect are investigated. It is also concerned at the lack of an integrated system of services and that problems of child abuse and neglect are often solely addressed in an ad hoc manner by NGOs . . .

* * *

40. The Committee is concerned that there is no legislation explicitly prohibiting corporal punishment, and that it is practised in the family, in schools and in other public institutions, including alternative care contexts.

41. The Committee recommends that the State party take action to address ill treatment and abuse committed against children in the family, in schools, in the streets, in institutions and in places of detention through, inter alia:

* * *

(f) Taking all the necessary steps to enact legislation prohibiting the use of corporal punishment in schools, institutions, in the family and in any other context;

* * *

(i) Taking into account the Committee's recommendations adopted at its day of general discussion on violence against children within the family and in schools (CRC/C/111).

* * *

43. (b) Undertake a comprehensive review of all legislation, policies and administrative decisions related to children within the family in order to assess their impact on the family as a whole with a view to the adoption of a family policy. The Committee further encourages the State party to adopt a family policy including a minimum of social security for the child and the family, housing and social services, consistency between parents' work and child care, women's and single parent's status, child maintenance, maternity and paternity leave and other family-related issues;

(c) Adopt and implement international and domestic legislation to address these concerns, including the 1973 Hague Convention No. 24 on the Law Applicable to Maintenance Obligations.

Concluding Observations: Iceland. Committee on the Rights of the Child[16]

Violence/abuse/neglect/maltreatment 28. The Committee welcomes the adoption of the 2002 Child Protection Act, which contains a comprehensive set of provisions to protect children from neglect and ill-treatment in the home. It also notes the establishment of Children's House to treat sexually abused children.

29. The Committee recommends that the State party:

(a) Raise awareness among parents, other caretakers and the public at large of the prohibition of corporal punishment – including in the family – under existing legal provisions;

(b) Continue to strengthen and expand the coverage of the Children's House concept throughout the State party;

(c) Conduct public education campaigns about the negative consequences of ill-treatment of children, and promote positive, non-violent forms of discipline as an alternative to corporal punishment;

(d) Allocate sufficient resources for the provision of care, recovery and reintegration of victims;

(e) Train teachers, law enforcement officials, care workers, judges and health professionals in the identification, reporting and management of cases of ill-treatment, including with respect to interviewing techniques which are the least harmful to child victims of abuse.

Committee on the Rights of the Child Concluding Observations: Libyan Arab Jamahiriya[17]

Violence/abuse/neglect/maltreatment

33. The Committee welcomes the prohibition of corporal punishment in schools and takes note of the information that measures have been adopted to report and investigate maltreatment of children. Nevertheless, it is concerned at the lack of information on the actual situation in the State party with respect to ill-treatment of children within the family. Further, it regrets the lack of information on prevention and awareness-raising activities.

34. The Committee recommends that the State party:

(a) Conduct a comprehensive study to assess the nature and extent of ill-treatment and abuse of children, as well as other domestic violence, and use the results to design policies and programmes to address this issue;

(b) Carry out preventive public education campaigns about the negative consequences of ill-treatment of children and promote positive, non-violent forms of discipline as an alternative to corporal punishment;

(c) Take the necessary measures to prevent violence against, and abuse of, children;

(d) Establish effective child-sensitive procedures and preventive mechanisms to receive, monitor and investigate complaints, including through the intervention of social and judicial authorities where necessary, to find appropriate solutions, paying due regard to the best interests of the child;

(e) Give attention to addressing and overcoming sociocultural barriers that inhibit victims from seeking assistance;

(f) Train teachers, law enforcement officials, care workers, judges and health professionals in the identification, reporting and management of ill-treatment cases; and

(g) Seek assistance from, among others, UNICEF and WHO.

Committee on the Rights of the Child Concluding Observations: San Marino[18]

Protection from abuse and neglect

21. The Committee welcomes the information that article 234 of the Penal Code also includes the prohibition of corporal punishment, but is concerned at the lack of any concrete statistical data and other information on the prevention and prevalence of and intervention in cases of child abuse and neglect.

22. The Committee recommends that the State party undertake awareness-raising campaigns on the negative impact of corporal punishment. Furthermore, the State party should undertake studies to assess the prevalence and nature of violence against children and develop a comprehensive plan of action based on this study for the prevention of and intervention in cases of child abuse and neglect, including the provision of services for recovery and social reintegration of victims, taking into account the recommendations of the Committee adopted at its days of general discussion on children and violence (see CRC/C/100, para. 688 and CRC/C/111, paras. 701-745).

NGOs

NGOs have also recognized violence against children as a human rights issue, as set out in the excerpt below.

Save the Children[19]

> *What we do/Exploitation & Protection/Violence* Violence is a fact of life for many children around the world. It can take many forms, such as physical punishment at home or in school; sexual abuse; trafficking for sexual exploitation; or dangerous and exploitative labour. There is a higher risk of violence in emergencies. Some groups of children are at particular risk within their communities, such as those living without their families, children living and working on the streets, and disabled children. Sometimes violence is a result of traditional customs or discriminatory beliefs that are harmful to girls or boys.
>
> Save the Children works to raise awareness of children's rights and the effects of violence. We promote ways of protecting children in their communities. We also work directly with children, helping them to understand their rights and the risks they face, and to find ways of reducing their vulnerability to violence.

9. A Possible Approach to the Problem

This problem highlights the tension between children's right to be free from 'all forms of physical or mental violence' under Article 19 of the Convention on the Rights of the Child, on one hand, and parents' rights to family 'privacy' under Article 17 of the Civil Covenant, on the other. The issue is an extremely sensitive one, especially where, as in the Problem, the children have suffered no physical injury (except for Ari's minor bruises) which would implicate their right to health under Article 12 of the Economic Covenant.

Under the recent decision of the Israeli court in Plonit, discussed in Section 7, Miriam may well face criminal sanctions, especially if, like the mother there, she smacks the children regularly. Thus, the situation should be reported to the police. At the same time, it is not clear that prosecuting their mother will improve family life for the children, whom Miriam may blame for her legal problems. As an attorney with a prominent children's rights NGO, you might inquire within your organization about possible support services, government-sponsored or private, which might help the family. Miriam needs to learn other ways of managing her children. The children need to understand their rights and to find ways of reducing their vulnerability described in Section 8.

For Further Research

1. Nuack, B. (1994), 'Note: Implications of the United States Ratification of the United Nations Convention on the Rights of the Child: Civil Rights, The Constitution and the Family,' *Cleveland State Law Review*, Vol. 42, pp. 675-706; Young, K. (1999), 'An Examination of Parental Discipline as a Defense of Justification: It's Time for a Kindlier, Gentler Approach,' *Naval Law Review*, Vol. 46, pp. 1-66.

2. In their cogent introduction to a survey of International Family Law, Geraldine Van Bueren and Randini Wanduralaga aptly observed that, 'particularly in relation to

international human rights law, there are emerging trends which will have an impact on the family. Broadly, the areas concern the competing interests of individual family members within the family and cover such issues as access to medical treatment, the elderly and the role of the family in the eradication of child labour.' For their discussion of these issues, see Van Bueren, G. and Wanduragala, R. (2000), 'Annual Review of Family Law,' in Bainham, A. (ed.), The *International Survey of Family Law: 2000 Edition*, Jordan, Bristol, pp. 1-9. For country-specific surveys, see Shulz, R. (2001), 'Child Protection in the Israel, Supreme Court: Tortious Parenting, Physical Punishment and Criminal Child Abuse,' Bainham, A. (ed.), *The International Survey of Family Law: 2001 Edition*, Jordan, Bristol; Grosman, C. and Iñigo, D. (2000), 'The Overriding Interest of the Child in Legislative Policy and Judicial Decisions in Argentina,' in Bainham, A. (ed.), *The International Survey of Family Law: 2000 Edition*, Jordan, Bristol, pp. 9-19.

3. There are a growing number of useful web sites addressing international human rights issues from a range of perspectives. Some noteworthy examples follow.

ASIL Guide to Electronic Resources for International Law: Human Rights
http://www1.umn.edu/humanrts/bibliog/bibllios.htm

Fordham O Wara: Bibliographical Pathfinder: African System for the Protection and Promotion of Human Rights (2002)
http://www1.umn.edu/humanrts/bibliog/africanpathfinder.html

Bibliography on Crimes of Honour
http://www1.umn.edu/humanrts/bibliog/honour.html

Bibliography for Research on Human Rights in Asia
http://www1.umn.edu/humanrts/bibliog/contents.html

Bibliography: Human Rights in the African Context
http://www1.umn.edu/humanrts/africa/african.html

Council of Europe bibliography http://civnet.org/civitas/coe/document/hrbible.htm

The Human Rights of Women: A Reference Guide to official United Nations Documents
http://www1.umn.edu/humanrts/instree/women/engl-wmn.html

UN Human Rights Documentation, A Guide to Country-Specific Research
http://www1.umn.edu/humanrts/bibliog/guide.htm

Violence Against Women Bibliography
http://www.sigi.org/Resource/vaw_bib.htm

Womens Human Rights Resources Database (Toronto)
http://www.law-lib.utoronto.ca/diana/

Notes

[1]   G.A. Res. 217A (III), U.N. Doc A/810 at 71 (1948).
[2]   G.A. Res. 2200A (XXI), 21 U.N.GAOR Supp. (No. 16) at 49, U.N. Doc. A/6316 (1966), 993 U.N.T.S. 3, entered into force Jan. 3, 1976.
[3]   G.A. res. 44/25, annex, 44 U.N. GAOR Supp. (No. 49) at 167, U.N. Doc. A/44/49 (1989), entered into force Sept.2 1990.
[4]   September 15, 1994, *reprinted in* 18 Hum. Rts. L.J. 151 (1997).
[5]   OAU Doc. CAB/LEG/24.9/49 (1990), entered into force Nov. 29, 1999.
[6]   Ct. App. 456/98.
[7]   CRC/C/83/Add.6. (State Party Report).
[8]   Thirty-second session Consideration of Reports Submitted by States Parties under Article 44 of the Convention, http://www.unhchr.ch/tbs/doc.nsf.
[9]   (CRC/C/51/Add.8).
[10] A/56/488, Annex.
[11] Thirty-second session Consideration of Reports Submitted by States Parties under Article 44 of the Convention, http://www.unhchr.ch/tbs/doc.nsf.
[12] CRC/C/15/Add. 197.
[13] CRC/C/15/Add. 198.
[14] CRC/C/15/Add. 203.
[15] CRC/C/15/Add 200.
[16] CRC/C/15/Add. 201.
[17] CRC/C/15/Add.209, 4 July 2003.
[18] CRC/C/15/Add.214, 27 October 2003.
[19] http://www.savethechildren.org.

Index